AMERICAN PROBLEMS OF TODAY

Other Works by the Author

THE UNITED STATES SINCE 1865
(with Benjamin B. Kendrick)

THE FARMER IS DOOMED

A SHORT HISTORY OF THE NEW DEAL

THE UNITED STATES
A GRAPHIC HISTORY

AMERICAN PROBLEMS OF TODAY

A HISTORY OF THE UNITED STATES

SINCE THE WORLD WAR

LOUIS M. HACKER

F. S. CROFTS & CO · NEW YORK

1938

MANUFACTURED IN THE UNITED STATES OF AMERICA
BY THE VAIL-BALLOU PRESS, INC., BINGHAMTON, N. Y.

TO

MY WIFE

PREFACE

THE institutional apparatus of our contemporary American state becomes more complex and bewildering every day, so that even the expert finds difficulty in keeping abreast of the times. What, therefore, can be expected of the intelligent layman? Within the past decade, the American state, under the dispensation of what all of us have come to call the New Deal, has taken on so many new functions, has branched out into so many hitherto unexplored regions, that a simple compilation and analysis of its agencies becomes a chore of no mean proportions. And when one seeks to understand the intention and tactics of these agencies and to measure (by whatever clearly conceived standards) their achievement, then one is launching upon a task that almost impinges upon the impossible.

Our state has become transformed—almost overnight. Formerly, it concerned itself almost exclusively with civil administration and national defense, and when it intervened in other realms it for the most part acted in the capacity of umpire between equals. This, at any rate, was the theory of such an outstanding example of state intervention as the passage of the Federal Trade Commission Act. Today, however, the state is operating to defend the underprivileged, to increase the national income, and to effect a more equitable distribution of that income among the various categories of producers. To achieve these ends not only has the American state taken on the whole job of assuring social security, but it has also become a participant in and an initiator of business enterprise. Our state, in short, has become the capitalist state, where only yesterday it was the *laissez-faire*, or passive, state: it protects the young, weak, and aged; it constructs and operates plants; and it buys and sells goods and services, lends money, warehouses commodities, moves ships, and operates railroads. In one sense, the state is seeking to erect safeguards for the underprivileged against exploitation; in another, it is competing with and replacing private enterprise—without, however, parting company with capitalist relations.

To attempt to follow the state through the intricate maze it has created in the past few years is, as I have said, a bold task. Yet there is the responsibility upon all of us to do exactly that. We are living in a democracy; and if our democracy is to continue to function, it is incumbent upon us to realize that this new Leviathan of state capitalism is not our master but our servant. We must understand—no matter how difficult, at first blush, the whole matter may appear to be—precisely what the state's plans and methods are, so that we can be in a position to criticize honestly for the purpose of controlling fully.

It was with some such thought in mind that the present work was undertaken. I have sought, employing always and consciously a critical apparatus, to present as clearly as I know how the reasons why American capitalism entered into a state of crisis beginning with 1930. I have also sought to understand and describe the rationale and tactics of the New Deal administrations. And I have tried to evaluate the achievement in terms of credits and debits, at the same time erecting a number of signposts for the guidance of the American citizen in his career as intelligent critic.

This book is written as a history and not as a polemical work. It tells in detail, but always employing a non-technical language, the story of the events of the last two decades. It is concerned with domestic politics, legislative program making, the establishment and functioning of administrative agencies, and foreign relations. But I would be less than honest if I claimed an Olympian objectivity. On this point I agree completely with Charles A. Beard that an historical work inevitably is conditioned by the environmental and educational influences to which the writer has been subjected, as well as by his own preferences and hopes. I have, therefore, written this book around what I consider to be the central problems of our time, that is to say: (1) the apparent inability of capitalism to continue to function in terms of a free market; (2) the necessity for erecting proper defenses against possible oppression at the hands of the bureaucracy of state capitalism; and (3) the danger of our involvement in foreign war. And if I express certain hesitancies and doubts, it is not because I am concerned over our common future so much as I am about the means currently being employed to assure it.

I should say that in conception this is a completely new book. However, at certain points, particularly in the opening chapters, I have drawn upon other writings of my own; for, having said a thing once to the best of my ability, I have found it difficult—and perhaps unnecessary—to attempt to repeat the same thought in another form. About one-fourth of the book has been taken from *The United States Since 1865* (written with Benjamin B. Kendrick) and my own *A Short History of the New Deal*. In every case this material has been brought up to date by me. I wish to express my deep obligation to Professor Kendrick not merely because he has consented to the use here of material appearing under our joint names, but because he was oncc my teacher and has always been my real friend and honest adviser. He has read this book in manuscript and offered me the benefits of his ripe wisdom; what faults I have committed have been in spite of rather than because of his counsel.

Louis M. Hacker

Columbia University, New York City

CONTENTS

PART ONE

THE GOLDEN TWENTIES

CHAPTER PAGE

I. POLITICS IN THE NINETEEN TWENTIES
The Election of Harding 3
The Administrations of Calvin Coolidge 9
The Engineer in Politics. 18

II. LEADING LEGISLATIVE PROBLEMS OF THE NINETEEN TWENTIES
The Tariff Acts of 1922 and 1930 21
Creating a Merchant Marine. 26
The Railroad Problem 28
The Public Debt and Tax Reduction 32
Providing for the War Veterans. 34
The Regulation of Power 36

III. AMERICA IN TWO HEMISPHERES
The United States and Latin America 41
Renewal of the Peace Movement. 48
Naval Limitation 53
Interallied Debts and Reparation Payments 57
Russian Relations 62

PART TWO

IMPERIAL AMERICA IN THE MACHINE AGE

IV. CAPITAL AND LABOR
The Growth of the Population 69
The Growth of Industry. 71
Mass Production 75
Productivity 76
The Position of Labor 79
The Supreme Court and Property 90
Mergers and Anti-Trust Legislation. 94

V. FOUR OUTSTANDING PROBLEMS OF THE TWENTIES AND THIRTIES
Prohibition 99
Immigration Restriction 107
The Decline of Agriculture 113
Economic Imperialism 127

CHAPTER PAGE

VI. LIFE, LETTERS, AND ART IN THE MACHINE AGE
Characteristics of the American Scene 146
Some Aspects of American Society 148
Science in America 157
Literature, the Arts, and Taste 162

PART THREE

AMERICA FIGHTS DEPRESSION

VII. CAPITALISM IN CRISIS
The Course of the Depression 177
The Causes of the Depression 179
What to Do? 191
The Election of 1932 193

VIII. FROM AN OLD TO A NEW DEAL
The First Steps of Recovery 197
The Theory of the New Deal 198
The Tactics of the New Deal 200
The Politics of the New Deal 204

IX. THE NEW DEAL AGENCIES
Agriculture 207
Industry and Labor 217
Social Security 229
Currency and Credit 234
Power and Housing 244
Railroads and Shipping 253
Foreign Trade 257
Public Works and Relief 264
Financing the New Deal 273
State Capitalism and the Problem of Bureaucracy 276

X. THE NEW DEAL MAKES PROGRESS SLOWLY
The Course of Recovery to Midsummer, 1937 282
The Election of 1936 292
The Supreme Court Fight 295
Labor Organizes 299
The "Recession" of 1937–1938 305
The Foreign Policy of the New Deal 315
America in Two Worlds 330

BIBLIOGRAPHY 335

INDEX 345

MAPS AND CHARTS

PAGE

The United States in the Caribbean . . . . *facing* 42

Intergovernmental Loans and Reparation Payments 61

Map of 1930 Population in the United States . . . . *facing* 70

Action and Reaction on Prohibition, 1920–1930 103

Systems of Liquor Control, 1938 104

Imperial America . . . . *after* 132

The Federal Government 1934 189

Wholesale Price Indexes 209

The Federal Government 1938 . . . . *after* 276

Farm Indexes 283

Indexes of Prices Received and Prices Paid by Farmers . . . 284

Banking Activities 287

Index of Business Activity 307

Selected Business Indicators 311

PART I

THE GOLDEN TWENTIES

PART I

THE GOLDEN TWENTIES

I. POLITICS IN THE NINETEEN TWENTIES

THE ELECTION OF HARDING

THE directors of the Republican party, when they foregathered in convention at Chicago on June 8, 1920, had every reason to look forward to the coming Presidential contest with confidence. The result was a spirited pre-convention campaign, from which there finally emerged as the favorites General Leonard Wood, Governor Frank O. Lowden of Illinois, and Senator Hiram Johnson of California. A quiet boom had been started for Senator Warren Gamaliel Harding of Ohio by his friend National Committeeman Harry M. Daugherty, but its strength came from local sources entirely. The convention proceedings were dominated by the conservatives in the party, who wrote a platform which committed the party to a domestic policy reminiscent of the McKinley era in its conservatism. In their arraignment of the foreign policy of the Democratic administrations the Republicans indicated a return toward isolation. Specifically, they pledged themselves to protect the rights and property of American citizens in Mexico, and declared that the Covenant of the League of Nations failed to promote those agreements among countries that were necessary for the preservation of the peace of the world. However, they did not condemn the idea of international cooperation entirely but vaguely promised to bring about "such agreement with the other nations of the world as shall meet fully the duty of America to civilization and humanity in accordance with American ideals and without surrendering the right of the American people to exercise its judgment and its power in favor of justice and peace."

The balloting for the candidates began on June 11, and on the ninth ballot Harding pulled ahead of Wood, Lowden, and Johnson. On the next roll call the Senator from Ohio was nominated.

As his running mate, the convention chose Governor Calvin Coolidge of Massachusetts.

The Democrats met at San Francisco on June 28, with Wilson absent and Bryan hovering only in the background. The leading aspirants for the nomination were William G. McAdoo, late Secretary of the Treasury and the son-in-law of Wilson; Attorney-General A. Mitchell Palmer of Pennsylvania; and Governor James M. Cox of Ohio. The platform was reported out on July 2 and, like the Republican avowal of faith, had nothing of significance to say concerning domestic questions. Clearly the old zeal for reform had run its course. But in relations with the outside world idealism persisted. The Democrats defended the President's Mexican policy, sympathized with Ireland in its aspirations for self-government, and promised independence to the Philippines and territorial status to Porto Rico. The League of Nations was declared to be "the surest if not the only practical means of maintaining the permanent peace of the world"; the Treaty ought to be ratified immediately "without reservations which would impair its essential integrity"; however, the Democracy was not opposed to "the acceptance of any reservations making clearer or more specific the obligations of the United States to the League of Nations." Forty-four ballots were necessary before a choice of a standard bearer could be made. On the thirty-eighth roll call Palmer released his delegates and the drift set in toward Cox. He was named on the forty-fourth ballot, and with him was nominated Franklin D. Roosevelt of New York, Assistant Secretary of the Navy.

The Socialists met at New York on May 8 with the right wing completely in control of affairs. Debs was named for the Presidency for the fifth time; the platform, in addition to the customary revisionist program of socialism by the ballot, supported industrial unionism. A Farmer-Labor ticket also made its appearance, with Parley P. Christensen of Utah named for the Presidency and Max S. Hayes of Ohio for the Vice-Presidency. La Follette would have been a natural choice for this new third-party attempt, but his insistence that the platform be his own and not that of the labor element made him unacceptable to the trade unionists. The Farmer-Labor platform was a right socialist document. It called for government ownership of railroads, mines and national resources; the lifting of the blockade against Russia; American withdrawal from the Treaty of Versailles; and the enactment of the kind of social codes that had so prominently figured in the Progressive platform of 1912.[1]

The canvass of 1920 was a spiritless affair. At the urging of Wilson, the Democratic National Committee proclaimed the campaign a "solemn referendum" on the question of American entrance into the League and Cox devoted a greater part of his attention to the Treaty and the Covenant. The Democratic candidate toured the country in a hopeless effort to evoke some enthusiasm for his cause. Harding's campaign, on the other hand, was conducted in the best Republican tradition. He greeted visiting delegations from the front porch of his home at Marion, Ohio, and addressed them in a series of orations which were dignified, conciliatory, and for the most part pointless. On the issue of joining the League of Nations, it was difficult to understand where the Republican candidate stood. In one breath he denounced the Treaty and all its works; in another he spoke of amending the Covenant of the League "so that we may still have a remnant of the world aspirations of 1918 builded into the world's highest conception of useful coöperation"; in still another he spoke of our participation in some vague "association of nations."

Harding was elected by an overwhelming majority, but the indifference of the American people showed itself in the fact that less than half of the eligible voters went to the polls. Observers agreed that it was not so much a victory for the platitudes and ambiguities of the Republican candidate as a vote in rejection of everything Wilson had stood for. Harding's popular vote was nearly twice that of his Democratic opponent, while in the electoral college Harding received 404 votes against Cox's 127. The Republican victory in the Congressional elections was equally impressive. Truly the voters seemed to crave that return to "normalcy" which the new President promised.

Warren Gamaliel Harding had been born in Ohio in 1865. In Marion, a community of some 30,000 souls, he had become the

[1] The Farmer-Labor party was formed by the union of three groups. The first was the so-called Committee of Forty-eight, made up of middle-class intellectuals. The second was the the National Non-Partisan League, which was distinctly a farmer organization, very much like the earlier Farmers' Alliances of the eighties. Its chief strength lay in North Dakota and Minnesota; its titular head was A. C. Townley. The third element in the triad was the National Labor party, which had been organized in 1919 and which drew its strength entirely from trade-union ranks. It was headed by Max S. Hayes, once a vice-president of the American Federation of Labor and the holder of a membership card in the Socialist party.

proprietor of the daily *Star*, and had collected local items, written editorials, and solicited advertising and job printing. He prospered, and before long was a member of the little local group of select persons who controlled the town banks, public utilities, churches, and philanthropies. He became a follower in Senator Foraker's train, was prominent in state election contests and went to the state senate during 1900–1904, becoming its presiding officer as lieutenant-governor during 1904–1906. Once he ran for governor, but he was defeated. In 1912, he placed Taft in nomination at the Republican convention; in 1914, he went to the United States Senate; in 1916, he was chosen permanent chairman of the Republican National Convention. As a Senator, Harding's record was negligible: he made speeches for his constituents to read, and he voted at the direction of the party whips. In the words of William Allen White: "He was a voice through which the Republican organization spoke. In Ohio, it was the Ohio gang; in the country, the Republican National Committee."

President Harding surrounded himself by a Cabinet that both cheered and dismayed the elder statesmen of his party. The state portfolio went to Charles E. Hughes; the Treasury office to Andrew W. Mellon, wealthy banker of Pittsburgh; the Commerce Department to Herbert Hoover, who had been Wilson's Food Administrator and who had later been in charge of American relief work in Europe. The chairman of the Republican National Committee, Will H. Hays of Indiana, was made Postmaster-General. Albert B. Fall of New Mexico, who as a Senator had bitterly fought the Wilson Mexican policy and was openly friendly with the country's large oil interests, was made Secretary of the Interior. Harry M. Daugherty of Ohio, director of the President's pre-convention campaign, was placed in charge of the Department of Justice. To the other Cabinet posts men as undistinguished as these last three were appointed.

Harding's conception of the Presidency was a modest one. He was to be a spokesman for policies determined by others; the bearer of olive branches; and the guest of honor at conferences, the laying of corner-stones, and the opening of public buildings. Hughes was the Secretary of State: he was therefore the person to handle foreign affairs. Mellon was Secretary of the Treasury: he could be trusted to evolve public finance policies. Hoover was the Secretary of Commerce: problems that concerned the world of business were to have his thought and planning. Over these mighty ones Harding presided only in name. Further, Harding's ultimate loyalties were not to the traditions of the American government but to his party, not to the American people but to his small coterie of Ohio friends. In other words, Harding was unable to rise above his origins as had Presidents Arthur and McKinley, for example. He remained the Ohio politician to the end, regarding public office as the just reward of his followers and public possessions as the spoils that had fallen to the victors. It is not unjust to measure Harding's stature by the persons with whom he associated himself.

A dreary feature of the Harding administration was a crop of major scandals, those in the Veterans' Bureau and the Departments of the Interior and of Justice being particularly noisome. The Veterans' Bureau affair led straight to its director Charles R. Forbes, who was found, by a Senate investigating committee, to have been guilty of reckless waste, misconduct, and dishonesty in the handling of construction contracts and the purchase of supplies. According to the counsel for the Senate committee, out of the billion dollars appropriated for the rehabilitation and care of sick and disabled war veterans, during the two years Forbes had been in office, fully one-fourth had either been stolen or been meaninglessly squandered. In 1925, a federal court declared Forbes, who had been driven out of office early in 1923, to be guilty of taking part in a conspiracy to loot the Veterans' Bureau.

The disgraces involving the Department of Justice directly implicated Attorney-General Daugherty. A Senate investigating committee, headed by Smith Brookhart of Iowa, found a trail of illegal withdrawals of alcohol, of suddenly enriched persons (Daugherty not the least among them), and of criminal neglect of duty. According to one of the members of the Senate committee, the morale of the Department of Justice staff was shattered as unfaithful persons were raised in rank and others were demoted or dismissed for fidelity to their duties. Daugherty was asked to resign in March, 1924, by President Coolidge on the technical charge of refusing to open his Department affairs to Senator Brookhart and his colleagues. One of Daugherty's friends, Thomas W. Miller, who occupied the post of Alien Property Custodian, was dismissed from office and in 1927 was found guilty of conspiring to defraud the government in the transactions arising from the sale of the assets of the American Metal Company, an alien enemy concern. Daugherty was tried on the same charge but the jury could arrive at no decision; in the case of Miller, the verdict of guilty brought a penalty of eighteen months' imprisonment and a fine of $5000.

The taint of oil besmirched the Departments of the Navy and the Interior. In 1912, by the executive order of President Taft, there had been set aside an oil reserve, for naval purposes in time of emergency, in the Elk Hills district of California. This was known as Naval Oil Reserve No. 1 and consisted of 38,000 acres. A second such reserve, at Buena Vista Hills, California, was created in 1912, and this consisted of 29,000 acres. President Wilson followed his predecessor's example and in 1915 created Naval Oil Reserve No. 3 at Teapot Dome, Wyoming. This comprised 9500 acres. By an executive order in May, 1921, which Harding signed and which had the approval of Secretary of the Navy Denby, the administration of these naval reserves was transferred from the Navy to the Interior Department and fell into the hands of Albert B. Fall. Fall set to work at once to enrich his friends E. M. Doheny and Harry F. Sinclair. On April 7, 1922, secretly and without troubling to obtain other bids, Fall leased the Teapot Dome Reserve to Sinclair; and on April 25, 1922, by one agreement, and on December 11, 1922, by another, Fall leased the whole Elk Hills Reserve to Doheny. With regard to the Teapot Dome transaction, Fall later justified himself by saying that the government oil was being drained off by the diggings of oil operators on adjoining lands. And as for the Elk Hills lease, Fall stoutly contended that Doheny's promise to build storage tanks for fuel oil at Pearl Harbor, Hawaii, would be of greater service to the Navy, in time of a Pacific war, than the 250,000,000 barrels of oil that were lying untapped in the California oil fields.

The secrecy attending the leases and the sudden wealth of Fall, who was known to have been in financial straits, led to a Senate committee investigation. Under the able direction of Senator Thomas J. Walsh of Montana, the unsavory details of the affair were gradually disclosed. It was found that Sinclair had made a number of heavy contributions to the Republican campaign fund, that he had personally befriended Fall and had showered him with gifts; that Doheny had made a "loan" of $100,000 to Fall without security or interest; that Fall had gone to considerable pains to conceal the fact that this large sum of money had been borrowed from the oil magnate, evolving a number of fanciful tales to account for the money in his possession. The final results of the scandal were the following: Denby and Fall resigned their Cabinet offices; government civil suits to recapture the oil reserves were ultimately crowned with success in 1927, when the Supreme Court ordered them returned to the government and branded Sinclair and Fall as being guilty of "fraud, conspiracy, and corruption"; Fall was found guilty, in 1929, of accepting a bribe from Doheny and was sentenced to pay a fine of $100,000 and to serve a year's jail sentence.[2] The major actors in the drama, that is to say, Sinclair and Doheny, were acquitted in a criminal prosecution for conspiracy, although Sinclair was subsequently compelled to serve a short prison term at Washington for being in contempt of the Senate and for hiring private operatives to shadow members of the jury sitting on his case.

Under the weight of these scandals, Harding sank. When he left on a trip to Alaska, in June, 1923, the facts concerning the corruption in the Veterans' Bureau and Prohibition Bureau were more than suspected; of the criminal conduct involving his Cabinet officers more than idle gossip was abroad. Observers reported that the President was troubled and not the genial, confident person he had always been. He sickened and died on his way home from Alaska and Calvin Coolidge succeeded him as President of the United States on August 2, 1923.

The Administrations of Calvin Coolidge

Calvin Coolidge was fifty-one years old when he took the Presidential oath. He had been born at Plymouth, Vermont, had been graduated from Amherst College, had read law at Northampton, Massachusetts, and there had settled down to practice at the bar. With the law had gone the inevitable interest in politics, and slowly he had climbed the ladder of political success: first as municipal councilman, then as state legislator, then as mayor of Northampton for a year, then as a member of the state senate for three terms. In 1916, Coolidge had been elected lieutenant-governor by his adopted state; in 1919, he was governor of the Commonwealth of Massachusetts.

Then, in September, 1919, there had taken place one of those curious turns of fortune's wheel, and the name of the local poli-

[2] Fall began serving his term in July, 1931.

tician, the discreet, cautious party servant, became one to conjure with. In 1919, the Boston police force, suffering under the weight of low salaries and heavy occupational expenses, sought to ameliorate its condition by organizing. Instead of forming the customary benevolent society, the policemen applied for a trade-union charter to the American Federation of Labor and obtained it. The refusal of the police commissioner to treat with his men and his dismissal of their leaders precipitated a crisis, with the result that on September 9 the greater part of Boston's uniformed force went out on strike. Not a little disorder followed. The very next day the mayor moved to take the situation in hand by calling out on police duty those companies of the Massachusetts militia stationed in the city. By the morning of September 11, order had been restored. It was not until that afternoon that Governor Coolidge, who had refused to intercede with the commissioner and who had rejected the mayor's request for militiamen when the strike threatened, appeared on the scene. He assumed control; poured into Boston militia units from other parts of the state; and sent to President Gompers of the American Federation of Labor a tart telegram in which he declared: "There is no right to strike against the public safety by anybody, anywhere, any time." Friends of law and order rushed to hail Coolidge's action as the courageous deed of a cool public servant; he was reelected governor of Massachusetts by a great plurality; his name was prominently mentioned during the deliberations of the Republican convention of 1920; and he was nominated for the Vice-Presidency almost by acclamation.

As President, Coolidge was able to save the reputation of his party despite the discreditable events in which its leaders had figured. Not that he ever denounced the wrong-doing of his predecessor; nor did he give aid or comfort to those undertaking to bring the culprits to justice. On the contrary, he did all he could to shield the malefactors from punishment and regarded their prosecutors with ill-concealed dislike and contempt. But personally, he was honest and eminently respectable. More important, he was a conservative, a Hamiltonian, a friend of Big Business. He had the support of the overwhelming majority of the press, which taught the country to regard the prosperity of the decade of the twenties as somehow being, if not exactly his work, certainly in large measure the result of his policy of hands-off as far as business was concerned. Because the years of his administrations marked a golden age in American annals, well-to-do Americans paused every now and then to do honor to the man during whose Presidency all these wonderful things were coming to pass.

Although the President did suffer a number of rebuffs at the hands of Congress his strength was not seriously impaired. When the Republican convention met at Cleveland on June 10, 1924, Calvin Coolidge, though having held office but ten months, was almost the unanimous choice of his party. On the first ballot he received 1065 votes as against 34 votes for La Follette and 10 votes for Johnson. For the Vice-Presidency, General Charles G. Dawes of Chicago was named after Lowden had refused the nomination. The Republican party platform was frankly a conservative document. It pledged its standard bearers to a program of rigid governmental economy; championed progressive tax reduction; favored American membership in the World Court; continued to regard with hostility entry into the League of Nations; promised continued support to the principles of high protectionism; and had something to say of agriculture, railroads, a merchant marine, war veterans, selective immigration, child labor, the eight-hour day, and independence for the Filipinos when they were ready for it.

The Democrats assembled on June 24 at New York and sat almost continuously until July 10. A serious disagreement broke out among the members of the resolutions committee, and the fight was taken to the floor of the convention to divide the delegates into two hostile camps. The platform was not reported out until June 28, and then it was accompanied by two minority reports. The first called for American entry into the League of Nations; this resolution was defeated by a vote of 353½ yeas to 742½ nays. The second called for the denunciation of the Ku Klux Klan by name. After a prolonged debate the resolution was also lost, the vote standing 541.85 for naming the Klan and 546.15 against naming it. The accepted platform spoke of a scientific tariff and tax reduction; stressed the need for honesty in government; promised farm relief without committing the party to a definite program; declared in favor of a readjustment of railroad rates to give agricultural, coal, and ore shippers lower tariffs; and favored government ownership and operation of a merchant marine and immediate independence for the Philippine Islands. The Democrats championed military and naval armaments reduction by joint agreement with other nations and spoke of their confidence "in the ideal of world peace, the League of Nations, and the World Court of Justice as together constituting the supreme effort of the statesmanship and religious conviction of our time to organize the world for peace." They, however, recommended that the question of joining the League be submitted to a popular referendum. The platform also supported collective bargaining and the child labor amendment. As for the Ku Klux Klan, which had stirred up so much antagonism among the delegates, the platform said merely: "We insist at all times upon obedience to the orderly processes of the law and deplore and condemn any effort to arouse religious or racial dissension."

On June 30 the balloting commenced, with McAdoo of California and Smith of New York the leading contestants and, incidentally, the chiefs of those two groups that had struggled so bitterly over the naming of the Klan in the platform. Supporting McAdoo were the rural, dry, evangelical Protestant Democrats of the South and the West; clustering about the standard of Smith were the Democrats of the great city machines, who had many Catholics and Jews in their ranks, who were hostile to the Eighteenth Amendment, and who saw that the Negroes of the North were a great political force to be reckoned with and to be won over to the Democracy, if possible. An impassable gulf separated these two factions. Finally, after other efforts to make possible the withdrawal of the chief contenders had failed, it was announced on July 8 that Smith was prepared to release his candidates if McAdoo was. McAdoo's reply that he would let his followers decide for themselves was regarded as tantamount to acceptance, and on the one hundred and third ballot, John W. Davis of West Virginia and New York was nominated. With him was named Governor Charles W. Bryan of Nebraska, the Commoner's brother.

In 1924, the West was aflame once more, as it had been in 1896, though this time it was a revolt in the ranks of the Republican party. The fact is, insurgent Republicans had held the balance of power in the politically close Sixty-eighth Congress, elected in 1922. The Republicans had been nominally in control, but in the Republican majority in the Senate there were five Republican Senators, headed by La Follette, who were consistently at odds with their party's chiefs; and these formed a bloc which, by combining with the Democrats, was able to frustrate Secretary of the Treasury Mellon's tax plan and other Republican party measures. In the House, the situation was largely the same. There was a strong possibility that this disaffected Republican group would join hands with a powerful labor body, which, at last, was ready to try its independent fortune at the polls. And so it turned out to be.

Reference has been made to the Farmer-Labor party in the election of 1920. By 1924, it, along with its component elements, had largely disintegrated. But there had appeared in its place the Conference for Progressive Political Action, backed by the powerful railroad brotherhoods. Here was a labor movement that held in it the promise of political success: it represented organized labor, was right wing in its tendencies, and was not likely to permit itself to be involved in the sort of factional disputes which had rent the Socialist party. The Conference for Progressive Political Action originally met in February, 1922; at a second meeting, it closed its doors to Communists; at a third, it decided to enter the political lists; and at a fourth, on July 4, 1924, it offered its nomination to Senator La Follette on his own platform.

La Follette accepted, helped choose as his running mate Senator Burton K. Wheeler of Montana (who was a Democrat), and wrote a platform which gained the endorsement, at the same time, of the Socialist party and the executive council of the American Federation of Labor. This, then, was the first Presidential campaign in which organized labor had formally taken part and in which Socialists, middle-class intellectuals, farmers, and organized workers were to fight under the same banner. La Follette's platform was directed largely at monopoly, that same monopoly which had been troubling the agrarian West for the last half-century. In other words, his was an agrarian program rather than a Socialist one. Thus, the first paragraph of his articles of faith read:

> The great issue before the American people today is the control of government and industry by private monopoly. . . . In violation of law, monopoly has crushed competition, stifled private initiative and independent enterprise and without fear of punishment now exacts extortionate profits upon every necessity of life consumed by the public.

The platform went on to promise the cleaning out of official corruption; the return of the naval oil reserves; public ownership of water power; the fixing of railroad rates on the basis of prudent investment; public ownership of railroads as the only solution to the transportation problem; tax reduction for moderate incomes only; abolition of the right of the Supreme Court to nullify acts of

Congress; popular election of the federal judiciary; tariff revision downward; prohibition of gambling in agricultural futures; reconstruction of the Federal Reserve Board and the Federal Farm Loan Board to provide real public control of the nation's financial and credit facilities; adequate laws to guarantee to farmers and industrial workers the right to organize and bargain collectively; the creation of a governmental agricultural marketing corporation; an anti-injunction law; adoption of the child labor amendment; the direct nomination and election of the President; the use of the initiative and referendum in federal affairs; the use of a popular referendum when war threatened; revision of the Treaty of Versailles; the outlawing of war, the abolition of conscription, and the reduction of armaments—these last to be effected by international treaties. La Follette ran under various party designations. In some states he was compelled to make his canvass under the Socialist emblem; in others he used the name of the Farmer-Labor party; in still others he ran as the head of the Progressive or Independent or Labor ticket, as the case might be. But in no states, outside of Wisconsin, North Dakota, and Minnesota, did he have state organizations of any value to help him.

Despite La Follette's presence in the campaign and the uncertainty attending the three-cornered contest, only 51.1 per cent of the eligible voters went to the polls. Coolidge's majority over his two rivals was an impressive one. His popular vote was 15,725,000, against 8,386,500 for Davis, and 4,822,900 for La Follette. The electoral vote was as follows: Coolidge 382, Davis 136, La Follette 13. Davis's vote came from the Solid South and Oklahoma; La Follette's from his native Wisconsin. It is important to note, however, that the combined Davis–La Follette popular vote was greater than the Coolidge vote in the Border states of Kentucky, Maryland, and Missouri; that Coolidge won by only a plurality vote in seven far western states; and that La Follette ran ahead of Davis in eleven western and far western states. However, in none of the eastern or middle western states was Coolidge threatened. In the Congressional elections, the Republican triumph was sufficiently great to insure that in the Sixty-ninth Congress the insurgents would no longer hold the balance of power. Henceforth, for six years, the party *par excellence* of Big Business would wield complete control over the country's destinies.

The Conference for Progressive Political Action did not survive for long. The American Federation of Labor leaders regretted their support of a third-party movement, and the railroad brotherhoods regarded the five million votes La Follette had received as too disappointing to hold out promise for immediate success. A last convention was held in February, 1925, and when the railroad men announced their withdrawal from the party the Conference adjourned sine die.

President Coolidge's good fortune did not desert him during the full term of his second administration. The country's phenomenal prosperity continued; business had the encouraging support of the administration's officers, Secretaries Mellon and Hoover in particular; industrial conflicts, except for a series of strikes in the anthracite and bituminous coal fields, were few and unimportant; and peace and plenty reigned over the land. The President continued to receive the applause of large business groups because of the energy with which he promoted the policies of which they approved and frowned upon those they disapproved.

On August 2, 1927, four years after he had become chief executive of the United States, Coolidge fluttered the political dovecotes by issuing a cryptic statement to the press which read, in its entirety, as follows: "I do not choose to run for President in 1928." Coolidge refused to amplify his message or to deny the report of his more zealous followers that he would make the canvass if drafted by the Republican convention. His continued silence kept the important delegations from New York, Massachusetts, and Pennsylvania unpledged and prevented the growth of booms for Lowden and Dawes, both of whom had expressed themselves in favor of farm-relief legislation and both of whom, therefore, Coolidge regarded as unfriendly to the policies of his administration. It began to become increasingly apparent that Secretary of Commerce Hoover was being groomed as the heir-apparent of the administration.

The readers of portents were not to be mistaken. The Republican convention assembled at Kansas City on June 12 and, although Lowden had shown considerable pre-convention strength, Hoover met with little organized opposition. He received the nomination on the first ballot, as did Senator Charles Curtis of Kansas for the Vice-Presidency. The Democrats met at Houston, Texas, on June 27, with Claude G. Bowers delivering the keynote address. Governor Alfred E. Smith's strength, despite the animosities that had been revealed at the 1924 convention, had been steadily growing over the four years, with the result that objection to his choice was slight. He was named on the first ballot and Senator Joseph T. Robinson of Arkansas was nominated to make the contest with him.

The campaign of 1928 presented many curious anomalies. For one, there was little to choose between the platforms of the two parties. The Republican campaign document praised the achievements of the Coolidge administrations, lauded protectionism, and approved the Department of State's foreign policies with respect to Mexico, Nicaragua, China, and the League of Nations. With regard to agriculture, the Republicans gave their approval to none of the Congressional panaceas for farm relief; as for Prohibition, they promised merely continued "vigorous enforcement." The Democrats, in their turn, avoided major issues quite as successfully. Although Coolidge's do-nothing policy for agriculture was bitterly arraigned, no definite program was advanced as a promised cure. The Democrats also pledged themselves to enforce the Eighteenth Amendment. The tariff question was straddled, the platform speaking of a tariff program that would "maintain legitimate business and a high standard of wages" and that would impose duties to "permit effective competition" and "insure against monopoly."

If the dissimilarities between the two party platforms seemed negligible, the Republican and Democratic standard bearers appeared to be as far apart as the poles. However, what seemed to be striking disparities resolved themselves into only superficial differences: on the points of heritage, training, and career, the two men furnished interesting contrasts; with regard to their social and economic views, there was in reality little to choose between them. Both had come from humble origins, Hoover having been born on an Iowa farm and Smith in New York City's slums. But from birth onward, their paths had stretched in different directions. Hoover, orphaned in childhood and befriended by well-to-do relatives, had studied engineering at Stanford University and then, during his early manhood, had quickly accumulated a fortune as a mining and railroad expert and promoter. His work had taken him into obscure byways of the globe; and, too, he was as much at home in Peking, Cape Town, and London as in his adopted state of California. He had proved himself to be a capable office chief and had shown his mettle as Belgian Relief head, Food Administrator, Chairman of the American Relief Administration, and Secretary of Commerce.

In all these posts, Hoover had learned to give orders; he had never been compelled to meet stubborn opposition or to reconcile differences. Smith, on the other hand, had moved in a political environment from very childhood. He had had little formal schooling, had worked at a variety of unskilled occupations and then had become a Tammany stalwart, learning his statecraft as Lincoln, McKinley, Theodore Roosevelt, and Coolidge had done, from practical situations and his daily intercourse with his fellow beings. He had been showered with the favors of his party, and at four different times had been elected governor of New York State. He was a man of the cities and a man of the people—human in his relationships, humble in speech, a "hard-headed, hard-working realist"—but he was no proletarian as Debs and even the young Bryan had been.

Governor Smith conducted a gallant fight, and the outpourings of crowds, which greeted him all over the country, attested to his personal popularity. There were, however, certain great disabilities he labored under. For one he had no economic program of dissent, having nothing particular to offer labor and agriculture. Again, he was a "wet" as far as Prohibition was concerned, a position unquestionably abhorrent to the old Bryan country of the South and West. Further, he was a Tammanyite. In the fourth place, he was a Roman Catholic. Finally, the golden era of prosperity stood in the way of a Republican upset, no matter how great the personal gifts of the Democratic nominee. The result was, Smith's presence in the campaign brought out the greatest vote to figure in an American election—and the Democracy suffered its most humiliating defeat. Smith lost his own state of New York as well as the southern states of Virginia, North Carolina, Tennessee, Florida, and Texas. He did not carry a single Border state. He almost failed in Alabama. The Far West, which had voted for Bryan and Wilson, disowned him. His total electoral vote was 87 and consisted of only Alabama, Arkansas, Georgia, Louisiana, Mississippi, and South Carolina in the erstwhile Solid South and the largely Catholic states of Massachusetts and Rhode Island.[3] Hoover's electoral vote was 444. The popular votes were as follows: for Hoover, 21,392,000; for Smith, 15,016,000. The Seventy-first Congress, elected at the same time, also was overwhelmingly Republican.

[3] Smith carried the great cities of New York, Boston, Cleveland, St. Louis, and San Francisco. He also ran well in Chicago, Detroit, and Philadelphia.

The Engineer in Politics

Herbert Hoover had carried his engineering habits into his business life with great success. He was to bring these same views over into politics, and their lack of success in this sphere was at once to become apparent. He was a firm believer in American industrialism and the opponent of any sort of political or social change that might, even remotely, smack of socialism. He placed his faith in the sort of individualism that Carnegie had sung; he knew of America's great wealth in her natural resources and was certain that, possessing these, we were the masters of our economic fate. With graphs and columns of statistics he had watched our extraordinary material progress during the entire decade of the twenties and he had come to believe sincerely that the benefits of this continued prosperity had seeped down even to the lowest strata of society and that want was being eradicated. He visioned a capitalist world in which factory wheels were kept incessantly turning, in which more and more goods were being produced and consumed, in which workingmen were always being employed and were coming to live in better houses, use more automobiles and radios and buy more electrical appliances. Such a society needed few governmental controls and even less social interference. Out of economic views such as these, the political opinions inevitably stemmed: if mankind was guided by an enlightened self-interest, if the processes of the economic life could be plainly charted and their future just as plainly predicted, if, in short, society was rational, then there was no place in it for the arts of accommodation. The facts always pointed to irrefragable conclusions: all one had to do was to collect the data, and opinions—based on prejudice, cupidity, fear—could be at once relegated to the realm of the irrational where they properly belonged. Government, therefore, was not a matter of give and take, of compromise, reconciliation, bargaining: government was one vast agency for gathering facts and for writing Q.E.D. after plainly-arrived-at conclusions.

Before the first half of his administration was over, Herbert Hoover was to taste the bitter dregs of defeat. Politicians were stubborn in the face of facts and demanded legislation for their local constituencies; business men refused to regard America's economic life as a closely integrated whole and clamored for support and tariff protection for their particular industries; and the capitalist world itself, with its self-adjusting laws of supply and demand working as inexorably as the ebb and flow of the tides (at least, so it seemed), simply collapsed in 1930 and where there had been once plenty there was soon to be destitution and gaunt poverty. The world and men, after all, were much more irrational than Herbert Hoover ever believed them to be. The problems of Prohibition, farm relief, crime, international peace, waterpower control, a war veteran policy were no nearer solution in December, 1931, than they had been in March, 1929. Added to this lack of accomplishment was the failure of the Hoover administration to adopt even palliatives for the handling of the country's staggering unemployment problem. And from December, 1931, to March, 1933, the President was to be confronted by a hostile Congress.

President Hoover met his first setback in the political arena. He was compelled to give ear to partisan considerations in the choice of his Cabinet, with the result that astonished Americans were to see his official family not made up of highly skilled experts but of Republican party stalwarts, many of them previously unknown. The State Department was filled by Henry L. Stimson, the Treasury office by Andrew W. Mellon, the Labor office by James J. Davis. These names were familiar; the rest were not. The Senate was openly hostile toward many of the Presidential appointments. It rebelled, though unsuccessfully, at the confirmation of Charles E. Hughes for the chief justiceship of the Supreme Court; it refused to approve the naming of John J. Parker, a "lily-white" Republican of North Carolina, to the same tribunal; and it challenged, in the courts, the make-up of the Federal Power Commission.

Once more, in the Hoover administration, Republican insurgency raised its head. The insurgent bloc, led in the Senate by Norris of Nebraska, opposed the President on his tariff, waterpower, and farm relief programs, united with Democrats to override his vetoes, and made common cause with Democratic Senators in the fights on Hughes, Parker, and many of Hoover's lesser nominations.

Again, Herbert Hoover was to learn that tariffs were not scientific devices adjusted after a careful weighing of production costs and cost-of-living standards, but documents whose schedules were written on the basis of trades between politicians and a continuous yielding to the needs of the least advanced rather than the most progressive manufacturers. The result was the writing, and the signing by the President, of the Tariff Act of 1930, with the highest schedules of rates that the protectionist interests had yet gained.[4] And this in the face of the protests of almost all the outstanding academic economists in America, the threatened reprisals of foreign nations, and the inevitable harm such a policy must visit on our export trade!

Finally, there came the stock market crash of October, 1929, and the catastrophic economic depression that set in with the beginning of 1930. By the spring of 1931 even administration spokesmen admitted that the total of unemployed in the country was in the neighborhood of 6,500,000 workers. Bread lines existed in all the great cities, and hundreds of thousands of families were barely subsisting on the meager doles granted them by charitable agencies. The steel industry was operating at one-third of capacity; crude oil production had reached the lowest point since 1926; the prices of copper, silver, cotton, and other commodities almost daily touched new lows; and as for the condition of agriculture, the lot of the farmer might be summarized plainly enough by the simple statement that wheat was selling at less than fifty cents on the Chicago market in the summer of 1931. Laissez-faire had broken down, and the forecasts of the business astrologers, which had promised such happy events when Herbert Hoover took the Presidential oath on March 4, 1929, were so many meaningless and bitter words that Americans remembered when they turned to look at the uninspired man in the White House. The electorate used the only means it had in its power to show a loss of confidence: in the Congressional elections of 1930 the American voters returned the House to Democratic control and reduced the Republican membership of the Senate to a bare plurality.

[4] See below, page 24.

II. LEADING LEGISLATIVE PROBLEMS OF THE NINETEEN TWENTIES

The Tariff Acts of 1922 and 1930

With the Republican party again in control of the Presidency and Congress in 1921, it was inevitable that business men should demand and legislators grant an immediate revision of the Democratic Tariff Act of 1913. While the Democratic tariff principles had never been fairly tested under normal conditions, it was argued that low duties were unfavorable to business. Again, something had to be done for agriculture, which, since the war's outbreak, had overexpanded its acreage and was confronted by great surpluses and by falling prices. It was the hope of farmers and their representatives in Congress that the domestic market, at least, might be secured by the raising of duties on farm products. A number of new American industries had sprung up since 1913, and these were out-spoken in their demands for protection.

The result was that the Sixty-seventh Congress, which Harding had called in special session immediately after his inauguration, passed an Emergency Tariff Act in May, 1921. This raised the duties on agricultural articles, wool, and sugar and devoted particular attention to the new chemical industry. An embargo was placed on German dyestuffs and those products that could not be made here were put on a licensing basis. Also, stringent clauses were written into the act to prevent foreign dumping. Meanwhile, the House Ways and Means Committee and the Senate Finance Committee were recasting the whole tariff structure, schedule by schedule. It was soon apparent, as the debates became public, that protectionism had few real foes in either party. The reason was plain: industrialization had made giant strides during the war, nowhere greater than in the South and West, where once low tariff principles had prevailed. Therefore, it was no surprise to anyone that the Fordney-McCumber tariff bill, when it finally emerged from the Senate Committee in April, 1922, proved to contain the highest rates in American tariff history up to that time. In rare instances only were rates cut below the duties of 1913; the general tendency was to approximate the levels of 1909 and to set prohibitory duties for the benefit of the new industries. With little genuine opposition, and then only from a few Western Progressives and a score or so of old-fashioned Southern Democrats, the new tariff bill became law on September 19, 1922.

The administrative features of the 1922 tariff were unique in two particulars. 1. The ad valorem duties were to be assessed on the foreign value of the goods or their export value at the port of shipment, whichever happened to be higher. 2. The act explicitly stated that the principle underlying American protection was to be that of the equalization of the costs of production between American products and those foreign articles entering into competition with ours. In other words, the tariff was to be a flexible one henceforth; and provision therefore was made for the creation of a Tariff Commission. This Tariff Commission was to ascertain what these differences in production costs were; was to investigate complaints of unfair practices by foreign competitors; and was to draw up new schedules of rates, as its investigations determined their necessity. To the President was given the power of proclaiming the new rates upon information furnished by the Tariff Commission. He did not, however, have to follow the Commission's recommendations; and such changes as he saw fit to make were not to be more than 50 per cent higher or lower than the rates written into the Tariff Act of 1922. In this fashion, the Republican tariff makers could claim that their guiding thought was to protect American industry from foreign dumping and American workers from the competition of the "pauper labor" of Europe. That the flexibility provision was to break down lamentably and that we were no nearer scientific tariff making in the twenties than we ever had been, time was quickly to reveal.

By 1928, dissatisfaction with the existing tariff was again general, and when the Seventy-first Congress met in special session, on President Hoover's call, the Congressional committees once more proceeded to a thorough overhauling of the protective system. The reasons advanced for tariff tinkering, in this instance, were the following: President Hoover, in his campaign addresses, had promised a limited revision, with particular attention to the needs of agriculture. The farmers, at the close of the decade of the twenties, were worse off than they had been at its opening. Higher rates, to the Republicans, again seemed to be the proper solution, although this time the farmers themselves were less sure about the efficacy of high protection than they had been in 1921. A number of special interests deemed the rates of the 1922 act inadequate, and these combined, through their Congressional representatives, on the basis of the familiar system of trade and barter, to scale all the schedules upward. There was general criticism directed against the breakdown of the flexibility feature of the 1922 act. Despite the elaborate investigations of the Tariff Commission, the only result had been the raising of rates. Opponents of high protection, particularly those whose economic well-being depended upon the creation of a healthy foreign trade (investment bankers, importers, and automobile manufacturers were three groups in this class), hoped that the spirit of nationalism had somewhat abated and that the tariff wall would be lowered. They regarded President Hoover, because of his economic training and his interest in the stimulation of American foreign trade, as sympathetic to their point of view. Much to their amazement, they were to see the "Little Americans" again firmly perched in the saddle, the same disregard expressed for the maintenance of an international division of labor, and the same intention displayed to shut our doors to European wares, even in the face of threatened reprisals. And they were to see President Hoover yielding to this party. The only solace the President could offer the friends of international trade was the promise that the flexibility provision would be employed to adjust such inequalities as the new tariff act contained.

The House Ways and Means Committee reported out the Hawley bill on May 7, 1929, and on May 28, so smoothly did the organization machine run, the bill was passed by a vote of 264 to 147. Duties on farm products and on raw materials were raised; minerals received particular attention; the rates on textiles and on dyestuffs were again scaled upward; compensatory duties were placed on manufactured articles the raw materials of which were taxed. But this time the Senate was less willing to follow the House's lead and insurgent Republicans from the Far West again revolted, as they had over the Payne-Aldrich bill in 1909. Insurgent Senators first tried to restrict the Senate Finance Committee to a consideration of the agricultural schedule only; this maneuver failing, they succeeded in incorporating two radical amendments into the Smoot bill. The first provided for an export debenture, or bounty, on all farm products exported, in order to make the tariff on foodstuffs effective; the second vested the administration of the flexibility power in the hands of Congress instead of the President. Despite the protests of President Hoover, the Senate bill was passed with both these amendments and in this fashion went into Conference Committee.

If the President could not crack the whip over the Senate, he could over the House, with the result that the House conferees refused to accept the Senate bill. Matters were thus deadlocked until May, 1930, with neither side yielding on the debenture or Congressional flexibility. Finally, on May 19, the Senate voted to untie the hands of its conferees. How completely the Senate had broken away from Hoover's leadership may be seen in the closeness by which the act was accomplished. The vote to give up the export debenture plan was 43 to 41, with fourteen Republicans voting or paired against the resolution.[1] The vote to place the flexibility tariff power in the hands of the President was 43 to 42, with Vice-President Curtis casting the deciding ballot for the resolution. These differences out of the way, the Conference Committee was able to agree on its report. On June 13, 1930, the Senate passed the Smoot-Hawley bill by a vote of 44 to 42, eleven Republicans voting against the bill and five Democrats voting for it. On the next day, the House did similarly, the vote being 222 yeas to 153 nays. On June 17, 1930, President Hoover affixed his signature and the Tariff Act of 1930 was law.

The rates were higher under the new act than ever. In a large number of cases, the duties on raw materials ranged from 50 to 100 per cent greater than those in the 1922 schedules; generally the average ad valorem rate for all the schedules was 40.08 per cent as compared with 33.22 per cent in the 1922 Act. It is interesting to note that the tariff makers refused to pay heed to those interests that wanted no protection at all. Thus, the automobile manufacturers had to accept a duty of 10 per cent although they themselves had agitated for the placing of automobiles on the free list.

As in the 1922 Act, the Tariff Act of 1930 provided for the appointment of a Tariff Commission (expanded to six members)

[1] Nothing more plainly revealed that tariff writing was the work of local interests than the vote against the debenture provision. Thus, six Democrats voted with the Republican majority and all these came from states that were interested in the passage of a tariff bill.

with power to investigate production costs and to recommend to the President the lowering or raising of rates. It was largely upon the retention of this provision, with its promise of flexibility, that President Hoover appealed for popular support for the new measure. However, the experiences with the flexibility power, as exercised by Presidents Harding and Coolidge, had been none too reassuring. Thus, from 1922 to June, 1929, Harding and Coolidge had proclaimed thirty-seven changes in rates: thirty-two of these had provided for higher duties; five for lower ones. The five different commodities receiving the benefits of lower duties were the unimportant ones of millfeeds, bobwhite quail, paint-brush handles, cresylic acid, and phenol. And when, in 1924, a majority of the commission had recommended that the sugar duty be lowered, President Coolidge had simply filed their report and done nothing. Critics pointed out, too, that the consuming public had no representation before the commission and that the body had heretofore been a football of politics and had, indeed, been packed in the interests of high protectionist groups.

While the Hawley-Smoot bill was still before Congress, no signs were wanting that a large and increasing body of Americans were impatient with, if not actually hostile toward, the excesses of log-rolling, bartering, and lobbying which entered into legislative tariff making. More and more people were beginning to realize that the American economic life was international in its scope and could not be confined within high Chinese walls. The widespread and favorable reception accorded to the manifesto, signed by more than one thousand trained economists and made public in May, 1930, which called upon President Hoover to veto the bill if it should ever get out of Conference Committee, showed the changing temper of the American people. The points made by the protesting economists were these: An increase in restrictive duties must tend to raise prices for the American consuming public. High tariff duties only encouraged wasteful concerns and unnecessary industries to continue in operation. A high tariff would limit the export of both agricultural and manufactured goods by the restrictions it would place on foreign trade. Protection could not help the growers of agricultural staples because their own surpluses helped to fix the world price. A high tariff would affect injuriously American investments abroad and prevent payment by debtor nations of interest and principal on loans made by Americans. Reprisals by foreign nations would be inevitable. This last turned out to be no idle prophecy. While the tariff bill was still being considered in Congress, European trade associations, from every important country on the Continent, filed protests against it with American consular and diplomatic representatives. And after the Tariff Act of 1930 was signed by the President, foreign governments proceeded to enact retaliatory measures. Before 1931 closed, fully twenty-five countries either had made extensive tariff revisions, had increased specific duties, or had threatened to do so. In almost every important case, the justification advanced was the necessity for fighting the United States with her own weapons.

There could be no question, as the nineteen thirties progressed, that an important reason for the continuance of world-wide depression was to be found in the artificial barriers erected to impede the international flow of goods and services. Everywhere, economic nationalism—which meant national self-sufficiency—was being fostered by governments. And the United States had been a leader in creating such devices, of which the protective tariff was the most important.

Creating a Merchant Marine

The merchant marine, which the United States Shipping Board and the Emergency Fleet Corporation had provided the nation during the years 1917–1920, was owned, and in considerable measure also operated, by the government. However necessary such a "socialist" scheme might be in war-time, under normal conditions it was repugnant to the spirit of American individualism. Of course, it was being argued, the government should give every encouragement, but if we were to put our carrying trade on such a sound basis that it would meet effectively the competition of British and German shipping companies, the merchant fleet must be operated by private owners.

In line with such ideas, there were therefore enacted the Merchant Marine Act of 1920 and the Merchant Marine Act of 1928. Under both of these measures the Shipping Board and the Merchant Fleet Corporation were continued. Under the first law the Shipping Board was to dispose of the war-time merchant fleet, as quickly as possible, to private operators. Every precaution was taken to see that the ships did not fall into the hands of foreign companies. Easy terms of payment were to be granted to purchasers. The Merchant

Fleet Corporation was to have these functions: it was to operate those ships it could not sell to private groups; it was to establish new shipping routes and keep ships in these services until private capital could be induced to take them over; it was to make loans to such shipping companies as were willing to operate over these new routes. To perform these tasks, the Merchant Fleet Corporation was given the use of a revolving fund of $25,000,000.

Between 1920 and 1928 the Shipping Board sought to interest American capital in the development of a merchant fleet that would be capable of carrying at least half of the country's overseas trade. It laid out some thirty different trade routes over which regular service was to be furnished. And it set out to establish shipping companies where none had existed before. Because American capital was timid to venture into a new field, the Shipping Board continued to lower purchase prices on its vessels and even went so far as to guarantee the losses of those operators who were willing to work the new routes. However, it became apparent that none of these new shipping companies was accumulating enough surpluses for capital replacements. The only remedy was subsidy, and this, in a measure, was offered by the Merchant Marine Act of 1928.

The law of 1928 renewed the declaration of a privately owned and operated merchant marine. It maintained the same administrative agencies. The Merchant Fleet Corporation was to continue to operate the government-owned ships until they could be disposed of, and was also given the power of replacement and repair so that the portion of the merchant fleet which was still government-owned would not become obsolescent. Subsidy was provided for through three means, two of which were directly indicated and one of which was implied: 1. There was set up a revolving fund of $250,000,000 from which construction loans up to three-fourths of the costs of building were to be made to private operators. 2. Private owners were to be given, as an encouragement to ship building and operation, long-term mail carrying contracts. That this was subsidy may be seen from the fact that up to February 1, 1930, there were awarded to seventeen steamship lines postal contracts totaling $5,588,000 annually, when the cost of carriage of the mails actually to be carried would have been but $92,000. The ratio of government-contract price to normal-rate price was therefore sixty to one. That operators regarded the postal contracts in the light of subsidy one may see, too, from the fact that during 1928–1930 postal contracts called for the construction of sixty-eight ships, valued at $281,000,000, which were to operate over thirty-nine new shipping routes. 3. The price at which the Shipping Board was selling its vessels to private operators constituted an indirect subsidy. So, from 1925 to 1930 the Shipping Board sold to ten lines a total of one hundred and four vessels for something less than $23,000,000. The total cost of construction for these one hundred and four ships had been $258,000,000; that is to say, the sale price to the private owners, in the aggregate, represented 9 per cent of the cost of construction to the government.

On December 31, 1930, there were registered under the American flag 1778 ocean-going ships of 1000 gross tons or more, of which 1345 ships were privately owned and 433 ships were still controlled by the Shipping Board's Merchant Fleet Corporation. The gross tonnage owned privately was 7,136,746; that owned by the government, 2,462,095. The outcome of this government interest was an extraordinary increase in the American merchant marine, and we were gradually freeing ourselves from a dependence upon British bottoms for the carriage of our exports and imports.

However desirable such an outcome might be regarded (and there were some who disputed its desirability), the question inevitably presented itself: Could not the government have attained the same end, at no greater cost, and at the same time provided lower rates for shippers and better working conditions for seamen and longshoremen, had it continued to own and operate the ships it had built at such great expense? But such a consideration was given no serious attention; and in subsequent legislation, as we shall see, the United States continued, with heavy public subsidies, to support a privately owned and operated merchant marine.

The Railroad Problem

The Railroad Administration of 1917–1919 was designed to be only a war expedient, with the result that on December 24, 1919, President Wilson announced that on March 1, 1920, the railroads of the country would be restored to private management. Congress gave considerable thought to the problem and the Transportation Act of 1920, which was signed by President Wilson on February 28, turned out to be a complete overhauling of the Interstate Commerce Act. The new law incorporated all the suggestions that reformers had been demanding for the past two decades, and government regulation over the railroad net, as far as Congress could legally go, was now complete.

The Transportation Act of 1920 reorganized the Interstate Commerce Commission. The law provided for a bipartisan board of eleven commissioners, who were to be appointed by the President with the consent of the Senate for seven-year terms.

The commission was given the power of establishing and maintaining rates which were to yield "a fair return upon the aggregate value of the railway property of the country."

The more prosperous roads were to share their profits with the less prosperous. All carriers enjoying a net railway operating income in excess of 6 per cent of their property value were to set aside half of the excess in their own reserve funds and were to turn over the other half to the commission to be applied to a railroad contingent fund. From this contingent fund, the commission might make loans to less fortunate carriers for capital expenditures. This was the so-called recapture clause.[2]

The long and short haul clause was amended, and the rules of procedure the commission had been employing were put into statutory form.

For the first time since its creation, the commission was given the power to prescribe minimum rates.

The twilight zone between state and federal control was removed. The commission was authorized to adjust rates and eliminate discriminations in those cases where persons engaged in intrastate commerce appeared to have obtained advantages over persons engaged in interstate commerce.

The commission was empowered to draw up a plan for the consolidation of the railroad lines of the country into a limited number of systems. Such combinations were to be exempt from the restrictions of the anti-trust laws; were to be on economic and not on geographic bases; and were to be made with an eye to the maintenance of competition between the carriers in the existing channels of trade.

[2] It was in a contest over this recapture clause that the Supreme Court in 1929, in the O'Fallon case, handed down its famous decision in which it declared that the Smyth v. Ames rule of "reproduction cost new" was to be given consideration in the determination of the valuation base for railroad rate-fixing. See below, page 93.

The anti-pooling clause of the original act was radically amended to permit the commission to authorize pools, for the division of traffic, if better service could be attained or economies of operation effected.

The commission was given the right to approve the formation of the Railway Express Agency out of the four great express companies then existing.

The commission was at last given authority to regulate the issuance of railway securities and to supervise the use to which the proceeds from their sales were to be put. After December 31, 1921, no person could be an officer or director of more than one carrier without the commission's consent. Even stronger was the prohibition against participation by directors in the sale of securities for their roads.

The administrative powers of the commission were enlarged to include control over "car service" (i. e., equipment) and terminals, and over embargoes and priorities; its supervision over accounts was extended; it could have access to all books and documents belonging to the carriers; it was to enforce rigorously a provision that carriers should be paid in cash and at once for freight shipments.

Elaborate machinery for the mediation of disputes between the railroads and their employees was set up. While compulsory arbitration was discarded, attempts were made to check industrial conflict through the creation of a Railroad Labor Board. This board was to sit in consideration of disputes which had not been settled by conference between the interested parties or by hearings before local boards of adjustment. The board was to make its decisions public and was to depend upon public opinion for their enforcement. In 1926, however, the Railroad Labor Board was abolished and in its place was established a Federal Board of Mediation which was to act on disputes only when asked to do so by one or another of the parties involved.

Between 1920 and 1926, the commission seriously concerned itself with the preparation of a plan for that consolidation of the country's railroad systems which the act of 1920 had authorized. Finally, an outstanding railroad authority, Professor William Z. Ripley, drew up a scheme calling for the grouping of the railroads into nineteen great systems. But the opposition on the part of the carriers was so marked that the commission was compelled to announce a change of program. It would permit the railroads themselves to originate schemes for consolidations, reserving to itself the right to accept or reject such proposals, or to modify them. Up to the present (1938) no important consolidations have been made under the terms of the act, although a number of proposals have been advanced and debated.

In the half-century of government regulation of the railroads the wheel of fortune had taken a strange turn. In the first three-fourths of the period, the railroad managers had steadfastly opposed attempts at public control: they had, with every weapon at their command, fought valuation, rate-fixing, and supervision over security issues by the government's agency, the Interstate Commerce Commission. In the last quarter of the period, however, the railroad managers were to appear in the rôle of humble petitioners praying for protection from the competition of new rivals. For the railroads were being menaced from strange quarters. Pipe line companies were not transporting the crude petroleum alone but beginning to carry gasoline and refined oil as well; interstate bus and motor truck lines had made their appearance to carry passengers and freight, if not as quickly, certainly as comfortably, more cheaply, and often with greater mobility, for the question of terminals did not trouble them; coastal and interior waterways steamship and barge lines were furnishing a type of competition not met with before. From 1920 to the end of 1929, railroad freight traffic (measured in ton miles) had increased but 8.8 per cent; passenger traffic (measured in passenger miles) had decreased 34.2 per cent. This was a serious relative decline, for from 1900 to 1910 the percent increase in gross ton miles of freight carried had been 80.1 per cent, and from 1910 to 1920, 62.2 per cent; from 1900 to 1910 the increase in passenger miles had amounted to 101.6 per cent, and from 1910 to 1920, 46.5 per cent. On the other hand, over 1920–1930, passenger motor car registrations had increased 181.1 per cent; motor truck registrations had increased 235.9 per cent; motor bus registrations had increased 825 per cent; intercoastal tonnage through the Panama Canal had increased 637.3 per cent; and traffic moved on inland waterways (exclusive of the Great Lakes) had increased 93.5 per cent.

To seek relief from the unregulated competition of bus and motor truck companies, from pipe lines and from coastal and interior waterways vessels, became a leading concern of the railroad executives of the nineteen twenties and thirties, and they came to urge upon Congress a large variety of measures which, they contended, were necessary to prevent the railroad industry from suffering serious harm. Thus, regulation was not over; it was to continue and, apparently, to develop in new directions. But that the railroads should now regard themselves as vulnerable and should agitate for government assistance was a development that would have amazed the anti-monopolists and grangers of the eighteen seventies, had they been endowed with the gift of peering into the future.[3]

The Public Debt and Tax Reduction

In 1900, the interest-bearing public debt of the United States had been $1,023,479,000, or a per capita distribution of $13.47. In 1914, the debt had been $967,953,000, or a per capita distribution of $9.88. At the end of the fiscal year June 30, 1920, as a result of the costs of the war, the public debt stood at $24,061,000,000, or a per capita distribution of $228.00. Secretary of the Treasury Mellon, aided and supported by Presidents Harding, Coolidge, and Hoover, reduced this burden 33 per cent in the decade of the twenties with the result that on June 30, 1930, the public debt stood at $16,185,000,000, which was a per capita distribution of $134.00.

Tax reduction was one of the leading preoccupations of the government during the decade of the twenties, and the Congresses of the Harding and Coolidge administrations were regularly called upon to bend their energies in this direction. At first there appeared considerable objection to Mellon's program of lifting the tax burden from the shoulders of the wealthy. Small attention was accorded to his argument that those who had to pay such a large proportion of their profits into the Treasury in the shape of income surtaxes were retarded from engaging in new industrial enterprises. But before long Congress yielded, and Democratic lawmakers joined with their Republican colleagues in enacting the administration revenue acts. The Revenue Act of 1921 repealed the war-time excess profits tax and raised the corporation income tax from 10 to 12½ per cent; asked by Mellon to reduce the maximum surtax from 65 to 32 per cent, Congress contented itself with cutting it to

[3] The railroads were particularly bitter about the work of the government-owned agency, the Inland Waterways Corporation, which had been set up in 1924 and which was operating a series of federal barge lines on some of the country's important navigable streams. In 1930, these barge lines collected almost $6,000,000 from freight revenues.

50 per cent. In the writing of the Revenue Act of 1924, Congress was still recalcitrant. The normal income tax rate was cut from 4 per cent to 2 per cent on the first $4000 of net income. The maximum surtax was lowered to 40 per cent; the minimum surtax was made to apply beginning with incomes of $10,000 in place of the former $6000. However, the maximum estate tax was raised from 25 to 40 per cent, a new tax was placed on money gifts, and a provision calling for publicity for income tax returns was written into the law. In addition, a whole variety of the war-time excise taxes was repealed. This law also made a distinction between earned income (derived from salaries and personal effort) and unearned income (derived from property) and allowed the former a rebate of 25 per cent. President Coolidge called this measure a "political bill," but he signed it in the end.

Beginning with the writing of the 1926 Revenue Act the administration had little difficulty in obtaining its way. The law of 1926 reduced the normal tax to a 5 per cent maximum and the surtax to a 20 per cent maximum; lowered the estates tax; repealed the tax on money gifts and the publicity provision; increased the exemption for heads of families from $2500 to $3500; and cut away another group of excise taxes. The process was continued in 1928 and in 1929. In the earlier year, the corporation income tax was again lowered and the tax on passenger automobiles was repealed; in the 1929 law, the normal income tax rate on personal incomes was reduced from 1½ to ½ per cent, that on trusts was reduced from 3 to 2 per cent, that on corporations from 12 to 11 per cent.

So, for a decade, Secretary of the Treasury Mellon had his way and the nation was to witness what seemed to be a miracle in public financing. Surtaxes were reduced; yet the governmental expenditures remained at a high level while surpluses piled up and the national debt was being paid off.[4] The depression of 1930 abruptly terminated the happy round and at once proved that the Treasury's policy had been woefully short-sighted. By radically diminishing surtaxes, the government had not made more private funds available for productive enterprise but had really given a spur to speculation; by failing to apply itself more assiduously to the national debt's reduction, through the maintenance of high income taxes in the

[4] The following were the total ordinary expenditures of the federal government for the indicated fiscal years: 1899–1900, $520,861,000; 1913–1914, $735,081,000; 1929–1930, $3,392,077,000.

upper brackets, it was compelled to face the fact that Americans for generations to come would be called upon to meet the costs of the World War as well as of the depression of the nineteen thirties.

Providing for the War Veterans

It was the hope of legislators, when they expanded the powers of the Bureau of War Risk Insurance in 1917 and made provision for the permanent care of totally disabled war veterans, as well as the sale, on easy terms, of life insurance by the government to all men under arms, that scandalous pension agitation, such as that which followed the Civil War, would be effectively prevented. But the hope was illusory. The original act had provided for hospitalization and rehabilitation treatment for those who had suffered injuries in the war; in addition, all totally disabled veterans were to receive compensation of $30 monthly, while increased allowances were made for dependents. But the compensation provisions were liberalized in 1918 and 1919. In 1921, all affairs pertaining to veterans were concentrated in a single agency known as the Veterans' Bureau. In 1924, liberalization of the existing code was further extended. This law declared that neuropsychiatric, tubercular, and certain other disabilities existing prior to January 1, 1925, were to be regarded as being of service origin and that veterans suffering from these ailments were to receive full compensation. Further, the scale of compensation was raised generously. Thus, a fully disabled veteran was to receive $80 monthly; if he was married, he was to receive $90; if he was the father of dependent children, he was to receive an additional $5 a month for each such child. Increases in compensation were provided for veterans possessing partial disabilities, too.

The first step toward a civil disability pension law was taken in 1930, a brief twelve years after the war's end. The law provided that certain non-service physical and mental disabilities from which war veterans were suffering on January 1, 1930, were to be held as being of service origin and such veterans were to be compensated by monthly payments ranging from $12 to $40, according to the degree of disability. Observers quite justly pointed out that once the principle of pensions for civil disabilities was accepted, the grant of service pensions pure and simple would follow as a matter of course. That had been the experience of post-Civil War Congresses, and apparently post-World War Congresses were to travel the same road, despite the grant of a bonus and the heavy annual expenditures of the Veterans' Bureau.

At the close of the World War, a discharge bonus, totaling in all $256,000,000, was paid to all service men. Not content with this gift, the friends of the veterans pressed for further grants and introduced bonus bills in Congress during the period 1920–1924. Finally a bonus bill was passed only to be vetoed by President Coolidge on May 15, 1924. However, the supporters of the bill were strong enough to muster the necessary two-thirds votes in both houses, with the result that the measure was enacted over the President's veto on May 19, 1924. The law provided for the issuance of adjusted service certificates in the form of twenty-year endowment policies. Against these certificates the veterans might borrow money from the government. The size of the certificates depended upon the length of service of their holders, with $1.25 per day being the credit for overseas service and $1.00 per day the credit for home service. Because the certificates were to bear compound interest at 4 per cent, the face value at maturity was to be, on an average, considerably more than $1000 for each veteran. At the end of 1930, the total face value of the outstanding certificates was three and one-half billions, and such promises to pay were held by almost three and one-half million veterans. Against these certificates, up to 1931, the government had already lent $330,000,000. In the winter of 1930, there appeared an agitation for the immediate redemption of these certificates. The arguments advanced were these: great numbers of veterans were in dire need because of unemployment, the drought, and agricultural distress; also, the addition of such a large sum of money to the country's currency would help break the depression by adding to the nation's purchasing power. Against such a proposal the Hoover administration sternly set its face. Even the compromise measure—providing for the increase of the loan value of the certificates from the then-existing proportion of 22½ per cent to 50 per cent, and the reduction of the interest charge from 6 to 4½ per cent—was opposed by the President and the Secretary of the Treasury. Nevertheless, even the usually compliant House disregarded the President's wishes and in February, 1931, Congress passed the Bonus Loan bill in the form indicated. The President promptly vetoed the measure; in less than twenty-four hours both House and Senate had overridden the Presidential veto by record majorities.[5]

The Veterans' Bureau had been established to supervise the medical and hospital care of disabled veterans, provide for their rehabilitation through occupational therapy, furnish employment, and supervise payments of compensation and insurance claims. In 1930 a further step toward the centralization of activities applying to returned soldiers was taken with the consolidation of the Veterans' Bureau, the Pension Bureau, and the National Home for disabled volunteer soldiers to form the single Administration of Veterans' Affairs. For the fiscal year ending June 30, 1930, the government spent close to half a billion dollars on the work of the Veterans' Bureau. During the fiscal year 1930–1931, the new Veterans' Administration was spending $65,500,000 monthly. Up to the end of 1930, the care of World War veterans—for disability compensation, insurance payments, adjusted service certificates, vocational training, allotments to dependents, medical and hospital care—had cost the American government five and one-half billions of dollars.

The Regulation of Power

For the three decades preceding the outbreak of the World War the two leading domestic questions which had engrossed the attention of the American public were the regulation of railroads and the regulation of large-scale corporate business. The problems of the rails and of corporate business still remained vexing ones: to their company, by the nineteen twenties, was added the problem of power supervision. And there was no definite body of experience, no mode of public control which had been completely tested by time, upon which legislators and the American public could draw. The result in the case of power was the same sort of uncertainty, the same kind of unsatisfactory hit-or-miss tactics, that had attended governmental efforts to cope with the rails and the so-called trusts. That something had to be done, a large group of persons were agreed, for the generation of electricity for heat, light, and power had become one of the most significant and essential American industries. And this had occurred practically overnight. Thus, in 1902, there had been produced by water power and by fuel 4768 million

[5] For later veteran legislation, see below, page 238.

kilowatt-hours of electrical energy; by 1912, the production had increased to 17,572 million kilowatt-hours; by 1929, to 97,352 million kilowatt-hours. In short, over the period 1902–1929, the production of electrical energy had increased more than twentyfold. In 1931, the electrical industry, which at the turn of the century was only in its infancy, was in possession of an investment worth twelve billions of dollars. Into the bargain, the industry was characterized by holding-company management and control, as a result of which small groups of individuals—usually associated with finance capital—were able to dominate, as a rule through minority stock ownership, vast operating properties.

The federal government, despite the fact that by 1930 from one-tenth to one-seventh of the total electric power being generated in the nation was moving across state lines and therefore lay in that twilight zone where it was amenable to no controls as to rates and services, was slow to formulate any program. Only in the case of water power produced on navigable streams were some efforts at regulation made, and even here Congress did not move until 1920. The Federal Water Power Act of that year created the Federal Power Commission, which was to consist of the Secretaries of War, Interior, and Agriculture and which was to perform its functions through the staffs of the different departments. An executive secretary for the commission was provided, however. The Federal Power Commission was invested with the following functions:

It was empowered to issue licenses to citizens of the United States for the purpose of "constructing, operating, and maintaining dams, water conduits, reservoirs, power houses, transmission lines, and other projects necessary or convenient for development and improvement of navigation." Such licenses were to apply only to contemplated projects on the navigable waters of the United States, the public lands, and Indian reservations.

It was to prescribe rules and regulations governing the accounting practices of such licensees; might examine the books and papers of those companies; and require the licensees to submit full information bearing on their assets, capitalization, and the net investment in their plants.

Licenses were to be issued for a maximum period of fifty years.

In the issuing of licenses or permits, preference was to be given to states and municipalities; also, licenses could not be transferred without the consent of the commission.

Licensees were to pay an annual charge; but states and municipalities furnishing power to the public without profit were to be exempt from these payments.

After the expiration of a license the commission had the power of recapture of any project upon the payment to the owner of the net investment in the property plus such severance damages as might exist (i. e., damages to property dependent upon the project recaptured). If the commission failed to exercise its rights to recapture, the licensee might ask for a renewal.

The commission was given the right to regulate the rates which the licensee, a subsidiary corporation or any corporation buying power from it charged for power sold across interstate or international boundaries. The commission, similarly, was given the right to regulate security issues. The commission also was to have jurisdiction over the rates and security issues of its licensees in those states which had not yet created their own public utilities commissions.

By 1930 it was apparent that a commission made up of Cabinet officers was unable to cope with the many and intricate problems that were regularly coming to its attention. The result was the creation, in June, 1930, of a full-time Federal Power Commission to have the status of the Interstate Commerce Commission and the Federal Trade Commission. This new commission was to be made up of five commissioners to be named by the President with the consent of the Senate, and was to create its own organization.

Between 1920 and 1930 the Federal Power Commission licensed 449 projects, of which 43 were in the eastern region and 406 were in the western region; 107 were regarded by the commission as major enterprises. The extent of the commission's control over water power may be seen from the fact that on June 30, 1930, one-fourth of all the horsepower capacity of hydro-stations in the country was under its supervision.

During the nineteen twenties, the demand for the extension of federal jurisdiction over power companies grew. Investigations by the Federal Trade Commission indicated that there were new problems in the industry pressing for solution: through the device of holding companies, particularly, there had developed a form of complex accounting methods which was being employed to appreciate property book values as a basis for rates to be charged. By 1930, too, it was seen that the Federal Water Power Act was not without its loopholes. Power companies could, for instance, escape the rigorous supervision of the Federal Power Commission by building their plants on the non-navigable tributaries of navigable rivers and by asking for "minor-part" licenses to cover only that portion of the project affecting the navigable streams. However, the Coolidge and Hoover administrations did not regard kindly the extension of federal regulation of power. President Hoover was particularly outspoken. He was opposed to government operation of power projects, like Muscle Shoals, and he looked forward to the time when the whole task of the control of power companies could be regarded as being a state, as against a federal, function.

If the Hoover administration was hostile to further federal interference, the proposals for tightening up the Water Power Act, for extending governmental control over all power companies, and even for governmental operation of important waterpower sites were not wanting for friends. A party in the Senate, headed by Couzens of Michigan, called for federal regulation of all interstate power corporations, with particular attention to holding companies. Another Senatorial party, headed by Norris of Nebraska, was favorably disposed toward government operation of the principal sites. The Norris group made a test case of federal operation of the Muscle Shoals plant in Alabama (on the Tennessee River), and twice, in 1928 and 1931, Congress passed resolutions providing for government operation, only to have the measures killed by the vetoes of Presidents Coolidge and Hoover.

In 1917, because of the need for nitrates in the manufacture of explosives, the government had authorized the construction of two nitrate plants at the foot of Muscle Shoals. Both plants were to be worked by the so-called cyanamide process. Plant No. 1 was to have a capacity of 8000 tons of fixed nitrogen annually and Plant No. 2's capacity was to be 40,000 tons annually. To provide the electrical energy needed for these plants it was also decided to construct a series of dams on the Tennessee River. Plant No. 1 was completed before the Armistice; Plant No. 2 was finished a few weeks after. The Wilson Dam was finished by 1925. The total investment of the government at Muscle Shoals was $145,000,000, of which more than two-thirds went to build the nitrate plants, neither of which was used after January, 1919. From 1925 on, the station was kept in operation by the United States Corps of Engineers, and most of the power generated was sold to the Alabama Power Company for distribution in the neighboring communities. But the return from the private company was small, in fact was not much in excess of $1,000,000 annually.

Congress, therefore, began to concern itself with the creation of a program which would call for the adequate use of both the nitrate plants and the hydro-electric station. In 1928 both houses passed the Norris-Morin resolution, which was largely the work of Senator Norris. This measure called for the completion of the various power units at Muscle Shoals and the creation of a government-owned corporation to work the nitrate properties (for the manufacture of agricultural fertilizers) and sell the surplus power. The resolution had, almost completely, the support of the South and the West; it was, on the other hand, opposed by the industrial East. On May 25 the resolution was sent to President Coolidge, who proceeded to kill it by a pocket veto.

In 1930–1931, the friends of government operation again were successful in the Senate and a Norris resolution, embodying substantially the provisions of the 1928 bill, was once more passed by both Houses. President Hoover was as unbending as his predecessor in his opposition to the government's engaging in the power business in competition with private enterprise. In a stinging veto message on March 3, 1931, he said:

> I hesitated to contemplate the future of our institutions, of our government, and of our country if the preoccupation of its officials is to be no longer the promotion of justice and equal opportunity but is to be devoted to barter in the markets. That is not liberalism; it is degeneration.

The President's acceptance of the gage of combat indicated that the power question was to play an important part in the Presidential election of 1932 and was to be no small concern of the F. D. Roosevelt administrations.

III. AMERICA IN TWO HEMISPHERES

The United States and Latin America

President Wilson's Mexican program had established the principle that intervention was abhorrent to American policy. After some serious errors, the Coolidge administration eventually was to build upon this foundation. In 1921, Secretary of State Hughes sought to exact pledges from Mexico that lands owned by Americans would not be confiscated, that the agrarian decrees and Article XXVII of the Mexican constitution would not be made retroactive, and that all properties seized since 1910 would be restored to their original owners. Only then would recognition be accorded. But this high-handed attitude met with a storm of protest in the United States with the result that the State Department became distinctly conciliatory and on September 3, 1923, diplomatic relations were once more restored.

But Hughes's policy, apparently, was not entirely satisfactory to his successor Frank B. Kellogg, who had followed him into the State office in 1925. Kellogg, in an unnecessarily threatening statement, charged that the new Calles government was not exercising itself to protect American lives and property rights. The statement issued by the American Secretary of State had, indeed, an ominous ring. Said one passage:

> The government of Mexico is now on trial before the world. We have the greatest interest in the stability, prosperity, and independence of Mexico. We have been patient and realize, of course, that it takes time to bring about a stable government, but we cannot countenance violation of her obligations and failure to protect American citizens.

The enactment of the Mexican Petroleum Law and the Alien Land Law, in December, 1925, only increased the tension that Kellogg's sharp warning had created. The first measure vested the ownership of all Mexican petroleum deposits in the Mexican nation; called upon all companies holding titles prior to May 1, 1917, to apply for confirmation of these before December 31, 1926, upon pain of forfeiture; and offered in exchange for the titles fifty-year concessions, to be dated from the time when exploitation had first commenced. The second law carried into effect the provisions of Article XXVII of the 1917 Constitution. Kellogg once again protested on behalf of American oil interests, but the oil and land regulations were put into effect, nevertheless; although, it is to be noted, the Mexican government did not proceed to annul the titles of those companies not complying with the registration law.

Beginning with the year 1927, relations between the two countries definitely took a turn for the better. From public threats, the American State Department turned to accommodation, and every effort was made to indicate that Washington believed that such differences as existed could be settled amicably. Ambassador Sheffield, who had not been particularly successful in gaining the confidence of Mexicans, was recalled in October, 1927, and in his place was sent Dwight W. Morrow, partner in J. P. Morgan and Company and personal friend of the President. Morrow was all that could be expected of a diplomatist: he was tactful, ingratiating, and genuinely friendly. He exercised himself in the interest of American rights without offending the national pride of the Mexicans; at the same time, the zeal with which he and the members of his family applied themselves to gaining Mexican good will, by a close study of the problems and aspirations of the people of that land, produced an effect that was altogether gratifying. Mexicans, apparently, were appreciative, for they began at once to make sweeping concessions. In November, 1927, the Mexican Supreme Court rejected that part of the land law which limited to a term of years the titles in subsoil deposits acquired and worked before 1917. The Mexican Congress proceeded to legislate to this effect; the laws were further liberalized by decree, the claims of foreign corporations as well as nationals being recognized. The American State Department in 1928 expressed itself as satisfied with these concessions and advised Americans that henceforth they should seek protection of their rights in the Mexican courts. In 1929, the Mexican government, which for the preceding three years had been carrying on a heated controversy with the Catholic Church and threatening to seize all church properties and secularize education, adjusted this difficulty, too, on the basis of a compromise; and in 1930 the Mexican churches were once again opened to worshipers. By this step, American Catholics, who had become the bitter foes of the Mexican gov-

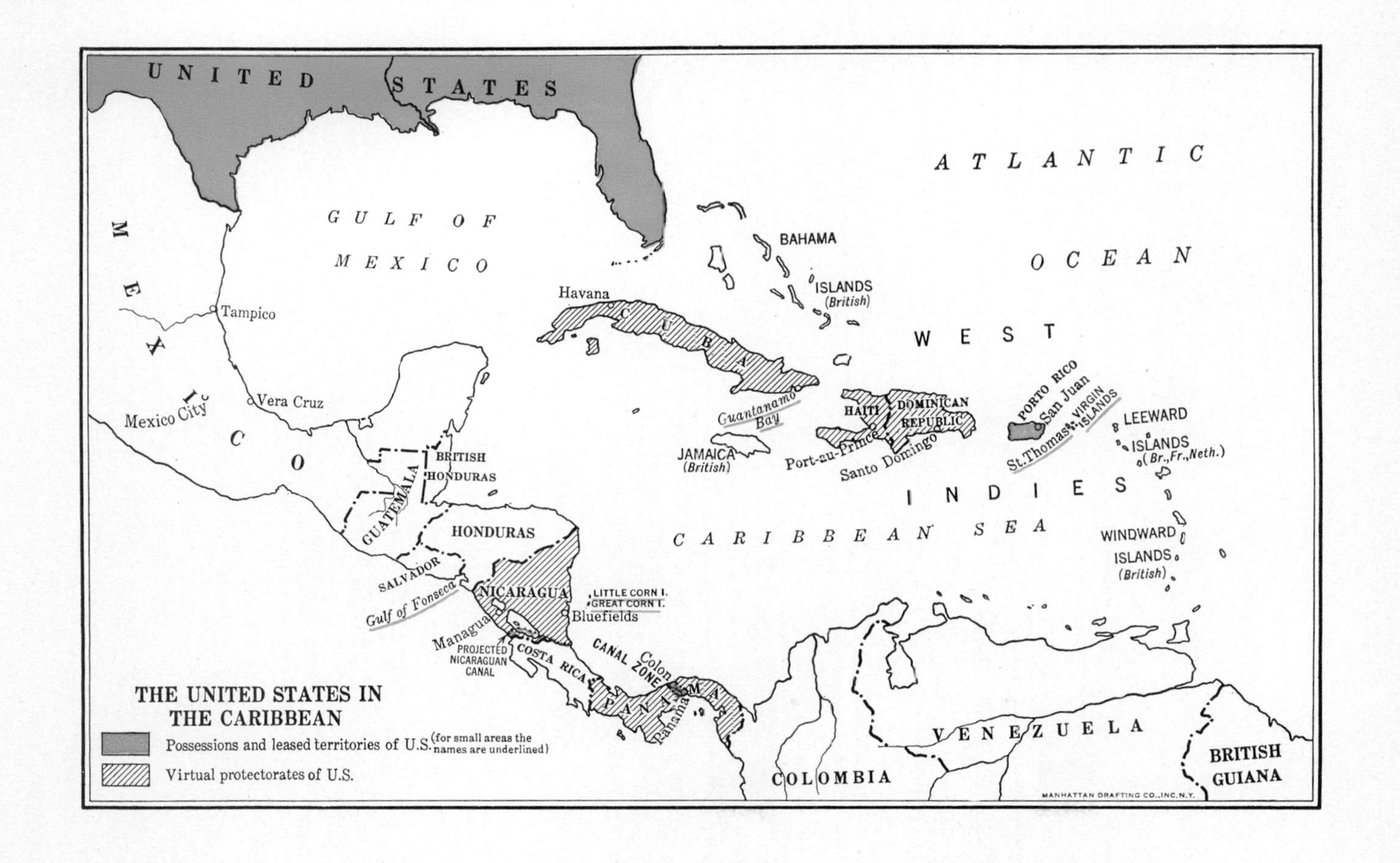

THE UNITED STATES IN
THE CARIBBEAN

Possessions and leased territories of U.S. (for small areas the names are underlined)

Virtual protectorates of U.S.

ernment and who in 1926 had joined the intervention party, were propitiated somewhat.

Events in the twenties pointed, as well, to a clarification of the country's Caribbean policy. The military intervention that had taken place in the Dominican Republic in 1916 was terminated September 18, 1924. In Haiti, the process of American withdrawal was slower. From 1922 to 1930, the Haitians were actually governed by the American occupation. In the earlier year, the loose administrative machinery set up under President Wilson was entirely recast and the island republic took on the definite form of an American protectorate. An American high commissioner was appointed to supersede the minister to Haiti, and in this official's hands was centralized control over the treaty officials and the expeditionary force. Parliamentary government was suspended, while an American bureaucracy of some two hundred and fifty persons ruled over Haiti's financial offices, its gendarmerie, its public works and its public health, agricultural, and legal activities. In 1930, however, President Hoover indicated that the American occupation would definitely terminate with the lapsing of the treaty arrangements in 1936.[1]

In the case of Nicaragua, too, there took place the liquidation of the old policy of active American occupation. Under the watchful eye of American officials the Nicaraguan congress in 1925 proceeded to elect a new president who was installed with the consent of the State Department. The new incumbent possessed, however, no more security than his predecessors had had, and the presence in the country of large bands of insurgents forced the Coolidge administration to take formal cognizance of the situation. In January, 1927, President Coolidge reported to Congress the reasons for our continued concern over the Nicaraguan situation. We were compelled to intervene, he said: (1) to protect American life and property; (2) to enforce the Central American treaty of 1923 under which the five Central American republics of Guatemala, Honduras, Salvador, Nicaragua, and Costa Rica had pledged themselves not to recognize any administration which had seized political control as a result of a coup d'état, "so long as the freely elected representatives of the people thereof have not constitutionally reorganized the country"

[1] This policy was subsequently affirmed when American commissioners in 1933 pledged the United States to a policy of non-intervention in the "internal or external affairs" of the other American states. The Senate ratified this treaty in 1935.

(the leader of the successful revolt, or anyone intimately connected with him, could not be designated president of the new administration); [2] (3) to safeguard our canal rights in Panama and in Nicaragua; (4) to forestall interference by other powers.

The result was the dispatching of Henry L. Stimson to Nicaragua in 1927, in an effort to find a formula which would be satisfactory to the various local factions. That same year, under Stimson's guidance, an understanding was reached that was acceptable to all parties except Augusto Sandino, who took to the jungle and for the next two years carried on a desultory guerilla warfare against the Nicaraguan government and the American expeditionary force. The warring factions (except Sandino) surrendered their arms and the elections of 1928 were held; similar elections, under the eye of American marines, were held in 1930 and again in 1932. In 1933, however, President Hoover, in line with an earlier promise, withdrew the American forces.

There was no doubt that under Presidents Coolidge and Hoover the policy inaugurated by Theodore Roosevelt and followed by Taft and Wilson, that is to say, physical occupation by armed American forces, had been terminated. It was not that postwar America was more liberal than prewar America: our State Department had merely become more realistic. It was evident to American statesmen, in the late twenties and the thirties, that American purposes in the Caribbean could be effected just as completely, with more dispatch, and certainly with less friction or awakening of outside hostility, through a compliant native officialdom. In brief, it was not hard to find Cubans, Haitians, Dominicans, and Nicaraguans who could be depended upon to watch as carefully over American interests in their own lands, to work hand in glove with our State Department, as could any expeditionary force and American treaty bureaucracy. This was mature, imperialist statecraft functioning quietly, effectively, and pervasively. It tended to still opposition at home, gain the friendship of the politicians of the Caribbean lands,

[2] While this treaty was not signed by the United States, the State Department announced in June, 1923, that it would be guided by the same principles in its policy of recognition. It will be observed that this was a Central American policy and not a Latin American one. Thus, we refused to recognize successful revolutionary leaders in Nicaragua in 1926 and in Guatemala in 1930; but we did recognize the Argentine, Brazilian, Bolivian, and Peruvian revolutionary governments of 1930.

and silence criticism of American purposes abroad, particularly in South America.

The question of our real interest in the Caribbean requires some examination. It is to be doubted whether American public policy was governed to an exclusive, or even a major, extent by the fact that financial investments of American citizens had grown so greatly in the decade and a half following the outbreak of the war. That our economic stake in the Caribbean countries was sizable was, of course, apparent; but that Washington was regularly exercising itself on behalf of American property rights, expending large sums of money on naval demonstrations, expeditionary forces, and the maintenance of elaborate treaty establishments, is a matter less easy to believe. The following figures indicate the nature of America's economic interest in those lands of the Caribbean in whose affairs we had been actively interfering, that is to say, the Central American countries, Haiti, and the Dominican Republic.

America's Economic Interest in the Caribbean

	1913	*1929*	*Increase*
Investments	$49,000,000	$218,186,000	345.3%
Imports from U.S.	36,686,000	81,843,000	123.1%
Exports to U.S.	28,466,000	51,345,000	80.4%

It is plain, from such figures as these, that the increase in the American–Caribbean trade had not been nearly in proportion to the increase in investments. In other words, it may be doubted whether American capital had flowed southward because of the belief on the part of our investment bankers that here were markets which could quickly be taught to absorb or produce more goods. It is more reasonable to suppose that American capital in the Caribbean followed in the wake of a diplomatic or political interest rather than the reverse. We may say, therefore, that the reasons for American intervention in the Caribbean up to the end of the nineteen twenties had been the following, somewhat in the order indicated:

We had intervened in the Caribbean to protect our Isthmian policy. This policy was one of naval strategy entirely and revolved about the belief that the lands adjoining the seagoing approaches to the Panama Canal and the proposed Nicaraguan canal were points from which our national security could easily be threatened. Mr. Stimson had phrased this Isthmian doctrine in this fashion:

The failure therefore of one of these [Caribbean] Republics to maintain the responsibilities which go with independence may lead directly to a situation imperilling the vital interest of the United States in its seagoing route through the Panama Canal. Out of this situation has followed our national policy—perhaps the most sensitive and generally held policy that we have—which for half a century has caused us to look with apprehension upon even the perfectly legitimate efforts of European nations to protect their rights within this zone.

We had intervened to protect American lives, property, and investments against local disorders and the depredations of armed bands.

We had landed troops upon the express invitation of the native governments.

We had intervened to preserve internal peace, to instruct the Caribbean peoples in the methods of orderly government, and to help them cope with their problems in a civilized fashion. Our motive had been in part humanitarian, in part economic, for it was fully appreciated that only through the cultivation of the arts of peace could these backward lands reach a higher industrial plane.

It may be said that in recent years this Isthmian policy has been in process of liquidation, largely because of State Department acceptance of the idea that European powers no longer were threatening American rights in the Isthmian Canal region. By the nineteen thirties American policy once more was based on the Monroe Doctrine (modified, of course, by our special rights in the Canal Zone and in the proposed Nicaraguan canal project). Indeed, the American protectorate over Cuba was ended in 1934 when President Franklin D. Roosevelt by an executive agreement terminated both the Platt Amendment and the protectorate. Similarly, in 1936, a treaty was signed between the United States and Panama under which our virtual protectorate over Panama also was surrendered.

More important as an earnest of American intentions in the Caribbean has been the repudiation of the "Roosevelt corollary" of the Monroe Doctrine, that policy which made the United States stand in the rôle of guarantor for the nations of the Western Hemisphere —that they would preserve the peace, pay their debts, and meet their obligations to European countries. In March, 1930, the State Department made public a memorandum on the Monroe Doctrine written in 1928 by J. Ruben Clark, at that time Undersecretary of

State. In this document, the Monroe Doctrine was defined as possessing the following attributes: 1. It is unilateral. "The United States determines when and if the principles of the Doctrine are violated, and when and if violation is threatened. No other power of the world has any relationship to, or voice in, the implementing of the principles which the Doctrine contains." 2. "The Doctrine does not concern itself with purely inter-American relations." 3. "The Doctrine states a case of the United States versus Europe, not of the United States versus Latin America." 4. The United States has always used the Doctrine to protect Latin American nations from the aggressions of European powers. "So far as Latin America is concerned, the Doctrine is now, and always has been, not an instrument of violence and oppression, but an unbought, freely bestowed and wholly effective guaranty of their freedom, independence, and territorial integrity against the imperialistic designs of Europe." 5. The Roosevelt corollary is not properly a part of the Doctrine itself, nor does it grow out of the Doctrine: ". . . it is not believed that this corollary is justified by the terms of the Monroe Doctrine, however much it may be justified by the application of the doctrine of self-preservation." [3]

The Clark memorandum served to clear the air not a little: so did the success of American diplomacy in Mexico, the decisions to withdraw from Haiti and Nicaragua, and the admission by the United States of the World Court's right to jurisdiction in disputes involving nations of the American continents.[4] These developments were positive tokens of good will and were a harbinger of the time when Latin American suspicions of "Yankee imperialism" would largely

[3] It is to be noted that Stimson, writing in 1927, foreshadowed this pronouncement when he declared: ". . . there are certain geographical considerations which impose upon us a very special interest as to how certain ones of those [Caribbean] nations fulfil the responsibilities which go with sovereignty and independence. . . . This situation does not arise out of the Monroe Doctrine but from certain broad principles of self-defense which govern the policy of the United States. . . . These principles in part underlie the Monroe Doctrine although they were not at all created by it. They bear a very much closer and more tangible relation to what I may call, for want of a better name, our Isthmian policy than they do to the Monroe Doctrine itself." In a public speech on February 7, 1931, Stimson, this time as Secretary of State, gave the same limited interpretation to the Monroe Doctrine. Using almost Clark's words, he said: "The Monroe Doctrine was a declaration of the United States versus Europe—not of the United States versus Latin America."

[4] The debate over the World Court is discussed below. See page 51.

be dissipated. It was a good sign also that the policy inaugurated by Secretary Stimson was continued by Secretary Hull with the active support of President Franklin D. Roosevelt.

Renewal of the Peace Movement

The United States had expressed its decision against entry into the League of Nations in the "solemn referendum" of 1920: throughout the twenties, therefore, there was little effort exerted, by political leaders, to bring again to a head the question of American participation. Nevertheless, for a time it seemed as if the United States, quietly and unobtrusively, would be drawn closer and closer into the League circle. Thus, the State Department took to dealing directly with the League's Secretariat; unofficial American observers were sent to sit with League committees discussing non-political matters; then official delegations replaced the unofficial observers. In 1924, formal American delegates were named to represent the United States at the second opium conference: thus the ice was broken, and between 1924 and 1930 the United States had official representation at more than twenty League gatherings. Naturally, because discretion rested with the State Department, and attendance was not obligatory, a uniform course was not pursued; but after 1925 the United States sent delegations to most of the important conferences and even signed several of the draft conventions, relating to non-political matters, that these conferences drew up. Indeed, in February, 1929, the United States Senate ratified the first of these, that relating to slavery and forced labor.

But the events of the nineteen thirties confirmed the American suspicions: the League was no more and no less than an instrument for the maintenance of the iniquitous Versailles system in the interests of the victors. During the twenties Britain and France, notably, had refused to relax their pressure on Germany; they had failed to recognize that their triumphs in North Africa, the Near East, and the Far East were making it just so much harder for the imperialist-capitalist economies of Italy and Japan to continue expanding peaceably. In the thirties these economically unappeased nations, now in the form of totalitarian states, challenged the status quo: and the League stood helpless in the face of aggression in Ethiopia, China, and Central Europe. More and more, Americans were beginning to recognize that efforts to check aggression by the imposition of economic sanctions alone—for aggressor states were preying upon the territories of weaker neighbors exactly because the logic of their capitalist economies required expansion—were likely to prove fruitless; for economic sanctions could not but end in war. As long as the world (in terms of territory and economic opportunities) continued to be shared out unequally, it was futile to believe, Americans came to see, that the pious and well-intentioned gestures of such an agency like the League could carry any weight. And Americans were becoming increasingly loath to pull the chestnuts out of the fire for the sated British and French imperialisms.

The failure of the Briand-Kellogg Pact to maintain world peace pointed to the same conclusion. In August, 1928, as a result of preliminary negotiations conducted between Premier Aristide Briand of France and Secretary of State Kellogg, there was signed at Paris, by the principal nations of the world, a pact which committed the high contracting parties to a mutual engagement for the outlawing of war. The pact had originated from Briand's suggestion, in April, 1927, that the United States and France enter into such a bilateral understanding; in December, Kellogg had proposed that the treaty be made multilateral and that, in time, all the nations of the world be invited to subscribe to it. Kellogg had pushed the matter with such energy that, by the summer of 1928, fourteen countries, namely, France, Belgium, Czechoslovakia, Great Britain, the other members of the British Commonwealth, Germany, Italy, Japan, and Poland, had signified their willingness to participate along with the United States. On August 27, 1928, therefore, the Pact of Paris had been solemnly signed.

The treaty consisted of three articles. Article I outlawed war "as an instrument of national policy." Article II committed the high contracting parties to settle all disputes, of whatever nature, by pacific means. Article III provided that the treaty was to go into effect as soon as the ratification of its signatories had been deposited at Washington. The convention, however, was to remain open for adherence by all the nations of the world. On January 15, 1929, the United States Senate, by a vote of 85 to 1, ratified the pact without reservation. However, the Senate did adopt the report of its Committee on Foreign Relations, which declared: that the treaty did not curtail America's right to self-defense; that the treaty was not incompatible with the Monroe Doctrine, which was "part of the national security of the United States"; that the treaty did not commit the United States to engage in punitive expeditions against aggressor states. On July 29, 1929, the Pact of Paris was proclaimed to be in force.

That the State Department meant to carry out the articles of the Pact of Paris in good faith (despite their violation by European and Asiatic signatories) was demonstrated by the fact that it proceeded to write a new group of bilateral arbitration conventions and to create the machinery for making the Bryan treaties for compulsory investigation effective. In 1928, Washington began to replace the Root conventions of 1908–1910 by another series which called for the arbitration of those international disputes that were justiciable in their nature. The first of these was written with France; by the middle of the thirties, a total of twenty-seven such agreements had been signed with almost all the important powers, the exceptions being Great Britain, Spain, Japan, and Russia. These new Kellogg treaties specifically exempted the following topics from arbitration: matters within the domestic jurisdiction of either of the contracting parties; matters involving the interest of third parties; matters affecting the Monroe Doctrine; matters involving the obligations of the other contracting party under the Covenant of the League of Nations.

At the same time, Secretary Kellogg began to extend the scope of the Bryan conciliation treaties. It will be recalled that Secretary Bryan had negotiated a number of treaties that called for the creation of permanent peace commissions empowered to investigate those disputes not submitted to arbitration. It was not until 1928 that the United States began giving thought to the erection of these investigating commissions or to the completion of the round of treaties. By the middle of the thirties, there existed in all some thirty-five of these agreements. Interestingly enough, Japan signed neither an arbitration nor a conciliation convention with the United States.

With Latin American nations, the understandings reached in 1929 were even more specific. The two conventions signed at Washington provided for the following: First, compulsory arbitration of legal disputes arising out of the interpretation of treaties, questions of international law, and the existence of those facts which constituted violations of international law. Such disputes were to be submitted for arbitration to the World Court, to the Hague Tribunal, or to special bodies to be created as disagreements arose. Second, the conciliation of all disputes, not submitted to arbitration, by commissions made up of members of the states involved. In cases of emergency, such differences were to be referred to committees at Washington or Montevideo, made up of diplomatic representatives accredited to those capitals. These two conventions were signed by the American government without reservation being made as to the Monroe Doctrine; they meant, in effect, that the United States was willing to forego the right of intervention and to submit all difficulties involving it and Latin American nations to arbitration or conciliation. By the middle of the thirties the United States and sixteen other nations had ratified the conciliation convention and the United States and thirteen other nations the arbitration convention.

During the twenties, the United States moved steadily in the direction of membership in the World Court. It is interesting to note that while American opinion was indifferent toward affiliation with the League, the contrary was the case as far as participation in the World Court was concerned. In fact, from its inception in September, 1921, American jurists had sat on the tribunal. John Bassett Moore had been chosen to the original bench of nine judges and had been a member from 1922 to 1928; Charles Evans Hughes had sat from 1928 to 1930, when he had resigned to accept the post of Chief Justice of the United States Supreme Court; Frank B. Kellogg had been named in 1930; and in 1935 he had been replaced by Professor Manley O. Hudson of Harvard.[5]

So real was American interest in the World Court that President Harding, in February, 1923, submitted its protocol to the Senate for ratification, accompanied by a group of reservations prepared by Secretary of State Hughes. The Hughes reservations were the following: 1. Adherence to the Court was not to imply the creation of a legal relationship between the United States and the League of Nations. 2. The United States was to have the right to appoint representatives to the League Council and Assembly when those bodies sat to elect judges. 3. The United States was to pay its fair share of the Court's expenses. 4. The statute of the Court was not to be

[5] The World Court has these two different sets of functions: 1. It may sit in judgment on cases between states and hand down binding decisions. Such cases come before the Court as the result of agreements between countries calling for the Court's arbitration. Again, nations accepting the so-called Optional Clause of the Court's statute bind themselves to compulsory arbitration by the Court in certain types of legal disputes. 2. It may issue advisory opinions when called upon to do so by the League Assembly and Council.

amended without the consent of the United States. A fifth reservation, added by President Coolidge later, declared that none of the Court's advisory opinions was to be binding upon the United States, unless such opinions were specifically requested by us. About this last reservation, much of the subsequent discussion was to revolve. The Senate Committee on Foreign Relations, however, was definitely hostile, and for fifteen months, despite Harding's and Coolidge's insistence, it refused to take action.

President Coolidge returned to the attack in his Congressional message of December, 1923, and met with a partial success. In May, 1924, the Senate Committee on Foreign Relations reported out the protocol; but the Senate failed to consider it. In 1925, the agitation was again taken up, even the House of Representatives joining the Court supporters when, by an almost unanimous vote, it went on record as favoring American adherence. Finally, on January 27, 1926, the Senate, by a vote of 76 to 17, adopted a resolution favoring American participation. The reservations that accompanied the resolution, in large part, followed the lines of those laid down by Hughes and Coolidge. The first three reservations were very much as Hughes had drawn them up; the fourth provided for American withdrawal at will and for amendment of the Court's statute only with American consent; the fifth, touching on advisory opinions, was greatly amplified. This reservation declared that no advisory opinions could be rendered unless they were publicly given and until all the signatories to the protocol had been notified; further, the Court was not, without the consent of the United States, to "entertain any request for an advisory opinion touching any dispute or question in which the United States has or claims an interest."

In September, 1926, the forty-eight signers of the World Court protocol signified their willingness to accept the first four reservations and the first half of the fifth reservation which the Senate had outlined; to the American claim for a veto right over requests for advisory opinions touching American interests, they would not yield, however. Here the matter rested until the winter of 1929, when Elihu Root, at the invitation of the League Council, was able to work out a formula that was acceptable to World Court members and American State Department alike. These were the amended protocols that President Hoover once again submitted to the Senate in December, 1929. The Root formula called for submission of all requests for advisory opinions to the United States; for the discussion of American objections to such opinions with the parties concerned; and for American withdrawal from the Court, without prejudice to its interests, if the other powers refused to concede that the United States had a vital national concern in the rendering of such opinions. In brief, as long as we were to be members of the World Court, the Court was to be prevented from handing down opinions affecting questions "in which the United States has or claims an interest." The Senate did not take action until January 7, 1935, and then by a vote of 52 for and 36 against (seven votes less than the necessary two-thirds), it rejected ratification. Despite its interest in peace and its concern with bilateral conventions and multilateral pacts (notably as affecting Latin America), the United States was reluctant to enter the international system that originated in the Versailles peace.

Naval Limitation

In another direction, the decade of the nineteen twenties saw an effort made to secure world peace: this was with regard to the limitation of naval armaments by the United States, Great Britain, and Japan principally, and by France and Italy to a lesser extent. At the Washington Conference of 1921–1922 and at the London Conference of 1930 treaties were written that were designed to stop the competition in the building of dreadnoughts, to establish a system of ratios for capital and auxiliary ships, and to recognize that naval parity existed between the United States and Great Britain. But by 1938, when even the United States had launched upon a naval race, this effort had been proved fruitless.

The call for the Washington Conference was issued by President Harding in the summer of 1921, invitations being extended to Great Britain, France, Italy, and Japan for the purpose of discussing the question of limitation of armament; and to Belgium, the Netherlands, Portugal, and China (in addition to the great powers) for the purpose of discussing questions affecting the Pacific and the Far East. The first plenary session met at Washington on November 12, 1921, and the last on February 3, 1922, the conference writing two sets of treaties: the first group related to naval limitation; the second to matters rising out of Far Eastern questions.

The following understandings emerged from these meetings: The powers agreed to the scrapping of a number of battleships which were either afloat or still in the process of construction. They agreed to a holiday, until 1931, in the building of capital ships and settled the battleship construction program of the United States, Great Britain, and Japan for the decade of the thirties. They also agreed to the following ratios of capital ship tonnage: 5 (United States): 5 (Great Britain): 3 (Japan): 1.67 (France and Italy). On this basis, these figures for capital ships were accepted: United States, 525,000 tons; Great Britain, 525,000 tons; Japan, 272,000 tons; France and Italy, 175,000 tons each. The United States, Great Britain, and Japan signed a convention in which these powers pledged themselves to the maintenance of the status quo as far as fortifications and naval bases in the Pacific Ocean were concerned. Specifically, Japan promised to limit the fortifications of certain of her islands in the Pacific; and the United States promised to do similarly as regards the Philippine and Aleutian Islands. But the conferees could come to no decision on the matter of auxiliary craft; no treaty, therefore, was drawn up.

The agreements reached with regard to the Far East were the following: First, on December 13, 1921, the representatives of the United States, Great Britain, Japan, and France signed, together, a Four-Power Treaty, whose purpose was "to respect their rights in relation to their insular possessions and insular dominions in the region of the Pacific Ocean." This convention went on to stipulate that any controversies arising among the high contracting parties, which could not be settled by diplomacy, were to be submitted to joint conferences of all the signatories for their consideration and adjustment. The Treaty meant, in effect, the severance of the Anglo-Japanese Alliance and the replacement of that understanding by one involving all the major Pacific powers; too, it committed the United States to compulsory conciliation of disputes arising out of Pacific questions. Second, on February 1, 1922, China and Japan succeeded in arriving at an agreement concerning Shantung, under which Japan consented to return the German rights in the Peninsula to China. Third, there was also signed a Nine-Power Treaty (in which the five powers were joined by Belgium, the Netherlands, Portugal, and China) that guaranteed the territorial integrity of China with continued recognition of the Open Door principle. It was to be a widened Open Door, however, which promised equal opportunity for the industry as well as the commerce of all nations, and which pledged the powers not to seek special rights or privileges for their own nationals at the expense of the nationals of other countries. Finally, another nine-power treaty established the principle of China's control over her own tariff. This convention, too, called for the creation of a commission to study the question of the abolition of the extraterritorial rights of foreigners in China. Without too much controversy, the Senate proceeded to ratify the treaties that the American delegation had signed.

In 1928, our State Department wrote a treaty with the Chinese Nationalist Government in which we agreed to accept exclusive Chinese tariff control; but we did not consent to the relinquishment of our extraterritorial rights. In a measure, therefore, we proceeded to accept the spirit of the Far Eastern settlement. Not as much could be said for the other signatories of the Nine-Power Treaty. In September, 1931, Japan invaded Manchuria and in February, 1932, she set up the puppet state of Manchukuo, completely under her domination. This was clearly in violation of the Briand-Kellogg Pact and the Nine-Power Treaty; and in a note to Japan Secretary Stimson said so, at the same time pointing out that the United States could not recognize the new state. But the great European powers were unwilling to back up the United States. It was becoming increasingly clear to Americans that the powers were prepared to talk of world peace only when their own vital interests were not concerned. The Stimson doctrine as regards the Far East, which insisted that the Washington treaties were to be regarded as a unity, was stated as follows by him on February 24, 1932:

> It must be remembered also that this treaty was one of several treaties and agreements entered into at the Washington Conference by the various powers concerned, all of which were interrelated and interdependent. . . . The willingness of the American government to surrender its then commanding lead in battleship construction and to leave its positions at Guam and in the Philippines without further fortification was predicated upon, among other things, the self-denying covenants contained in the Nine-Power Treaty, which assured the nations of the world not only of equal opportunity for their eastern trade but also against the military aggrandizement of any other power at the expense of China. One cannot discuss the possibility of modifying or abrogating those provisions of the Nine-Power Treaty without considering at the same time the other promises upon which they were really dependent.

While the subsequent Roosevelt administrations did not in so many words reaffirm the Stimson doctrine, American policy in the Far East was guided by it.[6]

In this way, a part of the work of the Washington Conference was undone in a decade; the other part, that concerned with naval limitation, too went by the board—in this case, in a decade and a half.

It was appreciated by Washington that the Conference of 1921–1922, although it had traveled far, had not gone quite far enough: an armament race was still not unlikely, with light cruisers as the participants instead of capital ships. The expectation was quickly fulfilled and, before the decade was over, interested nations were to see Great Britain and Japan engaged in a cruiser-construction race and the United States, itself, launched on a great building program. Between 1922 and 1930 other conferences had met—at Rome in 1924, at Geneva in 1927: all had ended in failure. It was plainly apparent that another agreement was in order. This time, Great Britain took the initiative and toward the close of 1929 invited the signatories to the five-power naval treaty of the Washington Conference to meet in London to discuss, again, naval armament limitation.

The London Conference's first plenary session met on January 21, 1930; its sixth and last on April 22, 1930. The London Naval Treaty, which resulted from the deliberations, was a three-power pact and was signed by the United States, Great Britain, and Japan, and proclaimed in force October 27, 1930.

We may sum up the achievements of the London Conference in this fashion: 1. The Conference established parity between Great Britain and the United States, once and for all. 2. It continued the capital ship construction holiday to the end of 1936. 3. It did not provide for a cessation in the building of auxiliary craft; but it did fix limits on such building within a system of ratios. In fact, during 1930–1936, the London Naval Treaty permitted the following new tonnage to be laid down: United States, 401,664; Great Britain, 330,924; Japan, 88,780. It was estimated that the cost of this additional construction to the United States would run from three-quarters of a billion to a billion dollars. Thus, the Conference did not bring limitation so much as it brought a stop to uncontrolled competition in building among the leading naval powers. 4. It con-

[6] See below, page 323.

tained an "escalator clause," under which any contracting party could build additional ships in any category if a non-signatory should launch upon a new building program out of line with its relative naval position. (By 1936, as will be indicated below, the treaty powers were ready to invoke the "escalator clause" because of new building by Germany and Italy. Indeed, on December 31, 1936, the London Treaty was a dead letter and a new naval race was taking place all over the world.) [7] 5. The treaty set up what was, to Japan, a satisfactory American-Japanese ratio. At the Washington Conference, the ratio of capital ships agreed upon had been 5:3. At the London Conference, for big-gun cruisers it was 10:6; for small-gun cruisers 10:7; for destroyers 10:7; and for submarines 10:10.

Interallied Debts and Reparation Payments

During the war, and in the two years immediately thereafter, the United States government had lent to the Allied powers a total of $10,350,000,000. It is important to note that of this amount, a total of $3,273,000,000 was lent after the Armistice. In 1922, Congress proceeded to set up a machinery for the refunding of these war debts. A World War Foreign Debt Commission was created, conditions for refunding operations were laid down, and negotiations were at once entered into with the various debtor states to hasten the liquidation of the principal and unpaid interest of the gigantic sum owed us by twenty nations. Washington made it plain, however, that the conditions for refunding would be adjusted with every consideration being given the debtors' different abilities to meet their obligations. Between June, 1923, and May, 1930, seventeen of the twenty nations came to terms with us, Russia, Armenia, and Nicaragua alone failing to arrange refunding operations. The table on page 58 presents the various refunding arrangements that were reached.

But from what source were these interallied debts to be satisfied? Plainly, from German reparations. During the whole decade of the twenties, the Allies sought to perfect a formula that would allow the collection of the greatest possible sum from the vanquished nation and at the same time not cripple her economic and financial life. In 1921, the Reparation Commission, created by the Treaty

[7] See below, page 328.

THE REFUNDING OF THE WAR LOANS

Country	*Amounts of original loans*	*Amounts of funded debts*	*Average interest rates over whole period*
Armenia *	$ 11,959,917	$ —	—
Austria	24,055,708	24,614,885	3.3%
Belgium	379,087,200	417,780,000	1.8%
Cuba †	10,000,000	—	—
Czechoslovakia	91,879,671	185,071,023	3.3%
Estonia	13,999,145	13,830,000	3.3%
Finland	8,281,926	9,000,000	3.3%
France	3,404,818,945	4,025,000,000	1.6%
Great Britain	4,277,000,000	4,600,000,000	3.3%
Greece	27,167,000	32,497,000	3.3%
Hungary	1,685,835	1,982,555	3.3%
Italy	1,648,034,050	2,042,000,000	0.4%
Jugoslavia	51,758,486	62,850,000	1.0%
Latvia	5,132,287	5,775,000	3.3%
Liberia †	26,000	—	—
Lithuania	4,981,628	6,432,465	3.3%
Nicaragua *	431,849	—	—
Poland	159,668,972	178,560,000	3.3%
Roumania	37,922,675	66,560,560	3.3%
Russia *	192,601,297	—	—
Total	$10,350,490,597	$11,671,953,489	2.1% ‡

* Debts unfunded.
† Debts paid.
‡ Average for all settlements.

of Versailles, fixed the bill at $33,000,000,000. It soon became apparent that the burden was too great and within a year the initial reparation payments had been defaulted. A second effort met with no greater success and the so-called Dawes Plan, drawn up by an international committee of experts, was in operation for but four years, namely, 1924–1928.[8]

In 1929, in another attempt to find the key to a very vexing problem, a second committee of experts was constituted, under the chairmanship of the American Owen D. Young. After four months'

[8] This Committee was named after its American chairman, Charles G. Dawes.

labor, the Young Plan was submitted to Germany as the new basis for reparation payments. This called for the following: First, thirty-seven annual payments, averaging $512,500,000, were to be made, to be followed by twenty-two further annual payments averaging $391,250,000. Actually, over the fifty-nine years, Germany was to pay twenty-seven and one-half billions of dollars; but the annuities, capitalized at 5 per cent, represented a reparation amount totaling only $9,272,000,000. Second, of each annuity payment in the first group of thirty-seven years, $165,000,000 was to be unconditional and to be earmarked to meet the reconstruction costs of the Allies. The conditional part was to be scaled down in proportion to any adjustments that might be made in the interallied debts. That is to say, if the United States reduced the amounts the Allies were to pay her, the Allies in turn would reduce the conditional payments to be made by Germany. In the second group of twenty-two annuities, there was to be no unconditional portion; therefore these entire payments were to be adjusted to the interallied debts. Third, Germany was to obtain the sums needed for the annuities from two sources; namely, from a mortgage on the German railroads, and from ordinary receipts in the governmental budget. Fourth, a Bank for International Settlements was set up to handle the reparation funds and to have certain other fiscal functions.

Thus the Young Plan definitely joined reparation payments and interallied debts together. But our State and Treasury Departments consistently refused to regard the two as inseparable, even going so far as to decline American representation on the directorate of the Bank for International Settlements. Secretary of State Stimson voiced the American policy in May, 1929, in this fashion:

> . . . this government does not desire to have any American official, directly or indirectly, participate in the collection of German reparations through the agency of this bank [the Bank for International Settlements] or otherwise. Ever since the close of the war the American government has consistently taken this position; it has never accepted membership on the Reparation Commission; it declined to join the Allied Powers in the confiscation of sequestered German property and the application of that property to its war claims.

Nevertheless, the relationship existing between the interallied debts and the reparation annuities was only too apparent. The Allies had made loans to one another, usually estimated to amount to

$21,613,000,000. But in view of the liberal terms on the basis of which the intergovernmental loans had been refunded, the capitalized value had been scaled down to $10,814,000,000. On the other hand, the capitalized value of the German reparation annuities was $9,272,000,000. Thus the two accounts largely balanced each other. As Professor S. F. Bemis remarked in 1936:

> . . . in reality, the payment of war debts was made to rest upon the payment by Germany of reparations. And, in reality again, Germany's payment rested on her capacity to borrow from private foreign capital, over a third of it American.[9]

By 1931, it was generally recognized that the Young Plan was no more satisfactory than its predecessors: it far outran Germany's ability to pay. Then, in the middle of the year, when the whole German financial structure was threatened with ruin and it was evident that the annuity for 1931–1932 could not be met, President Hoover was compelled to bow before the inevitable: after an exchange of views with the principal nations affected, Washington announced the establishment of a moratorium, for a single year, on all intergovernmental debts and reparation payments. The two financial operations were now officially linked and we could collect from the Allies only as much or as little as they, in turn, could collect from Germany.

Indeed, in 1932, our former Allies made this an explicit policy when, at a conference at Lausanne, they agreed to write off 90 per cent of the German reparations due under the Young Plan, provided that "a satisfactory settlement is obtained between them [Germany's creditors] and their own creditors [the United States]." The United States took no official cognizance of this understanding; and here

[9] How the Allies managed to skim what cream there was may be noted from the following. Germany paid in all on the various reparation accounts $4,470,000,000. The Allies paid to the United States, against the war debts, $2,606,000,000. On the other hand, it was made possible for Germany to finance her payments in considerable measure out of private loans which continued until 1931. Of the estimated total of $6,000,000,000 lent to Germany, $2,500,000,000 came from the United States. Under the Nazi regime, repatriation of German dollar bonds began to take place, largely through the use of blocked *Reichsmarks,* and at a discount frequently as much as 70 cents on the dollar. In other words, Americans got almost nothing when the transactions were balanced. On the other hand, Europeans got more cash out of Germany, lent her less, and into the bargain got more favorable terms in the settlement of the private-loan accounts.

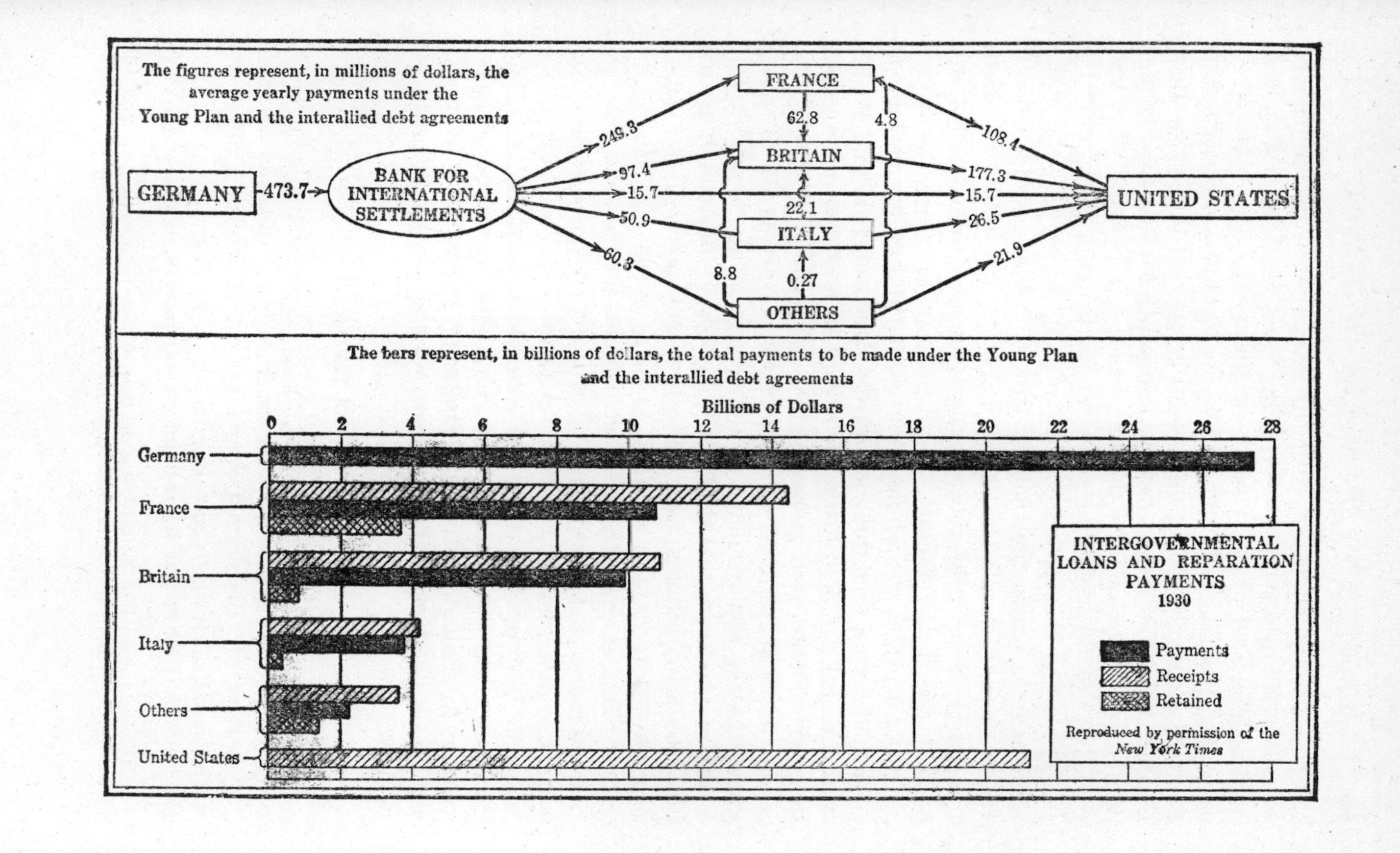
The figures represent, in millions of dollars, the average yearly payments under the Young Plan and the interallied debt agreements
GERMANY
473.7
BANK FOR INTERNATIONAL SETTLEMENTS
249.3
97.4
15.7
50.9
60.3
FRANCE
BRITAIN
ITALY
OTHERS
62.8
4.8
22.1
8.8
0.27
108.4
177.3
15.7
26.5
21.9
UNITED STATES
The bars represent, in billions of dollars, the total payments to be made under the Young Plan and the interallied debt agreements
Billions of Dollars
0
2
4
6
8
10
12
14
16
18
20
22
24
26
28
Germany
France
Britain
Italy
Others
United States
INTERGOVERNMENTAL LOANS AND REPARATION PAYMENTS 1930
Payments
Receipts
Retained
Reproduced by permission of the New York Times

the matter continued to rest with "token" payments being made up to 1933 and then even these stopping.[10]

With the Nazi party in power in Germany, after midsummer 1933, and pledged as Hitler was to the termination of reparation payments, it was becoming increasingly clear that the payments on the war loans had ceased finally. Americans viewed this state of affairs with bitterness. On the one hand, our former Allies continued to expend staggering sums for rearmament purposes at the same time that they protested their inability to pay. On the other, there was the realization that the cost of "making the world safe for democracy" during the years 1914–1920 in considerable measure was to be borne by future generations of Americans in terms of an increased tax burden.

To what extent the whole question of the funding of the war debts had been a doubtful joke on the American people from the beginning has not been made the subject of adequate historical inquiry. When that time comes, it may be revealed that American financiers, including the Secretary of the Treasury, Mr. Mellon, knew all along that the debts would never be paid, but deliberately kept alive the fiction that they would in order to make more palatable Secretary Mellon's reduction of income taxes in the higher brackets.

One thing, at any rate, the United States learned, and that was that our purse strings were not to be loosened again so easily. In 1934, Congress passed the Johnson Act, which forbade foreign governments in default on their debts to the United States to float public issues in this country. The Neutrality legislation of 1935–1937, as we shall see, extended the same prohibition to belligerents, outside of the Western Hemisphere, whether or not they were in default.

Russian Relations

The United States, alone among the great powers, failed to establish diplomatic relations with Russia during the nineteen twenties. Not only would the State Department not grant recognition, but it steadfastly declined to encourage trade by private individuals with the Soviets. The following influences and beliefs, as guiding Wash-

[10] The little country of Finland was the only one to continue the payments (she did so in full each year) on the interallied loans.

ington's Russian policy during the twenties, are to be noted particularly:

The State Department refused to consider the Communist rule in Russia as being aught but temporary. Recognition, therefore, awaited the collapse of Sovietism.

Administration officials declined to become enthusiastic about the potential significance of the Russian-American trade. Thus, Secretary of Commerce Hoover said in March, 1921:

> The question of trade with Russia is far more a political question than an economic one so long as Russia is under the control of the Bolsheviki. Under their economic system, no matter how much they moderate it in name, there can be no real return to production in Russia, and therefore Russia will have no considerable commodities to export and consequently no great ability to obtain imports. . . . That requires the abandonment of their present system.

It was held at Washington that Russian labor, in particular industries, was often conscripted. According to our tariff laws, therefore, commodities produced under such conditions could not be imported by Americans. In 1931, the American Treasury Department placed an embargo on Russian lumber and pulpwood on the ground of the use of forced labor.[11]

The Soviets had repudiated the Russian state debt, had confiscated the property of American citizens, and had refused to satisfy the claims of American nationals against the Russian government. The United States had advanced $192,000,000 to the Kerensky government in 1917, and this debt had never been funded. American bankers, in 1916, had sold to the American investing public $75,000,000 worth of Russian imperial bonds. These had been defaulted. In addition, Americans had claims totaling some $430,000,000, against the Russian government for losses suffered in the revolutions of 1917 and as a result of property confiscations.[12] Washington's position on the question of the Russian debts was put by President Coolidge, in December, 1923, as follows:

[11] But it would not ban the importation of manganese (needed in steel production). Thus the lines of economic necessity and political principle often cross, to the complete confusion of the latter.

[12] Of course, these claims have never been critically examined. Claims commissions would probably scale them down radically.

> Whenever there appears any disposition to compensate our citizens who were despoiled and to recognize that debt contracted with our government, not by the Czar but by the newly-formed republic of Russia . . . our country ought to be the first to go to the economic and moral rescue of Russia.

There never could be friendly relations between the two nations as long as Russia carried on Communist propaganda against American institutions, either through the American Communist party or through its own trade agencies.

Thus, we may say that the State Department insisted upon the presentation of tangible evidences of Russian good faith and ability to meet obligations as conditions precedent to the opening of negotiations. European governments, on the other hand, recognized first and negotiated later. Nevertheless, if official Washington was critical toward Russia, the American people certainly were interested in the Russian experiment and, beginning with the late twenties, books and reports on Russia, depicting the efforts of the Soviet governments to carry out their gigantic industrialization program, were being widely read. It is true that the State Department would neither countenance the floating of a Russian loan in this country nor give its encouragement to the extension, by Americans, of credits to the Soviets. This did not prevent American citizens and corporations, however, from entering into commercial relations with Russia at their own risk. Long-term credits were granted by outstanding American manufacturers, American technicians helped build and start off Soviet enterprises, American promoters sought to acquire concessions for the exploitation of Russian raw materials. The result was that Russian-American trade grew to considerable proportions in the late twenties. So, in 1913, American exports to Russia were worth $26,465,000; in 1930, they were worth $136,307,000. In 1913, American imports from Russia were worth $29,315,000; by 1930, at $24,386,000, they were almost at the prewar level. That these economic factors would ultimately have altered Old Guard Republican policy, even had there been no New Deal, is a safe assumption.

The anomalies of this situation and the fact that Japanese maneuvers in the Far East were drawing the United States and Russia together (at any rate, as far as Eastern foreign policy was concerned), prompted President Franklin D. Roosevelt to seek an accommodation. At his invitation the Russian Commissar for Foreign

Affairs, Maxim Litvinoff, came to Washington; and after a series of conversations, formal diplomatic relations were declared resumed on November 16, 1933. The basis was an exchange of notes between President Roosevelt and Mr. Litvinoff.

The notes committed both governments to respect the territorial integrity of each other and not to tolerate within their borders organizations which had as their aim "the overthrow of, or bringing about by force of a change in the political or social order" of the other. (The reference here, obviously, was to the Communist, or Third International, which presumably was not to carry on its propagandist activities in the United States.) Further, Russia assured Americans the right to worship in their own churches; and each country agreed that in the event of the arrest of their respective nationals in the other's country the consuls would be notified at once by the authorities and fair trials granted on the basis of most-favored-nation treatment. Russia waived all claims for American military activities in the Eastern Siberian intervention after the World War, while other financial claims and counter-claims were to be negotiated between the new Russian ambassador to Washington and the State Department. Despite the fact that ambassadors were appointed in 1934, by 1938 the claims question still remained unsettled.[13]

[13] In 1935, the United States and Russia signed a trade agreement under which the U.S.S.R. pledged herself to purchase a minimum of $30,000,000 worth of American goods annually. (The low point in U.S.–U.S.S.R. trade was reached in 1933, when American exports totaled only $10,674,000.) In August, 1938, the agreement was renewed with the minimum this time raised to $40,000,000. The policy was successful: for, in 1935–1936, American exports to the U.S.S.R. were worth $39,224,000; for 1936–1937, they were worth $40,513,000. And for 1935–1936, American imports from the U.S.S.R. were worth $20,674,000; and for 1936–1937, $23,230,000. (In 1933, imports from the U.S.S.R. were worth $12,114,000.)

PART II

IMPERIAL AMERICA IN THE MACHINE AGE

PART II

IMPERIAL AMERICA IN THE MACHINE AGE

IV. CAPITAL AND LABOR

The Growth of the Population

Between 1871 and 1900, the population of the United States had almost doubled in size; during the thirty years from 1901 to 1930, the gain had been but a little more than 60 per cent. The slowing up of the country's population growth was a definite characteristic of the twentieth century and was due largely to the following factors: (1) the restriction of immigration; (2) the movement from the country to the cities; (3) a wider exercise of birth control, particularly by the country's urban populations. The gain in population for the decade 1861–1870 had been 26.6 per cent; for the next two decades, the gains were much the same; from 1891 to 1900, it had dropped to 20.7 per cent; from 1901 to 1910, the gain was 21.0 per cent; from 1911 to 1920, 14.9 per cent; and from 1921 to 1930, 16.1 per cent. In 1900, the population of the United States was 75,994,575; in 1910, 91,972,266; in 1920, 105,710,620; in 1930, 122,775,046. In the last decade, the gains in population had hardly been distributed equally. In fact, more than one-fourth of the total increase over 1921–1930 was concentrated in the two states of New York and California. Each of these states had gained more than two millions; Michigan, Texas, and Illinois had each gained more than a million; Florida had increased its population by one-half, New Jersey by more than one-fourth, and North Carolina by one-fourth. The primacy of New England was now a thing of the past: indeed, the three Pacific states seated a greater total population than the six New England states.

The country had increasingly become urbanized in the thirty years since the opening of the new century. In 1900, 40 per cent of the population was urban (living in communities having 2500 or more inhabitants); in 1910, 45.8 per cent; in 1920, 51.4 per cent; in 1930, 56.2 per cent. America's population had been unable to resist the pull of the cities. Chief among the reasons for the great growth of our urban population were the following: the advances of industrialization, which had attracted millions of families away from the countryside; the country's large immigrant population had naturally gravitated toward the cities to join kinsmen and to take up anew the old community life of their native habitats; Americans, in growing numbers, had come to demand the fuller satisfactions of living—the modern apartment houses, the amusements, educational facilities, outlets for aesthetic enjoyment, the excitement and movement of crowds—which only the cities could offer. Nothing more typified the civilization of America in the postwar era than metropolitan New York, where, within a radius of fifty miles of Manhattan Island, were closely planted two hundred and ninety cities, boroughs and villages seating a population of more than ten millions. These were all part of New York City's urban life: they came here to work, play, shop; they read the New York newspapers, attended the New York schools and colleges, had New York's heroes and spoke New York's slang. And what was true of metropolitan New York was also true in only less degree of nearly a score of other metropolitan centers.

Not that a countervailing tendency was not beginning to evidence itself. If the great cities were glamorous, they were also crowded and impersonal; their transportation facilities were becoming taxed well-nigh beyond endurance; their living quarters were so many huge barracks that shut out the sky and the sun and put to an end that pleasant friendliness and community of feeling which had been so characteristic of provincial America. The city dweller had a small circle of intimates, but he had no neighbors. He had his personal problems, but the affairs of his community were remote and unreal. Municipal administration had become institutionalized, along with so much of industry and commerce, and public opinion was a small still voice. By the twenties, here and there a few Americans were beginning to quit the great cities, in protest against these dehumanizing tendencies. But the movement toward a decentralizing process could not go very far because the countryside and semi-rural communities still failed to offer opportunities for individual advancement comparable to the metropolitan centers. Thus, despite the fact that rural America was becoming a more attractive

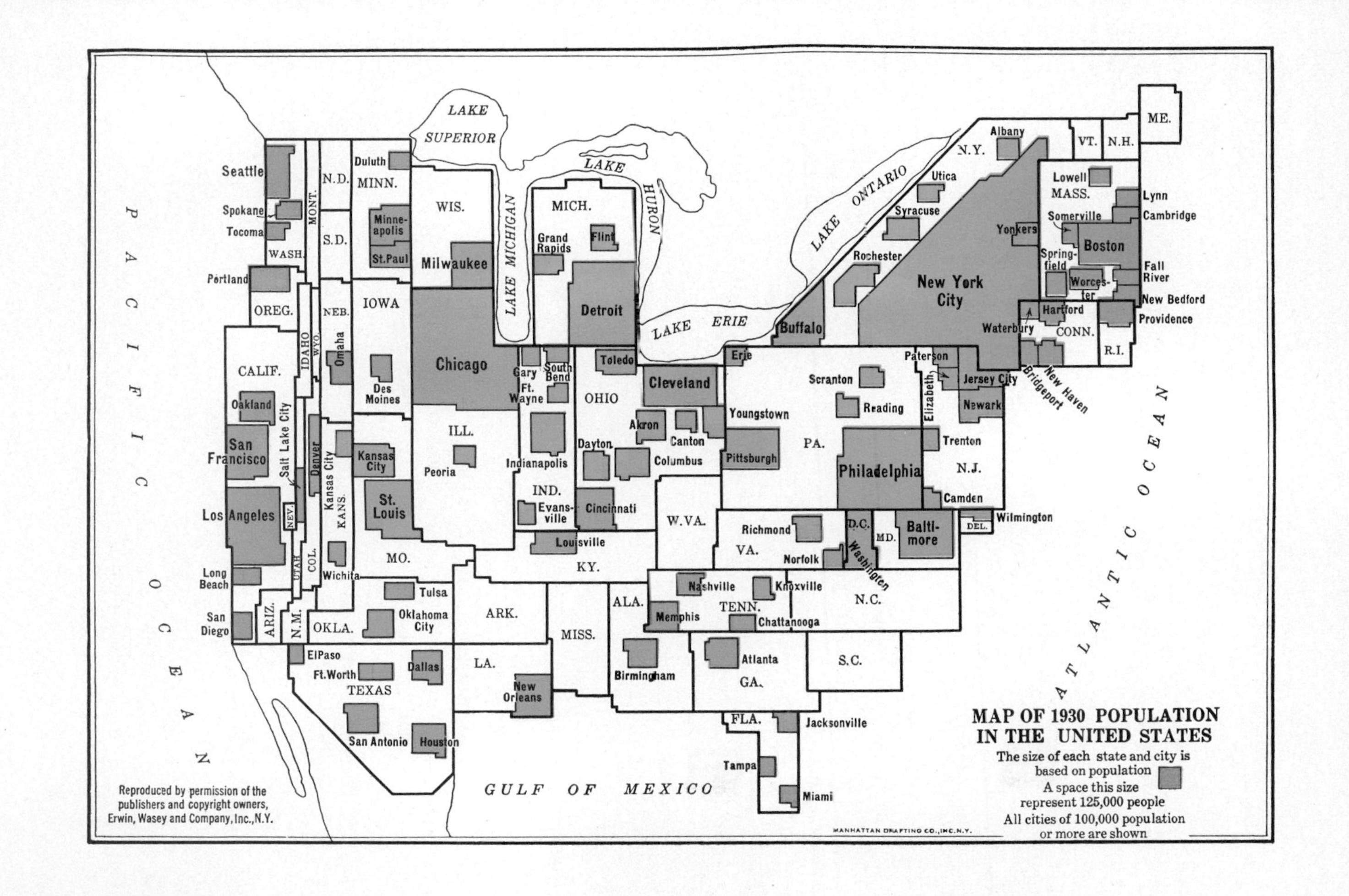
MAP OF 1930 POPULATION IN THE UNITED STATES
The size of each state and city is based on population
A space this size represent 125,000 people
All cities of 100,000 population or more are shown
PACIFIC OCEAN
ATLANTIC OCEAN
GULF OF MEXICO
LAKE SUPERIOR
LAKE MICHIGAN
LAKE HURON
LAKE ERIE
LAKE ONTARIO
Seattle
Spokane
Tocoma
WASH.
Portland
OREG.
CALIF.
Oakland
San Francisco
Los Angeles
Long Beach
San Diego
IDAHO
MONT.
WYO.
NEV.
UTAH
ARIZ.
Salt Lake City
Denver
COL.
N.M.
N.D.
S.D.
NEB.
Omaha
KANS.
Kansas City
Wichita
OKLA.
Tulsa
Oklahoma City
TEXAS
ElPaso
Ft.Worth
Dallas
San Antonio
Houston
MINN.
Duluth
Minne-apolis
St.Paul
IOWA
Des Moines
MO.
Kansas City
St. Louis
WIS.
Milwaukee
ILL.
Chicago
Peoria
MICH.
Grand Rapids
Flint
Detroit
IND.
Gary
South Bend
Ft. Wayne
Indianapolis
Evans-ville
OHIO
Toledo
Cleveland
Akron
Canton
Youngstown
Dayton
Columbus
Cincinnati
KY.
Louisville
ARK.
LA.
New Orleans
MISS.
ALA.
Birmingham
TENN.
Memphis
Nashville
Knoxville
Chattanooga
GA.
Atlanta
FLA.
Jacksonville
Tampa
Miami
S.C.
N.C.
VA.
Richmond
Norfolk
W.VA.
D.C.
Washington
MD.
Balti-more
DEL.
Wilmington
PA.
Erie
Pittsburgh
Scranton
Reading
Philadelphia
N.J.
Paterson
Elizabeth
Jersey City
Newark
Trenton
Camden
N.Y.
Buffalo
Rochester
Syracuse
Utica
Albany
Yonkers
New York City
CONN.
Hartford
Waterbury
New Haven
Bridgeport
R.I.
Providence
MASS.
Lowell
Somerville
Spring-field
Worces-ter
Boston
Lynn
Cambridge
Fall River
New Bedford
VT.
N.H.
ME.
Reproduced by permission of the publishers and copyright owners, Erwin, Wasey and Company, Inc., N.Y.
MANHATTAN DRAFTING CO., INC. N.Y.

place to live in than it had been but two decades back, flight from the metropolis generally stopped in the suburbs, where the slave of the 8:17 fondly believed he was enjoying the freedom of the country without relinquishing the advantages of the city.

The Growth of Industry

As we have seen, by 1900 the machine had become an important factor in American life. But in the three decades following, the machine was to become mightier and have a more pervasive influence—it was to produce more, furnish more comforts, conquer new domains, until by 1930, Americans began to regard it very much as the hallmark, the peculiar, distinguishing sign, of our whole civilization. The machine was ruthless: it broke down privacy, swept away ancient trades, destroyed skill, created technological unemployment, wasted natural resources, standardized and sometimes vulgarized taste, quickened the tempo of men's lives and brought in a crop of new psycho-neurotic disorders, made warfare a horror and an inferno, constricted the size of the world until men almost everywhere were performing their daily tasks in the same way, employing their idle moments in much the same fashion, and very largely thinking the same thoughts. Yet the machine was beneficent, too: it was releasing mankind from the bitter, back-breaking labor of centuries and was making life comfortable for the toiling masses; it was producing, if only slowly, more leisure time; it was turning out more goods. True, great inequalities in wealth and income still existed; and periodic breakdowns, or business crises, continued to occur, during which production slowed down and large numbers of persons were thrown out of work to suffer privations and often real want. The fault, however, lay not in the machine but in the nature of its ownership and the uses to which it was put by business.

The machine, too, made for more color and variety in our daily lives; it put amusements within the reach of all; it dressed the humblest shopgirl in clothes whose designs, at least, were the work of the smartest Paris salons. It was making life healthier and more secure against the ravages of nature; it was making men bolder and more certain of themselves; if it was destroying old crafts—glass blowers, weavers, cabinetmakers—it was creating new groups of artisans—radio mechanics, sanitary engineers, chauffeurs, steel construction workers. Thus the machine worked for both good and ill, and toward which side the balances tipped only a rash or a prophetic person might venture to say.

Such were the general characteristics of the period in which Americans were moving in the postwar era. What were the more particular attributes of this machine age? The writers in *Recent Economic Changes,* that great Domesday Book of industrial America, in 1930 singled out the following as having particular significance: 1. The machine had led to a greater productivity per worker. 2. There had been an increase in the physical volume of power. 3. There had been a great increase in the number of prime movers. 4. There had been a great increase in the fixed capital assets of industry (buildings, equipment, machinery). 5. Industry had been spending princely sums on industrial research. 6. New manufacturing methods and processes had made their appearance. 7. Yeoman work was being done in the elimination of waste. At the end of the single decade after the war, each American worker, on the average, was turning out half again as much goods as he had turned out at its beginning. From 1900 on, the national output of goods and services had doubled and in some instances trebled, while the country's population was not much more than half again the size it had been thirty years before.

Between 1900 and 1929, the wealth of the country had risen from eighty-eight billions of dollars to three hundred and sixty-one billions of dollars, and the per capita distribution had almost trebled.[1] There were definite signs to be read of the bettering of the national well-being: increases in savings bank deposits; the great growth of life insurance policies; the appearance and flourishing of the building and loan associations (which made home ownership possible); the great increase in school attendance; a widespread diffusion of goods once regarded as luxuries but by the end of the twenties considered part of the daily round of living (for example, the automobile, the telephone, electrical lighting and household appliances, modern plumbing, and central heating). The total realized income grew from $27,100,000,000 in 1909 to $66,000,-000,000 in 1922 and $84,000,000,000 in 1929. In terms of 1913 dollars, these incomes were as follows: 1909, $28,200,000,000;

[1] One should have in mind, of course, that figures of this sort are only the roughest kind of estimates; also, that they make no correction for the changing value of the dollar. But there can be no question that the trend of national wealth and income was sharply upward.

1922, $40,400,000,000; 1929, $52,500,000,000. In 1929, the per capita wealth was $2977 and the per capita income was $692.

The tabulation that follows presents the data for manufacturing establishments in selected years over the period being discussed.

GROWTH OF MANUFACTURES IN THE UNITED STATES *

(In thousands)

Year	*No. of establishments*	*Wage earners*	*Value of products*	*Value added by manufacture*
1899	208	4,713	$11,407,000	$ 4,831,000
1914	273	7,024	24,217,000	9,858,000
1919	214	8,998	62,000,000	24,803,000
1921	196	6,944	43,619,000	18,327,000
1927	192	8,350	62,718,000	27,585,000
1929	207	8,743	69,417,000	31,687,000

* For 1899 and 1914, the figures relate to factories (excluding hand and neighborhood establishments), whose products were valued in excess of $500; for subsequent years, only factories whose products were valued in excess of $5000 are included.

Which were America's great industries at the end of the decade of the golden nineteen twenties? The following were the outstanding: textiles and products; machinery; steel and products; food products; paper and printing; chemicals; transportation and equipment; lumber and products; stone, glass and clay; nonferrous metals. In short, we were turning out vast quantities of capital, or producer, and consumer goods. We were happily circumstanced: thanks to our great wealth of raw materials, our great capital plant, our technological skills and our magnificent domestic market, we were—or seemed—safe from those perils that constantly threatened the older economies of European nations. The twenties, also, had seen pioneering in new fields to employ new capital investments and create job opportunities for fresh skills and part of the workers displaced by advancing mechanization in older industries. During the twenties the radio, aviation, motion pictures, natural gas and chemical industries had suddenly appeared and as quickly grown to maturity; while the advance of the automobile had brought in its train a whole host of new industrial activities and services—the hard-surfacing of roads, garages and repair shops, road stands, the tourist camp.

Nothing was more indicative of the new day than the growing

industrialization of the South. Attracted by the nearness of raw materials, abundant power resources, low taxation, the absence of restrictive factory codes, the presence of a cheap and complaisant labor supply, northern capital and industry flocked southward so that, before the twenties were over, southern cotton mills were operating more spindles than were those of New England, the South's iron and steel mills had become significant factors in the country's industrial life, her tobacco, cigar, and cigarette industry was responsible for most of the production in this field. Indeed, it was not hard to see that southern industry had taken on the characteristics of the American machine age. The section was seating a great factory population, its towns and cities were increasing and expanding, accumulations of wealth were piling higher and were showing a disproportionate distribution as millionaires and wage toilers made their appearance and great corporations (particularly in the electric power and light field) and powerful banks came to exert their ramified influences over legislatures and the press. But the South, reaping the benefits of its new industrialism—in its good roads, better schools, more governmental services—was not to be spared its tares. In the late twenties, industrial combat broke out in many of the mill towns of Tennessee, North Carolina, and Virginia; Communist organizers poured into disaffected communities; unions sprang up to demand shorter hours, better wages, the end of speeding-up systems. Capital fought back with night riders, local strong-arm organizations, injunctions, state troops, spies, and wholesale dispossesses from company houses. The South, it was apparent, was not to skip that dark cycle of violence so characteristic of the industrial development of other sections of the nation.

The processes of marketing, too, had undergone a complete transformation. One might mention the following phenomena as being recent developments of our changed industrial society: 1. Instalment selling. During the years 1923–1929, the amount of instalment purchasing was estimated to be in the neighborhood of five billions of dollars annually. Automobiles, used cars and trucks, furniture, pianos and radios, and all those electrical appliances with which the average American home was being equipped, were being marketed in this fashion. 2. The growth of the practice of hand-to-mouth buying. This had a profound effect on style changes and on the great increase of marketing costs, particularly in the expenditures for advertising. 3. The mounting volume of advertising. It was estimated that a billion and one-half dollars was being expended annually during the twenties on this form of marketing. 4. The appearance of the chain store, notably in the five-and-ten-cents, groceries, drugs, tobacco, and candy fields. In a number of cities studied by the Census Bureau it was found that chain stores handled from one-fourth to one-third of the total retail sales. 5. The willingness of the American buying public to experiment with and purchase new wares, on a mass scale. This was true of the radio, the use of rayons, cosmetics, novelty shoes for women, electric stokers, oil-burning furnaces, electrical refrigerators.

Mass Production

The machine was the emblem of the time; and mass production of goods, of standardized design, uniform quality, interchangeable parts, was what flowed from the machine. Nothing was more symbolical of our era than the chassis assembly line of American automobile plants, where every process was routinized and the men performed their single functions with the precision of automatons.[2]

To produce units in the rhythm of the machine, power was necessary, and our use of power, therefore, quadrupled in the short period after the turn of the century. After the war, America was using as much electrical energy as all the rest of the world put together. America's supremacy in the realm of power is revealed by the following comparative figures: the capacity of America's prime movers was 700 million horsepower; Great Britain's was 175 million horsepower; Germany's was 175 million horsepower; and France's was 70 million horsepower.

Standardization, under a machine economy, was a prime requisite, and the standardizing of products was pushed with a zeal that leveled all barriers before it. Mr. Hoover's Department of Commerce, during the twenties, pointed the way, and industrialists were not slow to follow, even at the risk of surrendering that individuality of design which had been the basis of much of their earlier claims to survival as entrepreneurs. Not only were models standardized, but sizes, lengths, and thicknesses: the varieties of paving brick

[2] According to Stuart Chase, it cost Henry Ford $100,000,000 to change from the Model T Ford to the Model A. Almost half of the production machinery in the Ford plant had to be replaced or supplemented. This change from Model T to Model A in not much more than a year in a way epitomizes the whole story of mechanization in postwar America.

were reduced from 66 to 4, of sheet steel from 1819 to 261, of range boilers from 130 to 13, of invoice, inquiry, and purchase order forms from 4500 to 3. In a short ten years the Department of Commerce could report that under its auspices more than one hundred plans for standardization had been adopted in as many industries, and that the estimated annual saving to the manufacturers involved was a quarter of a billion dollars. Standardization meant that further mechanization was possible, of course, but it also made easier the replacement of parts and permitted the integration of allied industries.

Our acceptance of machine production had other results. The reduction of waste and the development of new materials and products went hand in hand with simplification and standardization. The entrepreneurs of the twentieth century were less willing to depend upon chance and the work of individual erratic genius to blaze new trails for them and furnish other outlets for their great accumulations of capital. They subsidized scientific foundations, kept up a ceaseless round of experiments, and carried on their pay rolls large staffs of laboratory workers who puzzled over problems of pure as well as applied research. The great industrial laboratories of the Du Pont companies, those maintained by the Westinghouse Electric and Manufacturing Company, the General Electric Company, the American Telephone and Telegraph Company, the Mellon Institute of Industrial Research, produced new industrial processes and a bewildering array of products which were totally unfamiliar to the world a generation before. There was little likelihood of raw materials failing the machine age when this constant questing for substitutes and the reduction of waste kept up its ceaseless round. One might mention the following processes and products which had come out of the laboratories of industry: the hydrogenation process for extracting gasoline from coal, oil shale, and other minerals; the cracking of gasoline; the development of sheet cellulose (cellophane) as a dustproof and waterproof wrapper; dry milk, corn syrup, cellulose sausage casings, viosterol; carbon dioxide ice; new types of steel; lacquer, laminated bakelite, rayon, pyrex (glass substitute), fabrikoid (leather substitute).

Productivity

Nowhere did the influence of the machine display itself more startlingly than in the increased productivity of labor in industry.

Here we are brought face to face with the nature of that new industrial revolution that had set in during the nineteen tens, had been accelerated during the twenties and, indeed, was continuing at an unchecked pace during the thirties. The machines were producing more goods—and were requiring less and less manpower for their operation. Nothing has revealed this change of affairs more convincingly than the figures collected by the National Resources Board, a New Deal agency. The following index figures, based on 1920 as 100, present experiences for selected years for output, man-hours worked, and employment needs per unit of production.

INDEXES OF OUTPUT, EMPLOYMENT, AND UNIT-LABOR REQUIREMENT

(1920 = 100)

Industry	*1920*	*1925*	*1929*	*1932*	*1934*
Manufacturing:					
Output	100.0	116.9	140.6	78.3	94.4
Man-hours	100.0	91.9	98.1	43.0	52.5
Unit-labor requirement	100.0	78.6	69.8	54.9	55.6
Mining:					
Output	100.0	96.8	105.5	54.0	65.4
Man-hours	100.0	85.8	82.8	40.4	52.8
Unit-labor requirement	100.0	88.6	78.5	74.8	80.7
Steam railroads:					
Output	100.0	95.3	99.2	52.1	59.2
Man-hours	100.0	83.2	79.8	43.7	44.0
Unit-labor requirement	100.0	87.3	80.4	83.9	74.3

An examination of the tabulation indicates that between 1920 and 1929 the whole of manufacturing, in terms of unit-labor productivity, became 30 per cent more efficient; mining became more than 20 per cent more efficient; and steam railroading became 20 per cent more efficient. In the case of manufacturing, notably, the advance was continued right through the depression years 1930–1934.[3]

Here was one of the crucial points on which examination of our industrial society required focusing. Greater productivity per unit of labor meant obviously the utilization of new machine techniques and therefore the creation of new investment opportunities for capital.

[3] See below, page 291, for another treatment of this concept of the productivity of labor.

(Although, of course, it should be said parenthetically, that increased output frequently was achieved by improvements in the layout of plant, routing of materials, more comfortable and healthful conditions of work, and the like.) On the other hand, greater productivity made for labor displacement. Was there not a need for so-called buffer employment while men were shifting gradually from those industries from which they were being separated to new ones in time requiring more hands? The nineteen twenties could afford to disregard the problem in view of the fact that the total of unemployed and the smaller total of disemployed as a result of technological advance were not very great.

It should be pointed out here that unemployment figures were never recorded by a public agency, and estimates had to be resorted to. That unemployment continued to exist, even in boom periods, was generally recognized. It was estimated, for example, that during the years 1922–1929, the average annual figure was between two and two and one-half million workers. Unemployment was generally due to the seasonal characteristics of trades, the shutting down of plants, industrial disputes, and voluntary quitting. To these more or less temporary forms was added that grimmer kind already referred to—technological disemployment.

What the toll of technological disemployment was, we did not know. But that its figures were large and that the forced shifting of labor from old to new forms of employment was accompanied by great travail were generally recognized. So, from 1919 to 1929, industries employing 40 per cent of the country's wage earners were using 900,000 fewer workers. In manufacturing, in that single decade, productivity had increased 30 per cent, while the number of workers had declined 546,000; in railroad transportation, productivity had increased 20 per cent, while the number of workers had declined 253,000; in mining, productivity had increased 22 per cent, while the number of workers had declined 100,000. In the same period the country's population had increased seven millions. In short, almost eight million new job seekers were compelled to look for work in lines of endeavor outside of manufacturing, the railroads, and mining. That there should be a residue, because of the excess of job seekers over new opportunities presented, was inevitable. Wesley Clair Mitchell placed this shrinkage in jobs for the years 1920–1927 at 650,000.

Americans in the twenties, dimly as they were aware of this

problem, were beginning to see nevertheless that our greater mechanization was bringing about marked changes in the position of labor. For example, younger men were replacing older men, and age forty-five, for the worker out of employment, verged closely on superannuation. It was growing harder for men permanently laid off to find new work, because of the competition for jobs. Temporary employment was getting more difficult to obtain. As a result of industrial superannuation, the burden of support of the idle worker fell on other members of the family, causing a lowering of living standards. Displacement by a machine meant a loss to society of skills built up by years of application. A worker thus displaced was forced to learn laboriously a new craft or to accept work, at lower wages, as an unskilled laborer. Isador Lubin, studying 754 dispossessed workers in 1928, found that more than half of those obtaining employment were compelled to take positions in different occupations where new skills had to be learned; too, almost the same number found it necessary to accept reductions in pay. Reabsorption into industry, with its accompanying lower standards of living, if not actual dependency, was painfully slow.

The Position of Labor

That the upper strata of labor, as well as capital, enjoyed the fruits of the prosperity of the twenties there was ample evidence to prove. American standards of living were considerably superior, in the postwar period, than any prevailing, certainly since the Civil War; that the margin between those of America and Europe was widening was apparent as well. There was a diffusion of creature comforts. If we look at automobiles, for example, we find that in 1910 there was one passenger car to each two hundred and sixty-five persons in the country; a short eighteen years later, there was one to every six persons. In 1913, but one in every ten non-farm homes was equipped with a stationary bathtub; in 1928, the ratio was one in every five. In 1913, but one in every twenty non-farm homes was equipped with a residence telephone; in 1928, the ratio was one in every ten. In 1913, but one in every twenty non-farm homes was wired for electric light and power; in 1928, the ratio was one in every five. While at the end of the twenties the average income of a workingman's family was only between $1300 and $1500 a year (upon which he supported a family averaging four persons), still, apparently, it was possible to provide with it not a few of the amenities of life.

The gains of the working class—in higher wages, lower hours, better working conditions—were, as has been said, generally confined to the so-called aristocrats of labor, that is to say, the well-organized skilled craft workers. There was an outstanding reason for this: the upper levels of the workers also profited from the creation of expanding opportunities for capitalist enterprise outside of the boundaries of the United States. From the nineteen hundreds on and notably with the outbreak of the World War, America had become an imperialist nation as, more and more, our exports began to consist of manufactured goods and investable capital. Skilled workers were in a superior bargaining position and with the tacit consent of employers they were able to create virtual job monopolies as a result of which they could obtain real concessions. This, of course, was a condition that could exist only during a period of growing foreign trade; and such was the case, with only minor and temporary setbacks, from 1915 to the end of the twenties.

It was no accident, therefore, that the years in question were years of waning trade-union militancy. Class collaboration was the keynote of traditional trade unionism; and the unskilled were compelled to fend for themselves. One finds therefore that whereas membership in American trade unions grew fairly steadily until the end of the World War, it began thenceforth to decline. Industrial disputes also decreased in numbers and duration. In 1897, there had been 447,000 American trade unionists; in 1900, 868,500; by 1914, 2,716,900; and in 1920—the all-time peak until 1937—5,110,800. By 1922, the trade unions had lost a million members; and in 1929 the total membership was 4,330,000.

The American Federation of Labor, the outstanding federation of workers' organizations, continued during the period wedded to its philosophy of "pure and simple" unionism—of craft organizations, wage consciousness, job monopoly, and business opportunism. That it should lose in prestige and remain stationary in membership, during the twenties, was inevitable. The Federation remained a congeries of craft unions: of boilermakers, bricklayers, carpenters, printers, quarry workers: these jealously clung to their jurisdictional rights and sought, in the interest of job monopoly, to limit their numbers by long apprenticeships and high initiation fees. New fields the American Federation of Labor was unable to explore: it could not organize the white-collar workers, the steel workers, the automobile workers, the mill workers in the new southern textile area. Why was this?

Some of the reasons for organized labor's inability to grow in the postwar years were the following: 1. The traditional policy of voluntarism, first laid down by Samuel Gompers, which held that labor's advance could be furthered only by its own economic power. Hence, organized labor continued unwilling to organize for political action or to demand the intervention of the state in such vital matters as those pertaining to wages, hours, and social insurance. 2. The adoption of a class-collaboration program. Voluntarism, on its other face, called for working-class militancy; and this the leadership of the American Federation of Labor eschewed. In the words of David J. Saposs, the keenest student of the problem of the period:

> . . . union-management cooperation was elevated to a cardinal principle, and was substituted for belligerency as the program of voluntarism. The new procedure was to sell unionism to the employer. If he recognized the union and permitted his workers to join it, the union in turn would cooperate in setting up machinery which would cooperate with the employer in increasing his profits through reducing costs and enlarging his markets. . . . The union now became a service agency equally interested not only in its own welfare but in that of the employer.

This program, however, was successful only with lesser employers; the great mass industries refused the proffered hand of friendship. 3. Mechanization, which was destroying rapidly the skills of the old-time artisans and hence rendering the old craft distinctions obsolete. With organized labor's refusal to shift from a craft to an industrial basis, its chances for winning over the country's great body of workers became increasingly slighter. 4. Welfare capitalism (that is to say, company health, recreational, and insurance programs), which sought to give the workers at least the same benefits as were offered by the conservative unions. 5. Open shop movements and company unions. 6. Yellow-dog contracts, as a result of which unions might be enjoined from organizing those individual workers who had signed such agreements with their employers. 7. The refusal on the part of most of the A. F. of L. unions to admit into their memberships Negro workers. 8. Labor injunctions, which placed serious obstacles in the path of unions engaged in industrial disputes. These last two phenomena we must examine at greater length.

In the fifteen years beginning with 1915, fully one million Negroes poured into the industrial centers of the North and West to work in West Virginia and Illinois coal mines, Chicago and Kansas City packing plants, Detroit automobile factories, Pittsburgh, Cleveland, and Joliet steel and iron mills. In considerable measure, the northern factory managers began by regarding the Negroes as an industrial reserve, who, because they had no class consciousness, could be used to break the strikes of the white craft unions. The Negro was not averse to strikebreaking for a number of reasons: In the first place, the wages, living conditions, and opportunities for leisure that the northern factory communities offered him were immeasurably superior to anything he had enjoyed in the South. Again, the Negro's slave heritage—strengthened in the period following the Civil War by the preachments of such leaders as Booker T. Washington, by the Negro churches, and by northern white philanthropy—made him regard the white worker as a natural foe and the white employer as a trusted friend and well-wisher. In the third place, the great majority of the Negroes coming from the cotton country were really completely unfamiliar with trade unionism and class solidarity, if not with factories themselves. Most significant of all was the failure of the craft unions to admit into their ranks these new industrial laborers. Openly or not, the policies of the international and national craft unions were based on exclusion. And from 1890 on, the American Federation of Labor itself gave support to this attitude by refusing to bring pressure to bear on its constituent organizations and by seeking to unionize Negroes not as locals in the national unions but as weak federal locals under the direct aegis of the Federation itself. The class-conscious Negro worker scabbed because of his hatred for such tactics and because of his desire to pay back the white unionists in their own coin.[4]

The chief weapon against organized labor, in the armory of capital, was not violence or counter-organization so much as the use of a peculiarly American legal device, that is to say, the injunction. Appealing to federal and state courts sitting in equity (on the ground that substantive law was deficient) employers in increasing numbers, beginning with the nineties, took to suing for

[4] See Sterling D. Spero and Abram L. Harris, *The Black Worker* (1931).

injunctions to prevent labor unions and striking workers from committing irreparable injury to their property. The courts were quick to grant the type of relief requested. Also, the process was a swift and a successful one. During the nineteen twenties, the most common forms of injunctions, sued for against workers and their representatives the trade unions, were the following: from engaging in strikes (whether local, general, or sympathetic); from assembling to act or organize for a strike; from paying strike benefits; from engaging in boycotts; from picketing; from adopting rules against the handling of goods made by nonunion labor; from making trade agreements with employers stipulating the employment of union labor only and the production of goods under union conditions; from making trade agreements for the limitation of production; from sabotaging and the use of violence.

Such procedure received the sanction of the Supreme Court, curiously enough, on the basis of its interpretation of the Sherman Anti-Trust Law. The Sherman Law was invoked by the federal government itself against the striking railroad workers in 1894 and Eugene V. Debs's jail sentence for contempt was upheld by the Supreme Court. It was true that the Court had not specifically rested its judgment in that instance on the Sherman Law. Nevertheless, the way was open to the general use of the injunction against strikers on the plea of irreparable property damage. In 1908, the Supreme Court definitely decided that organized labor might be regarded as a conspiracy in restraint of trade, and hence that the Sherman Law could be made to apply to its activities as well as to those of industrial monopolies. From 1908 to the end of the twenties, the Supreme Court proceeded to add to the list of labor activities that might be regarded as in restraint of trade, and therefore illegal under the anti-trust laws. We may review here the outstanding cases by which this was accomplished.

In Loewe v. Lawlor, 1908 (208 U.S. 274), the Court held that the secondary boycott being used by the United Hatters of America against Danbury hat manufacturers, for their refusal to recognize the union and employ the union label, was illegal and punishable under the Sherman Law. The Court authorized the injured hat manufacturer to sue for the relief provided for in the Sherman Law, and a subsequent action ended with an award to him of $252,000, which was levied against the union's funds and the individual members of the hatters' union. In 1917, the hat company was finally able to collect the damages it had been awarded.

In Gompers v. Bucks Stove and Range Co., 1911 (221 U.S. 418), the Court declared that officers of the American Federation of Labor could be called to account for encouraging boycotts against nonunion manufacturers. As a result, the Federation's officials—Samuel Gompers, Frank Morrison and John Mitchell—were haled before the lower court and sentenced to jail for contempt. While the Supreme Court, on appeal, did dismiss the contempt charges on technicalities, in an obiter dictum it declared that "any act, however peaceful, which was part of a conspiracy to restrain interstate trade unlawfully, itself partook of the illegal nature of the conspiracy."

In Hitchman v. Mitchell, 1917 (245 U.S. 229), the Court upheld a writ granted by a federal district court in West Virginia in 1907 which enjoined the United Mine Workers of America from undertaking to unionize miners who had signed yellow-dog contracts. This was one of the most significant decisions in American labor history. Besides furnishing capital an easy means of checking unionization, i. e., through the yellow-dog contract, it also recognized the applicability of the Sherman Law in the case of production in an individual state, where interstate commerce was not directly affected.

Against these practices, which it regarded as a misinterpretation and a perversion of the Sherman Law, organized labor raised its voice in heated protest. It pointed out that the decisions of the federal and state courts were acting in the interests of capital when: they classified business as property; they disregarded the theoretical limitations on the issuance of injunctions (that is to say, that the plaintiffs were to enter the courts with clean hands); they deprived labor of the only effective weapons it had against capital (that is to say, the strike and the boycott) without disarming capital of its weapons (that is to say, the black list and the lockout); they employed the temporary injunction to abridge labor's constitutional rights of freedom of speech, assembly, and trial by jury.

The force of these arguments could not easily be disregarded; and the result was the writing of the Clayton Act, in 1914, to release labor from the oppression of the Sherman Law. The Clayton Act, with its plain-spoken Articles 6 and 20, indeed had every appearance of promising the long-sought relief. Labor leaders were not to be blamed for looking upon the new law as excepting trade-union organizations from action under the Sherman Law and as limiting severely the right of injunction-issuance in labor disputes. Article 20 seemed to say that injunctions could not be issued to prevent persons from quitting work, from engaging in peaceful picketing, from carrying on primary and secondary boycotts, from collecting and paying out strike benefits, from assembling and, in fact, from doing all those things which they could legally do in times of no industrial disputes. By 1921, labor was profoundly disillusioned. Not only had the Clayton Act, the Supreme Court was to show, not freed organized labor from the weight of legal displeasure but it had even added an additional burden, to wit, that injunction proceedings could be brought against trade unions by private individuals (instead of by the federal Department of Justice alone, as under the Sherman Law). The Supreme Court, in the following typical decisions, deprived labor of the relief the Clayton Act had seemed to promise.

In Duplex Printing Press Co. v. Deering, 1921 (254 U.S. 443), the Court denied that the Clayton Act had legalized secondary boycotts. The action had been brought by the plaintiff (a Michigan corporation) to enjoin the union from persuading other trade unionists in and around New York to boycott the corporation's products, i. e., in hauling, installing, repairing, etc. The petition for an injunction had been denied by the lower courts. But the Supreme Court reversed these decisions and in its opinion said: "Congress had in mind particular industrial controversies, not a general class war."

In United Mine Workers v. Coronado Coal Co., 1922 (259 U.S. 334), and in Coronado Coal Co. v. United Mine Workers, 1925 (268 U.S. 295), the Court put serious obstacles in the way of the union's activities in carrying on its organization work in the nonunion coal fields by deciding that a trade union, though an unincorporated association, might be sued for damages under the anti-trust laws. The Court, in its 1925 decision, further declared that interference with production within a state constituted a conspiracy in restraint of commerce, if intent to restrain and if a substantial restraint could be proved.

In Bedford Cut Stone Co. v. Journeyman Stone Cutters' Association, 1927 (47 Sup. Ct. Rep. 522), the Court ordered the issuance of an injunction against the union despite the fact that in no instance had the men acted in an unlawful manner. The case arose out of the refusal of members of the stone cutters' union, which included both quarrymen and the workers installing the cut stone on buildings, to handle the products of quarrying companies where nonunion labor was employed. The lower courts refused the grant of the injunction but the Supreme Court ordered one issued on the ground that a secondary boycott was being employed. Said the Court: "Where the means adopted are unlawful, the innocent general character of the organizations adopting them or the lawfulness of the ultimate end sought to be attained, cannot serve as justification."

Renewal of agitation for real protection finally resulted in 1932 in the passage by Congress and the signing by President Hoover of the Norris-La Guardia Federal Anti-injunction Law. This measure effectively stopped the misuse of the federal judicial power. The law forbade the federal courts to issue injunctions in the following situations: (1) when workers ceased or refused to perform work; (2) on a worker's becoming a member of a trade union; (3) upon the payment of strike or unemployment benefits to strikers; (4) the giving of publicity to a strike, "whether by advertising, speaking, patrolling, or by any other method not involving fraud or violence"; (5) peaceable assembly. It also outlawed yellow-dog contracts; revoked the judicial rule laid down in the Danbury Hatters' case that union members could be held liable for damages caused by other members; changed the procedure so that orders could not issue without testimony in open court; called upon the complainant to come into court with clean hands; and required that cases of contempt of court arising out of disregard of injunctions be tried before juries.

One of the most interesting aspects of labor's history in this period was the diminishing number of industrial disputes. Records between 1906 and 1915 are lacking; within the decade and one-half 1916–1930, however, there was to be seen almost a steady diminution of the number of disputes and the number of workers involved in them. (This is true except for the year 1919, which was the most violent in American labor annals.) The following table presents the situation for typical years.

STRIKES IN THE UNITED STATES

	Number of—		*Index (1927–29 = 100)*	
Year	*Strikes*	*Workers involved*	*Strikes*	*Workers involved*
1916	3,789	1,599,917	509	514
1919	3,630	4,160,348	488	1,337
1920	3,411	1,463,054	458	470
1925	1,301	428,416	175	138
1929	921	288,572	124	93
1930	637	182,975	86	59
1931	810	341,817	109	110
1932	841	324,210	113	104
1933	1,695	1,168,272	228	376

In the light of such a state of affairs there was excellent reason for the generally held belief that American organized labor constituted the most conservative workingmen's force in the world.

What was true of the industrial sector was equally true of the political. The decline of the Socialist party, to which, in the prewar era, there had been attracted a sizable body of workers, was an outstanding phenomenon of the times. The entry of the United States into the war resulted in a split in its ranks; the Russian Revolution completed the work of destruction. What was left was a small centrist group which refused to adhere to the Third (Communist) International and which looked to the attainment of a socialist state by the ballot. In 1924, the Socialist party endorsed the candidacy of La Follette; in 1928, it again put forth its own ticket in the national canvass by nominating Norman Thomas of New York. But in 1928, despite the doubling of the electorate through woman suffrage, the Socialists received only 267,400 votes, as compared with 919,800 in 1920 and 897,000 in 1912.

That certain groups of workers should grow impatient with the evolutionary tactics of the Socialist party and the business opportunism of the American Federation of Labor was not surprising. The banner of radicalism, in the first three decades of the twentieth century, was carried by two different organizations: the first was the Industrial Workers of the World (or I.W.W., as it was more generally known), which flourished from 1905 to about 1924; the second was the Communist party, which was organized in 1919 and which, in effect, inherited the revolutionary doctrines of the earlier movement.

Radical trade unionism raised its head in the West in 1905, when the I.W.W. was formed, and for a decade and a half this militant body led no fewer than one hundred and fifty strikes, most of them characterized by a turbulence and hostility more like real warfare than the well-ordered, peaceable tests of strength engaged in by the American Federation of Labor unions. Because it was distrustful of all political activity and advocated the use of the methods of direct action (that is to say, the general strike and sabotage) to attain the workers' commonwealth, the I.W.W. had much in common with European syndicalism. But in reality it was an indigenous movement, growing out of a peculiarly American situation: for it had its roots and flourished in the labor camps of the western country, where the unstable conditions of employment had led to the appearance of a large body of migratory laborers. The western metal mines, harvest fields, and lumber camps were worked by casuals who drifted from job to job with the seasons; they were homeless men, most without families, who labored under particularly arduous conditions; more frequently than not they were unskilled in any craft. It was perfectly understandable that the job philosophy of the American Federation of Labor unions should have no appeal for these men and that they should find more to their liking the doctrines of industrial unionism and the overthrow of capitalism, the two major tenets of the I.W.W. Such were the recruits who filled the ranks of the organization. Its leading spirit was William D. Haywood, at one time an officer of the Western Federation of Miners, although in its earlier years Daniel De Leon and Eugene V. Debs also had been associated with the movement.

In over a little more than a decade, the I.W.W. issued a million membership cards, about one hundred thousand of which were held by Negroes. But at no one time did its membership exceed sixty thousand. In 1912 the I.W.W. came east into the textile districts of Lawrence, Mass., Paterson, N. J., and Little Falls, N. Y., to lead desperately fought strikes in an effort to organize the sweated mill workers. None of these strikes succeeded, but the organization gained numbers of adherents.

In 1917, the state governments began to strike at the I.W.W. through the passage of criminal syndicalist laws. In all, sixteen states, for the most part in the West, inscribed acts on their statute books to outlaw the activities of the I.W.W., and the wobblies (as the members were popularly called) were proceeded against with unusual severity in Arizona, California, Michigan, and Washington. In 1918 the federal government broke the back of the movement when it arrested and tried for conspiracy one hundred and thirteen I.W.W. leaders. Haywood and ninety-two others were found guilty and sentenced to jail for terms of from one to twenty years. Haywood never served his sentence but fled to Soviet Russia, and this, too, contributed to the decline of the organization. By 1924 the I.W.W. had to all intents and purposes vanished from the scene, many of the rank-and-file membership joining the Communist party.

The Communist party, as the American section of the Third (Communist) International, was organized in 1919 at Chicago. Because it was frankly a revolutionary party and openly espoused the tenets of the Russian-inspired Red International, it was proceeded against with vigor by the federal Department of Justice and up to 1924 was compelled to carry on its activities underground. In 1924, the repeal of war-time legislation and the cutting of the Department of Justice's appropriations put an end to the Red hunts of the Attorney-General's office. The Workers' party, which had been organized in 1921 to take the place of the outlawed Communist party and which advanced a more or less traditional left program of political demands, was now superseded by the Workers' (Communist) party of America. In 1928, all surface pretense was discarded and the group again took up its old title of Communist party and candidly avowed that it was the American section of the Third International. While the paid membership of the party was small—estimates, in 1931, putting it at between 7500 and 15,000—it exerted an influence far beyond the strength of its regular adherents.

More important, even, than the fact that it was obtaining a fairly large political support were the following other phases of Communist activity of the twenties and thirties: (1) the persistent propaganda carried on by Communists, through their own press, through so-called "innocent" organizations, which presumably were nonpolitical but which the Communists dominated, and by public mass demonstrations; (2) their dual-union labor program; (3) their work among young people; (4) the general interest being evidenced by Americans in the outcome of the Russian experiment. The fact that American Communism was a branch of international Communism and that its philosophy and tactics stemmed straight from Russia gave it a prominence and importance it could scarcely have claimed had it been only another radical system like syndicalism or anarchism.

The original Communist labor program called for the capture of the A. F. of L. unions by a policy of boring from within. This work was conducted by the Trade Union Educational League. Boring from within—that is to say, the seizure of the conservative unions by Communists and their employment as a revolutionary weapon—initially was attended by small gains. In some cases local and regional unions were won. But the vituperative campaign launched against individuals and the costly and unsuccessful strikes embarked upon led to retaliations: wholesale expulsions took place and many international unions amended their constitutions to forbid their members from being members of the Communist party or its affiliates. In the meantime, trade unions had purged themselves of their extreme leftist groups; the result was, the boring from within tactic ended in failure. In 1929, therefore, the Communists adopted a dual-unionist program based on industrial lines This work was conducted under the Trade Union Unity League, which, in the early nineteen thirties, had affiliated with it some twenty industrial unions, most of them not much more than paper organizations. This new line, like its predecessor, was also a failure. The ineffectualness of the tactic here and abroad and the advent of Hitler to power in Germany—with his threat to the U.S.S.R.—caused still another shift. The U.S.S.R. began to woo the so-called democracies (Great Britain, France, the United States) in order to create a coalition against the so-called fascist states (Germany, Italy, Japan). At the same time, Communist parties were instructed to surrender their intransigence and join forces with progressive, or at any rate non-reactionary, groups for the purpose of setting up so-called People's Front governments in order to check the growth of fascism at home and the advance of fascism on the continents of Europe and Asia.

The American section of the Third International, therefore, during 1935 proceeded quickly to dismantle the Trade Union Unity League and order its members back into the A. F. of L. unions. On the political front, the Communist party in the United States gave up all pretense of agitating for socialism and, beginning with the Presidential election of 1936, proceeded to render President Roosevelt uncritical support. This was largely due to the fact that President Roosevelt, in his foreign policy, seemed to be leaning toward a program of cooperative action among the "democracies" against the aggressor (i. e., "fascist") nations.

The Supreme Court and Property

Between the decisions of Lochner v. New York (1905) and Bunting v. Oregon (1917) the Supreme Court receded from the bold position it had taken in defense of property rights during the eighties and nineties of the preceding century, and adopted a more conciliatory attitude. It gave its approval to a great number of state and federal laws growing out of the enlarged interpretation of the police power and a more liberal reading of the Fourteenth Amendment. Statutes affecting hours of labor, pure food codes, injuries suffered by employees, workmen's compensation, the Adamson Eight-Hour Law, rate-fixing by legislatures and commissions of the services of public utilities corporations—these received the judicial imprimatur. The Supreme Court became more popular than it had been for a generation, and if its attitude toward labor was not too generous (as we have seen above), at any rate the general outcry against the Court's arrogation of power was temporarily stilled. But the peaceful interlude was a brief one and by 1930 the Court was again being fiercely attacked on the score that it was employing its prerogative of judicial review to exalt property rights at the expense of human rights. A review of the outstanding decisions of the Supreme Court, from 1917 through the twenties, shows plainly the heightening of its conservative temper.

In Hitchman Coal Co. v. Mitchell, 1917 (245 U.S. 229), the Court held that the existence of a yellow-dog contract could be used to prevent the unionization of coal miners.

In Hammer v. Dagenhart, 1917 (247 U.S. 251), the Court found the federal Child Labor Law unconstitutional.

In Eisner v. Macomber, 1920 (252 U.S. 189), the Court found that stock dividends were not income and therefore denied the right of the government to tax them.

In Federal Trade Commission v. Gratz, 1920 (253 U.S. 421), the Court found a "cease and desist order" of the commission illegal because there "existed no unfair method of competition" despite the proved unfairness per se of the methods being employed.

In Duplex Printing Press Co. v. Deering, 1921 (254 U.S. 443), the Court denied that the Clayton Act prevented the issuance of injunctions in labor disputes.

In Truax v. Corrigan, 1921 (257 U.S. 312), the Court declared unconstitutional an Arizona law prohibiting the issuance of injunctions in labor disputes.

In Adkins v. Children's Hospital, 1923 (261 U.S. 525), the Court declared the District of Columbia's minimum wage law for women unconstitutional.

In Burns Baking Co. v. Bryan, 1924 (264 U.S. 504), the Court declared a bread standard-weight law, for the purpose of protecting buyers from short weights, unconstitutional.

In Gitlow v. People, 1924 (268 U.S. 652), the Court upheld New York's criminal anarchy law, making possible the prosecution of Communists.

In Schlesinger v. Wisconsin, 1925 (270 U.S. 230), the Court declared unconstitutional a Wisconsin law which sought to check possible evasion of its inheritance-tax statute. (This law construed all gifts made six years prior to death as evasion.)

In Weaver v. Palmer Bros. Co., 1925 (270 U.S. 402), the Court declared unconstitutional a Pennsylvania law aimed against the use of shoddy in comfortables.

In Whitney v. California, 1927 (274 U.S. 357), the Court upheld California's criminal syndicalist law.

Rulings such as these choked off the right to political dissent; refused to allow labor relief against the injunctive process; and again, by invoking the Fourteenth Amendment, interfered with the states in their use of the police power to protect life, health, and morals. In another body of decisions, in which the Court passed on the rate-making functions of state public service commissions and the Interstate Commerce Commission, the Court sided with property, when it answered the questions, "What shall be a reasonable rate?" "What shall constitute the rate base for public utilities?" definitely in property's favor. Agitation for the regulation of the railroads, begun in the eighteen seventies, had met with a partial success in 1887 with the passage of the Interstate Commerce Commission Act. But it was not until 1920 that the abuses against which shippers had protested had finally been brought under control. In fact, thanks to the work of the elder Senator La Follette, from 1906 on, liberals in Congress had kept their eyes steadily on the single, ultimate goal: the vesting in the Interstate Commerce Commission of the power to fix rates on the basis of a physical valuation of the carriers. A part of that victory had been achieved in 1913 with the passage of the Physical Valuation Act, the final part through the passage of the Transportation Act in 1920. Beginning with 1923, however, the Supreme Court proceeded to nullify, to a large extent, the effects of this legislation when it ordered public utility commissions and the Interstate Commerce Commission to give consideration, when fixing the rate base, not merely to original cost or prudent investment but also to the reproduction cost new of the properties.[5] By taking this stand, the Supreme Court rendered the whole procedure of government regulation, so painfully built up after an agitation of almost half a century, almost futile. The following were the decisions by which this was accomplished.

[5] Justice Brandeis in his dissent in the O'Fallon decision in 1929 defined prudent investment as "the reasonable and necessary investment in the property."

In Southwestern Bell Telephone Co. v. Public Service Commission of Missouri, 1923 (262 U.S. 276), the Court held (with Brandeis and Holmes dissenting) that a rate base for a reasonable rate must take consideration of reproduction cost new and that a return of 5⅓ per cent was confiscatory. The decision was based on the rule promulgated in the Smyth v. Ames case of 1898. Justice Brandeis' dissent attacked the rule in these words: "The so-called rule of Smyth v. Ames is, in my opinion, legally and economically unsound. . . . The Constitution does not guarantee to the utility the opportunity to earn a return on the value of all items of property used by the utility or any of them. . . . The compensation which the Constitution guarantees an opportunity to earn is the reasonable cost of conducting the business. Cost includes not only operating expenses, but also capital charges. Capital charges cover allowance, by way of interest, for the use of the capital, whatever the nature of the security issued therefor, the allowance for risk incurred, and enough more to attract capital."

In St. Louis and O'Fallon Railway Co. v. United States, 1929 (279 U.S. 461), the Court held (with Brandeis, Holmes and Stone dissenting) that the Interstate Commerce Commission, in fixing the valuation of the railroads for the purposes of recapture as prescribed in the Transportation Act of 1920, was to give consideration to the factor of reproduction cost new. The Commission itself, in fixing the value of the O'Fallon Railway, had divided, and the majority had refused to give this factor of reproduction cost new full value. But the Supreme Court sided with the opinion of the Commission's minority. Said the Court's opinion: "The question on which the Commission divided was this: When seeking to ascertain the value of railroad property for recapture purposes, must it give consideration to current or reproduction costs? The weight to be accorded thereto is not the matter before us. . . . But Congress has directed that values shall be fixed upon a consideration of present costs along with all other pertinent facts; and this mandate must be obeyed."

In United Railways v. West, 1930 (280 U.S. 234), the Court held (with Brandeis, Holmes, and Stone dissenting) that the plaintiff, a Baltimore street railway company, was right in its contention that a return of 6.26 per cent was inadequate and that anything less than 7.44 per cent would be confiscatory. The Court extended the Smyth v. Ames rule by permitting the company to subtract from its net income a depreciation charge on the basis of reproduction cost new. The inclusion of the value of the company's franchise, for the calculation of the rate base, was also allowed.

The bitter fight which was launched by Senators during February 10–13, 1930, against the appointment of Charles E. Hughes, to succeed the late W. H. Taft as Chief Justice of the Court, was not a personal one, entirely. The opposition pointed to Hughes's long record, before the Supreme Court itself, in the rôle of advocate for some of the country's most powerful corporations and insisted that in his decisions he could not but be influenced by his close association with great wealth. For this reason the appointment was attacked by both insurgent Republicans and Democrats and in the final balloting on Hughes's confirmation eleven Republicans voted against the man who had been their party's standard bearer in the election of 1916. Senator Borah's speech against Hughes plainly showed that since 1896, when Bryan had first raised the flag of revolt, there had been little progress in the Court's recognition that Americans were confronted by a new world. Said Borah, in one passage:

> Bear in mind that at the present time coal and iron, oil and gas and power, light, transportation and transmission have all practically gone into the hands of a very few people. The great problem is, How shall the people of the United States be permitted to enjoy these national resources and these means of transportation, free from extortion and oppression? I can conceive of no more vital question than this, which has long divided our Supreme Court. It has divided the Court not because one group of justices is less or more conscientious in their views but because of a wide difference in viewpoint. I am deeply imbued with the wisdom and justice of the viewpoint of the minority. I do not want to strengthen the viewpoint of the majority.

Mergers and Anti-Trust Legislation

The movement toward consolidation, which reached such a heightened tempo in the years immediately following the close of the nineteenth century, slowed down for a little more than a decade. Roosevelt's public campaign against the trusts and the energy with which the Department of Justice under Taft and Wilson pushed prosecutions against large combinations, contributed much to check the attempted formation of monopolies. Just as important was the appearance of new fields of enterprise to welcome capital legitimately: the automobile, electrical goods, telephone, electric power and light industries.

But in the postwar period, the trend toward consolidation again evidenced itself and the vigor of the movement was perhaps even greater than the earlier one. These new combinations were frequently effected to obtain additional capital; to permit of the exploitation of the national market, instead of merely sectional or local ones; to bring about important economies, through the use of common sales agencies or capital equipment or management. Another important motive was to be found in the fact that their creation provided opportunities for promotional profits for investment bankers on the one hand and avenues into which could flow capital savings not otherwise employed in legitimate productive enterprise on the other. This was particularly true of holding companies.

It was evident, at the end of the twenties, that such supercorporations were playing a part of the first importance in the American industrial life. The following tabulation, prepared by J. T. Flynn, indicates the financial strength of the merged groups in a selected number of industries.[6]

AMERICAN MERGERS, AS OF DECEMBER 31, 1929

Industries	*No. of mergers*	*No. of controlled companies*	*Market value of securities of the mergers*
Copper	12	67	$ 1,450,000,000
Chemicals	17	189	1,902,177,000
Agricultural implements	10	87	641,899,000
Iron and steel	25	217	2,114,115,000
Automobiles	23	187	2,630,359,000
Tires, rubber	13	115	945,062,000
Electrical equipment	11	71	2,319,000,000
Railroad equipment	17	131	845,139,000
Telephone and telegraph	3	627	4,433,643,000
Moving pictures	6	74	393,296,000
Automobile equipment	33	160	658,784,000
Food products:			
Baking flour	9	95	637,090,000
Candy, soft drinks	9	43	392,595,000
Dairy products	6	236	530,118,000
Foods	15	119	1,471,142,000
Meat-packing	8	203	291,049,000
Totals	217	2,621	$21,655,468,000

[6] From the *New Republic*, July 2, 1930, by permission of the *New Republic* and J. T. Flynn.

Many of these consolidations, or mergers, had the characteristic intention of the earlier trusts, that is to say, the achievement of monopoly control over prices, production, and the flow of new capital into plant expansion. During the twenties, business also turned to another agency to effect the same end, and through the so-called trade associations, which began to flourish in the second decade of the century, members of the same industry were openly exchanging price, production, and credit information. Originally inclined to view such activities with suspicion, the Supreme Court on June 1, 1925, in two decisions, gave the trade associations what was tantamount to a clean bill of health.[7] The Court held, in effect, that the members of such organizations were not actually agreeing to fix prices or curtail production; therefore, it was incumbent upon the Department of Justice to prove that arising out of the open circulation of trade data there resulted an unlawful restraint of competition.

Not only did the Supreme Court relax its severity, as far as monopolies and corporate practices were concerned, but the Department of Justice and the Federal Trade Commission also became more friendly toward the methods of Big Business. This was particularly true in the postwar period. It is not to be understood that the number of prosecutions under the anti-trust laws showed a falling off. The fact is, the records of the Harding, Coolidge, and Hoover administrations were every whit as impressive as those of Roosevelt, Taft, and Wilson. The difference between the prewar and postwar decades was one of attitude, largely: in the decade of the twenties, the Department of Justice refused to be alarmed by the growing size of corporations, expressed itself as being perfectly willing to offer opinions on the legalities of projected mergers, and

[7] Maple Flooring Manufacturers' Assn. v. United States, 268 U.S. 563. Cement Manufacturers' Protective Assn. v. United States, 268 U.S. 588.

By 1927, according to the Department of Commerce, there existed some one thousand of these trade associations, many of which were engaged in all of the following activities: collection of statistics, cost accounting practice, industrial research, commercial research, simplified practice or standardization of products, publicity, trade relations, exchange of credit information, insurance, employer-employee relationships, traffic problems. It should be noted that Mr. Hoover, as Secretary of Commerce, not only gave the trade-association movement his blessing but frequently took the lead in promoting such organizations. In this institutional development the New Deal's NRA (except for its labor provisions) was clearly foreshadowed. See below, page 217.

exerted itself almost entirely in proceeding against what it deemed unlawful trade practices.

The same was true of the Federal Trade Commission. It will be recalled that the Clayton Act had placed the following specific practices under the ban: price discrimination (Section 2), exclusive contracts (Section 3), stock acquisitions by corporations (Section 7), interlocking directorates (Section 8). The Commission was soon to show that it had little faith in its ability to check such activities and during the twenties its "cease and desist orders," under Sections 2, 3, 7, grew fewer and fewer. In fact, during its whole history it did not issue a single order under Section 8. More and more the commission devoted its energies to the enforcement of Section 5 of the Federal Trade Commission Act—that dealing with unfair methods of competition—but even here, certainly after 1925, it voluntarily imposed serious limitations on its own powers. In 1925 and 1926, over the protests of a minority group (the members of which, when their terms expired, were not reappointed), the Commission indicated that it was more cordially disposed toward business: by defining closely the types of complaints it would consider; by encouraging settlements and thus checking the filing of formal complaints; by placing limitations on the publicity heretofore given "to cease and desist orders." How narrowly the Commission was interpreting its duties may be seen from the fact that in the late twenties and early thirties, three-fourths of its "cease and desist" orders were directed against only these five unfair methods of competition: misbranding, false and misleading advertising, misrepresentation, passing off, resale price maintenance.

With practices of the following nature, whose evils certainly outweighed any of those already mentioned, there was no disposition on the part of governmental agencies to interfere: (1) the issuance of non-voting or non-par stock by corporations, with the result that companies were controlled not by their stockholders but by inner cliques; (2) the inadequate and often unintelligible reporting methods used by corporations; (3) the development of the holding company device, particularly in the fields of the electric power and light industry, railroading, and banking. By means of the holding company, insiders were able to gain control over huge properties although they themselves possessed but small minority interests; and state commissions regulating public utilities were frustrated, inasmuch as courts held that holding companies were not utilities and therefore were not liable to control. The holding company, too, because of its great complexity, lent itself easily to manipulation, stock-watering, speculation by syndicates, and the like.

Thus, after forty years of experience, the relations between government and business, particularly Big Business, were as ill-defined as in the beginning. Monopoly controls, notably as they affected prices, struck at the very heart of the capitalist system which could function only in the climate of a free market. The reformism of the Square Deal of Theodore Roosevelt and the New Freedom of Woodrow Wilson had been without avail in finding solutions to this vexing problem; the reformism of the New Deal of Franklin D. Roosevelt, as we shall see, was to be no more successful.

V. FOUR OUTSTANDING PROBLEMS OF THE TWENTIES AND THIRTIES

Prohibition

The end of the second decade of the twentieth century saw the victorious culmination of an agitation which had had its beginnings in the early days of the Republic: with the proclamation of the Eighteenth Amendment on January 29, 1919, the movements against the saloon and intemperance were crowned with success. By the end of 1914, state-wide prohibition existed in but eleven states. If local option areas were added, still there were less than half of the American people living in regions where the open sale of intoxicating liquors was prohibited. However, the demands for the curbing of the liquor traffic took on new impetus in the next five years. More states joined the roll of dry commonwealths; America's entry into the war gave plausible justification for federal restriction on the use of grains in the making of beers and hard liquors; the appearance of the automobile and further mechanization in industry pointed up the claims of dry advocates that inebriated persons were a menace to others on public highways and in factories; the ever-growing pressure being applied on politicians by temperance societies was a force that could not be denied. By the end of 1918, the eleven dry states of four years earlier had been joined by eighteen others and two-thirds of the American people were living in Prohibition areas.

With the capture of Congress by the dry forces as the second decade opened, federal action, it appeared, could not be long delayed. In 1913 both houses repassed over President Taft's veto the Webb-Kenyon Interstate Liquor Shipment Act, which forbade the transportation of liquor from wet states into dry; in January, 1917, the Supreme Court upheld the constitutionality of the law; late in the same year Congress adopted a resolution submitting to the states, for their ratification, a Constitutional amendment aimed at the establishment of national Prohibition under the aegis of the federal government. The first section of the proposed amendment was drastic in its provisions. It read:

After one year from the ratification of this article the manufacture, sale, or transportation of intoxicating liquors within, the importation thereof into, or the exportation thereof from the United States and all territories subject to the jurisdiction thereof for beverage purposes is hereby prohibited.

In little more than a year, the legislatures of three-fourths of the states had adopted the amendment, with the result that its proclamation followed on January 29, 1919. On January 16, 1920, Prohibition went into effect without any compensation for the owners of distilleries, breweries, saloons, and factories making bar fixtures, in short, all those persons who had had a proprietary interest in the manufacture, sale, and transportation of beers, light wines, and hard liquors. The National Prohibition Act (known generally as the Volstead Act after its sponsor), enacted by Congress over President Wilson's veto on October 28, 1919, was as rigorous as the Eighteenth Amendment itself: it defined as an intoxicating liquor all beverages containing more than one-half of one per cent alcohol; placed under severe regulations the manufacture and sale of alcohol for industrial, medicinal, and sacramental purposes; provided for the denaturing of alcohol to prevent its conversion into beverages; and ringed around, with formidable licensing restrictions, every conceivable phase of the remaining legitimate liquor industry. By amendment, in 1921 and 1929, the National Prohibition Act was further strengthened to circumscribe the activities of physicians, druggists, and shippers of alcohol and to make harsher the penalties for the criminal infringement of the law.

To create an adequate enforcement machinery was more difficult. The first Prohibition unit was organized as part of the Bureau of Internal Revenue of the Treasury Department; detection of offenders and control over licensed manufacturers and venders of alcohol were in its hands. But prosecutions were the affair of the Department of Justice, while cooperation in carrying on the work of enforcement had to be sought from a large number of other governmental agencies. To make confusion worse confounded, the Prohibition unit quickly became a football of politics with the result that its heads, its agents, and even its policies were at the mercy of every idle political breeze that swept over Washington. Not until 1927 was appointment to the Prohibition Bureau placed on a merit basis; not until 1930 was some plan introduced into enforcement with the transfer of the Prohibition activities proper from the Treasury Department to the Department of Justice. However, control over industrial alcohol was still vested in the Treasury Department.

Prohibition, under the Eighteenth Amendment, had been designed to eradicate two evils, the saloon and intemperance. The saloon, with its open drinking and its encouragement to idleness and even the more criminal forms of vice, had been eliminated. But with its going there sprang up in its place a group of more vicious institutions—the speakeasies, beer flats, and blind pigs—which, being illegal, could flourish only because they were founded on an open contempt for the law by their proprietors and patrons and because they had the protection of a corrupt local officialdom. As for universal temperance, not only was that ideal never attained but it appeared, a decade after Prohibition had gone into effect, that America was drinking almost as much as it had been before 1914.

In addition, by the end of the twenties, the hostility to the Eighteenth Amendment was no longer covert. Interestingly enough, in the acrimonious debate which ensued, the opponents of Prohibition were able to take a high moral ground: Prohibition, they said, was bringing about an open contempt for all law; it was the chief reason for the flourishing of crime; it was debauching police, prosecuting authorities, and the courts; it was depriving government of important sources of revenue and filling the pockets of an undesirable element in the community. Also, the anti-Prohibition forces were increasingly making themselves heard in the national political arena. The Democratic national convention of 1924 was the scene of a struggle between the drys led by McAdoo and the modificationists led by Smith. In 1928, Smith, as the Democratic standard bearer, openly appealed for city support by favoring a return to state home rule. In the Congressional elections of 1930, many seats were contested solely on the wet–dry issue, and the Seventy-second Congress saw the dry forces in it considerably weakened.

It was the opinion of President Hoover's Law Enforcement Commission, in its report of January, 1931, that enforcement of Prohibition had broken down.[1] The commission, after having examined the question for eighteen months, declared that it was op-

[1] This commission was generally known as the Wickersham Commission, after its chairman, George W. Wickersham, Attorney-General in President Taft's Cabinet.

posed to the repeal of the Eighteenth Amendment, to the restoration of the legalized saloon, to the federal and state governments going into the liquor business, and to the modification of the Volstead Act in order to permit the manufacture and sale of light wines and beer. However, state aid was necessary to insure enforcement; the public was not obeying the law; the present organization for enforcement was inadequate; if, after further trial, enforcement was still impossible, the Eighteenth Amendment ought to be revised to give Congress the power to "regulate or prohibit" the manufacture, sale, and transportation of intoxicating beverages. Americans were quick to note that of the eleven commissioners only four, in appended statements, suggested further trial for the Eighteenth Amendment. Five of the others advocated modification and two favored outright repeal.

What was standing in the way of enforcement? These three factors, reported the commissioners. 1. A great margin existed between the cost of producing or importing illicit liquor and the price such liquor commanded when sold. In other words, the liquor traffic was a highly remunerative industry, and because it represented such a great economic stake it was inevitable that it should encourage bootlegging, highjacking, gang wars, and official corruption. 2. The public, in many localities, was either hostile or, at best, completely indifferent to enforcement. In the case of the enforcement of the narcotic laws, for example, public opinion was favorably disposed, with the result that the traffic in drugs had been driven underground. On the other hand, the drink traffic flourished openly because the American people refused to regard it as a criminal enterprise. 3. The general feeling prevailed that enforcement of the Eighteenth Amendment was the task of the federal government exclusively, and many states gave only lip service to the need for enforcement.

The chief factor in the development of illicit distilling was the appearance of new and cheap materials that could be employed, notably corn sugar, but also cane and beet sugar, molasses, corn meal, and other grains. Further, it was the expert guess of the Prohibition Bureau's director that for the fiscal year ending June 30, 1930, the illicit production of wine and malt liquors had been 118,-320,000 and 683,032,000 gallons respectively. This was not much less than 40 per cent of the actual legitimate withdrawals in 1914

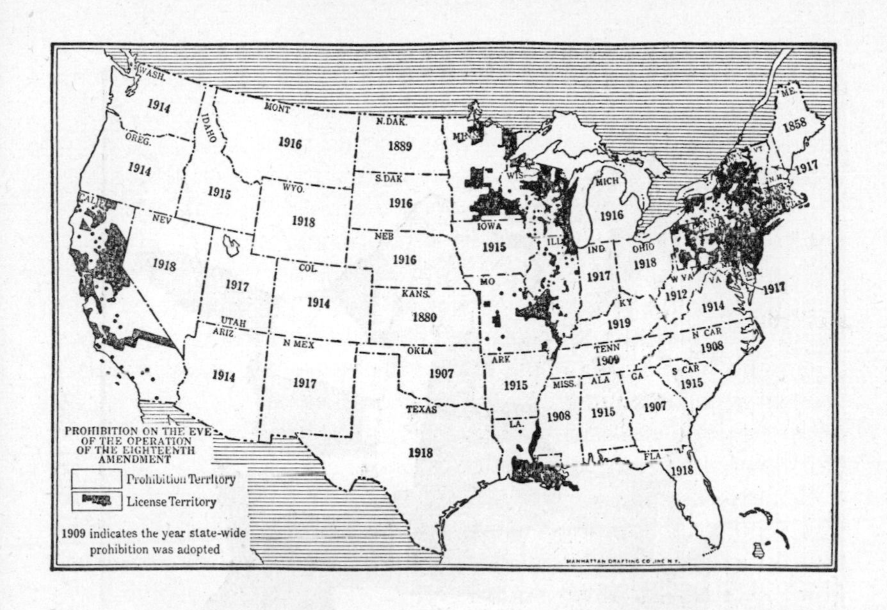

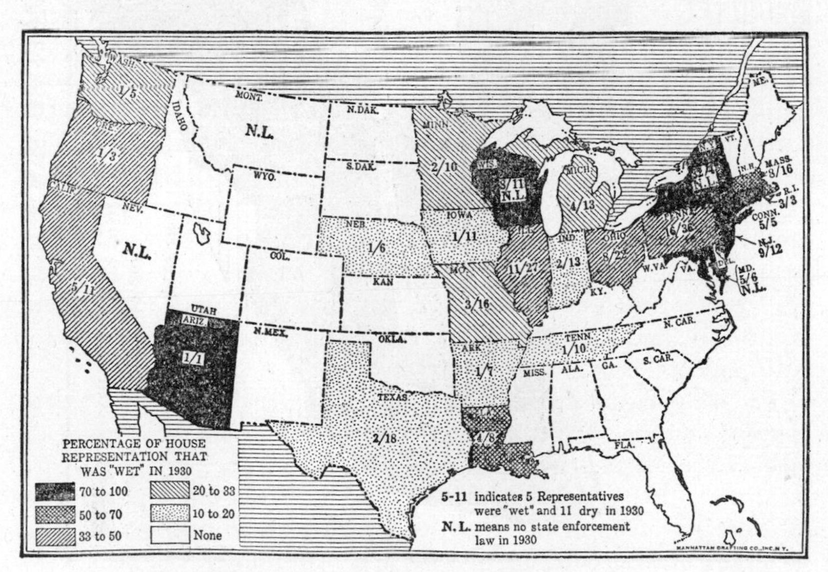

ACTION AND REACTION ON PROHIBITION, 1920–1930

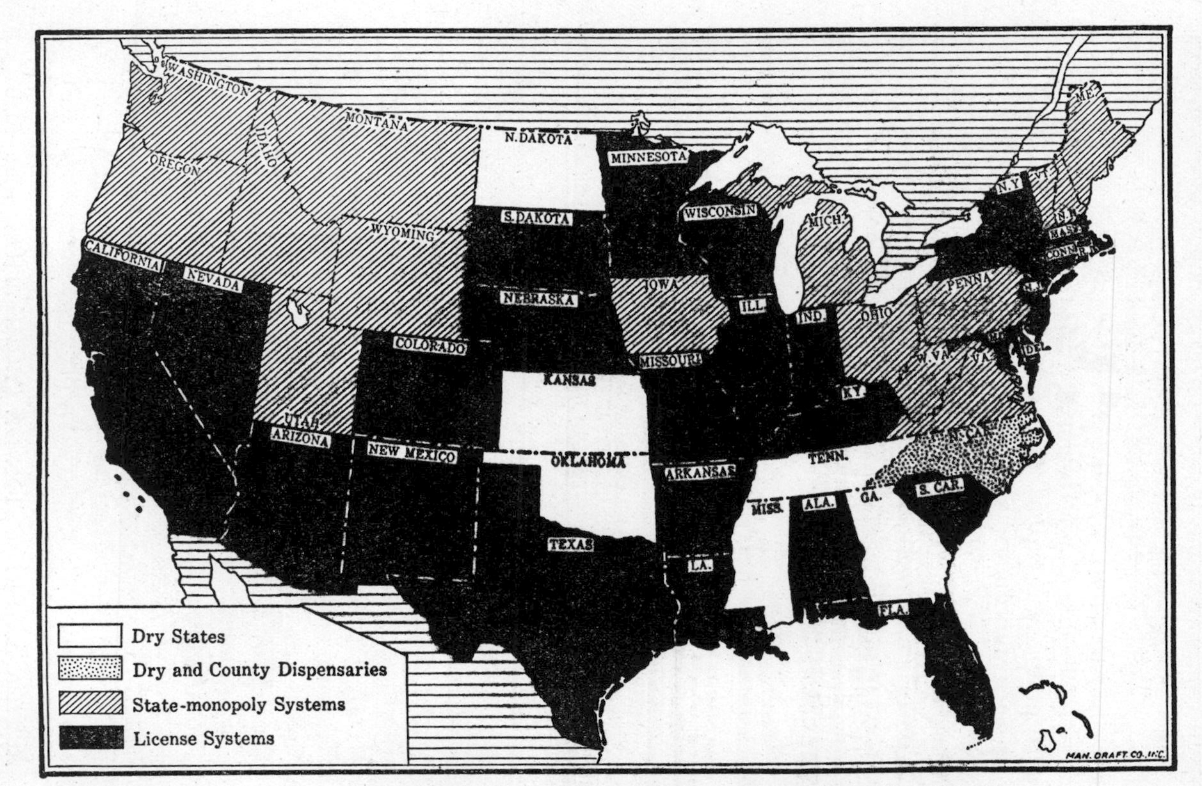

SYSTEMS OF LIQUOR CONTROL, 1938

and still took no account of other forms of liquor diversion. This, too, in the face of a heightened enforcement effort.[2]

The country's first decade of experimentation with Prohibition thus ended uncertainly. And the end of the twenties had seen opposition to Prohibition definitely emerge into the open. The effect on national politics was curious. National politicians watched the contest between wets and drys uneasily. Would they be compelled to take sides on a question that had so many elements of danger in it—for them? Would the Democratic party, to hold its urban following, have to become wet—and risk the loss of support in the agrarian South and West? Would the Republican party, to hold its farmer constituencies, have to remain dry—and lose the support of the middle classes in the great cities? The directors of both parties, as the Presidential year 1932 approached, spent many anxious moments scanning the heavens for a sign. While politicians pondered the question, it became increasingly evident that Americans were wearying of the debate. For citizens were beginning to understand, as the full effects of the depression of 1930 and after made themselves felt, that the Prohibition question was not really very important; indeed, it was serving only to distract attention from more serious concerns. The Prohibition discussion, in short, seemed to be very much like a red herring drawn across the trail of every vital public question with which Americans of the twenties should have been concerning themselves.

The Democrats finally took the plunge; and in their 1932 party platform they called for the legalization of beer, the repeal of the Eighteenth Amendment, the prevention of the saloon's revival, and the return of control to the states. Mr. Roosevelt's election was regarded as a mandate, with the result that steps were at once taken by Congress to repeal the unpopular amendment; also, in March, 1933, the manufacture and sale of 3.2 per cent beer was legalized. The joint resolution for repeal passed through both houses of Congress in February, 1933; by December of the same year 36 states had ratified the new (Twenty-first) Amendment and it was therefore proclaimed by the Secretary of State. The amendment, in addition to repealing the Eighteenth, promised such states as wished

[2] The commission enumerated and described five other sources from which the nation got its illegal drink, as follows: (1) importation, from Canada, the Caribbean, and Europe; (2) the diversion of industrial alcohol; (3) illegal brewing of beer; (4) diversion of medicinal and sacramental liquors and wines; (5) home brewing.

to continue dry federal protection against the transportation and importation of intoxicating liquors into their areas.

The sale of liquor became immediately legal in 19 states; in the remaining, constitutional or statutory provisions prevented the dispensing of alcoholic beverages. But within the next two years, such provisions were repealed in all the states but Alabama, Georgia, Kansas, Mississippi, North Dakota, Oklahoma, and Tennessee; and Alabama joined the column of wet states in 1937. It is to be noted that even the six remaining were not bone-dry, for the sale of beer was permitted. The states moved so swiftly because of the insistent pressure of public opinion, on the one hand, and because new revenue sources had to be opened up in order to make possible the local carrying of the heavy relief burden resulting from the depression. The states this time, however, did not forget that the sale of liquor had to be ringed about by all sorts of regulations in order to prevent the recurrence of a dry agitation. The results were the following: in 15 states, state-monopoly systems were set up under which the sale of liquor was made a public business managed by liquor-control commissions; in 26 states, central licensing bodies were provided for and invested with the responsibility of regulating the private liquor trade; and in all the jurisdictions where liquor could be sold new means were devised for taking the curse off the business. Chief among these were: (1) The separation of the package sale of liquor from the sale for on-premise consumption; (2) arrangements for the sale of non-intoxicating beer on a different basis from that applying to the sale of wines and spirits; (3) the limiting of the on-premise sale of spirits and heavier wines to bona fide restaurants and hotels; (4) the requirement that licensed places for on-premise consumption be open to full public view.

The federal government also assumed its share of the burden by establishing the Federal Alcohol Administration to which was assigned the function—and one, incidentally, which it performed with a high degree of success—of creating proper business standards for the liquor (but not beer) industry and promoting fair trade practices in the interests of producers and consumers.

The results of repeal five years after were still hard to chart. Public opinion as to the return of the saloon was mixed, although it was generally conceded that the free sale of package liquor for home consumption was meeting with little disapproval. Also, the high expectations of public authority regarding the revenues to be realized from legalization and licensing were doomed to disappointment, for the returns were surprisingly small. Indeed, many jurisdictions were discovering that they were in danger of killing the goose that laid the golden egg (slight as it was), for as taxes on liquor and licenses were increased, bootlegging and speakeasies and blind pigs began to make their return.

Immigration Restriction

The movement, inaugurated in the eighteen nineties, for the barring of undesirable immigrants and for the restriction of immigration on a selective basis continued with unflagging zeal into the new century. Almost continuously, Congress was called upon by labor representatives, eugenists, charity workers, and sociologists to enact legislation for the control of the immigration stream. Certainly, to those who believed that America's future development depended entirely upon the creation of a homogeneous population, the situation was a bewildering one. In the first decade of the twentieth century, 8,795,000 newcomers were admitted at American immigration stations; during the next five years (1911–1915), the new arrivals numbered 4,460,000; even during the war period (1916–1920), the number of immigrants was 1,276,000. A radical immigration-restriction policy was inaugurated, finally, in 1921, but even this did not bring about complete stoppage. So, during 1921–1925, 2,639,000 new arrivals were admitted; during 1926–1930, the total was 1,468,000. It remained for the Department of Labor, during the thirties, with the support of the State Department and without necessity of Congressional sanction, to discover how the bars could be raised so high that to all intents and purposes immigration was checked altogether. Indeed, for a number of years during the thirties, the country's net emigration exceeded its net immigration. We must review, in some detail, the history of immigration legislation over the thirty-odd years since 1901.

As a result of the work of the Industrial Commission of 1898, and of the increased public agitation, the country's immigration code was completely overhauled in 1903 and again in 1907. The Bureau of Immigration was transferred from the Treasury Department to the newly created Department of Commerce and Labor (1903); to the already long list of undesirable foreign born were added epileptics, persons who had once been insane, professional beggars, anarchists, and procurers; the head tax was raised from fifty cents to two dollars and then once again to four dollars; the steamship companies were compelled to assume responsibility for the return carriage of foreign born in the excluded classes (thus forcing them to conduct examinations of immigrants at the ports of embarkation). Finally, to blaze the trail along which further selective policies were to be developed, the law of 1907 called for the establishment of a Congressional investigating committee to scrutinize closely the whole immigration problem. This Immigration Commission conducted the most elaborate inquiry yet carried on by an American governmental agency and in 1911 published its report and conclusions in some forty-odd volumes.

In discussing principles for further immigration legislation, the commission set up these chief signposts: Care was to be taken that "immigration be such both in quality and quantity as not to make too difficult the process of assimilation." A slower expansion of American industry, "which would permit the adaptation and assimilation of the incoming labor supply, is preferable to a very rapid industrial expansion which results in the immigration of laborers of low standards and efficiency, who imperil the American standard of wages and conditions of employment." To bring about these ends, there were recommended: the more effective barring of the excluded classes; a better administrative machinery; efforts to guard the immigrant against exploitation; measures to discourage immigrant remittances abroad; a governmental plan for the better geographic distribution of new arrivals; the encouragement of permanent residence and naturalization; the restriction of unskilled labor. As for the favored device of the advocates of selection, that is to say, the literacy test for foreign born, a majority of the commission recommended its adoption.

Once again, therefore, the friends of a literacy test sought the passage of such an act. Cleveland had vetoed the first such measure in 1897; in the next decade a number of similar bills was again passed by either house of Congress; in 1913, the Smith-Burnett bill, embodying the Immigration Commission's recommendations, also called for the use of this standard as the basis for immigration selection. President Taft vetoed the bill in 1913; President Wilson vetoed another such bill in 1915, and still another in 1917. But this was the last stand of the Executive against the Legislative will. In

May, 1917, southern representatives joined hands with the restrictionists from New England and the West and passed the immigration bill over the Presidential veto. The 1917 Immigration Act made far-sweeping concessions to the demand for a program of selective immigration. Its literacy-test provision required that all immigrants be able to read thirty or forty words in some language. It added to the list of debarred foreign born all persons who possessed "constitutional psychopathic inferiorities," who suffered from chronic alcoholism, and who were vagrants or stowaways or likely to become public charges. It excluded all Asiatics. It tightened the Department of Labor's control over the resident foreign born by increasing the deportation period from three to five years and by making foreign born convicted of felonies liable to return to their native lands. It raised the head tax from four dollars to eight dollars.

Yet the 1917 law failed in its purpose, and by the fiscal year ending June 30, 1921, 805,228 new immigrants had entered America. Of these, 63.8 per cent came from the countries of Southern and Eastern Europe and, despite the rigorous supervision of the immigration service and the many groups of excludable persons, only some 14,000 prospective immigrants could be turned back. And only 10 per cent of this small number were denied admission because of failure to pass the literacy test. The demand for drastic restriction, on a selective basis, now became the foremost public question of the day. The old arguments of the eighties and nineties were refurbished; new ones were advanced; and economic need (because of the world-wide depression of 1921) strengthened the hands of organized labor and the patriotic societies. The result was, the writing of the immigration legislation of the twenties on the basis of the selective principle. The device employed was the so-called quota system and to its perfection the Congresses of the early twenties devoted a large part of their attention.

The first immigrant quota bill was passed by the Sixty-sixth Congress in the closing days of its last session, but President Wilson's pocket veto compelled the incoming Harding administration to take up the problem anew. The result was, the passage of the Emergency Quota Act of 1921. The life of the act was to be but one year. It provided that a system of quotas was to be set up, for newly admitted foreign born, under which the total of any particular nationality to be granted admission was not to exceed 3 per cent of the number of persons of that same nationality living in the United States in 1910. The basis of the system was to be land of birth, not the land of last residence, and it was to apply to all countries except those in the Western Hemisphere. Certain efforts were made to soften the sweeping character of this restrictive measure. So, foreign born who were resident for one year in a country of the Western Hemisphere were exempted from the quota provision. Similar exemption was granted the minor children of American citizens. And the following groups were given preferred quota status: the wives, parents, brothers, sisters, minor children of declarants and World War veterans. In May, 1922, the Emergency Quota Law was reenacted for two years more with but one important change: the quota exemption for foreign born living in countries of the Western Hemisphere was made conditional on a five years' residence period.

From the point of view of the selectionists, however, the results of the law were not entirely satisfactory. While the gross number of immigrants was cut sharply in the first year, it had begun to mount again by 1923–1924. Again, the new law, while it did succeed in checking considerably the flow from Southern and Eastern Europe, did not encourage markedly immigrants from Northern and Western Europe. In particular, there was a large incease in the number of immigrants from Canada and Mexico, who in considerable measure were made up of European foreign born residents who were taking advantage of the relaxed quota restrictions.

The debates attending the writing of the new Immigration Quota Law in 1924 sought to clarify these and similarly complex problems. As completed by Congress and signed by President Coolidge, the new law accepted the principle of selection on the basis of racial stock. The quota base, from July 1, 1924 to June 30, 1927, was to be 2 per cent of the foreign born of each nationality resident in the country at the time of the 1890 census. After July 1, 1927, the quota base was to be "that proportion of 150,000 which the number of persons of a given national origin residing in the United States in 1920 bears to the country's total population in 1920."

The quota system was to apply to all countries, with the exception of Canada, Mexico, and the independent nations of Central and South America.

The minimum quota from any one country was to be 100. There

were to be entirely excluded all foreign born who were ineligible to citizenship or who were inadmissible under the Immigration Law. (This provision was aimed at the Chinese and Japanese.)

Quota preferences, up to 50 per cent of the total from any one country, were to be granted to the unmarried children (18–21 years) and to the parents and husbands of American citizens; also to skilled agriculturists, their wives, and minor children (under 16 years).

The non-quota classes were to include: the unmarried children (under 18 years) and the wives of resident American citizens; persons born in the Western Hemisphere; ministers, professors, and bona fide students under 18 years; resident aliens returning from visits abroad.

The immigration flow was to be controlled at the ports of embarkation. American consuls, by means of visas, were to certify those immigrants whom the steamship companies might transport; also, American health officers were to attest to the physical and mental fitness of quota immigrants before passage could be booked.

The 2 per cent and 1890 quota base was continued until June 30, 1929, because the so-called national origins base was so difficult to determine. The intention was that this device should preserve the present character of the American population on the basis of ratios already existing. But the committee—the Secretaries of State, Commerce, and Labor—charged with preparing this scientific analysis of the composition of the country's population on a number of occasions frankly confessed its inability to do so; and Mr. Hoover, both as Secretary of Commerce and as President, appealed to Congress to be released from what had turned out to be an impossible mandate. Congress was adamant, however, and after the calculations had been revised a number of times, they were proclaimed by the President, reluctantly, on March 22, 1929. The new system limited the number of quota immigrants to 150,000 annually; it was particularly partial to prospective immigrants from Great Britain and Northern Ireland, did not seriously affect the comparative status of arrivals from Southern and Eastern Europe, but did lower sharply the quotas for Germany, Irish Free State, and Scandinavia.

By the end of the twenties, therefore, selective immigration had become a definite reality and the new accretions to our population were coming from those lands whose racial stocks had been prominent in settling America. The following table shows the change that took place in the character of our immigration over the thirty years 1901–1930.

IMMIGRATION BY COUNTRIES OF ORIGIN
(Figures in per cents)

Period or year	*From N. & W. Europe*	*From S. & E. Europe*	*From Asia*	*From Canada & Newfoundland*	*From Mexico*	*From West Indies*	*From other countries*
1901–1910	21.7	70.8	2.8	2.0	.6	1.2	.9
1911–1915	17.7	67.4	2.8	8.0	1.8	1.4	.9
1916–1920	16.3	29.3	5.4	30.3	10.7	4.6	3.4
1921–1925	26.6	37.4	3.0	20.5	8.9	2.1	1.5
1926	41.5	9.6	1.1	30.7	14.2	1.1	1.8
1927	37.8	12.4	1.1	25.3	20.2	1.2	2.0
1928	37.9	13.7	1.1	24.5	19.2	1.3	2.3
1929	40.9	15.8	1.3	23.8	14.4	1.5	2.3
1930	40.2	20.8	1.9	27.0	5.2	2.2	2.7

During the thirties, it became plain that Washington, under the wide latitude allowed it by the immigration laws, might put an end to immigration entirely. Exercising the legal right to exclude all prospective immigrants likely to become public charges the State Department proceeded to deny visas to large numbers of applicants; while the Department of Labor deported foreign born on a wholesale scale. Also, many foreign born, despairing of finding employment here during the years of depression and denied relief by local authorities because of the presence of archaic settlement laws on statute books, began to leave the country voluntarily. Not only had the tide ceased flowing; it had begun to ebb: for during 1932–1935, more persons quit America than arrived here. The figures below

Year ended June 30	*Immigrants admitted*	*Emigrants departed*	*Net gain or loss*
1930	241,700	50,661	+ 191,039
1931	97,139	61,882	+ 35,257
1932	35,576	103,295	– 67,719
1933	23,068	80,081	– 57,013
1934	29,470	39,771	– 10,301
1935	34,956	38,834	– 3,878
1936	36,329	35,817	+ 512
1937	50,244	26,736	+ 23,508

give numbers of immigrants admitted for permanent residence and emigrants abandoning domicile during the depression years.

Thus was ending another epoch in American history: the doors of the United States, as the historic haven of the oppressed in all lands, were being swung shut.

A word should be said of Mexican immigration. In the decade of the twenties 459,000 Mexicans were admitted into the country, to the growing concern of our Southwest. Fear of the appearance of another racial problem led to agitation for the restriction of this group, and bills to that effect were introduced into Congress in 1928. But Washington had profited from earlier blunders of this character: to check the entry of Mexicans by exclusion would mean not only offending a friendly nation but also closing off entirely the only source of unskilled labor still left us. Mexicans constituted, in large part, a floating labor supply and were useful in railroad construction camps and mines and for farm labor in the Southwest's vegetable, sugar beet, fruit, and cotton fields. But in time of economic stress, when native unemployment was particularly marked, Mexicans might very well be denied admission. This the Department of Labor was able to effect through exercise of the powers vested in it by the immigration laws: on the ground that Mexicans were likely to become public charges, most of them, beginning with 1929, were turned back at the immigration stations on the southern border. So, in 1927–1928, 59,000 were admitted; and in 1928–1929, 40,000. But in 1929–1930, only 13,000 Mexicans were permitted to enter the country, and in 1936–1937, only 2347. Whether American labor would be satisfied with the deposit of such great powers in the hands of an administrative official (who could, just as easily, flood the country with unskilled labor by the simple issuance of a countermanding order), once full economic revival set it, remained to be seen.

The Decline of Agriculture

For two decades, from 1900 to 1920, the pressure on American agriculture—a pressure that had appeared in the eighteen eighties and that had reached an unbearable pitch in the middle nineties—was relieved. American industry was ready for the exploitation of the home market and thanks to an open immigration policy our urban population increased by leaps and bounds; the old immigrants from Western and Northern Europe largely, who had been attracted to the public lands, were supplanted by the new immigrants from Southern and Eastern Europe, who thronged to the cities. Industry, aided immeasurably by the rapid strides it was making as a result of mechanization, was able to furnish them with work and house, clothe, and equip them cheaply.

But if industry and trade profited enormously, so did agriculture. Mechanization on a large scale had not yet come to the farms, so that the output of farm products did not increase in proportion to the output of other consumer goods or the increase in urban population. More and more agriculture found itself in that happy position where it was being limited to the domestic market needs (at least, for cereals and meat products), without the consequent disorganizing effects of world prices. The results were therefore the following: a comparative decline in the rural and farming populations; a smaller exportable surplus of cash crops; a comparative rise in the price of farm products; and an increase in the value of the national farm plant. Between 1900 and 1910, the aggregate value of all farm property doubled; the total value of all cereals raised in the country, between 1899 and 1909, increased 79.8 per cent, while the total yield increased only 1.7 per cent; the value of all food exports declined from $545,474,000 in 1900 (39.8 per cent of total) to $369,088,000 in 1910 (19.1 per cent of total). Nothing showed more plainly the protected state of American agriculture during these few years than the index of farm prices as compared with the index for the prices of all commodities. The following tabulation presents the figures for selected years (1900 = 100):

Year	*Prices of all commodities*	*Farm prices*
1896	82.5	78.3
1900	100.0	100.0
1901	98.8	105.8
1905	106.3	111.6
1910	123.8	149.3
1911	118.8	134.8
1914	125.0	149.3

The tale of the next half-decade was even more splendid, for during the war years the American farmer actually became affluent. The demand of the Allies for foodstuffs and cotton, the requirements of our own mobilized forces, the needs of postwar Europe before war-torn lands could be reclaimed—these factors, during 1915–1920, sent prices of crops and agricultural lands dizzily upward so that the farmer, as a producer of foodstuffs and staples and as a land speculator, grew rich and contented. American agriculture, therefore, expanded and opened marginal and submarginal lands, using irrigation and dry farming to overcome inadequate rainfall. Thus, between 1910 and 1920, the acreage increased 9 per cent, whereas over the preceding decade it had increased but 5 per cent; the land in farms in the Mountain states more than doubled; and there was an increase of five million acres of irrigated lands in the same ten years. The money values of American farms mounted, in some regions doubling, in others trebling their prices. Before the war (in 1910), land in Iowa, for example, was worth $82 an acre; after the war (in 1920), the same acre was worth $200. Spring wheat, in 1913, was selling at Chicago for 93 cents a bushel; the price in 1919 was $2.76. Corn, in 1913, was selling at Chicago for 70 cents; in 1919, for $1.59. Cotton, in 1913, was selling at New York for 13 cents a pound; in 1919, for 38 cents. Lulled by a sense of security, the American farmer pushed out his horizons: he increased his improvements, bought machinery for the first time on a large scale, invested in an automobile and auto trucks, installed a telephone, electrified his house and barn, and clamored for the extension by his state and county governments of the social services—better roads, consolidated schools, county hospital and nursing units, old-age pensions, local farm bureaus, and university extension activities. To the accompaniment, of course, of an ever-mounting tax rate.

Alas, boom times were all too brief and the bubble of the farmer's content was pricked with a suddenness and completeness that left him shaken to his depths. The era of deflation, which set in toward the end of 1920, left its mark on industry and agriculture alike, but whereas industry began to recover with 1922, agriculture remained permanently depressed. Land values plunged downward until in 1929, that year of golden prosperity for industry, they were not much higher than they had been before the war; crop prices dropped until, in some instances, they were lower than they had been for almost half a century; agriculture was left with a heavy burden of debt and taxation as a result of overexpansion of acreage, improvements, and public budgets. The depression of 1930 and after merely served to sharpen the outlines of a situation that had been steadily getting bleaker as the decade of the twenties progressed. Put simply, farm prices had been deflated, while farm costs—necessaries for home and field, mortgage debt, taxes—were still highly inflated. The farm account could not be balanced.

The bare statistical exhibits in themselves tell a startling story. In 1919, the total farm property of the nation had been valued at $78,000,000,000; by 1929 this value was $57,604,000,000, and by 1932, $44,000,000,000. In 1919, the total farm income was $15,000,000,000; by 1929, $12,000,000,000, and by 1932, $5,200,000,000. In 1919 (with the average for 1909–1914 as 100), the prices paid by farmers for the commodities they needed stood at 206; the prices they received, at 205, making a ratio of prices received to prices paid of 99. That is to say, the farm dollar was worth 99 cents. But in 1929, it was worth only 89 cents; and in 1932, only 47 cents!

The efficiency of American agriculture was being hampered not only because of declines in gross and relative income. What was more serious was the fact that fixed charges were eating up a larger and larger share of the farmer's earnings so that he was compelled to divert the use of income from the improvement of his techniques to the payment of taxes and interest on mortgages. In 1910, tax payments took 3 per cent of gross income; in 1920, 3.6 per cent; in 1930, 6 per cent. In 1910, interest on mortgages took 3 per cent of gross income; in 1920, 4 per cent; in 1930, 6 per cent. In short, total fixed charges absorbed 6 per cent of gross farm income in 1910 and 12 per cent in 1930: this was indeed a heavy price to pay for land ownership. Farm mortgage debt in particular had become a millstone about the necks of American agricultural producers. In 1910, the mortgage debt on American farm land and buildings made up 27.3 per cent of the value of properties; in 1920, 29.1 per cent; and in 1930, 39.6 per cent. Inability to meet mortgage payments and to pay taxes was converting many farm owners into tenants or croppers or forcing them off the land altogether to enter the industrial reserve army of America's urban population.

Nothing proved the decline of agriculture more certainly than this state of affairs: the inability of farm tenants to pull themselves up by their own bootstraps and become farm owners. Formerly, tenancy had been of the ladder variety: younger sons, grandsons, and sons-in-law, as well as immigrants, starting out as tenants, accumulated savings and in time became owners. This upward climb had now ceased. More and more tenants were remaining permanently in that inferior status and were doomed to inadequate incomes and insecurity. In 1880, 25.6 per cent of all the farms in the country were being operated by tenants; in 1930, 42.4 per cent. The differences among the various geographical sections were significant, as the following tabulation shows.

FARMS OPERATED BY TENANTS

(Figures are per cents of all farms)

Year	*Middle Atlantic*	*East North Central*	*West North Central*	*South Atlantic*	*East South Central*	*West South Central*	*Mountain*
1880	19.2	20.5	20.5	36.1	36.8	35.2	7.4
1930	14.7	27.3	39.9	48.1	55.9	62.3	24.4

Tenancy was on the increase in the great corn–hog and wheat raising areas of the North and in the great tobacco and cotton raising areas of the South. Indeed, in 1930, 73 per cent of farms growing cotton were operated by tenants, of whom half were sharecroppers. In 1930, there were 725,000 croppers in cotton, of whom half were blacks and half whites.

The unhappy effects of the growth of tenancy were to be found in economic and social maladjustments. Said a government report on this problem: [3]

The correlation between soil erosion and tenant occupancy is very striking. The reasons are obvious. The tenant whose occupancy is uncertain at best, and ordinarily does not average more than two years, can ill afford to plant the farm to any but cash crops. . . . The tenant who has no assurance of permanent occupancy can rarely afford to apply fertilizers beyond the amount which will give him most immediate return, or to plant soil-building crops.

The tenant who expects to remain but a short time on a farm has little incentive to conserve and improve the soil; he has equally little incentive to maintain and improve the woodlot, the house, barn, shed, or other structures on the farm. . . .

Erosion of our soil has its counterpart in erosion of our society. The one wastes natural resources; the others, human resources. Instability and insecurity of farm families leach the binding elements of rural community life.

We find the unwholesome spectacle of men, women, and children,

[3] Special Committee on Farm Tenancy, "Farm Tenancy" [75th Congress, 1st sess., House Document No. 149] (1937).

especially among the tenant families, moving from farm to farm each year. This social erosion not only wears down the fiber of the families themselves; it saps the resources of the entire social order. In the spring of 1935 there were more than a third (34.2 per cent) of the 2,865,000 tenant farmers of the nation who had occupied their present farms only one year. In many areas the proportion exceeded 50 per cent. White tenants move more frequently than do colored tenants. The incessant movement of tenant and cropper families and of migratory laborers from farm to farm and from community to community deprives these families of normal social participation. It lays a heavy hand upon the large numbers of rural children caught in this current, who find their schooling periodically interrupted, if not made impossible; they suffer from mental as well as economic insecurity.

Equally significant as an example of decline, was the debased position of agricultural real estate, that single factor which heretofore had always succeeded in redressing the balance. What happened to agricultural real estate is graphically indicated by the following index figures of the estimated value per acre for 1914, 1920, 1929, and 1933. (Average for 1912–1914 = 100.)

CONDITION OF AGRICULTURAL REAL ESTATE

	1914	*1920*	*1929*	*1933*
United States	103	170	116	73
East North Central States	103	161	100	62
West North Central States	103	184	112	64
East South Central States	103	199	129	79
West South Central States	104	177	136	82
Mountain States	100	151	101	69
Pacific States	106	156	142	96

Such were the outward signs of a deep-seated malady which was not a passing phase but had all the aspects of permanence. Let us see what were the reasons for the depression under which the country's agricultural interest labored in the decades of the twenties and thirties. They may be summed up in a single phrase: the foreign market contracted and the domestic market did not expand.

First, as regards the foreign situation. The great historical reason for the advance of American agriculture after the Civil War had been our debtor status. We were borrowing capital from Europe to help transform our capitalism from a merchant to an industrial base. As a result, we engaged in an heroic expansion of agriculture to permit payments on foreign borrowings and for those raw materials we ourselves could not produce. In brief, American industry was growing up behind high tariff walls with the assistance of foreign capital; and American agricultural surpluses helped make this possible.

By 1920 (as we shall see below in greater detail) the United States had become a creditor nation. But other countries, due to the staggering costs of the World War, because they were debtors, and because of the ambitions of their own capitalists, were now desperately trying to obtain foreign exchange. How help the process better than by the enlargement of their own agricultural operations? This was notably true of the newer lands—Canada, the Latin American countries, Australasia, the Far East—which could balance their international payments only by selling in the world market those foodstuffs and fibers which we ourselves kept pouring into Europe up to the end of the World War. What made the situation worse was the fact that European countries began to strive for agricultural self-sufficiency. By resettlement projects, by great grants of agricultural credits, by high tariff walls, import quota systems, and milling requirements, virtually every European country (including the United Kingdom!) was seeking to build up a domestic agricultural group large enough to supply at least the home food requirement. Why was this? The following reasons may be cited: (1) The fear of dearth in time of war; (2) the need to conserve foreign exchange for basic raw materials which could not be produced at home—oil, cotton, rubber, minerals, metals; (3) the political desirability of building up a rural conservative interest, supported by government, which could be used against the propertyless and dispossessed urban workers in the event of the threat of revolutionary overthrow.

The result was a vast expansion in the production of agricultural goods throughout the world during the nineteen twenties. Between 1913 and 1932, the United States increased its area devoted to major food crops from 290,000,000 to 320,000,000 acres, or more than 10 per cent; in the same period, Europe, Canada, Argentina, and Australia increased their acreage for the same crops from 631,000,000 to 724,000,000, or more than 16 per cent. As Messrs. Ezekiel and Bean pointed out in their study "The Economic Bases for the Agricultural Adjustment Act": "This increase in foreign competition and foreign self-sufficiency brought about a persistent decline in United States exports of food products from 1921 on, long before the 1929 collapse. The 1932–1933 export volume finally shrank below prewar levels. In the face of this shrinkage in foreign demand, acreage of important crops in the United States has been maintained about 10 per cent above prewar acreage."

Thus, the wheel had turned full circle in not more than sixty years, and America in the twenties was in the position England had been in when American agricultural surpluses first appeared in the world market. *Then*, English farmers had not been able to meet the competition of American grains and meats because they were burdened with heavy rents, labor costs, and capital charges. *Now*, we could not compete with Argentinian and Australian beef growers, Canadian and Polish bacon manufacturers, Argentinian, Australian, Canadian, Russian, and Manchurian grain farmers and Indian, Chinese, Russian, and Brazilian cotton producers for exactly the same reasons. The doors of the world market were slowly swinging shut.

Second, as regards the domestic situation. The possibilities of increasing domestic consumption of agricultural goods, in order to take in the slack, were remote. The following factors may be noted: 1. Our population growth was slowing down because of immigration restriction and birth control. 2. Because of these facts, the age distribution of our population was changing, with interesting repercussions upon the consumption of agricultural goods. Indeed, the two decades 1910–1930 witnessed a profound change in dietary habits as Americans shifted from a reliance on grains and beef to a greater use of pork, vegetables, fruits, milk, and sugar. The significance of the shift lies in this fact: grains and beef are largely the products of extensive cultivation; pork products, vegetables, fruits, and milk are the products of intensive cultivation requiring less land in use and more capital expenditures. And extensive cultivation was the method of production notably of the typical American farming unit, the family farm.

Also, the consumption of agricultural goods at home was not increasing proportionately because of changing habits in feeding and clothing. 3. Women were dieting and thus eating less calories. 4. Improved methods of heating homes, the wide use of heated automobiles, and the machine's growing elimination of the need for hard and back-breaking human toil also made it possible for men as well as women to dispense with foods with high caloric contents: for, as became generally known, calories were required largely to supply heat and replace rapidly wearing out body tissue. 5. Cotton was being replaced by rayons and other chemically produced fabrics. 6. Finally, agriculture itself had become more efficient, making it possible to produce more foods and fibers for each dollar of labor and capital expended. In fact, between 1919 and 1929, on a stationary cultivated acreage, the output of American farmers increased more than 20 per cent! There were notably three reasons responsible for this revolutionary advance: progress in the application of mechanical methods and the motorization of farm equipment (with an accompanying decrease of land use necessary for the provision of feed grains for horses and mules); increasing acre yields as a result of intensive cultivation, the improvement of crop strains, and the application of fertilizer; and the greater efficiency of milk and meat animals per unit of feed consumed. There was, therefore, a surplus of farmers in the United States.

Governmental programs for agriculture, during the nineteen twenties, were concerned only with details. There was no effort made to come to grips with the fundamental problems of high costs, heavy fixed charges, economic and social maladjustments springing from tenancy, and contraction of the market for agricultural goods. In the late twenties, a powerful political agrarian interest sought the passage of fundamental agricultural legislation; but these pressures Presidents Coolidge and Hoover resisted. President Hoover did make an effort to cope with the question of wheat and cotton surpluses by taking them out of the market—but to no avail. The actions of government must now be passed in review.

In August, 1921, after three years of debate in Congress, there was passed and approved by President Harding the Packers and Stockyards Act. This measure, designed to aid the cattle raisers, made it unlawful for the packers to engage in unfair practices, to combine to control prices and apportion markets, and to create a monopoly. Persons engaged in the operation of stockyards or market agencies were to register with the Secretary of Agriculture, to whom they were to furnish a statement of their scale of charges. These charges, according to the act, were to be reasonable and nondiscriminatory. The administration of the law was to be vested in the hands of the Secretary of Agriculture, who was to operate much as the Federal Trade Commission did in the case of unfair business practices, that is to say, by entertaining complaints, by holding hearings and by issuing orders to "cease and desist." In February, 1922, the Capper-Volstead Cooperative Act received the signature of the President. This law exempted, once and for all, agricultural associations or cooperatives from attack under the Sherman Law, for by it the cooperatives were granted the rights to process, prepare, handle, and market their wares in interstate commerce.[4] Here, too, the Department of Agriculture, and not the Federal Trade Commission, was granted the power of supervision.

In March, 1923, to the Federal Reserve Act of 1913 and the Federal Farm Loan Act of 1916, there was added the Federal Intermediate Credit Act. The purpose of this law was to make still easier the extension of credits to farmers by setting up a system of federal intermediate credit banks for the purpose of handling agricultural paper exclusively. By the act the Federal Farm Loan Board was authorized to grant charters to twelve new institutions, to be known as the federal intermediate credit banks. These were to be established in the same cities as the federal land banks and were to have the same officers. But they were to be separate corporations. Each bank was to have a capital stock of $5,000,000 (with the government as the only subscriber) and each bank could issue debentures up to ten times its paid-up capital and surplus. The security for these debentures was to be the agricultural paper the banks were to rediscount. This rediscounted paper was to come from state and national banks, trust companies, agricultural credit corporations, and the like, and was to consist entirely of notes, drafts, and bills of exchange whose proceeds had been used for agricultural or livestock purposes. The intermediate credit banks could also lend directly to agricultural cooperatives on notes secured by warehouse receipts and bills of lading, for a period ranging from six months to three years and up to 75 per cent of the market value of the products that were pledged as collateral.[5] Also, in order to encourage greater banking facilities in agricultural regions, the act permitted the establishment, by private capital, of agricultural credit

[4] In 1926 the law was extended to permit such cooperative associations to exchange openly statistical, economic, and price information. In this sense, the agricultural cooperatives were given preferred status among the trade associations.

[5] Thus there were finally incorporated into law the essential details of the subtreasury scheme of the Populist agitation of the eighteen nineties. But by the nineteen twenties the agrarian problem had shifted from one of credit to one of surplus production and overexpansion of plant in the face of world competition.

corporations, which could lend money on agricultural paper, with a nine-months' maturity.

During the twenties, the outstanding proposals advanced by farmer interests for agricultural relief were the equalization fee and export debentures plans. These programs set it as their purpose to raise the level of domestic prices on agricultural products up to those points where the full advantages of the tariff duties on agricultural commodities could be obtained. This was to be achieved by segregating the domestic requirement from the exportable surplus. The former was to be sold at the inflated domestic price; the latter at the going world price. Under the equalization fee scheme, the difference between the artificial domestic price and the normal world price (on the surplus) was to be borne by the farmers of each particular commodity. Under the export debenture scheme, this difference was to be borne by the government out of customs receipts. In short, in both instances, price fixing was to be countenanced; in the case of the export debenture scheme, the growers of staples which entered the world market were to be directly subsidized.

The McNary-Haugen bill, which incorporated the equalization fee scheme, made its first appearance in the lower house in January, 1924, but twice failed of passage. In February, 1927, however, the farmers mobilized enough strength to jam the measure through both houses; they did not, however, have margins large enough to override President Coolidge's veto. The final test of strength came in the spring of 1928. The Senate passed the bill in April by a vote of 53 to 23; the House in May, by a vote of 204 to 121. Again President Coolidge rejected the measure and again Congress found it impossible to gather the necessary two-thirds for passage over the veto. The bill, in its final form, had these provisions: It provided for a federal farm board. The board was to have authority to make loans to cooperative associations for the purpose of assisting them in controlling seasonable surpluses in excess of domestic needs. The board was to collect an equalization fee from the grower of each staple sufficient to cover the losses, met with in the marketing of the surplus, due to the difference between the domestic price and the world price. A revolving fund of $400,000,000, to finance these operations, was to be set up.

The export debenture plan was first introduced in Congress in

January, 1926, reintroduced in 1928, and in 1929 was added by insurgent Republican Senators to both the Smoot tariff bill and the administration's agricultural marketing bill. In each case, the Senate was compelled to give way before the House's demand that the debenture be abandoned. The essentials of the proposal were the following: Export bounties were to be paid on wheat, corn, rice, cotton, tobacco, swine, and cattle. The rates specified in the 1928 bill were to be one-half of the tariff duties. In other words, the domestic price was to be the world price plus one-half of the duty on the particular commodity. These bounties were to be paid in the form of negotiable instruments known as debentures which were to be receivable in payment of import duties. That is to say, governmental revenues were to be reduced by the amount of export debentures or bounties issued for a particular year. A federal farm board was to be set up and its chief function was to regulate domestic production of agricultural staples by reducing or even canceling the debenture rates. So, if production by the farmers was increased, the bounty was to be cut; if the increase in production was more than 15 per cent over the average of the preceding five years, the debenture was to be revoked.

The Agricultural Marketing Act of 1929 embodied President Hoover's program for agricultural relief. The Seventy-first Congress had been called in special session to cope with the farm and tariff problems, and it turned its attention to the former first. The House passed the Agricultural Marketing bill with little discussion; but the Senate insisted upon the inclusion of the export debenture in its measure and, despite the President's disapproval, passed the bill in that form. Only after the House had voted down the Senate bill by a record vote did the Senate abandon the export debenture. On June 14, the Senate accepted the Conference Committee's report, and on the next day President Hoover affixed his signature. The Agricultural Marketing Act rejected the price-fixing and subsidy features of the earlier agricultural proposals. It was founded on the principle of voluntary cooperation under governmental auspices: that is to say, through the operation of nationwide cooperative marketing associations, and by the exercise of self-discipline, agriculture was to be redeemed. Agriculture, with its millions of small units, was to work as corporate industry did: curtail production to establish an equilibrium between domestic supply and demand, shift quickly from one form of activity to another as demands changed, rationalize its plant, seek a greater return from wages of management than from capital investments.

The new act's provisions were the following: 1. There was to be established a Federal Farm Board of eight members, to be appointed by the President, with the consent of the Senate, for six years. 2. This Board was to encourage the organization and development of agricultural cooperatives. 3. A revolving fund of $500,000,000 was set up, from which loans were to be made to the cooperatives. 4. The Board might institute advisory committees for the particular agricultural commodities, and on their application might recognize stabilization corporations. These stabilization corporations, through loans from the revolving fund, were to be enabled to control, handle, and market the surpluses of their particular commodities. 5. The Board might enter into agreements to insure the cooperatives and the stabilization corporations against loss because of price declines.

In the stimulation of cooperative marketing associations the Board, in its three years' work, met with a notable success. Through its efforts there were organized cooperatives for marketing nearly every sort of crop produced in the country. The Board, in its first year alone, received applications for loans from 206 cooperatives and approved loans to 132 of these, to which it granted $165,146,555. But more important than encouraging the processes of self-help was the injunction laid upon the Board of "aiding in preventing and controlling surpluses in any agricultural commodity, through orderly production and distribution, so as to maintain advantageous domestic markets and prevent such surpluses from causing undue and excessive fluctuations or depressions in prices for the commodity." In the cases of wheat and cotton such crises, in the fall of 1929, impended with the result that the Board was compelled to act. Proceeding on the assumption that the wheat crop of 1929 was a short one, and that, therefore, the market price was too low, the Board offered to lend wheat cooperatives $1.18 per bushel for all wheat held off the market. And in February, 1930, the Board created the first of its two stabilization agencies, the Grain Stabilization Corporation.

This organization entered the wheat market twice and in all bought some 330,000,000 bushels, the first operation being completed in the middle of 1930 and the second in the middle of 1931. Three results were apparent from these ventures by the Federal

Farm Board's subsidiary. 1. Its purchases succeeded in pegging the domestic price from 20 to 30 cents above the world figure, for something like half a year. But as soon as the Grain Stabilization Corporation abandoned the market permanently in June, 1931, the price of July wheat dropped to 57 cents, the lowest for the commodity since 1896. 2. The federal government was left in possession of the whole 1930–1931 carry-over, which menaced the price of the new crop. 3. What to do with the wheat surpluses? There was, apparently, nothing for the government to do but hold them. From July to November, 1931, the Federal Farm Board was able to sell abroad some 47,000,000 bushels; the rest was left on its hands to be disposed of piecemeal, while the storage charges mounted higher and higher to wipe out most of the value of the original investment.

The same procedure was repeated in the case of cotton. The Federal Farm Board lent to cotton cooperatives, for cotton held off the market, at an average price of 16 cents a pound. But cotton prices continued to drop so that here, too, resort was had to the creation of a stabilization agency. The Cotton Stabilization Corporation, formed in June, 1930, went into the market and in its efforts to sustain the price was compelled to buy the whole 1929–1930 carry-over, a total of 1,319,800 bales. The price could not be supported, however, with the result, at the end of November, cotton at New York was selling for 6.75 cents a pound. The second operation, the purchase of the 1930–1931 carry-over, left the Cotton Stabilization Corporation with a total supply of 3,250,000 bales in warehouses; and in 1932, cotton was selling at 5 cents. After its affairs were wound up, it was discovered that the Federal Farm Board had lost $150,000,000 in cotton alone.

As early as the summer of 1930, perhaps because it itself had little confidence in the program, perhaps because it appreciated that it was best to have two strings to its bow, the Federal Farm Board began an intensive campaign to urge the farmer to reduce acreage. Said the Board's members in public statements: The American farmer was overproducing; he ought to cut his acreage to the requirements of the domestic market; his surpluses entered a world market where they were compelled to compete with products raised by cheap labor, on cheap land, and shipped by cheap water transportation. But the American grower of staples would not, or could not, reduce acreage; and the crops for 1931–1932 and 1932–1933 were as bountiful as ever. There was another ironic element in the situation, and it was this: while the Federal Farm Board exhorted and cajoled, in an effort to obtain acreage reduction, the Department of Agriculture and the states, through their educational agencies and experiment stations, happily continued on their way teaching the farmers how to grow bigger and better crops! This paradoxical state of affairs continued until President Franklin D. Roosevelt took office.

Economic Imperialism

Great Britain had been launched on her imperialist career in the third quarter of the nineteenth century; Germany had followed in the wake of Britain a couple of decades later; it was not until the World War was over that America, abandoning her traditional isolation, set out upon the same course. We had, it is true, acquired oversea possessions as a result of the Spanish War and had begun to wrestle with the problems of colonial administration, in a somewhat half-hearted way, from the Presidency of Theodore Roosevelt onward. But we had not become imperialist, in the modern sense, until almost twenty years had elapsed after the fall of Manila. This new American imperialism meant an awareness of the fact that the domestic economy of the nation was inextricably tied up with world economy: that our movements and our decisions were being affected, sometimes to a very marked degree, by events taking place in remote corners of the earth. This, then, was the stuff of imperialism: raw materials that were vital to our industries and that we did not ourselves produce; outlet markets that could absorb our surpluses of manufactured goods; fields of investment for our saved capital; the maintenance of peace everywhere, lest fine adjustments be disturbed to hinder the steady supply of something we needed, close a market to our wares, or stop the interest payment on a governmental or industrial bond held by American rentiers. In the twenties of the new century, America was brought into unobtrusive conflict with the economic and financial groups of other nations, particularly those of Britain in Latin America and those of Japan in the Far East.

The United States was a mighty nation in the period following the World War, yet we were not altogether self-sufficient, for the list of those materials for which we were dependent upon outside sources was a long one. We had no nickel, for example, and no tin ore; we had no rubber, silk, camphor, and coffee; our local supplies of long-staple cotton, sugar, wool, hides, wood-pulp, and nitrates were inadequate for domestic needs. In addition, annually we were compelled to import large stores of the following important raw materials: antimony, chromite, cork, graphite, hemp, iodine, jute, flaxseed, manganese, manila, mica, nux vomica, opium, platinum, potassium salts, quicksilver, quinine, shellac, tungsten, and vanadium. To obtain these necessities for our factories, American merchants, engineers, geologists, agronomists, and investment bankers found it necessary to keep up a persistent search. It was inevitable, therefore, that we should be interested in Bolivia because tin was mined there, in British Malaya because rubber was grown there, in Brazil because of its manganese, Peru because of its vanadium, Canada because of its wood pulp. In addition, we had things to sell and saved capital to invest. To hunt out markets for these surpluses of our factories and annual incomes became another great concern of Americans in the decade following the end of the World War. Of the sale of our industrial surpluses and the investment of our saved capital, more will be said below. It is enough at this point to repeat that the three items of inadequate domestic raw materials, industrial surpluses, and saved capital changed our economy, made us an imperial nation, and forced us to regard with greater attention and occasionally real anxiety the progress of the rest of the world that lay beyond our thresholds.

It has been said that the consequences of the acceptance, by Americans, of their imperial destiny were serious. Whether they were to end unhappily; whether, indeed, it was possible to check our headlong career along the way once trod by Romans, Venetians, Dutchmen, and (only yesterday) Germans—these, after all, were questions for speculation only. This, however, was certain: our newfound grandeur had made us, as a people, disliked and envied; and had compelled all those interested in public questions to give thought to the implications of our wider destiny.

The reasons for America's unpopularity abroad, in the twenties, were the following: 1. Our continued insistence that the war debts be repaid. 2. Our high protective tariff. The only way Europeans (and other peoples) could meet interest and principal on governmental and private loans made to them by America was by the sale of goods. Yet the Tariff Acts of 1922 and 1930 had practically closed our market, placing well-nigh prohibitive rates on those foreign commodities that could compete with American industry. 3. Our aggressive business methods abroad. We had things to sell —often better made, for better values, more attractively put up— and not infrequently our sales agencies entered into competition with native manufacturers and distributors. Every time we wrested a market away from a native rival we made a series of enemies. 4. The Americanizing of the rest of the world. American motion picture films, soda fountains, penny slot machines, gasoline pumps, tin cans; American automobiles, safety razors, fountain pens, typewriters, weighing machines, scales—all those wares that our mechanized and standardized industry was turning out in an endless stream we poured into every conceivable corner of the earth to break down local habits and prejudices and reduce taste to the measurements we had decided upon. Not that our modern plumbing fixtures, central heating plants, and electrical supplies were bad for the inhabitants of other lands; very often, resentment was entirely due to the fact that it was the American who was making their daily lives more comfortable. 5. Our branch factories abroad. Because we had saved capital to invest we could tunnel our way under the tariff walls of other peoples by merely establishing plants within their own boundaries. True, the labor employed was native and some of the raw materials purchased came from local sources; but the profits went to America. 6. The great prosperity, sometimes the bad manners, usually the ignorance of and unconcern in the face of local habits and customs, of our tourists. Annually, American tourists spent abroad in the neighborhood of three-quarters of a billion dollars, and they often spent ostentatiously. Also, their greater wealth permitted them to acquire art works and rare books of great local sentimental value. The fact that these purchase and expenditures by Americans helped European nations to balance their international payments did not change matters for the man on the street, whose thinner purse and lower standard of living, in the face of such foreign splendor, produced a feeling of envy, both natural and inevitable. 7. Our immigration restriction policy. 8. Our great armament programs. True, as we have seen, the United States did not decide to build until the great powers had refused to join us further in the restriction of naval armaments. Where the shoe pinched was the fact that by our superior wealth we could force our policy upon them by outbuilding them all. 9. Our too easy habits of self-deception. We insisted that our intentions were pacific, that our chief desire was to live in amity with other peoples. Indeed, most Americans believed in this creed and personally conducted themselves to conform with it. Yet the cumulative effect was anything but that. Our marines in Nicaragua, Haiti, and Santo Domingo; our high-handed attitude toward Colombia; our flouting of the national honor of the Japanese; our refusal to accept a mandate for Armenia—these falls from grace did everything to destroy the effect of the good works of American philanthropy in a war-ridden and poverty-accursed world.

As our industrial and financial attitudes toward the world changed with the widening of our horizons, so, though more slowly and perhaps less consciously, our political attitudes changed with them. That we had become an imperial nation, at least industrially and financially, was plain; that our foreign policy was imperial, was not so easy to prove. For one thing, unanimity did not exist because there was definite opposition by statesmen at Washington to the relinquishment of America's traditional attitude of aloofness from the rest of the world; for another, there had not yet appeared a public leader to point up the doctrine of America's imperial destiny by openly proclaiming it (as, for example, Joseph Chamberlain had done in England, the Kaiser in Germany); for still a third, party distinctions were too loosely drawn in America to permit one or the other of the major parties to identify itself with the cause of America's interest overseas. But that, sooner or later, foreign and international policies would have to conform with economic interests, was a truism which few could deny after regarding the recent histories of the British, German, and French nations. It remained for the future to clarify the details of such an American policy whose general contours one found little difficulty in outlining.

First, our interest in raw materials and markets for our surplus goods demanded that our political leaders exert themselves to keep the trade channels of the world forever open. Second, our great capital investments abroad required that we take active steps for the preservation of the peace everywhere. Third, the danger of rivalry and the disputing of our economic supremacy by others required that we be prepared to meet all potential foes on the field of battle. We may now see which American foreign policies were definitely established, which still were uncertain or the subject of controversy as the nineteen twenties and thirties unrolled.

These foreign policies were being regarded by Americans as having been clearly defined, once and for all: the Monroe Doctrine; the Isthmian policy, which has turned the Caribbean into an American lake; peace by arbitration; restricted immigration; the Open Door. Only the last needs some amplification. The Open Door principle, in the decades of the twenties and thirties, meant not merely the equality of commercial opportunity enunciated by Hay; it signified in addition equality of financial opportunity for our investment bankers and the right to buy raw materials freely even in the face of world monopoly. So, our Department of Commerce, under Secretary Hoover, protested vigorously and often successfully when artificial means were created to inflate the prices of the following more or less monopolistically controlled commodities: long-staple cotton (Egypt), camphor (Japan), coffee (Brazil), nitrates (Chile), potash (France–Germany), mercury (Spain–Italy), rubber (British Malaya), sisal (Yucatan). And, as we shall see below, in the thirties Secretary of State Hull persisted in demanding the safeguarding of American commercial, financial, and philanthropic rights in China in the midst of the undeclared Sino-Japanese war.

The determination of the following questions still was unsettled during the twenties and thirties: 1. What was to be America's tariff policy? The "isolationists" were quite willing to shut out the wares of other peoples. The "imperialists" saw that an open exchange of goods was necessary to permit our debtors to pay interest and principal on the loans we had made to them out of our saved capital.[6] Thus, this latter group had not the slightest objection to America's becoming an importer of foodstuffs and raw materials and an exporter of manufactured goods and saved capital. The bearing of this difference of opinion on the state of our domestic agriculture is plain. The "isolationists" were prepared to save agriculture at any cost, subsidy being held a small price. The "imperialists" were

[6] I have used the terms "isolationists" and "imperialists" to express states of mind that were familiar to postwar America. By the thirties the issue had not yet been clearly drawn to allow for the appearance of groups who openly supported one set of views as against the other. That is to say, there were not—yet—"Little" Americans as against "Big" Americans. The whole debate in the thirties was being clouded by the emergence of another consideration: the possibility of another World War outbreak. In this connection, those in favor of maintaining American neutrality, in such an event, approximated the position of the "isolationists"; while those who favored American participation in efforts to achieve world peace—even at the expense of our entering the war as soon as it started (the so-called "collective securityites")—approximated the position of the "imperialists."

frankly indifferent to the claims of our native farming interest. The analogy between our present situation and the struggle in England over the repeal of the Corn Laws in 1846 is obvious. 2. What was to be our final attitude toward affiliation with the League of Nations and the World Court? The "isolationists" were suspicious of Europe and refused to regard its problems as our concern. The "imperialists" felt that only through the maintenance of peace in every corner of the globe could the delicate mechanism of American economic imperialism keep its equipoise. 3. What were we to do about the interallied or war debts? The "isolationists" demanded payment. The "imperialists" were willing to talk reduction or cancellation because they knew that these debts stood in the way of further financial operations overseas by our investment bankers. 4. To what extent might our investors abroad expect governmental assistance when their bonds or physical properties were jeopardized, or government cooperation in finding new fields for investment? The "isolationists" said never. The "imperialists" were not unaware of the fact that sooner or later government and financiers must come to an understanding, as had been the case in prewar Great Britain, France, and Germany, and was again true of postwar France and Britain. In both these countries the investment centers, as far as foreign lending was concerned, had virtually become annexes of the ministries for foreign affairs. Indeed, the American State Department had shown a definite interest in the character of the bond issues being floated by American bankers, as early as 1922, and had offered to pass an opinion on the desirability of any foreign loans being taken up by American investors. Of course, this was not supervision or control, but that it was a step in that direction could not be denied. For example, Secretary of Commerce Hoover had received loyal assistance from the State Department in his fight for the maintenance of the Open Door principle, when Secretary Kellogg had indicated that American loans to help the work of the Franco-German potash syndicate and the Brazilian coffee monopoly would be regarded with disfavor.

Such were the many perplexities confronting the thoughtful American when he turned his attention upon his country's international position. We must now review briefly how our surpluses of goods and saved capital changed our whole national economy. Before the World War, we had been a debtor nation, exporting

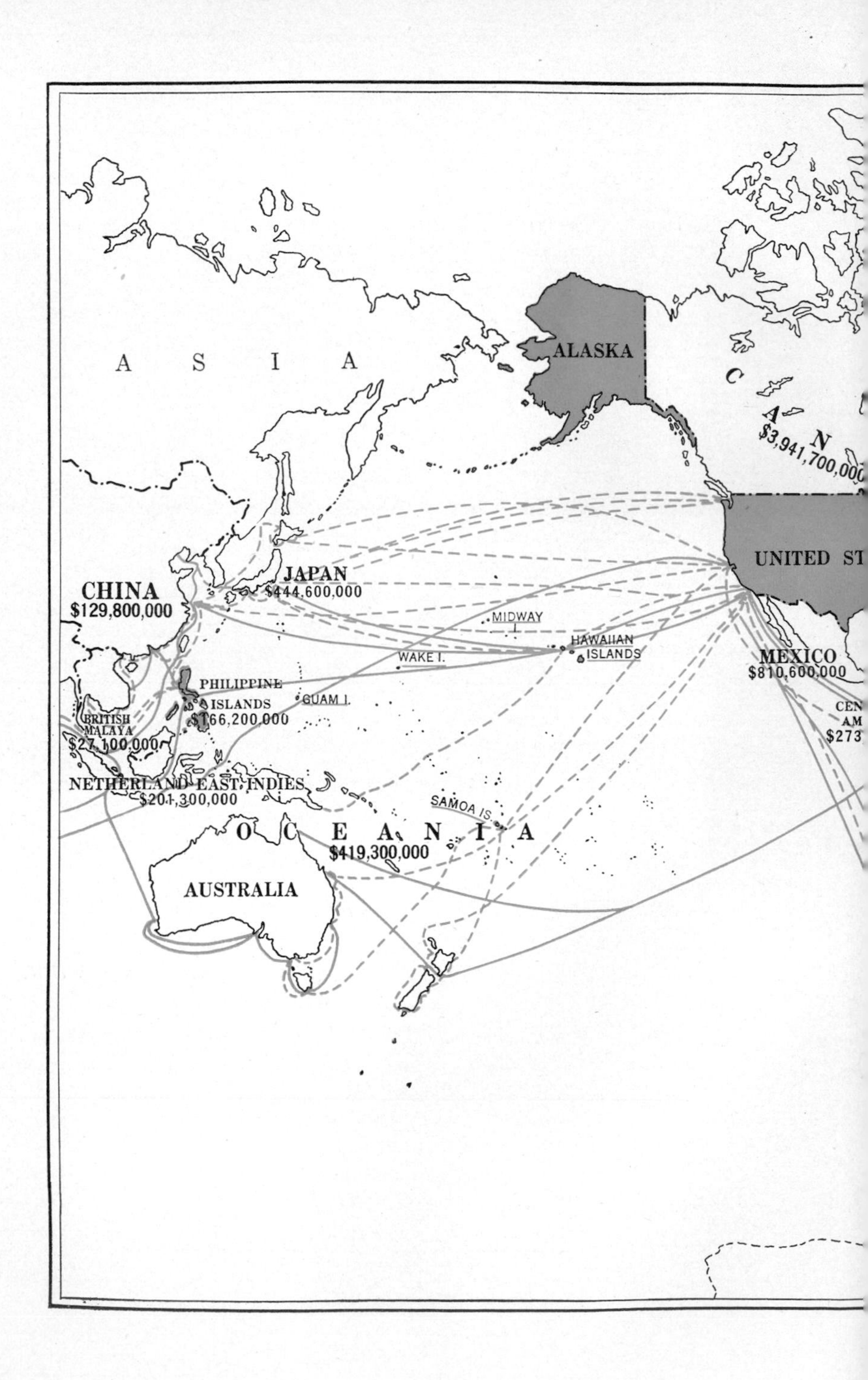

A S I A
ALASKA
C A N
$3,941,700,000
UNITED ST
CHINA
$129,800,000
JAPAN
$444,600,000
MIDWAY I.
HAWAIIAN ISLANDS
WAKE I.
MEXICO
$810,600,000
PHILIPPINE ISLANDS
$166,200,000
GUAM I.
BRITISH MALAYA
$27,100,000
NETHERLAND EAST INDIES
$201,300,000
SAMOA IS.
O C E A N I A
$419,300,000
AUSTRALIA

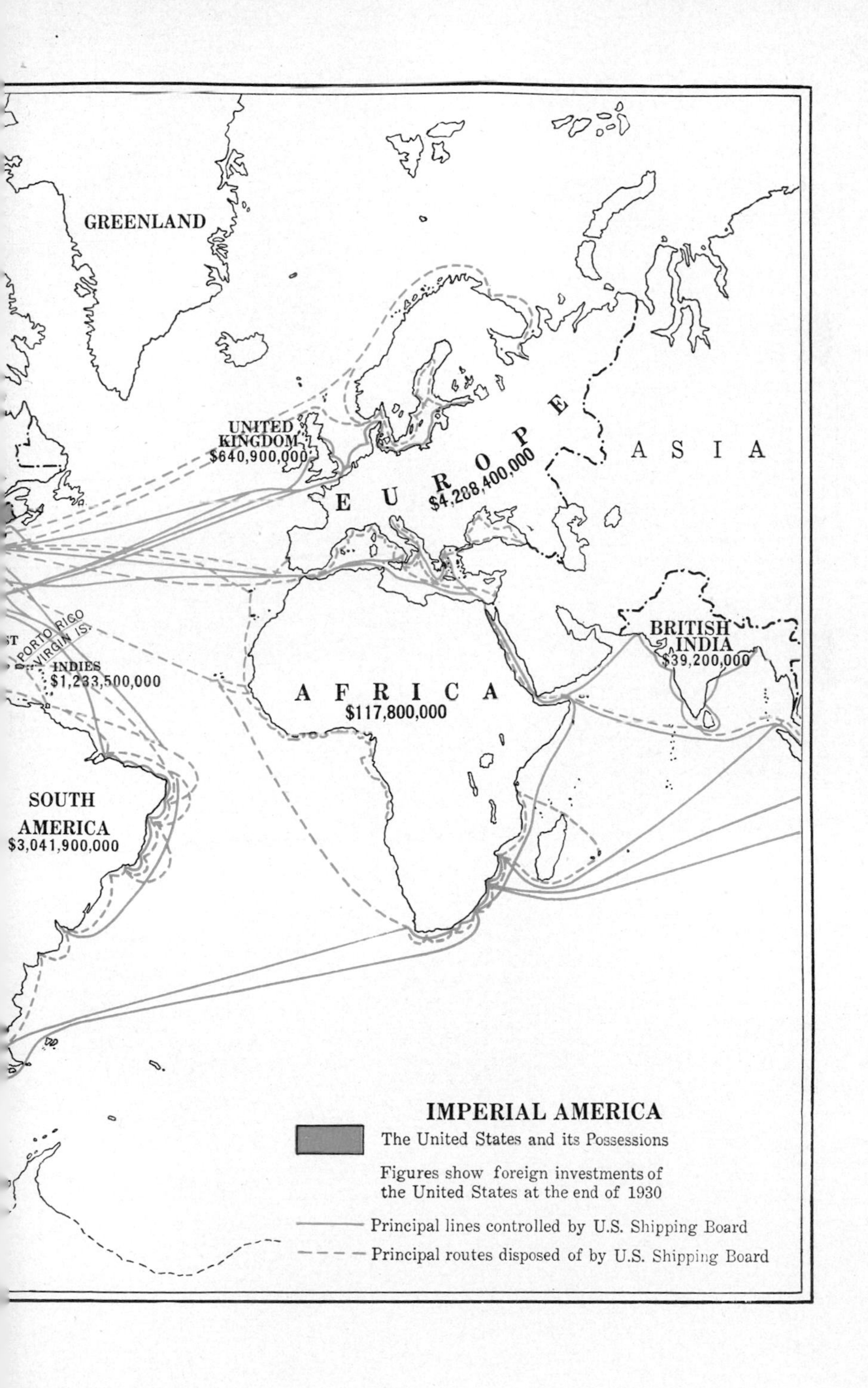
GREENLAND
UNITED KINGDOM
$640,900,000
E U R O P E
$4,288,400,000
A S I A
PORTO RICO
VIRGIN IS.
INDIES
$1,233,500,000
A F R I C A
$117,800,000
BRITISH INDIA
$39,200,000
SOUTH AMERICA
$3,041,900,000
IMPERIAL AMERICA
The United States and its Possessions
Figures show foreign investments of the United States at the end of 1930
Principal lines controlled by U.S. Shipping Board
Principal routes disposed of by U.S. Shipping Board

largely our agricultural wares to meet the charges on our foreign financial obligations; after the war, we became a creditor nation, exporting manufactured goods and capital and with the favorable balances forcing our economic penetration into every land on the face of the earth. Indeed, it may be said that an important key to the prosperity of the twenties was to be found exactly at this point. We had, in our foreign trade, a heavy commodity balance in our favor. On the one hand, to permit foreign nations to pay their balances, we extended them credits; and on the other, we bought from them their physical properties—their manufacturing plants, plantations, mines, public utility concessions, and the like. We may anticipate our story just a little by pointing out that when foreign peoples no longer could continue paying the services on the loans we made them, our commodity exports declined—and depression then set in in the American industrial sector.

Although, on the basis of visible items (that is to say, exports and imports of merchandise and specie), the international payments of the United States left the country each year in possession of a favorable balance, we were actually a debtor nation until the outbreak of the World War. This was due to the fact that the invisible items in our foreign transactions—interest payments on foreign capital invested here, American tourists' expenditures abroad, immigrants' remittances, freight charges, and insurance premiums—came to more than a half-billion dollars a year (average) over the eighteen years from 1896 to 1914. The fact is, over the eighteen years in question, the flow outward of goods, specie, and services added up to some thirty-two billions of dollars, while the flow inward had totaled considerably more than thirty-three billions of dollars. Thus, the balance against us was more than one billion dollars; and this amount was again added to the investments that foreigners had accumulated in American enterprises. At the turn of the century, such investments had totaled $3,330,000,000. By the end of 1914, these holdings of foreigners had amounted to four and one-half billions of dollars. Of course, in the same period, American capital had penetrated into Canada, Mexico, and the Caribbean lands, and these foreign interests of ours were worth in the neighborhood of one and one-half billion dollars. But when all transactions were balanced, the United States was still heavily a debtor nation in 1914.

All this the war changed. The warring nations of Europe needed

American foodstuffs, manufactured articles, and munitions of war. They paid for these by returning here American securities, by gold shipments, and by heavy borrowings. The result was, the end of the war period saw Europe deeply in our debt; and the subsequent years saw that debt steadily mounting, rather than otherwise. A series of circumstances contributed to the change in the balance of American international payments: our exports, particularly of manufactured goods, increased greatly; the revival of the American merchant marine reduced freight payments to foreign carriers; the restriction on foreign immigration began to cut heavily into immigrants' remittances; Europe began to pay us interest charges, instead of the reverse. In the transactions of the war years 1914–1918, alone, our favorable balance was almost eight and one-half billions of dollars; in each subsequent year until 1930, the balance in our favor was fully one billion dollars. Indeed, at the end of 1930, because there were no real offsets to counterbalance American export surpluses and the interest payments due us, the rest of the world was in our debt to the amount of sixteen billions, which took the form of private long-term American investments abroad in government loans and physical properties.

This, then, is what happened to the many billions of dollars making up America's favorable trade balances, particularly in the years following 1914. The capital was left abroad: to help finance the Allied cause; to rehabilitate the currency systems of Germany, France, and Italy; to maintain the Weimar Republic in the postwar years; to build harbors in Jugoslavia and strategic military railroads in Poland; to give Mussolini in Italy a chance to stabilize his position; to erect American branch factories in Canada, Ireland, Italy, and Scandinavia; to mine tin in Bolivia, drill oil wells in Mexico, Venezuela, and Iraq; to lay out rubber plantations in the Netherlands East Indies, banana plantations in Central America, and sugar plantations in Cuba. Thus the surplus products of the American farms, mines, and factories took us far afield and bound American destinies in a thousand and one intimate ties with the political stability of Latin America, Asia, and postwar Europe and with the maintenance of capitalist institutions everywhere.

At the end of 1930, according to the Bureau of Foreign and Domestic Commerce, American private long-term investments abroad amounted roughly to $16,000,000,000. Of this, half represented direct investments, that is, ownership of factories, mines, sales agencies, and the like; and half portfolio investments, that is, ownership of foreign securities of both a public and a private character. The table below shows the distribution of these various forms of investment, by principal world areas.

AMERICAN PRIVATE INVESTMENTS ABROAD AT END OF 1930

(In millions of dollars)

Area	*Direct*	*Portfolio*	*Total*
Canada	$2,048.8	$1,892.9	$3,941.7
Mexico, Caribbean, and Central America	2,002.9	562.0	2,564.9
South America	1,631.0	1,410.9	3,041.9
Europe	1,468.6	3,460.6	4,929.2
Asia and the Pacific	599.4	909.8	1,509.2
Africa	115.3	2.5	117.8
Total	$7,866.0	$8,238.7	$16,104.7

It is important to examine, because of their effects on domestic American economy, the nature of the industrial distribution of the direct investments. Fully a fifth of the total amount invested directly in other lands ($1,534,000,000) was to be found in manufacturing enterprises, which, for the most part, may be said to compete in the export markets with American industries manned by American labor. What were the chief economic reasons for this factory expansion beyond our own borders? These may be cited: 1. The nationalist protective tariff policies of other nations, which made importations from the United States to a large degree prohibitive as well as unpopular. In other words, our saved capital permitted us to tunnel under the high protective tariff walls notably of the European nations. 2. The desire, on the part of other countries, to build up native industry. 3. The stipulation, by many nations, that articles protected by their own patent laws were to be manufactured in local plants. 4. The economies that could be effected in distribution, marketing, and labor costs. 5. The nearness to raw materials or the presence of a particular type of local skill. (This accounted for American-owned cork factories in Spain, embroidery shops in Madeira, fancy glove works in France, and burlap plants in India.) 6. The absence of ample credit facilities, for purposes of rebuilding and expansion, in postwar Europe. (This factor made it necessary for many European industrialists to sell minority rights to American corporations or, to prevent their own submergence, to become the licensees of powerful American groups.) 7. Access to monopoly colonial markets (as in the case of the French possessions) or to national raw material monopolies (as in the case of camphor in Japan, potash in France and Germany, etc.). The result was that in 1932 American manufacturers of automotive vehicles had seventy-six foreign units; of radios and phonographs, thirty-one foreign units; of telephones, thirty-two foreign units; of agricultural implements, ten foreign units; of heating and ventilating equipment, forty-four foreign units; of petroleum refining, sixty-one foreign units; of rubber manufactures, forty-one foreign units. An incomplete count showed in the field of manufactures alone 1520 such branch and subsidiary plants employing more than a quarter of a million foreign workers.

In addition to direct manufacturing operations abroad, the following other foreign capitalist activities by Americans are to be noted: 1. Investments in sales organizations, worth $362,000,000. 2. Ownership of communication and transportation properties, worth $1,609,800,000. 3. Investments in oil lands, refineries, and petroleum distribution agencies, worth $1,117,900,000. (The petroleum lands were largely situated in Mexico and Venezuela, with significant holdings in Argentina, Bolivia, Colombia, Peru, Iraq, China, and Angola.) 4. Ownership of mines and smelters, worth $1,185,200,000. (Copper properties were held in Canada, Chile, Mexico, and Peru; iron mines in Cuba; nickel mines in Canada; vanadium mines in Peru; tin mines in Bolivia; nitrate deposits in Chile.) 5. Investments in agricultural lands worth $874,500,000. (In Cuba and Santo Domingo, Americans grew sugar; in other Caribbean areas, fruits; in the Far East, Brazil, and Liberia, rubber; in Mexico, guayule rubber and cattle.) 6. Investments in the paper and pulp industry, $278,900,000. 7. In miscellaneous enterprises (general merchandising, banking, ocean shipping under foreign registries, the motion picture industry, real estate, etc.), $907,000,000.[7]

This single fact is of the utmost significance to an understanding of America's world position in the postwar era: these extraordinary

[7] In 1938, when the Bureau of Foreign and Domestic Commerce presented new figures for American direct investments abroad, it was able to report an appreciable decline in only one sector—agricultural properties. And this was due almost entirely to the poor economic position of sugar.

capital operations were not an ephemeral phenomenon which grew out of the unprecedented prosperity of the decade of the twenties. They had become a permanent characteristic of the American capitalist-imperialist economy, as inexorable in their ebb and flow as the tides. The fact is, the depression of 1930 and after affected our position only in detail. At the end of 1936, the total of direct investments stood at $6,816,000,000, while the total of portfolio investments was at $4,741,000,000, and the grand total was $11,557,000,000. It will be noted that the shrinkage was largely in the portfolio investment category; and this was due to the sinking-fund operations and redemptions of dollar bonds by foreign governments. The table below shows the situation regionally.

AMERICAN PRIVATE INVESTMENTS ABROAD AT END OF 1936

(In millions of dollars)

Area	*Direct*	*Portfolio*	*Total*
Canada	$1,952	$1,647	$3,599
Mexico, Caribbean, and Central America	1,381	166	1,547
South America	1,466	1,354	2,820
Europe	1,245	1,949	3,194
Asia and the Pacific	528	623	1,151
Africa	93	2	95
International	26	.....	26
Total	$6,691	$5,741	$12,432
Add bank capital	125	.....	125
Deduct estimated net repurchases by foreigners	.....	1,000	1,000
Net Total	$6,816	$4,741 *	$11,557

* The reported value of American portfolio investments abroad represents almost wholly the par value of foreign dollar bonds held by investors in this country. In 1936, the market value as a per cent of par value of this class of investment was 74.7; thus the values were not inflated very much.

It is significant to note, as well, that despite depression American capital investments abroad were earning very large returns. So, in 1935, the total thus credited to our account was $521,000,000, and in 1936, $568,000,000. Only one aspect of the picture had changed: the great growth of foreign-held investments in the United States, occasioned by political uncertainties in Europe. Europeans, largely, were pouring long-term and short-term capital into this country—in 1936, foreigners here possessed property claims worth $7,600,-000,000 [8]—in order to buy American stocks and bonds, to maintain bank balances, and to acquire direct investments. On these accounts, in 1935, we paid out to foreigners $171,000,000, and in 1936, $238,000,000. The following table presents the comparative situation of these data for the twenties and thirties.

Annual average	*Interest and dividends paid by foreigners to U. S.*	*Interest and dividends paid by us to foreigners*	*Balance in our favor*
	(In millions of dollars)		
1921–1925	$381	$138	$243
1926–1930	865	328	537
1931–1935	525	114	411

What was the significance of these depression experiences? Two conclusions could be drawn and both were ominous: 1. That even in a period of sharp crisis American foreign holdings were not seriously jeopardized if they were controlled directly. In the light of such a situation it was possible to predict that the continuance of depression would have the result in time of turning American attention sharply outward in order to extend political or economic control over backward regions. For only so could the security of our great stake overseas be assured, the uninterrupted flow of interest and profits from plantations, mines, railroads, public utilities and branch plants in Latin America and the Far East guaranteed—and continued outlets for saved capital found. It was no accident, therefore, that President Franklin D. Roosevelt and Secretary of State Hull were so closely interested in what was occurring in China, Mexico, and Brazil. 2. That the presence of such heavy investments on the part of Europeans in the United States constituted a source of very real danger to us in the event of the outbreak of war in Europe. These investments could be sold by foreign governments here and in this way materials needed for war could be purchased; an industrial boom could thus be started; and before we would be aware of it our fortunes would be linked with those of our outstanding belligerent purchasers and creditors. In this fashion

[8] This was an official estimate. In 1938, unofficial estimates were putting the figure at considerably over eight billions of dollars!

we had been dragged into the first World War. Obviously, what was required was federal control of some sort over the operations of foreign capital in the United States, notably in time of war.

America's foreign trade almost doubled from the opening of the century to the year of the outbreak of the World War; by 1916, it had doubled again; and by 1929 it was, in value, four and a half times as great as in 1900. On the other hand, the extraordinary drop in our foreign trade after 1930 was an outstanding characteristic of continued depression. The accompanying table indicates, in summary form, this situation.

EXPORTS AND IMPORTS OF MERCHANDISE, 1901–1935

(Figures in thousands of dollars)

Yearly average	*Total exports & imports*	*Total exports*	*Total imports*	*Excess of exports*
1901–05	$2,426,000	$1,454,000	$ 972,000	$ 482,000
1906–10	3,124,000	1,779,000	1,345,000	434,000
1911–15	4,083,000	2,371,000	1,712,000	659,000
1916–20	9,879,000	6,521,000	3,358,000	3,163,000
1921–25	7,847,000	4,397,000	3,450,000	947,000
1926–30	8,810,000	4,777,000	4,033,000	744,000
1931–35	3,738,000	2,025,000	1,713,000	312,000

It is important to note two facts in connection with our foreign trade: that the proportion of the country's movable goods exported declined rather than otherwise; and that significant changes took place in the kinds of goods we bought and sold. The first phenomenon was due to the constant expansion of our domestic market; the second, to the fact that our national economy, from being largely an agricultural one, became more and more industrial in its characteristics. The table on page 140 shows the national output of movable commodities and the proportion exported, for selected years.

Before the turn of the century, America exported agricultural products largely and imported large quantities of manufactured and semi-manufactured goods. By the opening of the World War, the export of non-agricultural products had caught up with products of the farm and plantation; by the twenties, manufactured goods had outdistanced agricultural products. The result was, we were now exporting manufactured wares, and importing foodstuffs

PRODUCTION OF MOVABLE GOODS AND PROPORTION EXPORTED

(In millions of dollars)

Year	*Agricultural products*	*Manufactures*	*Mining*	*Freight receipts (R.R.'s)*	*Total*	*Exports U.S. merchandise*	*Per cent of total*
1899	$ 3,355	$ 4,831	$ 600	$ 981	$ 9,767	$1,253	12.8
1914	8,165	9,675	1,450	2,082	21,372	2,071	9.7
1919	17,677	24,748	3,158	3,625	49,208	7,750	15.7
1929	11,851	31,687	4,200	4,899	52,587	5,157	9.8
1933	6,128	14,538	1,750	2,529	24,945	1,647	6.6
1935	8,010	21,700	2,600	2,831	35,141	2,243	6.4

and raw materials. The percentages in the accompanying table reveal the profound change that had taken place in but thirty years.

EXPORTS OF MERCHANDISE, BY GROUPS

(In terms of per cents of totals)

Yearly average	*Total*	*Agricultural products*	*Non-agricultural products*
1896–1900	100.0	66.2	33.8
1911–1915	100.0	49.7	50.3
1916–1920	100.0	42.1	57.9
1926–1930	100.0	36.1	63.9
1931–1935	100.0	36.8	63.2

The following table indicates what were the ten leading exports of United States merchandise, on the basis of their 1936 ranking. The figures are those for values in millions and tenths of millions of dollars.

	1926–1930 average	*1936*
Cotton, unmanufactured	$765.7	$361.0
Machinery (inc. office appliances)	488.0	334.9
Petroleum and products	524.4	260.8
Automobile parts and accessories	406.2	240.2
Tobacco, unmanufactured	144.5	137.3
Chemicals	137.4	116.9
Iron and steel products	170.7	111.9
Fruits and nuts	122.2	80.6
Coal and coke	121.8	56.6
Copper (inc. ore manufactures)	150.0	50.7

There is a question that arises at this point: If in the past twenty-five years rarely more than 10 per cent annually of our total production of movable exports was exported, could we cut ourselves off completely from the rest of the world without seriously deranging the finely adjusted mechanisms of our capitalist system? The answer was, No; for when the crude figures for movable goods were broken down, it was possible to perceive at once that some of our basic agricultural, mineral, and heavy industries, as well as a great variety of newly developed light ones, were closely bound up with the existence of a world market. The following table shows the percentage of the product of certain industries exported.

	1914	*1929*	*1933*	*1936*
Tobacco leaf	47.2	41.2	39.3	33.4
Cotton	62.6	54.8	65.6	56.1
Phosphate rock	70.5	41.0	45.0	52.8 *
Meat products	10.5	10.2	6.6	2.0
Canned salmon	27.9	12.2	8.7	15.7 *
Wheat	19.7	17.9	5.4	2.5
Fresh apples	5.5	15.5	13.0	9.9
Dried fruits	19.7	46.0	39.1	†
Canned fruits	22.3	22.8	20.8	†
Gum resin	62.8	60.8	54.5	54.8
Refined mineral oils	37.9	19.6	11.9	9.9 *
Copper, refined	54.8	36.2	41.0	32.1
Printing and book-binding machinery	18.0	27.6	38.8	†
Office appliances	23.6	30.2	26.1	23.2 *
Agricultural implements and machinery	†	25.1	29.8	10.6 *
Automobiles	4.5	12.9	7.3	8.0
Aircraft and parts	†	11.6	30.2	29.2 *

* Data for 1935. † Not recorded.

Who bought our wares? Not Europe, largely, as had been the case in the second half of the nineteenth century, but the Western Hemisphere and Asia. To Europe still went our cotton, meats, and grains; to the other portions of the globe went our manufactured goods, and because this second category was becoming increasingly the more important, we were beginning to find the chief outlets for our products in the less developed countries of the earth. The following percentages show the changes that took place in our markets.

GEOGRAPHIC DISTRIBUTION OF EXPORT TRADE

(Figures in per cents)

Geographic sections	*Yearly average* 1896–1900	1921–1925	1926–1930	1931–1935
Canada and Newfoundland	6.9	14.3	17.4	14.8
Latin North America	5.6	10.1	8.4	8.0
South America	3.1	6.8	9.4	7.0
Europe	76.7	52.7	46.8	47.4
Asia	3.9	11.3	12.0	17.3
Oceania	2.3	3.2	3.7	2.4
Africa	1.5	1.6	2.3	3.1

What did we buy? The following tabulation indicates, by percentages, the character of the goods we imported in selected years over the period under examination. It is to be observed that in the categories "semi-manufactures" and "finished manufactures" copper, newsprint, and vegetable oils bulked large in the nineteen twenties and thirties, while they were comparatively insignificant at the turn of the century.

IMPORTS OF MERCHANDISE, BY GROUPS

(In terms of per cents of totals)

Yearly average	*Total*	*Crude materials*	*Crude foodstuffs*	*Manufactured foodstuffs*	*Semi-manufactures*	*Finished manufactures*
1896–1900	100.0	29.5	15.1	15.9	13.3	26.2
1921–1925	100.0	37.4	11.1	13.0	17.6	20.9
1926–1930	100.0	36.8	12.6	9.9	18.9	21.9
1931–1935	100.0	28.9	15.6	13.7	18.7	23.0

While we prided ourselves upon being a self-contained nation, indeed were so to an extraordinary degree (only Russia being our equal), American industry in reality depended upon many imported articles not merely for its continued prosperity but often for its very existence. Thus, in the manufacture of steel alone we imported some forty different commodities from more than fifty countries. Manganese, for instance, employed in the manufacture of high tensile steel, was imported from Russia, Brazil, the Gold Coast, and India, for the domestic output supplied but one-tenth of our annual needs. All our nickel had to be imported (from Canada), all our tin (from the Malay Peninsula, the Netherlands East Indies, and Bolivia), much of our iron ore (from Cuba, Sweden, Spain, and North Africa), and considerable parts of our antimony, pyrites, asbestos, ferrosilicon, asphalt, bauxite, and graphite. Our silk imports (from Japan and China) kept the wheels of a great domestic industry going; combing, clothing, and carpet wools (from Argentina, New Zealand, and Australia) were needed to supplement our local supplies; we imported long-staple cotton from Egypt and India; newsprint and woodpulp from Canada; crude rubber from the Malay Peninsula and the Netherlands East Indies; burlap from India; furs from Russia, Germany, and Belgium; palm oil from British West Africa; and copra from Oceania. All these, it will be noted, were necessary for American industrial requirements and did not include the imported foodstuffs, which in time of national crisis we might dispense with or find substitutes for.

The tabulation below shows the relations between imports and home production of some of the vital materials for which we were dependent upon outside countries. The figures give the proportion of apparent consumption during 1925–1929 that imports represented.

Commodities imported	*Imports as per cent of apparent consumption*
Minerals:	
Asbestos	100.0
Graphite (amorphous)	71.8
Graphite (crystalline)	80.6
Iodine	100.0
Magnesite	51.2
Mica (sheet)	73.9
Nitrates (Chilean)	100.0
Potash	86.5
Metals:	
Antimony	100.0
Bauxite	40.2
Chrome ore	100.0
Manganese	92.1
Nickel	97.7
Platinum	95.1
Tin	100.0
Tungsten	76.1
Vanadium	63.1

Commodities imported	*Imports as per cent of apparent consumption*
Agricultural wares:	
Camphor	100.0
Cattle hides	23.1
Coconuts	100.0
Flax fiber	100.0
Flax seed	49.6
Jute	100.0
Manila fiber	100.0
Rubber	100.0
Shellac	100.0
Silk	100.0
Foods:	
Bananas	100.0
Cacao beans	100.0
Coffee	100.0
Tea	100.0
Sugar (cane and beet)	82.5

We may obtain an idea of how large a part these vital imports played in the American economy by noting the values of the more important imports for the period 1926–1930 (the figure given in each case is the annual average): coffee, $281,700,000; cane sugar, $207,300,000; crude rubber, $294,400,000; raw silk, $368,200,000; newsprint, $134,200,000; paper and manufactures, $151,200,000; paper base stocks, $114,500,000; tin, $88,900,000; furs and manufactures, $114,800,000; hides and skins, $118,000,000; burlaps,

GEOGRAPHIC DISTRIBUTION OF IMPORT TRADE

(Figures in per cents)

Geographic sections	*Yearly average* 1896–1900	1921–1925	1926–1930	1931–1935
Canada and Newfoundland	5.0	11.5	11.9	13.8
Latin North America	10.3	14.9	11.4	10.3
South America	13.2	12.2	13.5	14.3
Europe	52.6	30.4	29.9	30.1
Asia	14.6	27.3	29.7	28.6
Oceania	3.1	1.6	1.3	.9
Africa	1.3	2.1	2.3	1.9

$72,300,000; wool and mohair, $78,800,000; cocoa, $45,500,000; flax, hemp, and ramie products, $44,300,000; tea, $27,000,000; nickel, $12,500,000.

As we might expect, in view of the changed character of our imports, the sources of our foreign-bought commodities changed markedly. How little we were really dependent upon Europe the tabulation at the foot of page 144 reveals with startling clarity.

VI. LIFE, LETTERS, AND ART IN THE MACHINE AGE

Characteristics of the American Scene

The splendor of the America of the Machine Age was everywhere visibly expressed. Never had there been a people in the history of civilization who might lay claim to possessing so much of this world's goods. The bountifulness of nature and the ingenuity of man had combined, it seemed, to make postwar United States a great, rich, happy land. Foreigners, visiting our shores for the first time, found much to astonish them: the dazzling shops, the comfortable homes, the ever-present automobile, the free spending and the high standards of living; these seemed common characteristics, to be viewed alike in the mighty metropolises and the smaller inland towns. That the pattern was not a uniform one, Americans themselves every now and then remembered: a short distance to the east or west of every Fifth Avenue in the land was still to be seen a wretched slum; while the Valley of Democracy's new industrial cities were beehives of activity, New England's mill towns were the helpless victims of a growing dry rot; America's new industries were keeping steadily employed millions of the working population, yet the share-cropper of Arkansas, the bituminous coal miner of West Virginia, and the wheat farmer tilling the submarginal lands of the Far West lived in a round of abject poverty and mute despair.

America was rich. Was there a better sign to be found than the zeal with which her well-to-do citizens vied with one another in disposing of large parts of their wealth? Certainly, only a confident expectation that fortune would continue to smile on their efforts could account for the munificence of American philanthropic endeavor. Well might the wealthy part with their surpluses: that their positions were secure could not be denied. Well might the toilers with hand and brain buy automobiles, radios, single-family houses, electric washing machines, and fur coats: that the machine's happy round would never cease was the expectation of every American who was living in the wonder days of the nineteen twenties.

The era of the machine brought great fortunes for the rich and put comforts within the reach of many workers. It was small wonder that the whole life of America should move in its accelerated tempo. One of the most interesting characteristics of the period was the fact that the whole country seemed to become a prolongation of what Sinclair Lewis so aptly denominated Main Street. The questing for money, the endless round of making goods and buying and selling them, evidently had become the peculiar hallmark of our civilization until America took on all the aspects of one great market place. One might travel almost endlessly through thousands of communities without truly appreciating that the outskirts of one municipality had been left behind and the heart of another already reached. Those real differences of local tradition and habit which had set the American towns of the nineteenth century apart from each other had been inexorably destroyed. We were no longer living in Concord or Camden or Glens Falls or Wichita but in Middletown: where we all listened to the same radio programs, saw the same motion pictures, traveled in the same automobiles, and read the same feature stories and columnists in the newspapers.

The machine had blotted out provincialism everywhere; and everybody was harnessed in the service of the machine. The Lynds, in that searching inquiry which they called *Middletown*, were moved to wonder by the spectacle of a people ceaselessly at work. The question they phrased was often on the lips of intelligent observers during the postwar era: "One emerges from the offices, stores, and factories of Middletown asking in some bewilderment why all the able-bodied men and many of the women devote their best energies for long hours, day after day, to this driving activity, seemingly so foreign to many of the most powerful impulses of human beings." Certainly not for leisure, for even pleasure was pursued with the same grim determination. Certainly not for security, for it was plainly evident that the working American spent his surpluses on semi-durable consumer goods—in fact, became heavily involved in the system of instalment buying in order to acquire those articles which every billboard assured him he could not do without.

Was it for culture? Indeed, there was to be found a serious preoccupation with the things of the spirit: America's educational plants, her scientific endowments, her research organizations, her great company of creative workers in all the arts made a mighty exhibit. In America, a true taste had appeared and was spreading. Yet, even here, two reservations were necessary. The observation was justly made by both foreigners and native Americans that much of the country's cultural life was sustained by its women. The machine had released the American woman from the drudgery of the kitchen, and the rich returns from industrial enterprise had poured into her purse available funds with which to indulge her caprices and nourish her tastes. The American woman, in short, was free and had money to spend. That Mrs. Francis Neilson should support that excellent critical journal the old *Freeman* and Mrs. Willard Straight should support the *New Republic;* that Mrs. H. O. Havemeyer, Mrs. Chester Dale, Miss Lizzie Bliss, Mrs. Gertrude V. Whitney, and Mrs. John D. Rockefeller, Jr. should be among the great art patrons of the day; that hundreds of thousands of women in the land, through their clubs, should make the vocations of literature and musical composition possible by the financial encouragement they gave America's artists—these were signs of the times.

Again, while so many phases of the country's institutional life were so rich and various, and there was so much in the America of the Machine Age of which one could be justly proud, the question could still be raised: Did the influences of all these shoot through and color our works so that ours was something more than a fortunate civilization? There were many doubters. Illiteracy, child labor, disease, economic insecurity, a corroding poverty—these still existed. And while they flourished side by side with material plenty, one found it hard to believe that America had already produced a creative and purposeful civilization. Our institutional modes were a scaffolding: it still remained for the future to erect that common life of which it could be said that it had enriched the heritage of man.

Some Aspects of American Society

It was generally held that in modern America the tradition of early Puritanism still survived. How otherwise account for the great memberships in the Protestant dissenting churches, their evangelical zeal both abroad and at home, and the crusades these regularly fostered against the saloon and intemperance, cigarette-smoking, and an "immoral" stage? A count in 1930 found that the total number of church communicants in the country was in the neighborhood of 50,000,000 persons, of whom 9,200,000 were members of the Baptist Church, 9,119,000 of the Methodist Church, 2,800,000 of the Lutheran Church, and 2,670,000 of the Presbyterian Church. It was true, too, that in certain areas of the country, particularly in the South and trans-Mississippi West, evangelical Christianity was a living force. But by and large it may be said that during the whole period of the early twentieth century, the influence of the country's churches was very rapidly slipping.

A number of reasons might be cited for this state of affairs. Protestant Christianity, particularly in the evangelical sects, was rent by a great doctrinal struggle between the Fundamentalists and the Modernists. The Fundamentalists, despite the teachings of modern science and the doubts thrown on the inspired character of the Testaments by biblical scholarship, still clung tenaciously to the tenets of primitive Christianity. So deadly in earnest was this party that during the nineteen twenties it succeeded in having passed in the legislatures of Tennessee, Arkansas, and Mississippi bills forbidding the teaching of the doctrine of evolution in all institutions of learning supported out of public funds. The Dayton (Tennessee) trial of 1925 of a young schoolman who had violated the anti-evolution law and the resulting conviction of the defendant brought the Fundamentalists world-wide notoriety. Opposed to the Fundamentalists were the Modernists, who surrendered entirely their belief in a literal interpretation of the Bible. Such schismatic disputes only succeeded in bewildering the average church attendant; if his attention was only half held by the Protestant churches, the fault was more with his leaders than with him. The inability of the Protestant churches to resolve their differences under the head of a real denominational union was another reason for the prevailing dissatisfaction with institutional religion. While the Federal Council of Churches of Christ in America did make its appearance in 1908 its achievement was not very significant. Americans continued to go to church—when the pull of the automobile and the golf links was not too great—but the influence of organized Protestantism among the contemporary vital forces was definitely of a minor character.

The position of Catholicism, certainly in its outward aspects, seemed to be more secure. Its numbers and its institutional life were impressive: in 1930, the Catholic population of the country was in excess of twenty million persons, of whom more than two million were children in regular attendance in parish schools; too, the Catholic hierarchy supported a ramified system of educational plants and eleemosynary institutions, and publicly avowed an advanced program of social action (though steadfastly conservative as far as divorce and birth control were concerned). The acceptance of the leadership of Rome and the important parts played by Roman Catholics in the politics of some of our Eastern and Middle Western municipalities made the faith conspicuous; nevertheless, the Church's influence on modern living was hardly commensurate with its numbers and the apparent devotion of its members.

André Siegfried, that acute French observer, summed up the place of religion in the United States of the Machine Age in these words:

> Thus, no matter where we turn, everyday materialism is tending to encroach on spiritual life. Neither Protestantism nor Catholicism is threatened from without by aggressive disbelief, for the agnostics, though numerous, maintain the Protestant vocabulary and the Protestant outlook on moral problems. They like its background and are not hostile in any way. . . . In America, the dominant force that is threatening to carry everything before it, Protestant, Catholic, and Jew, is the obsession for tangible and material accomplishments.

Another great institution to flourish during the period was philanthropy. By the third decade of the twentieth century, organized charity had become one of America's major activities. Charity had started out by being a simple process of good works, financed by benevolent individuals and conducted by generous souls who were touched by the sufferings of the poor. As Abraham Epstein has said of the pioneer social workers: "They were imbued with a spiritual yearning which was both contagious and inspiring. They blazed the trail to many most significant reforms. Prevention of distress and misery by fundamental programs of protection and social legislation was their dominant keynote." Such had been the impulses that had directed the work of Jane Addams, E. T. Devine, Owen Lovejoy, Simon Patten, and Graham Taylor. By the nineteen twenties it was apparent that charity had undergone a complete metamorphosis. It was no longer concerned with economic and social evils but with "individual maladjustments"; it did not try to cope with the great problems of dependency—unemployment, old age, invalidity—but it devoted itself to straightening out the personal psychological, functional, and vocational kinks of its "clients"; it was no longer occasional but organized and routinized like so much of the rest of our institutional round. In the Machine Age the social worker, from being something of a lay preacher, had become the active directing genius of a local community chest, which once a year raised a lump sum varying from $100,000 to $5,000,000 for distribution among a great host of charitable societies, of different degrees of usefulness. In the nineteen thirties, there were almost four hundred such organized groups in as many cities, spending as much as one hundred millions annually.

This was only one aspect of philanthropy's growing importance. The rôle of the foundation is not to be overlooked. From making regular and anonymous grants to individual charities, with the turn of the century wealthy men fell into the habit, increasingly, of setting aside a large sum in a single charitable trust usually to be devoted to a unified program. Andrew Carnegie led the way: he was quickly followed by John D. Rockefeller, Russell Sage, Julius Rosenwald, E. S. Harkness, and others until, by the thirties, there were some one hundred and fifty of these foundations or large charitable trusts in the land having a combined capitalization of one billion dollars! The Rockefeller Foundation, with a capitalization of $147,000,000, devoted itself to the "well-being of all mankind"; the Carnegie Foundation, with a capitalization of $135,000,000, was dedicated to the "diffusion of knowledge"; the Commonwealth Fund, with a capitalization of $30,000,000, spent its funds on child welfare projects; the Julius Rosenwald Fund, with a capitalization of $20,000,000, distributed principal and interest on Negro education, medical and hospital services, and other enterprises.

What were the reasons for these great benefactions? The slowness of American government to extend its activities into the whole realm of the social services, and the still generally accepted notion—at least, through the twenties—that failures in the economic race were to be regarded as objects of charity and not of public concern undoubtedly had much to do with the matter. In a land where "rugged individualism"—up to the inception of the New Deal, at any rate—was the key to social progress, the poor were inevitable and deserving. The rich frequently gave liberally from their surpluses in the belief that unrest among the masses was to be allayed in this fashion. The compulsory factor was not to be disregarded, for through the operations of organized charity, with its great publicity machinery, there were suggested threats of economic and social penalties to those who refused to participate. Finally and most important of all, there entered what Veblen has so illuminatingly called the element of conspicuous waste. Nobody was born to the purple in our middle-class America of the Machine Age, and being a millionaire had in it less claim to distinction than being the world's amateur golf champion, let us say. One of the surest ways of attaining recognition, and therefore community leadership, was through generous benefactions, no matter for what purpose.

Thus, through community chest drives, the grants from foundations, on private health, education, and other welfare-work programs—in other words, the whole business of philanthropy—the annual outlay was not far from one billion dollars. The benefits to be derived from this imperial munificence were easily apparent; but so were the evils. Philanthropy allowed for experimentation, the carrying out of activities in those spheres where public authority could not or would not enter, the relief of distress. Philanthropy, on the other hand, hindered the legitimate expansion of a public social program, too often expended its energies on blowing life into dead forms, and tied to its leading strings—making for regimentation and timidity—those educational and other institutions which were regularly dependent upon it for their growth, if not survival. Particularly in times of economic stress, one saw that philanthropy could scarcely scratch the surface of the problem of dependency. During the depression of 1930 and after, the burden of charitable relief of the unemployed fell not on private welfare agencies but on public authority: and another American institution virtually became a museum piece.

Greatest perhaps of all institutions was America's educational system. Public education had become firmly entrenched in the American scheme by the end of the nineteenth century, and the next three decades were to mark a steady progress onward. School attendance laws raised the compulsory school-going age until, in many jurisdictions, children through the age of sixteen were called upon to attend regular sessions; plants were modernized so that, often, the local public school took on all the aspects of a great athletic and social center, with fully equipped gymnasium, auditorium, swimming pool, and the like; a ceaseless experimentation was carried on in curriculums and special projects. Of marked interest were the development of the junior high school and junior college ideas and an effort to adjust the course of study to individual needs by the grouping of children according to their mental capacitics (through the use of the intelligence test). By the thirties, the public schools were well on the way to becoming significant laboratories for the study of child welfare problems, not merely educational but psychological and functional ones as well. The adding of child behavior clinics to public school systems, in the nineteen twenties, and the beginnings of serious experimentation with activity programs in the nineteen thirties, were notable achievements.

Secondary education made striking advances. From a half-million students attending high schools in the United States at the turn of the century there was by the end of the twenties an army of more than three and one-half million children enrolled in the same type of institutions. The curriculum here underwent less radical changes: formal disciplines were more closely adhered to, largely because the high school was still regarded as preparation for entrance into college; an entirely successful course of study had not yet appeared to meet the educational needs of boys and girls who were at school not by choice but because of the requirements of school attendance laws and the inability to obtain employment in industry. Yet public authority was making serious efforts to find the key to a puzzle which was not simple: the continuation school, the fully equipped technical high school, courses in art design, radio engineering, home economics, and the like, were common occurrences in the public secondary school systems of the modern era.

Nothing was more interesting to witness than the unanimity with which twentieth-century America accepted a collegiate education as a prime requisite for future success, whether the chosen career was to be in business, politics, or the professions. In 1900, but 224,000 young men and women were in attendance at colleges and universities; by 1930 their numbers had swelled to more than 900,000. Fully one-eighth of the country's population between the ages of 18 and 21 was registered in institutions of higher learning, at the end of the period we are examining; a boy or girl out of high school had almost one thousand halls of learning from which to choose, ranging from the great state universities and privately endowed educational centers (like the Universities of California, Wisconsin, Minnesota and Columbia, Harvard, Yale, Princeton), the scarcely less splendid half-dozen municipally supported colleges, to the more select smaller colleges (like Amherst, Smith, Vassar, Williams) and the many denominational colleges which dotted the East and Middle West.

That the colleges and universities should fit more and more into the institutional pattern of the times was no real occasion for surprise. Lay boards almost entirely supplanted the earlier clergymen who had directed the destinies of higher education in nineteenth-century America; the college curriculum was expanded to wide and perhaps strange limits as it tried to meet almost all the requirements of a complex mechanical age; in the place of the former presidents of the type of Eliot and Gilman one came to encounter more and more, at the helm of great institutions, resourceful, politically circumspect individuals whose chief task in many cases seemed to be the acquisition of physical properties, the piling up of endowments, and the wheedling of great budgets out of legislatures.

Certainly, the record was spotted—but only a rash individual would venture to say it was wholly black. If our college students appeared more frivolous than their European mates and athleticism was a high cult among them, one could also point to the little theaters, the real understanding of modern art movements, and the writing and editing of competent undergraduate literary journals. If, in an effort to be of service to all, many university courses were trivial, on the other hand it was not difficult to prove that the modern American university was better equipped for study and research in the physical, natural, and social sciences than any other similar plant on the face of the earth. Nor was it wanting for scholars. In the words of the Beards: ". . . they were right who claimed that learning in the American colleges of the Machine Age was more diverse, bolder, and more speculative, freer in spirit and more enlivened by the saving grace of humor than the same learning in earlier ages." Occasionally, a teacher whose views on social questions departed in a marked degree from the orthodox was dismissed; nevertheless it would be idle to believe that boards of trustees made it a practice to hunt out and punish all heresies. Finally, too, experimentation in the remodeling of curriculums was continuous.

Not only had churches, philanthropy, higher education become institutionalized: the same was true of the collection and dissemination of news and the creation of public opinion. Pulitzer and Hearst had found, by the turn of the century, that the conduct of a newspaper could be turned into an enterprise of Big Business, and although they did not part altogether with the traditions of personal journalism of the Middle Period they plainly indicated that the future of the newspaper lay in its ceaseless adaptation to the requirements of our mechanical age. And so it turned out to be. The successors of these earlier giants were commercial entrepreneurs first and journalists in but a limited sense. They banded newspapers together in great chains, placing before readers, every day, in Los Angeles, Omaha, New York, and Boston, the selfsame dish of Washington and foreign dispatches, feature articles, columns by syndicated writers, comics, and household hints; they bought up and abandoned local newspapers in order to reduce competition in particular cities; they depersonalized editorials and toned down opinion until it was scarcely possible to discern where a newspaper stood on the leading political, economic, and social questions of the day. More and more the American newspaper of the modern era came to regard itself as an agency for the informing and amusing of its readers rather than as a public tribune. That it became, also, a medium in which the wares of local merchants and to a lesser degree those of national corporations could be hawked was in a sense inevitable, for only from advertising revenues could the modern newspaper be supported. This state of affairs, at any rate, was the case up to the coming of the New Deal. Then, certainly from 1936 on, many newspapers became violently partisan once more, particularly when they were in opposition to President Franklin Roosevelt's policies. It really did not matter, however: for the election returns clearly showed that newspapers were no longer molding public opinion. In Chicago, for example, where three of the great dailies were anti-Roosevelt and but one paper, and a tabloid at that, supported the President, the Roosevelt majority was overwhelming.

That the *World* and the New York *Journal* of the nineties had not plumbed all the possibilities of popular journalism was demonstrated by another phenomenon of the age: the picture tabloid of the nineteen twenties. Sensing that there was a large group in the populace that cared neither for the complete news accounts nor for the rather intellectualized features of the standard papers, the publishers of the Chicago *Tribune* appeared in New York City, in 1919, with their *Daily News*—a smaller newspaper, made up of a maximum of photographs and a minimum of reading matter and devoted almost entirely to recitals of local occurrences. The *Daily News* became at once successful and was quickly followed by competitors: some ranged very low in an effort to gain the patronage of the illiterate and filled their pages with faked or so-called composite photographs, the confessions of notorious persons, the histories of gunmen, and scandal columns given over to the doings of the demimonde and the underworld. However, by the nineteen thirties, most of the more sensational tabloids had failed and the really competent ones—like the *Daily News*—became first-class newspapers.

The periodical press submitted to the same influences. In a hunt for a wider reading public (and therefore greater profits to be derived from their advertising columns) the magazines of the country definitely lowered their standards. From discussing seriously matters in the public eye and crusading for political and economic reform (after the fashion of the "muckraking" magazines), they become whole-hearted defenders of the reigning order of things, printing articles on the miraculous rise of humble boys to financial power, chanting the praises of politicians of mediocre talents, and purveying a type of standardized fiction in which the average American was made out to be a person who divided his time between gaining success in business, displaying his prowess on the golf links, and winning in marriage the beautiful daughter of his employer. The *Saturday Evening Post* and *Collier's* each brought these messages of cheer into more than two million American homes every week; every month the women's magazines—the *Ladies' Home Journal*, the *Woman's Home Companion*, *Pictorial Review*, and *McCall's*—did similarly. The so-called "quality magazines" were compelled to brighten up and popularize their pages in an effort to keep up with the times and make ends meet; not a few succumbed. There was a limited number of intelligent journals to which an educated American seriously interested in the art, literature, and public happenings of the day might turn; but survival among these, too, was hard in view of the fact that most of them were not self-supporting.

It has been said above that newspapers had become increasingly institutionalized; it is important to note, too, that the news they carried very frequently was colored by a peculiar and special-interest bias, not that of the newspaper proprietor necessarily but of the agencies upon which his editors and reporters were dependent for their information. With the growing complexity of our modern life, it was inevitable that large and articulate groups should appear that were particularly desirous of having their policies, methods, and intentions placed in their most favorable light before the American public. Whether it was a governmental agency in the midst of working out a costly program, or a philanthropy seeking financial support for a charity, or a labor organization confronted by an internal dispute, or a public utility corporation accused of levying a monopoly price on the consumers of its wares, or a reform society agitating for civic betterment—whatever the particular question of the moment, all found it to their interest to carry on their staffs "press agents" or "public relations counsels" or "publicity men" whose function it was to get into the news columns of the daily papers reading matter calculated to make friends and disarm criticism. It was only the person of rare discernment who could successfully, each day, as he made his way through the twenty or thirty pages of his newspaper, differentiate between the propaganda of the publicity offices and the news gathered by disinterested journalists. More and more, the average middle-class American was beginning to hold opinions that had been manufactured for him by the United States Department of Commerce or the American Legion or the American Federation of Labor or the American Railway Association or the Anti-Saloon League or his local chamber of commerce or community chest. To an extent, the fault was that of the newspaper proprietor, who had surrendered his independence to gain financial and social recognition; to an extent the fault could be placed on the doorstep of the typical American himself.

For the American of the Machine Age was a "joiner": never, apparently, was he so happy as when banded together with his neighbors and acquaintances in an association for the common furtherance of fraternal, business, moral, or athletic purposes. He lunched with an eating club, played golf or boated or swam at a country or yacht or beach club, heard business conditions discussed (often by a professional lecturer) at his chamber of commerce or the annual convention of his particular industry. He supported causes that were organized and incorporated; he agitated for social and political reforms because some astute person had flatteringly placed his name on the board of directors of an obscure, and often quite useless, society. And with each one of these associations, leagues, committees, and causes that he joined, he took over a new set of ready-made prejudices. This associational life the country's press sustained; and all these influences combined to make the articulate public opinion of the country routinized and deeply middle-class in almost all its loyalties.

Science in America

Where the wonders the machine performed were on all sides plainly in view, one had no cause for surprise at the large part that science played in the life of modern America. Every day patient workers in laboratories strove to perfect devices already in use or to invent new ones for the amusement, edification, and comfort of America's more than receptive buying public. The automobile, the airplane, the radio, the motion picture were but the more apparent triumphs of mind over matter in the period of which we are speaking. Of lesser social significance, but in their own ways equally important because they reduced physical labor or made life more secure or comfortable, were the advances made in physics, chemistry, biology, medicine, and the like. It is to be noted that the practical aspects of scientific progress are here stressed; although, in pure science, particularly in the nineteen twenties and thirties, Americans were making great strides. Our laboratory work was becoming the most significant in the world: and this was no cause for surprise, for pure research requires patronage—and patronage continued to survive in America despite the depression, for we had by no means reached the bottom of our resources.

It is to be recorded, however, that for the application of pure science to the uses of industry and commerce Americans apparently had a peculiar aptitude. The development of the automobile was particularly characteristic of our middle-class economy, both in the zeal with which mechanically gifted persons applied themselves to its improvement and in the readiness with which Americans accepted it as a vehicle for pleasure and business. In 1896 there were only four gasoline cars in the United States; by 1930, there were some 26,500,000 automobiles and trucks in general use. Americans did yeoman work in carrying on experiments with the early automobile; the names of Duryea, Haynes, Winton, Ford, Maxwell, Clarke, White, and Franklin stand out among those in a large gallery. With the perfection of the internal combustion engine, by the end of the first decade of the new century, the automobile was ready for commercial exploitation. How rapid the strides from then on were may be gauged from the figures for passenger car registration in the United States: 1910, 458,000; 1915, 2,310,000; 1920, 8,226,000; 1929, 23,122,000. The name of Henry Ford must always be joined with the great progress made by this new industry. In the early nineties he had completed his first car; just before the century closed he was manufacturing automobiles for commercial use; in 1908 he inaugurated a new era in American business when his now famous Model T went into quantity production. By 1915 he had produced a million cars; by 1925 his company was turning out two million cars a year; in 1928, Model T was discontinued shortly after car number 15,000,000 was completed.

In fact, America took to the road in the nineteen twenties and thirties, and the automobile, it almost seemed, became the center about which the economy of the average household revolved. It affected, in a hundred and one different ways, the life of the times: emptying the churches, profoundly coloring the habits of youth, making it possible for workers to seek jobs and work at them as much as fifty miles from their homes, facilitating the escape of criminals, placing serious if not insuperable obstacles in the way of the enforcement of Prohibition. It gave rise to the appearance of a whole host of new services: gasoline and repair stations, wayside refreshment booths and inns, curio shops, the operation of tourist camps. It made road construction a major industry in the United States. It turned us, as P. W. Slosson says, into a migratory folk and converted the whole country into the playground of the American people. Indeed, the recent settlements of Florida and Southern California were in large part due to the initial excursions taken by automobile tourists into these sunny lands. Finally, more than any other single influence, it leveled for all time the barriers of localism so that the United States of America became a cultural as well as merely a geographical entity.

The motion picture, too, as an industry and a social force reached maturity during the period we are examining. In the eighteen nineties, the experiments of Edison with his kinetoscope and the invention by Thomas Armat of the modern projector (1895) opened up the possibilities for the commercial exploitation of the films. First used merely as a novelty in the composition of vaudeville programs, the motion picture in a short time reached the stage of a fully formed and independent institution. Several factors contributed to bring this about, among which may be cited the following: 1. The realization that the films could be employed to depict a complete narrative instead of merely isolated incidents. "The Great Train Robbery," a one-reeler one thousand feet in length, was the first "story picture" successfully turned out (1905), and it was quickly followed by others. 2. The wizardry of D. W. Griffith, who developed a distinct technique in the direction and filming of motion picture productions. His use of the "close-up," "cut-back," and "fade-out," his handling of masses, and his heightening of effects through the introduction of a richness of detail, all definitely indicated that the motion picture's future history lay in paths that sharply diverged from those of the stage. Griffith's "Birth of a Nation" (1912) was a turning point in the history of the silent screen. 3. The introduction of the star system, largely as a result of the enterprise of Adolph Zukor. The popularity of the motion picture was firmly established with the development of such early stars as Mary Pickford, Lillian Gish, Douglas Fairbanks, and Charlie Chaplin. The star system undoubtedly hurt the artistic progress of the motion picture, but it was one of the contributing factors in making it an industry of major proportions, as the American public thronged to the movie houses to see its favorite actors perform almost always in the same dramas revolving about simple tales of romantic love, high adventure, and pathetic frustration. The motion picture producers had put a finger on two simple truths—that the average individual, the world over, was never so content as when he could identify himself with a young person happily in love or embarked on noble enterprise, never so superior as when he was permitted to witness an even humbler fellow than himself being made the butt of life's cruel jokes; and for this the producers reaped untold riches.

Toward the end of the twenties, the motion picture industry took on a new life as what had seemed a flagging attention on the part of the movie-going public was recaptured with the development of sound pictures. Before long, every motion picture theater was wired for sound; operas, musical shows, and spoken plays were being adapted or written originally for the screen; news reels brought living notables and the daily happenings before audiences—and the industry climbed to new peaks. In 1922, the average weekly movie attendance in the country was 40,000,000 persons; by 1930, it was close to 100,000,000. There were some 20,000 film "palaces" —not to mention a "cathedral" or two—in the United States; and the industry represented an investment of two billions of dollars.

The radio's entry into the common life of America was even more spectacular. Made a reality through the invention in 1906 by Lee De Forest of the audion, the radio waited until the twenties for successful commercial exploitation. In less than a decade, it had become an indispensable adjunct of fully half of America's homes. Every hour of the twenty-four, the person in search of entertainment or instruction might find a program on the air to suit his particular whim. Broadcasting stations, linked together in a few great chains, of which the Columbia and National broadcasting companies were the outstanding, and supported by heavy revenues derived from national advertisers, vied with one another in attracting to the microphone celebrities from the concert halls, the stage, and the world of sport. Politics, the churches, the newspapers, the universities—and in the nineteen thirties self-styled news commentators, in reality propagandists—were quick to grasp the potentialities of the radio and extended themselves to gain the attention of a great invisible public that nightly sat at home and waited, in comfort, to be harangued, amused, enlightened, and moved. The air in the United States was free, with a difference: while broadcasting was not made a government monopoly, as in most other lands, the operation of a sending station had become as expensive as the publication of a daily paper—and therefore as circumspect. Unpopular causes had few chances for a hearing; the voice of dissent was heard much less frequently than that of the established order of things. If America obtained good music as a result of the radio, it was getting almost no controversy of a fundamental nature.

Aviation added its contributions to make the contemporary life more exciting and complex. The experiments of the Americans, S. P. Langley and Wilbur and Orville Wright, with the heavier-than-air machine, were epoch making in the development of this mode of transportation, so that, by 1905, the airplane was making successful flights. The postwar decade saw aviation assuming all the characteristics of a full-grown industry. Airports were built, transport companies appeared, regular lines for mail, passenger, and express service—all heavily subsidized by the federal government—were laid out. In 1926, air operation provided 3715 miles of passenger route; in 1936, 60,451 miles. Not a few of the American heroes in the calendar of the day came from this field. Chief of all was Charles A. Lindbergh, who, during May 20–21, 1927, crossed the Atlantic alone in a single-motored plane. On May 9, 1926, Lieutenant-Commander Richard E. Byrd and Floyd

G. Bennett flew over the North Pole; in 1929, Byrd headed an elaborate scientific expedition into Antarctica; in June, 1931, Wiley Post circumnavigated the globe by air in the amazing time of seven days and eighteen hours; and this record was cut in half in July, 1938, when Howard Hughes and four companions flew around the world in three days, nineteen hours, and eight minutes!

Literature, the Arts, and Taste

It was no paradox that while material things, in the America of the Machine Age, had so many earnest votaries the arts should reach their highest expression. The artist and patronage have always been indissolubly joined: with wealth and leisure a society has ample opportunity to cultivate its tastes both for the intrinsic enjoyment to be derived from things of beauty and for ostentatious display. Not only did Americans scour every corner of the earth to collect the artistic treasures of earlier times and other civilizations, but they applied themselves seriously to the task of encouraging native talent. The result was the flourishing of such a company of novelists, poets, dramatists, painters, sculptors, architects, composers, and critics as was the match of any to be found elsewhere in the twentieth-century world. The United States, perhaps, had not yet produced individual painters as significant as Pablo Picasso and Henri Matisse, or novelists to rank with James Joyce and Marcel Proust. Americans did have the right to say, however, that the artistic endeavors of their more gifted fellow citizens were mature, serious productions that reflected, in a bewildering variety of forms, their individual reactions to the native scene. Could one doubt that American art had truly come of age, in the era of the machine, when one was called upon quite regularly to view such exhibits as *An American Tragedy, My Antonia, Babbitt, A Farewell to Arms, The Waste Land, Strange Interlude,* the buildings of Frank Lloyd Wright, and the water colors of John Marin?

True, conservative opinion still clung to the artistic canons of an earlier time: in literature, it refused to tolerate any deviation from classical outlines; in painting, a preoccupation with form and color alone and a subordinating of representational characteristics were disdainfully regarded; in architecture, the bold innovations of men who, abjuring Greco–Roman, Gothic, and Renaissance models, were seeking a style in the materials and construction of the age, were deemed barbarous. But more and more, voices were being raised to say that the academies, the elder critics, the learned pundits were wrong: that if modern art appeared to be freeing itself from the standards of other days, the same could be said of much of our modern living; and that each time, out of its own deep experience, had to evolve its criteria for the good, the true, and the beautiful.

In the field of the novel, there was much that merited serious attention. The productions of Upton Sinclair, Jack London, and Robert Herrick, in the early years of the twentieth century, marked the complete break with the past—with the complacencies of the Gilded Age and with the subservience of American writers to European models. If Jack London and Upton Sinclair, in particular, only too frequently ended by turning their novels into social tracts, the problems they set themselves were honestly faced, their characters boldly drawn. Here were signposts: the American novelist, by concerning himself with American life, had something to contribute to the world's literature. This early promise was fulfilled in the works of the so-called middle generation, which reached maturity in the nineteen twenties, with the result that the novels of Theodore Dreiser, Sinclair Lewis, Sherwood Anderson, Willa Cather, and James Branch Cabell were achievements of the first order; and in the works of the younger generation of the nineteen thirties, notably those of John Dos Passos, James Farrell, Ernest Hemingway, and Thomas Wolfe.

Certainly, Theodore Dreiser was a name to be taken seriously. Working in obscurity for almost twenty years, adding slowly to an impressive shelf his *Sister Carrie*, *Jennie Gerhardt*, *The Financier*, *The Titan*, and *An American Tragedy*, Dreiser was compelled to wait until the twenties for universal recognition. He showed himself to be a person having an extraordinary capacity for pity: the weak and poor men and women who filled his pages were held chained by circumstance and if they thrashed about helplessly, finally succumbing to their baser passions, theirs was not the blame. Living was bewildering, planless, and yet had a certain grand inevitability about it. Dreiser was no finished artist; he displayed his faults in his careless vocabulary and his inability to discard extraneous material. But these were not fundamental and his Jenny and his Clyde, to mention but two of his characters, rose out of the foggy pages as sentient beings.

Sinclair Lewis's chief literary tool was satire: except, perhaps, for his Martin Arrowsmith, his characters were hardly drawn to evoke the reader's admiration. Steeping himself in the manners, habits, morals, and speech of middle-class America, Lewis produced a series of social satires that were, at the same time, examples of highly skilful reporting and of real imaginative writing. For Lewis, despite his preoccupation with environmental detail, was not rebelling at American society so much: Main Street, with its artificial standards, its catch phrases, its worship of material possessions, was not the center of his attack. But Main Street had done something to its men and women: it had vulgarized them, turned them into empty drums, deprived them of sensibility and the capacity for honest expression: and on these Lewis visited his disdain. His novels, *Main Street, Babbitt, Elmer Gantry, Arrowsmith, Dodsworth,* were a gallery of such figures, and nearly every aspect of the America of the Machine Age has its representative, drawn full-length. In the nineteen thirties, Lewis to a certain extent rejected his early position, and this time he visited his scorn upon the youngsters because, in their hunt for new answers, they too quickly abandoned the values of their elders. What the critics were saying simply was that Lewis had become older and was identifying himself with his own generation. In 1930, Lewis was awarded the Nobel Prize for Literature, the first American to be thus honored.

Sherwood Anderson, too, dipped deeply into the American life. His short stories—for in this medium he was at his best—were moving documents of simple people who, frustrated by a too hard, objective world, were driven into themselves. They sought their expression in subterranean ways, sometimes their impulses became overpowering, and the result was a flash of aberrant conduct. In *The Triumph of the Egg, Horses and Men,* and *Winesburg, Ohio,* there were published collections of such tales. Willa Cather was perhaps the finest novelist of this middle generation, when judged by the rules of the literary craft. Her important books—*O Pioneers!, The Song of the Lark, My Antonia, The Lost Lady, Death Comes for the Archbishop*—were finely plotted, and their women characters, in particular, were drawn with a warmth and understanding for which there was no equal in contemporary literature. James Branch Cabell was at once the finest stylist of the period and its outstanding ironist. Equally at home in his native Virginia and in a fanciful medieval world, his books *The Rivet in Grandfather's Neck, The Cream of the Jest, Jurgen, Beyond Life*, showed a mastery over his materials that marks off the truly great comic writer. Parrington thus described his method: "He hates the cant and dishonesty of our bourgeois existence, and he refuses to take seriously the host of petty concerns that most of us are very serious about . . . but the spirit of comedy saves him and he contents himself with a jest. But the Cabellian jest uncovers depths of meditation that reveal the philosopher and the poet."

The decades of the nineteen tens and twenties were to see flourish, too, a number of gifted poets. The names of Edgar Lee Masters, Carl Sandburg, Vachel Lindsay, Edwin Arlington Robinson, Robert Frost were more than items in an American catalogue, important only because they were native. Their songs were like separate pieces of a mosaic. Masters's bitter, revealing flashes of the middle western life, Sandburg's poems in praise of millions of men toiling in wheat fields and steel mills, Lindsay's rhythmic chants of blacks and street-corner evangelists, Frost's quiet lyrics that gave meaning and verity to a rural New England almost forgotten by the rushing new age, Robinson's fine, muted narratives that were "a prolonged enquiry into the why of human behavior"—these, when put together, formed a complete whole. Here was American poetry finding itself in America: the vocabulary and the themes, while not Whitman's, were in every sense as fundamentally sound as those of the greater man. The writings of the younger poets who followed the middle generation—of T. S. Eliot, Robinson Jeffers, Hart Crane, Archibald MacLeish—were, in a sense, more limited in range, and yet they explored worlds unknown to their elders. The passionate protest of Masters and Sandburg, for example, they put by: they filled their lines with obscure and often personal allusions; they employed a phrasing that, as Newton Arvin has said, was "nervous, meager, metaphysical, and acrid." In other words, it was the poetry of disillusionment, of a generation living after the World War and in depression, which, measuring promises by performances and finding very little in the objective scene for which to be thankful, took refuge in the recesses of its own consciousness.

Critical writing was as much a part of the real literature of the period. In fact, the dean of the middle generation was Henry L. Mencken, who, first from the pages of the *Smart Set* and later from the *American Mercury*, encouraged his fellow craftsmen to greater efforts, and by his own attacks on American Philistinism profoundly colored the imaginative works of the day. If Mencken had no positive canons for the creation of a wholesome social life, he had what he called his prejudices: he hated the stupidities, the subterfuges, the hyprocrisies of a bourgeois society, which, mouthing political and moral platitudes, had in reality no decent rules of conduct. As Mencken grew older he became more conservative and made political and economic iconoclasm the butt of his barbs. Van Wyck Brooks and Randolph Bourne set themselves other tasks, but their achievements, too, were of the first importance. Bourne died when he was thirty-two; Brooks wrote little literary criticism after he was forty: yet, each, in a few intensive years, was responsible for a body of critical judgments that shaped in innumerable, subtle ways the development of the younger men and women. Brooks gave American writers an awareness of the unity of American culture, from its colonial beginnings to the reign of the machine; Bourne was the first to point out to young America, even while the World War was still raging, that a sterner discipline was needed than the cheery philosophy of their elders who talked so hopefully of progress and yet accepted war as a sure method of freeing the race of all its distempers. The places of these two, beginning with the middle twenties, were taken by worthy successors—Edmund Wilson, Lewis Mumford, and Waldo Frank—who, because art was life, did not permit their writings to be circumscribed by esthetic rules purely but ranged over the whole cultural and social history of America and Europe, both past and present.

In the realm of formal thinking, twentieth-century America might justly be proud of the record of John Dewey. It was his achievement to evolve a complete system out of that pragmatism (or instrumentalism, as Dewey called it) whose principles had first been laid down by Charles S. Peirce and William James. Logic was a tool or instrument to be used in the service of society and its problems, and no thinking was real that did not grow out of experience. In his outstanding writings—*School and Society*, *How We Think*, *Democracy and Education*, *Human Nature and Conduct*, *Experience and Nature*—Dewey set himself to drawing up the chief rules for a conduct that was to be guided by "the experimental method of knowing." Dewey was nothing if not a modern. As he himself put it, his philosophy stemmed from the "growth of democracy . . . the development of the experimental methods in the sciences, evolutionary ideas in the biological sciences, and the industrial reorganization." It was natural, therefore, that he should insist that the problem before us was the employment of ideas first in our adjustments to and then in the transformation of an empirical world. Thus he wrote: "The task of future philosophy is to clarify men's ideas as to the social and moral strifes of their own day. Its aim is to become, so far as is humanly possible, an organ for dealing with these conflicts."

John Dewey had no peers in the middle generation. Nor, among the younger men, did there seem to be emerging any who might claim a place in the line of succession. The same was true of social and economic thought, with but perhaps a single exception: Henry George, Henry Adams, and Thorstein Veblen, those giants of the Gilded Age, left but a single heir, Charles A. Beard, who was an historian, political scientist, and—above all—a humanist.

The plastic arts were to have worthy representatives in the creative life of the Machine Age. Most American painters went to school to France; and whether they left our shores or not, they could not but be influenced by the teachings of first Manet and his group and then Cézanne. This was not slavish imitation but a commendable understanding of the fact that the great Frenchman had revolutionized modern art and had freed the artist from stultification. To work honestly with materials, to express the significance of the subject rather than its outward semblance, to embody "the inner personal standard of the artist," to concern oneself with form, color, and design without regard for dead formulas: these meant release. The result was the appearance, in the middle generation, of a goodly company of painters all of whom had learned this lesson well, all of whom, nevertheless, were distinctly American. Robert Henri, John Sloan, George Luks, Maurice Prendergast, Kenneth H. Miller, Jerome Myers, William Glackens produced canvases that richly illuminated the life of the day; George Bellows's lithographs, particularly, attained the recognition that was their due; the black and whites of Boardman Robinson and Robert Minor gave distinction to the graphic arts.

Beginning with the second decade of the century, the name of Cézanne came to be writ large on the art life of America. Thanks to the encouragement of Alfred Stieglitz, whose personal influence had much to do in the shaping of the talents of a number of the younger artists, and to the support of a sizable body of wealthy collectors, American art was able to launch on the bold experiments of post-impressionism, cubism, and futurism and to seek to express that "significant form" which had become so truly the keynote of all the modern arts. Before the postwar decade was over, there had emerged a large body of contemporary painters and sculptors, and a notable group of craftsmen using other materials, whose productions indicated that modernism was exactly fitted to the American temper. Municipal museums bought their work, foundations sprang up to provide the gallery space for periodic displays, and young America began to talk as familiarly of John Marin's water colors, Georgia O'Keeffe's flower pictures, Thomas Benton's murals, and Gaston Lachaise's figures in stone and metal, as it did of the contemporary novels, poems and literary criticism.

Architecture did not break loose from the bondage of old forms until the first decade of the twentieth century was over. Louis Sullivan's lessons were, for a time, forgotten and, as buildings soared higher (under the compulsion of high ground rents), misguided architects sought to fetter the skyscraper. In the words of Suzanne La Follette: "They topped it with heavy cornices, they engirdled it with horizontal bands, they split it into sections with balustrades, surmounted by rows of pedimented windows. They encircled it with orders, at top or bottom, or both, and crowned it with cupolas and temples." It is not to be understood that all of the early skyscrapers were subjected to this uninspired handling. Cass Gilbert's Woolworth Building in New York (finished in 1913), for example, was a triumphant application of the pure Gothic principle to the tall building: but in this direction true progress could not be pushed much further. Happily, new vistas were opened largely because of an accident. In the midst of the World War, to prevent the growth of a city of perpetual twilight, New York's municipal assembly passed an ordinance requiring the "setting back" of tall structures after certain heights had been reached. With the resulting treatment of the skyscraper as a series of masses, in which the sparing decoration used was made to accentuate the vertical line, a new art form emerged—indeed, one of America's most important contributions to the life of the Machine Age. Ralph T. Walker's New York Telephone Company Building, Arthur L. Harmon's Shelton Hotel, William F. Lamb's Empire State Building, all in New York, Bertram Goodhue's Nebraska State Capitol and Los Angeles Public Library, and Eliel Saarinen's Cranbrook Foundation group at Bloomfield Hills, Michigan, were examples of modern architectural achievement, in which form, materials, and decoration were blended together to realize to the fullest the functional nature of the buildings.

Even more startling in their implications were the designs of Frank Lloyd Wright, a pupil of Sullivan and one of the great artists of modern times. Wright built houses, hotels and pleasure gardens, ever in keeping with his own dictum that "a building should be made to grow easily from its site, shaped to harmonize with its surroundings of Nature." He experimented with materials, he created revolutionary patterns: his was an ever-fruitful talent whose many bewildering forms gained the admiration of the contemporary world. Lewis Mumford, who has done so much to familiarize Americans with the significance of Wright's work, has said of him:

> No architect during the last century, probably no architect since the Renaissance, has perceived so many fresh openings, projected so many possible lines of attack. . . . He has explored new combinations of material and new methods of construction, and in his varied work in the Middle West, the Pacific Coast, the Southwest and Japan, he has shown that a modern architecture need not consist in a series of dull stereotypes, applied without respect to topography, atmosphere, landscape, historical traditions.

The American drama, too, reached full stature in the Machine Age. That the theaters were controlled by commercial interests and that only too frequently plays were presented for the sole reason that they attracted the "tired business man" were apparent. With the development of the motion picture, a large part of the theatergoing public vanished and the traveling company became quite as extinct as the Chautauqua. Nevertheless, more and more good plays were being written and were receiving intelligent, imaginative handling by producers; the employment of lighting, scenery, and effects was revolutionized; and the theater, if anything, became a more glamorous place for the creation of illusion than ever. Not the least element in the progress of the stage to be recorded was the fact that American dramatic writing belonged among the best of the creative literature of the time; indeed, it stood head and shoulders above the similar efforts of the younger English and Continental playwrights. To an extent this was due to the devotion to the stage of what came to be called the Little Theater groups and the summer stock companies, which kept up a steady round of experimentation and which furnished the opportunities for the development of budding talent; to an extent, too, the appearance of the Theatre Guild in New York, a non-commercial enterprise supported by a subscription list, which brought the best of current foreign dramatic writing first to the New York and then to other metropolitan stages, further the process of education. The chief reason, however, as was true in the case of the other arts, was the growth of taste. A public had appeared to demand good plays: it got many superlative ones.

The most important American dramatist thus to emerge was Eugene O'Neill, who, next to George Bernard Shaw, was the greatest living writer for the stage, with audiences not merely in America but in every great city of the world. His first works, a series of one-acters, were presented by the Provincetown Players (one of the leading Little Theater groups) during the years of the war. From then on he proceeded from triumph to triumph, boldly disregarding the classical unities and those later rules of the dramatic craft which insisted upon the presentation of pat situations whose artificial perplexities could be resolved in the space of two hours. He wrote "expressionistic" dramas in which the intent was to depict conflict not between men and men or men and ideas but between men and emotions; he used masks; he penned a nine-act play, to be presented at a single sitting, in which the characters were called upon to reveal, often unwillingly, their inmost and even unconscious thoughts at the same time that they phrased their everyday, humdrum desires and intentions. Other outstanding dramatists of the period were Maxwell Anderson, Elmer Rice, and Clifford Odets.

Music, in America, flourished as never before. Not only was there a sound tradition alive, which demanded the presentation of first-rate works, but every encouragement was given the native composer. Foundations nurtured him, symphony orchestras at once gave him a hearing, his intentions and achievements were as seriously studied as were those of other creative artists. If musical composition, in America, still lagged behind the other arts, it could not be claimed that neglect of the composer was the explanation. Yet the situation was full of hope and, as a result of the efforts of a number of serious workers in musical forms, there was every reason to believe that a true American music was in process of emerging. In the words of Paul Rosenfeld:

> We have an American music: there exists a body of sonorous work, not jazz, made by persons associated with the American community, to be grouped without impertinence with classic European works. Jazz may continue to bulk large and remain the most striking product of our direction toward the instruments of music. Still, side by side with it, and side by side with other products of energy directed toward the means of art, there continue to appear with an accelerating speed, compositions rooted in the American "soil"; exploiting the material of sound in characteristic ways and releasing a typical pathos.

To play the works of native Americans and to present the compositions of classical and modern masters there existed in the country such a host of symphony orchestras, chamber music groups, choral societies, and operatic companies as was not to be found in any other country. John T. Howard records the fact that in the early nineteen thirties (before the depression reached its depths) regular programs were being offered by seventy-three permanent symphony orchestras (of which eleven were of the highest grade), fifty-five chamber music societies, six grand opera companies, and more than five hundred choral groups. In addition, great music foundations provided able teachers for the young people who sought to enter the musical lists as writers, singers, and instrumentalists.

If, as far as truly great musical achievement was concerned, America was still compelled to look to the future, in the realms of light music and popular music native workers had no masters among their generation. The operettas of Victor Herbert and Reginald De Koven, of the first half of the thirty years of the new century, and the jazz pieces of George Gershwin, Paul Whiteman, Irving Berlin, and innumerable others, of the second half, amused and captivated not merely the United States but the whole civilized world. Particularly was this true of jazz and its later successor swing, which were as indigenous products as Model T. Indeed, the phenomena sprang very much from the same situation, for jazz and swing were peculiarly children of our modern mechanical age.

The thought has been stressed, here, that the significant achievements of American art in every field of creative endeavor, during the Machine Age, were made possible by the appearance of a sound taste. Of course, each nourished the other. But without a proper appreciation, guided by true canons, on the part of an art-loving public, the artist, no matter how lofty his genius, cannot flourish. What was interesting in America was that patronage—in the sense of support for art—was not the peculiar characteristic of the very wealthy: throughout much of the whole middle class there was arising an understanding of what sound artistic values really were. In fact, so widespread was the demand for real art that the New Deal, during the depression years, very wisely included art projects among the white-collar employments being sponsored by the WPA. The result showed itself in many interesting ways, particularly in the common modes of daily living. Domestic architecture, whether it leaned toward the modern or followed period lines, was more and more correct in all essential details; interior decoration was producing homes that were at the same time cheerful, handsome, and comfortable; the machine was being utilized to create new forms in furniture, to evolve new fabrics, to turn out in new patterns and designs age-old articles of utility. Never was there a time when color was used so tellingly, where there was so much real beauty in so many humble things.

This was achievement: yet it would be a grave error to hold that it was thoroughgoing or even enough. There still existed a great group in the population whose lives were scarcely ever touched by beauty: who lived not in charming colonial homes in a spacious suburb but in the miserable dumb-bell tenements of the Gilded Age; who were not daily surrounded by Renoirs, Cézannes, and Picassos, who indeed never penetrated into those galleries where such masterpieces were on display; who, if they heard good music, ever fingered good books, viewed handsome objects, did it without any emotional lift.

How could they? To cultivate and appreciate art, a civilization requires not only wealth and leisure but a sense of security, a feeling of the permanence of most essential things. The masses of the country, who toiled in factories, behind store counters, at desks, and as share croppers—most of the inhabitants of the land—had none of these things: the bare fact of living was too cruel to allow for pondering on the timelessness of a Chinese vase. Until beautiful things were part of the daily life of every person in its population, no matter how humble his gifts or station, no civilization could rightly lay claim to a true success.

PART III

AMERICA FIGHTS DEPRESSION

PART III

AMERICA FIGHTS DEPRESSION

VII. CAPITALISM IN CRISIS

The Course of the Depression

During the twenties, Americans witnessed the new and greater heights to which the machine could transport them. Never before in the history of the country had there been such widespread good times: such a high level of real wages, such capitalist expansion, such production and consumption of new goods. And the new day had its new prophets. Americans were told they could discard their old economic hesitancies and doubts; that with the revolution in machine production there had come a revolution in economics. These were the tenets of this modern faith that were being preached by not a few industrialists, investment bankers and brokers, and college professors: (1) that depressions and poverty were both on the way to abolition; (2) that the whole nation was becoming capitalist—witness the diffusion of stock ownership; (3) that the widespread speculation on the stock exchanges was healthy rather than otherwise; (4) that high money rates were not undesirable; (5) that there was no occasion for alarm in the diversion of funds to stock-market transactions; (6) that the valuation of stocks did not have to be reckoned at ten times earnings, but might go as high as twenty-five times earnings.

Thus encouraged, Americans launched into an orgy of stock speculation. Brokers' loans increased by four billions of dollars between 1927 and the fall of 1929; at the end of September, 1929, these reached the gigantic total of $8,549,000,000. Of this amount, non-bank loans to brokers (that is to say, money advanced by individuals, investment trusts, and corporations) totaled $5,377,000,000 or 63 per cent. The average daily volume of trading on the New York Stock Exchange, in 1929, was close to four million shares. On March 26, 1929, eight million shares were bought and sold; on October 24, 1929 (the first day of the panic), the total number traded in was 12,900,000 shares. Millions of persons had margin accounts—from the humblest stenographer to the most conservative bank president. From 1914 to 1929 the number of issues listed on the New York Stock Exchange doubled; and the New York Curb Exchange, now also housed in a magnificent building, further added to the opportunities for speculation.

The counsels of more cautious persons were forgotten, these in particular: First, that depressions were a normal characteristic of the business cycle. Second, that the steady diversion of the country's credits into stock exchange loans was bad for business. It meant the encouragement of over-speculation by the investing public and over-expansion by industry. Third, that certain auguries by the early part of 1929 were already unpropitious. The building boom had ended by the fall of 1928; automobile and steel production began dropping off in August, 1929; American oil wells were producing in excess of the market demand.

The raising of the English rates for money to 6½ per cent and the outward flow of European capital, in October, 1929, were the first indications that the speculative house of cards was sagging. Actual collapse came in the two weeks following October 24, when hundreds of thousands of margin accounts were liquidated, stock prices tumbled as much as 80 per cent below their highs for September, and almost twenty-five billions of dollars in market values were wiped out. On October 1, 1929, the market value of the listed stocks on the New York Stock Exchange was eighty-seven billions; on November 1, 1930, this had shrunk to fifty-five billions; and on March 1, 1933, to nineteen billions!

The recession that set in, in early 1930, was prolonged into a deepening depression, which, in the spring of 1933, touched the lowest point experienced in recent capitalist history. Between 1929 and 1932, the total physical output of goods was reduced 37 per cent; total labor income, 40 per cent; total property income, 31 per cent. In March, 1933 (with the monthly average of 1923–1925 as 100), the index of industrial production stood at 60; that of construction at 14; that of factory employment at 61; that of factory pay rolls at 38; that of wholesale prices (1926 as 100) at 60. The farmer's purchasing power was reduced 50 per cent. There were at least 15,000,000 unemployed persons. And with the unprecedented collapse in prices, the burden of debt had become intolerable.

The Causes of the Depression

As the depression dragged on, it began to become evident that this experience did not represent simply another downswing in the customary business cycle. There were fundamental faults in the capitalist economy; our institutional structure, in short, was not as sound as the sanguine had led us to believe. More and more, people were beginning to understand that what was happening to capitalism was this: It was saving and accumulating; it was investing its saved capital in capital goods industries at home and abroad; and the capacity to produce, notably more capital goods, was mounting higher and higher. On the other hand, the distribution of national income did not favor the ultimate consumers, for too large a part of the national income went to capital claims (rent, interest, profits) and not enough to wages of workers. The capital claimants and the large income-receivers did not spend enough of their income for consumer goods and saved too large a part of it for further investment. The wage earners, on the other hand, did not have enough income, or purchasing power, to buy all the consumer goods and services our productive plant was capable of turning out. Here was a dangerous gap that was widening: the gap that was represented by the gulf between capacity to produce and ability to consume; and in this gap our capitalist economy was living perilously.

It is important that an analysis of certain aspects of this economy be presented in greater detail.

First, despite all our wishful thinking to the contrary, we were living in a class society. No more did it really avail the humble producer—whether in agriculture, industry, or the service activities —to labor long hours and be abstemious; the possibilities of pulling oneself up by the bootstraps were remote. Broadly speaking, the postwar American world was coming to be divided into two groups: the owners of the means of production and those who worked for them. There was no longer a broad middle plain that connected the two, but an unbridgeable chasm. The typical American, in other words, worked for wages; while opportunities to become a member of the owner class were becoming narrowly contracted.

Some rough estimates of the change in the class structure of American society were made by Lewis Corey (*The Crisis of the Middle Class*, 1935). According to his calculations, in 1870, 44.8 per cent of the American population gainfully employed consisted of industrial and other wage-workers; by 1935, this proportion had increased to 59.3 per cent. In the same interval, the farming group shrank from 36 per cent to 14.5 per cent. The so-called middle class had undergone a curious transformation. Whereas in 1870 it had consisted of 18.4 per cent of the population at work, with 4.8 per cent salaried workers and 13.6 per cent independent entrepreneurs; in 1935 this middle class made up 25.5 per cent of the population at work, but now 20.2 per cent were salaried employers and only 5.3 per cent were individual enterprisers. Put simply, in 1870, the wage-and-salaried workers constituted about one-half of the working population; in 1935, above four-fifths.

In addition, as has been said, combinations in ownership were taking place. This led to concentration of corporate wealth and corporate income. According to President Franklin D. Roosevelt, in an extraordinary message delivered to Congress on April 29, 1938, in 1935 one-tenth of 1 per cent of all the corporations reporting to the Bureau of Internal Revenue owned 52 per cent of all the corporate wealth of the nation, and less than 5 per cent of them owned 87 per cent of all the corporate assets. As regards income in the same year, one-tenth of 1 per cent of the corporations earned 50 per cent of the net corporate income, and less than 4 per cent of the manufacturing corporations earned 84 per cent of all the net income.

This combination in ownership represented the monopoly stage of capitalism's growth. It was to be found, notably, in steel, automobiles, chemicals, meat packing, sugar refining, petroleum, public utilities, the manufacture of electrical equipment, rubber tires, aluminum ware, tobacco. At the end of the twenties, six companies owned 75 per cent of the steel-making capacity of the country; two giant integrations ruled the automobile industry; the electrical equipment industry was dominated by three great corporations; four companies were producing 70 per cent of the country's rubber tires; the various Standard Oil companies had under their rule 73 per cent of the pipe lines for transporting petroleum and its products.

Another phenomenon was characteristic of the period: as combination in ownership grew, leadership in business policies came more and more to be concentrated in the hands of finance. Finance capital's rôle was strategic. It amassed the great funds necessary to build up integrations; it furnished the short-term capital requirements; it had its representatives and spokesmen on the boards of directors of transportation, public utility, and manufacturing and commercial corporations. As early as 1912, the part played by finance capital was significant; by the end of the nineteen twenties it had become fundamental. It was not stretching the facts too far to say that a few dominant finance-capitalist groups—among which the Morgan and Rockefeller groups were the leaders—were controlling the destinies of a great part of the country's business life.

The position of the House of Morgan was typical. According to Anna Rochester (*Rulers of America*, 1936), on January 1, 1932, the partners of the banking firm of J. P. Morgan and Company sat on the boards of directors of thirty-five banks and insurance companies and sixty non-financial corporations; the total assets of these corporations were $30,000,000,000. If Morgan-dominated banks are included, as a kind of second ring of Morgan power, to this list must be added sixteen financial institutions and twenty-six miscellaneous corporations, with additional assets of $16,200,000,000. A third and outer ring may be included as falling under Morgan influence—where interlocking directorates put Morgan partners and men in close touch with corporate needs and policies. In this third group were to be found 145 banks and other companies with combined assets of about $15,000,000,000. Thus, some $61,200,000,000 of corporate assets, either directly or indirectly—representing nearly one-fourth of American corporate wealth—fell within the Morgan sphere of influence.

Apologists to the contrary, the great mass of the American people were not deriving additional income from ownership of stock shares in American corporations. According to Lewis Corey's estimates (*The Decline of American Capitalism*, 1934), in 1928 there were in the United States 3,750,000 owners of stock shares among the whole total of 47,000,000 persons gainfully employed. That this does not tell the full story of concentration is evidenced by the further fact that of these, 2,600,000 owned but 5.7 per cent of the capital worth of American corporations while 1,150,000 persons possessed the remaining 94.3 per cent. And, as regards income derived from stock ownership, the President's message, above referred to, indicated that in 1929, three-tenths of 1 per cent of the nation's population received 78 per cent of the dividends reported by individuals. To use the President's words: "This has roughly the same effect as if, out of every 300 persons in our population, one person received 78 cents out of every dollar of corporate dividends, while the other 299 persons divided up the other 22 cents between them."

Second, America was incapable of using its current plant, for the production of goods and services, up to full capacity. This meant, obviously, that the claims paid to capital were not the result of production but of ownership; it also meant—as has already been said—that productive capacity was in excess of consumptive ability. Two studies, made during the nineteen thirties, illuminated this situation. The first, by the Brookings Institution (*America's Capacity to Produce*, 1934), found that in 1929, at the peak of prosperity, existing plant could have created 19 per cent more of goods and services. Put in terms of money, if capacity had been completely used, we could have added $15,570,000,000 to the national income in 1929.

But the Brookings Institution imposed upon itself a series of significant reservations which made its estimates too low. The Brookings experts looked upon "unused capacity" entirely from the point of view of the current market's ability to absorb goods and services. Therefore, they gave consideration to the current nature of "the labor force, transportation facilities, and the supply of money and credit," as limiting factors; they also refused to envisage the use of capacity beyond, as a rule, one-shift operation of equipment and seasonality of production.

The second study (Harold Loeb, *Report of the National Survey of Potential Product Capacity*, 1935), started from the point of serviceability rather than vendibility. It was interested in ascertaining how many goods and services America's current plant could create if production were directed toward the satisfaction of the needs and reasonable wants of its population. In short, the only limiting considerations these experts accepted were those of physical factors and the present state of our knowledge: that is to say, our resources, man-power, and known technical skills.

Suppose, now, unused capacity had been largely employed under such guides to actions? In 1929, there would have been available goods and services for domestic consumption worth $135,516,000,000, or an increase of 44 per cent (instead of the Brookings Institution's 19 per cent) of what was actually turned out. This would have given the statistical average American family of 4.1 persons an income of $4370 a year at once. We shall see below that in 1929, 71.2 per cent of America's families were receiving less than

$2500 a year. In short, the use of plant for vendibility was leading to unused capacity up to two-fifths of America's plant possibilities.

Third, a very large share of the national income paid out was going to capital claimants. In 1929, the payments made to individuals in the form of wages, salaries, interest, dividends, entrepreneurial withdrawals (withdrawals of non-corporate business owners and professional people), and net rents and royalties, totaled $78,632,000,000; in 1932, $48,362,000,000. The capital claimants were those who received income from interest, dividends, and net rents and royalties. The following table presents the percentage distribution of natural income by types of payment.

NATIONAL INCOME PAID OUT, 1929 AND 1932
(In per cents)

	1929	*1932*
Total income paid out	100.0	100.0
Total compensation of employees	65.6	64.0
Total salaries and wages	64.4	61.7
Other labor income	1.2	2.3
Total dividends and interest	14.4	16.5
Dividends	7.6	6.7
Interest	6.6	10.3
Net rents and royalties	4.4	3.0
Entrepreneurial withdrawals	15.6	16.5

In short, even if all salaries and all entrepreneurial withdrawals were to be regarded as "earned," in the sense that wages were, these claimants in 1929 received but 81.4 per cent of the national income and in 1932 but 80.5 per cent. And as the depression continued, the relative positions of the claimants changed sharply. Thus, in 1932, the following payments were being made in terms of what had been paid in 1929:

To wages (in selected industries)	— 40.8 per cent of wages received in 1929
To interest	— 97.5 per cent of interest received in 1929
To entrepreneurial withdrawals	— 63.9 per cent of such withdrawals made in 1929
Total income paid out	— 61.5 per cent of total in 1929.

These conclusions thus emerge: first, that a large share of national income was going to claimants who were not earning it as a result of current productive effort; and second, that, during the depression, the capital claims going to interest continued to remain high, while wages paid to labor fell off sharply.

Fourth, the incomes received by the great proportion of American families were too low to sustain their purchasing power and to permit them to buy all the goods and services turned out by American production. The Brookings Institution (*America's Capacity to Consume,* 1934) indicated that in 1929 the following was the distribution of income by family groups:

DISTRIBUTION OF INCOME BY FAMILY GROUPS, 1929

	Families		*Income*	
Income group	*In thousands*	*Per cent*	*In millions*	*Per cent*
Under $1,000	5,899	21.5	$ 2,900	3.8
$1,000 to $1,999	10,455	38.0	15,364	19.9
$2,000 to $2,999	5,192	18.9	12,586	16.3
$3,000 to $4,999	3,672	13.4	13,866	18.0
$5,000 to $9,999	1,625	5.9	10,820	14.0
$10,000 and over	631	2.3	21,580	28.0
Total	27,474	100.0	$77,116	100.0

It will be seen that the heaviest family concentration in 1929 was to be found in the $1000 to $1999 group; in fact, the most frequent income was in the neighborhood of $1300 for a family group of 4.1 persons. At one end of the scale, over 42 per cent of the families in the United States were receiving apiece less than $1500; together, they got but 13 per cent of the total for the country's family population. At the other end of the scale were 0.23 per cent of all the families receiving apiece $50,000 or more; and these, together, got 14.8 per cent of the total for the country's family population.

The significance of this analysis is to be found in the following: given a family requirement of $2500 income a year for living in decency, health, and comfort, in 1929, 71.2 per cent of America's families were receiving income less than this amount.

Fifth, those who were saving were unable to invest their savings productively. The following table indicates that in 1929 savings took place largely among the upper-income family groups.

SAVINGS OF FAMILIES, BY INCOME GROUPS, 1929

	Families		*Savings*	
Income group	*In thousands*	*Per cent*	*In millions*	*Per cent*
Under $1,000	5,899	21.5	–$ 2,138	–15.0
$1,000 to $1,999	10,455	38.0	801	5.0
$2,000 to $2,999	5,192	18.9	1,490	10.0
$3,000 to $4,999	3,672	13.4	2,317	16.0
$5,000 to $9,999	1,625	5.9	2,549	17.0
$10,000 and over	631	2.3	10,120	67.0
Total	27,474	100.0	$15,139	100.0

The Brookings Institution's conclusion may be quoted:

About 2.3 per cent of all families—those with incomes in excess of $10,000—contributed two-thirds of the entire savings of all families. At the bottom of the scale 59 per cent of the families contributed only about 1.6 per cent of the total savings. Approximately 60,000 families at the top of the income scale, with incomes of more than $50,000 per year, saved almost as much as the 25,000,000 families (91 per cent of the total) having incomes from zero to $5000.

We may say, therefore, that the poorest American families not only did not save but that they fell into debt; while the well-to-do had more than enough for the satisfaction of current consumer needs.

To the savings of individuals must be added the savings of business corporations; and from both must be subtracted—if we want to know how much capital was available for new investment—the amounts used up on farms and in other personal enterprises and for direct capital extensions of corporate business. Making the necessary additions and corrections, Harold B. Moulton (*The Formation of Capital*, 1935) found that in 1923 and 1924 the amount of new money available for investments must have been around $8,000,000,000 or $9,000,000,000 annually, while in 1929 it was around $15,000,000,000. How were these savings used? In 1929, new capital flotations of corporations absorbed $10,200,000,000, and new mortgage financing $1,500,000,000, making a total of

$11,700,000,000. But corrections of this figure were necessary. 1. New securities were sometimes issued to provide working capital. 2. They were sometimes used—indeed, were being so used with increasing frequency during the nineteen twenties—to buy the securities or properties of other companies. The following table presents two corrected series: "net new financing" eliminates use of capital for working purposes; "net productive financing" eliminates use of capital for security and property purchases. The figures also exclude use of capital for refunding operations and purchase of U.S. government and foreign issues.

NEW CAPITAL FINANCING, 1923–1930

(Figures in billions)

Year	*Net new financing*	*Net productive financing*	*Net productive financing as per cent of net new financing*
1923	$3.8	$3.0	77.5
1924	4.5	3.5	76.2
1925	5.1	3.3	64.5
1926	5.2	3.2	60.8
1927	6.2	3.3	53.0
1928	6.7	2.9	44.1
1929	9.2	3.2	34.7
1930	6.1	3.4	57.2

Mr. Moulton now came to the following conclusion:

> Summarizing this discussion, we had funds available for investment ranging from around $8,000,000,000 or $9,000,000,000 in 1923 and 1924 to as much as $15,000,000,000 or $16,000,000,000 in 1929. On the other hand, the volume of new corporate issues for productive purposes, including mortgages, remained practically stationary at about $5,000,000,000. The amount of the savings that passed into the hands of business enterprisers for use in buying materials and hiring labor for the construction of new plant and equipment was thus about $5,000,000,000 annually.

The question obviously arises: What happened to the other two-thirds of the savings? Mr. Moulton's answer ran as follows: 1. Part of it went into the purchase of new security issues created by investment trusts and holding companies (for railroads, banks, public utilities, industrial and commercial corporations). 2. Part of it went to finance the purchase of inflated security values, that is to say, stock market speculation. 3. Part of it went into the purchase of foreign issues, that is to say, the operations of our capitalist-imperialism abroad.

And Mr. Moulton drew the following moral, notably as a result of his preoccupation with the second point made above:

> The rapid growth of savings as compared with consumption in the decade of the 1920's resulted in a supply of investment money quite out of proportion to the volume of securities being floated for purposes of expanding plant and equipment, while at the same time the flow of funds through consumptive channels was inadequate to absorb—at the prices at which goods were offered for sale—the potential output of our existing productive capacity. The excess savings which entered the investment market served to inflate the prices of securities and to produce financial instability. A larger relative flow of funds through consumptive channels would have led not only to a larger utilization of existing productive capacity, but also to a more rapid growth of plant and equipment.

Sixth, the cheap money policy of the Federal Reserve System during most of the twenties served to intensify the disorder in the financial markets. A quotation from a report by Winthrop W. Aldrich, chairman of the board of the greatest bank in the country, the Chase National, will point up the significance of this situation. Writing in 1938, Mr. Aldrich said:

> The real trouble in 1928 and 1929 was, I believe . . . an excess of bank credit going into capital uses and speculative uses due to the cheap money policies of the Federal Reserve System during the 1920's. When a prolonged period of artificially cheap money generates a volume of bank credit which outruns the needs of commerce and industry and runs over on a grand scale into capital and speculative uses, we inevitably lay the foundation for a crisis and depression, because we inevitably create a situation in which debt outruns production.

Seventh, as a result of combination and concentration—due to the growth of monopoly and finance-capitalist control—prices in a number of important sectors were being managed. Monopoly had three outstanding purposes: price control, production control, and control over new capital investments; and of these, price control had the most pervasive effects. In a period of depression the results of such a policy were well-nigh catastrophic, largely because the stickiness, or inflexibility, of prices occurred in those regions where monopoly was most effective, that is to say, in the heavy, or capital goods, industries. Diminished production in these industries meant smaller wage payments; lower consumer demand among the workers in the capital goods industries accelerated the processes of the depression in the light, or consumer goods, industries. In turn, *their* prices dropped sharply because they were less susceptible of being managed. But *their* costs for capital goods remained high. Wholesale failures and the speed-up of production in the consumer goods industries took place, thus further increasing the numbers of unemployed.

The following figures, compiled by Gardiner C. Means (*Industrial Prices and Their Relative Inflexibility*, 1935), point up the contrasts in the conduct of prices and production in the heavy and light goods industries during the first period of the depression. The percentage figures show price and production declines from 1929 to the spring of 1933.

PRICES AND PRODUCTION IN SELECTED HEAVY AND LIGHT INDUSTRIES

Heavy industries	*Per cent drop in prices*	*Per cent drop in production*
Agricultural implements	6	80
Motor vehicles	16	80
Cement	18	65
Iron and steel	20	83
Light industries		
Textile products	45	30
Food products	49	14
Leather	50	20
Agricultural commodities	63	6

From his statistical analysis, Mr. Means drew the following conclusion:

One may make the broad generalization . . . that for industries in which prices dropped most during the depression [i. e., the non-monopoly light industries] production tended to drop least, while for those in which prices were maintained [i. e., the monopoly heavy industries] the drop in production was usually greatest. Indeed, the whole depression might be described as a general dropping of prices at the flexible end of the price scale and a dropping of production at the rigid end with intermediate effects between.

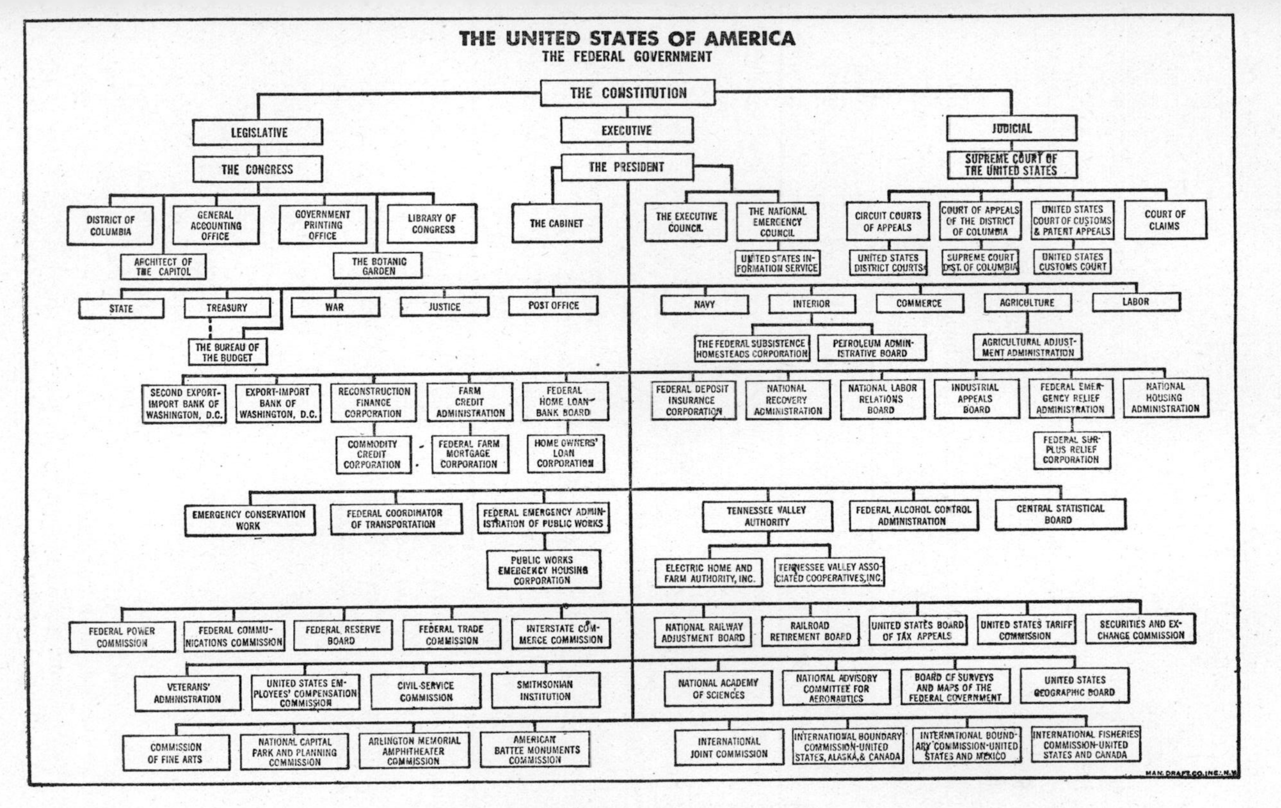

THE FEDERAL GOVERNMENT
1934

Eight, our whole expanded program of foreign trade was based upon our willingness to finance the purchases of countries importing from us; when these no longer could service their dollar loans, we stopped lending—and our export business accordingly fell off sharply. During the nineteen twenties, we convinced ourselves that we could both maintain a favorable commodity balance in our foreign trade and at the same time continue investing our surplus capital abroad. In other words, when we changed our status from a debtor to a creditor nation we also did not change our status from an exporting to an importing nation. The result was, countries which bought from us could not send their own goods in return; and the only means left them of financing their purchases was through the raising of public, or dollar, loans in this country. In this way, the continental European countries largely and some of the Latin American ones were able to buy American agricultural commodities on the one hand and machinery and durable and semi-durable consumer goods on the other. The round was not ever-lasting in view of the fact that our debtors had to sell to somebody in order to obtain foreign exchange with which to service the charges on American dollar loans; and with contraction of foreign trade the world over following 1929 European and Latin American countries began to default on their interest payments on American loans. We stopped making new loans, naturally; our debtors stopped buying; and, the result was, depression in those industries dependent upon foreign markets was accelerated.

The moral here was plain: a capitalist country could not forever continue to maintain in its foreign trade a favorable commodity balance at the same time that it was seeking to invest a good part of its annual savings in foreign regions. We were trying to be a raw-material producing and rentier people at the same time: and that meant, simply, that we were trying to have our cake and eat it too.

Ninth, continued depression in agriculture, from 1920 on, reduced the purchasing power of a large sector in the American population. With the value of the farm dollar, as we have seen, dropping regularly, it was impossible for fully one-sixth of the American population to continue purchasing its share of capital and consumer goods. Agriculture could not carry its part of the load as long as it was weighed down with heavy fixed charges, had to employ tenancy as an organizational form of production, and was confronted by surpluses which a contracting foreign market and a non-flexible domestic market could not absorb.

Tenth, due to greater productivity, job opportunities in industry, transportation, and trade were not expanding. Extended comment on this factor has already been made above.[1] See also below [2] for labor productivity and labor costs under the New Deal.

The situation that confronted America at the end of the nineteen twenties may now be put in the following general terms. Opportunities for capitalist enterprise, in new and promising fields, were contracting. Oversea markets were narrowing. Control over business policy had shifted definitely from industrial to finance capitalism; and the latter was concerned with the making of profits not as a result of the production of goods but through stock promotion and manipulation and the exploitation of investors. The gap between capacity to produce and ability to consume—a situation inherent in the process of accumulation, and therefore capitalism's fundamental contradiction—was widening. Imperialism was proving its inability to discover outlets for the absorption of all the savings of capitalist accumulation. The world market for American agricultural goods was contracting; and a decline in farm land values—sure sign of permanent agricultural depression—had set in. Finally, job opportunities for labor were dwindling because of extraordinary technological progress.

What to Do?

In previous downswings of the business cycle, the forces of depression had been permitted to spend themselves. Falling prices and tightening of credit had been followed by a liquidation of debts and the writing-down of capital values. Costs of production had dropped; surplus stocks of goods were consumed. Then there had taken place a revival of credit to pump new life into the system, and the capital goods industries began to resume production. With the stimulation of purchasing power in this sector, the consumer goods industries could raise their prices once more—and the cycle was ready for another upswing.

Certain barriers stood in the way of the normal movement of

[1] See above, page 77.
[2] See below, page 291.

the cycle this time: The heavy goods industries, largely, as we have seen, were already confronted by unused plant—the quick revival of capital goods production was therefore out of the question. Prices did not drop evenly, because of inflexibilities in those industrial sectors which had fallen under the control of monopoly. Bank credit could not easily be revived because so many banks were carrying speculative securities in their portfolios. Foreign trade could not be stimulated because of the increasing tendency toward economic nationalism, notably on the part of European countries.

To these obstructions, the Hoover administration added artificial ones. Despite the general assumption that the Hoover attitude was a do-nothing one, it is important to note that President Hoover formulated a program whose purpose it was really to check the natural blood-letting process. It has been pointed out that the very large share of the national income taken by capital claims had been a characteristic of American capitalism preceding the depression; that the burden of debt had become well-nigh intolerable, as prices fell; and that a normal procedure of previous depressions had been the reduction of capital claims. It was at this point that the Hoover program intervened. To help agriculture—not by sloughing off the greater part of its debt load, but by getting for it higher prices—the Federal Farm Board was set up in 1930. And to permit financial agencies and large borrowers to carry their debts, the Reconstruction Finance Corporation (RFC) was established in February, 1932. This agency, with an initial fund of $500,000,000 at its disposal and the right to borrow more money, was to make government credits available to release the frozen assets of banks and mortgage companies and to come to the assistance of the railroads.

Why had the Hoover administration intervened to prevent wholesale bankruptcy, which is, of course, the usual process by which capital claims are written down? At this point in the country's development, such a procedure would have been attended by too much risk: for the great investors now were the institutional savers—the savings banks, life insurance companies, building-and-loan associations. These were holding the farm and urban mortgages and the railroad and public utility securities of the country: and the failure of such institutions might have been fatal to capitalism. (It is significant to note that the Roosevelt attitude toward debt was largely the same, with this difference: debts were not to be sloughed off but to be borne; and to make their carrying easy, prices were to be raised. It is exactly at this point—if we may anticipate a little—that one of the cornerstones of the Roosevelt recovery program was set up.)

Further than this, however, President Hoover would not go. But in the minds of many defenders of the capitalist system, more drastic measures were necessary. Increasingly, the demand was raised for one form or another of governmental planning, that is to say, public intervention in order to speed revival. The usual proposals of the advocates of planning included the following. First, governmental control over capital allocations. If saved capital was flowing into regions where there was already unused plant capacity and if it was flowing also into speculative channels, then it was imperative that devices be created so that savings be used only for productive purposes. Second, governmental control over prices. The intention here, of course, was to prevent the continuance of monopoly controls over prices, particularly in the capital goods sector. Third, a fair writing down of capital claims. Fourth, a public works program, in order to stimulate the badly depressed construction industry. Fifth, increase in the purchasing power of labor. Sixth, government ownership in those regions where natural monopoly prevailed, that is to say, as a minimum, the railroads and the public utilities.

We shall have occasion to see to what extent the New Deal, as its program evolved, was able to satisfy these defenders of the capitalist system who, at the same time, insisted that drastic reforms were necessary to keep it a going concern.

The Election of 1932

The depression was in the middle of its third year when the Presidential contest of 1932 took place. There was no question of President Hoover's renomination, and his name and that of Vice-President Curtis were again formally placed before the electorate by the Republican convention. The platform pledged the continuance of the gold standard and the stabilization of commodity prices; it defended the tariff law of 1930; it promised to support any plan to raise agricultural prices provided it was "economically sound and workable"; and it had planks on taxation, veterans' benefits, the World Court, the St. Lawrence waterway, and the repeal of the Prohibition amendment.

With this platform and with his record as President Mr. Hoover sincerely believed himself entitled to reelection. At the beginning of the depression he was certain business was fundamentally sound and he urged business men to carry on as if nothing had happened. If they would refrain from cutting wages and prices, he maintained, confidence would be restored and fear brought on by the stock market crash would be banished. He sternly resisted "doles" to unemployed and direct relief to farmers. Along with other public and private authorities he constantly predicted that prosperity was just around the corner. When time proved the prophecies false and the casualties of the depression began to reach upward and threaten the financial stability of railroads, large city banks, life insurance companies, and the like, at the behest of Mr. Hoover Congress in February, 1932, as we have seen, established the Reconstruction Finance Corporation which became the chief prop of his recovery program.

In his campaign speeches Mr. Hoover pointed with pride to the RFC and maintained that through its beneficent operations the gloom of depression was already lifting. He also made much of the tariff, especially its agricultural features, of his administration's "economy" and its public works program, and he laid the blame for the continuance of hard times on unsettled conditions abroad. To help correct these he pledged his support to a proposed world economic conference. Some small evidences that conditions were on the mend appeared in July, August, and September when wholesale prices began to rise and production showed a slight increase. Whatever hopes these signs held out were dashed in October when the trend again turned downward and it became apparent that once more Mr. Hoover was a false prophet.

Governor Franklin D. Roosevelt of New York was the leading contender for the Democratic nomination and despite serious efforts to mass opposition against him he was named on the fourth ballot with the approval of all his opponents except Alfred E. Smith, who, after a period of apparent sulking, also finally accorded valuable support. One of Roosevelt's rivals, Speaker John N. Garner of Texas, received the Vice-Presidential nomination. The Democratic platform unequivocally pledged the party to repeal of Prohibition and the legalization of beer; and it promised a reform of the banking system, regulation of the stock and commodity exchanges, a federal economy program, a "sound" currency, an international monetary conference, a "competitive" tariff for revenue, reciprocal trading agreements, federal credit to the states for purposes of unemployment relief, the enactment of "every constitutional measure" to help farmers obtain prices above cost of production, reduction in the hours of labor, the regulation of security sales, adherence to the World Court, the independence of the Philippines, and a new veterans' program. The Socialists named Norman Thomas and the Communists William Z. Foster as their standard bearers.

Franklin D. Roosevelt was fifty years old when he was named to make the Democratic canvass. Although a Democrat he first appeared in New York state politics as a foe of Tammany Hall in 1910, when he was elected to the New York Senate. An early supporter of Woodrow Wilson for President in 1912, his reward had been the assistant secretaryship of the navy and thus at thirty-one he was occupying an administrative post in Washington of great importance in the ensuing war period. In 1920 he was Cox's running mate in the forlorn contest against Harding. A year later he was stricken with infantile paralysis, but, thanks to his great physical and mental courage, after seven or eight years of almost complete invalidism he was able to fight his way back to health. During these years Roosevelt kept his name fresh in the minds of countless party workers by means of an elaborate correspondence. In both 1924 and 1928 he gained attention by his speeches nominating his friend, Alfred E. Smith, at the Democratic conventions. Despite the fact that Roosevelt's cure had not yet been completed, Smith succeeded in prevailing on him to make the New York gubernational contest in the latter year in the hope that Roosevelt would help carry the state for the national ticket. This he failed to do but he did carry it for himself and during 1929–1932 he was a successful but not great governor of a pivotal state.

Roosevelt's campaign for President electrified the country. Beginning in the spring be traveled more than 25,000 miles and visited almost every state in the Union; every important economic question received his attention and, thanks to the assistance of a group of well-informed advisers (who came to be dubbed the "Brain Trust"), he discussed with clarity the problems of the depression. One clear-cut distinction between the positions of the two candidates began to emerge as the debate before the electorate progressed. As already noted, Mr. Hoover attributed the depression to international causes, while Mr. Roosevelt maintained that many of the country's difficulties were domestic in origin. While Mr. Roosevelt did not hesitate to interlard his remarks with general promises of a reordering of our economic society, a close reading of his addresses will show that he was not hostile to the capitalist system. But the operations of the system were to be hedged around so closely in the interests of the security of the working man, farmer, and small investor, and its activities were to be directed so completely to the attainment of social rather than individual ends that to many, who had been brought up on the automatic operations of the laissez-faire economy, a veritable revolution threatened. Mr. Roosevelt was a member of the capitalist class, of course, but his income had been derived largely from interest rather than from profits; it was not unnatural that the excesses of industrial competitive enterprise and the chances and penalties of the free market should appear repugnant to one who, as a rentier, had never exploited labor or wasted natural resources. Many efforts have been made to find parallels in comparative politics for Mr. Roosevelt's views. The most obvious one is his close approximation to the position of the British Tory Socialists, who, on the one hand, were prepared to make real concessions to labor at home while, on the other, they pushed a vigorous imperialist policy abroad.

Early indications promised a Democratic victory, but the results exceeded all expectations. The popular vote was 22,821,857 for Roosevelt, 15,761,841 for Hoover, 884,781 for Thomas, and 102,991 for Foster. The electoral vote was 472 to 59, Hoover carrying only the six states of Maine, New Hampshire, Vermont, Connecticut, Pennsylvania, and Delaware. The Democrats also elected heavy majorities to both houses of Congress. The way was now clear for the inauguration of that New Deal which Roosevelt and his advisers had so hopefully outlined.

VIII. FROM AN OLD TO A NEW DEAL

The First Steps of Recovery

As the country waited, it seemed almost as though all the wheels of industrial and financial activity were visibly coming to a dead halt. Not only were the depths of the depression reached in the first days of March, 1933, but imminent catastrophe seemed about to overwhelm the whole economic structure. Prices continued to drop; the unemployed were estimated at from 13,600,000 to 17,000,000; local private and public agencies were finding it impossible to carry the growing load of relief. The burden of public and private debts, in the face of declining prices, was becoming well-nigh intolerable and threatened to consume almost the whole income of the country; the wellsprings of credit appeared to have dried up. At first gradually, soon with increasing intensity, the banking system of the country began to sag and then to collapse. On the eve of Mr. Roosevelt's inauguration the panic had reached the great financial nerve centers of the nation, with the result that the day of the new President's inception into office saw banking operations practically at a standstill in every state and all security and commodity exchanges closed. Even with the generous aid of the Reconstruction Finance Corporation, the great credit and money organizations confessed themselves unable to maintain the unequal struggle.

Although Roosevelt had been critical of this agency, when he assumed office he did not ask for its liquidation but made it an integral part of his own recovery program. But unlike his predecessor he did not place almost his sole reliance upon the RFC. On March 5, he ordered every bank in the nation closed for four days and placed an embargo on the withdrawal or transfer for domestic or export use of gold or silver; on March 9, when the Seventy-third Congress met in special session, Roosevelt had ready for its consideration the Emergency Banking bill, which both houses passed the very same day. The intention of the measure was to permit the sound banks to reopen and to furnish them with currency for the purpose of liquefying their assets. In addition, the act provided that the Secretary of the Treasury could call in all gold and gold certificates in the country; and that the RFC was to be authorized to subscribe to the preferred stock, capital notes, and debentures of banks and trust companies.

While it is generally conceded that the President's measure halted the progress of panic, many liberals believed he had missed a golden opportunity to nationalize the credit institutions of the country or at least to force all banks to join a Federal Reserve system much modified in the public interest.

The second emergency measure of the administration was the so-called Economy bill whose passage Roosevelt demanded on March 10 for the purpose of balancing the budget. This was to be effected in two ways: by salary cuts of governmental employees and by paring down benefit payments under the pension and veterans' compensation system. The bill was passed by both houses and on March 20 received the President's signature.

A third recovery act, signed March 22, was the legalization of beer and wine with an alcoholic content of 3.2 per cent by weight, largely in the interests of obtaining additional revenue. A fourth, this one designed to cope quickly with more obvious aspects of the unemployment problem, was the signing on March 31 of a bill setting up the Civilian Conservation Corps. This agency was to put to work at once on reforestation, road building, and flood control projects some 250,000 unemployed citizens who were to be housed in special camps, paid $30 monthly, and were to be under the supervision of army officers. With immediate emergency questions thus out of the way the more enduring parts of the program were now ready for submission to Congress. Before these are examined, however, it is proper that some attention be given to the theory of reconstruction that, presumably, was at the heart of the New Deal legislation.

The Theory of the New Deal

Since the New Deal has been described as a revolution, it is important that its real nature be subjected to analysis. The natural history of revolutions in modern times has amply illustrated that they are relatively simple affairs. An economic society, in its youth, is one of very great vigor; not only has its tone been set by a leading class freshly emerged from triumphant struggle, but its purposes have also had the support of nearly all groups in the population. The old vestigial traces have been cut away, class antagonisms—because the opportunities for enterprise in hitherto unexplored regions are so many and so bewildering—have not yet had time to form. The life of the times moves to a new harmony in which what dissonances there are are faint and unimportant.

But as an economic society during the course of its evolution grows into maturity and old age: when the leading problem shifts from expansion into new fields to consolidation of those already won: when for the living energies of men there are substituted institutional patterns—then class lines harden. Revolution sometimes has been employed as a device for the destruction of the constricting molds of such class relations. It wipes them out once and for all and commutes their solidified forms into a new fluidity. The English Revolution, the American Revolution, the French Revolution, the American Civil War, and the Russian Revolution were such virtually clean breaks with the past.

Obviously, in terms of these definitions, the New Deal could scarcely be regarded as revolutionary. Its rationale may be stated in the following group of propositions. The New Deal recognized that the American economy had slowed down and that the forces within it were no longer in equilibrium. Opportunities for capitalist enterprise had contracted: the population had ceased expanding, there were few new great industrial fields to be opened up, oversea markets had been shut off by high tariff walls or were already being closely worked by rival imperialist nations. Business controls had shifted from industrial capitalism to finance capitalism. The spread between capacity to produce and ability to consume was constantly widening. The world market for American agricultural goods had largely disappeared. Not only had new jobs for white-collar and professional workers practically become nonexistent, but there was a surplus rather than a dearth of industrial labor as well. Class lines were being drawn clearly; the danger of class hostilities was no longer remote but already in evidence.

The New Deal, to put it baldly, assumed that it was possible to establish a permanent truce on class antagonisms. The private ownership of the means of production was to continue; but capitalism was to be stopped from exploiting, on the one hand, the producers of its raw materials and, on the other, its labor supply. Agriculture, despite its over-capitalized plant and its growing restriction to the domestic market, was to get a large enough return to allow for the meeting of fixed charges and the purchase of capital and consumer goods. Wage earners were to be assured employment and at least means of subsistence, if not incomes conducive to a decent standard of living. This idea of establishing a balance between American class relations occurred frequently in the writings and utterances of Mr. Roosevelt and his advisers. Thus, as late as March 5, 1934, the President stated the principle clearly:

> What we seek is balance in our economic system—balance between agriculture and industry and balance between the wage earner, the employer, and the consumer. We seek also balance that our internal markets be kept rich and large, and that our trade with other nations be increased on both sides of the ledger.

The Tactics of the New Deal

The devices employed by the New Deal, for the purpose of revitalizing the American economy, were the following.

First, the restoration of prices. The world-wide collapse that set in with 1930 had been characterized everywhere by a slipping of prices. This phenomenon was nothing new, but the situation took on real aspects of alarm because the great burden of private and public debts (which was new) could not be carried at the same time that prices were falling. According to the Twentieth Century Fund, the long-term debt of American public agencies totaled $33,000,000,000, while that of American corporations and individuals totaled $100,000,000,000. These debts were the real difficulty; to lighten them would have meant repudiation either through wholesale bankruptcy or unchecked inflation, and to avoid this dread alternative the New Deal chose what seemed the easier one of restoring buying power through the raising of the price levels. That the raising of prices was at the heart of the New Deal program and its "definite and determined" policy can be indicated innumerable times from the statements of the New Deal leaders. Thus President Roosevelt, in the speech above cited, said:

The National Industrial Recovery Act was drawn with the greatest good of the greatest number in mind. Its aim was to increase the buying power of wage earners and farmers so that industry, labor, and the public might benefit through building up the market for farm and factory goods. Employer, wage earner, and consumer groups are all represented on its boards with the government; all three groups with the government must have the interest of all the people as their main responsibility.

At one time or another, the New Deal used the following methods to raise prices: 1. By devaluation of the dollar and an increase in the amount of currency outstanding. 2. By gold purchases from abroad. 3. By seeking to establish parity prices (and also parity income) for agriculture, through corp limitation (with benefit payments) and commodity loans to farmers. 4. By codes of fair competition in industry, to eliminate price cutting.

Second, the revival and expansion of credit. An important characteristic of the crisis had been the slowing down of the movement of short-term and long-term credit into business. The commercial banks, because of their non-liquidity, were not in a position to extend loans for working capital and the purchase of raw materials. The agencies of long-term credit—the savings banks, the insurance companies, trust funds of one kind or another—seeing their earlier investments unproductive, feared to assume further risks until some elements of stabilization had appeared.

The New Deal used the following methods for this purpose: 1. By opening the banks and using the resources of the RFC to achieve liquidity quickly. 2. By putting the control of the open-market policy of the Federal Reserve Banks into the hands of the government itself, so that a public agency now could expand (and contract) credit through open-market operations. 3. By lowering (and raising) the minimum legal reserves required of member banks. 4. By giving the Federal Reserve Board the power to raise (or lower) the margin requirements for security purchases, thus controlling to an extent the amount of bank credit flowing into brokers' loans. 5. By cutting off security affiliates from the control of the commercial banks. 6. By direct loans made by the RFC to business men.

Third, the raising of the purchasing power of the workers. Labor, confronted by shrinking opportunities of employment, was forced to sell its services cheaply and to debase its standards.

Sweated industries once more had begun to flourish; child labor had increased; women had resumed homework. To make it possible for the workers to participate once more in the economic life of the nation, the following devices were employed: 1. The establishment of minimum wages and maximum hours in the codes of fair competition. 2. The abolition of child labor in the same codes. 3. The recognition of collective bargaining so that through self-help the same purposes might be achieved. 4. The passage of the Wages and Hours Act of 1938.

Fourth, the reduction of debt. Debt, as has been pointed out, had become onerous. The New Deal sought to come to grips with this problem in two ways, that is to say, by raising prices and by writing down the face value of debt in those places where price change itself could not be entirely and immediately effective. Reduction of debt was to be achieved through the following: 1. In agriculture, the creation of a new fiscal agency (the Federal Farm Mortgage Corporation) which was to make possible the exchange of privately held agricultural long-term paper for semi-public (or public-guaranteed) paper. 2. In the field of home ownership, the creation of a new fiscal agency (the Home Owners Loan Corporation) for a similar purpose. 3. The reform of the federal bankruptcy law to permit private companies and municipalities to come to an understanding with their creditors quickly and at small legal cost. It should be said, here, that in no case was debt reduction thoroughgoing.

Fifth, the revival of foreign trade. Another important characteristic of the crisis was the decline of foreign trade. The New Deal sought to revive American oversea commerce of course; but it was equally interested in the restoration of world trade generally. This dual policy it hoped it could achieve by getting Congress to make the writing of reciprocal trading agreements an executive function. The result was, the State Department was empowered to negotiate commercial treaties whose purpose it was to obtain the lowering of tariff barriers. In the interests of world trade, these agreements were to contain most-favored-nation treatment clauses.

Sixth, the relief of the needy. The crisis had taken a tremendous toll of the American population in undernourishment, illness, invalidism, and psychological maladjustments. The relief of distress was an imminent public duty; and the New Deal came to grips with this hydra-headed problem in the following ways: 1. The lending of money to the states for straight outdoor relief. 2. The creation of a federal agency (the Public Works Administration) which was to lend money to public and quasi-public authorities to finance long-term public construction projects. 3. The writing of social security legislation under which direct federal appropriations and federal matching grants-in-aid were to be made to the states to provide for the unemployables and the permanent needy (the aged, the blind, dependent and crippled children). 4. The provision of employment for the temporary needy, capable of work, in short-term projects financed by the federal government (under the Works Progress Administration).

The above plans were designed to speed recovery. In addition, the New Deal sought to strike at certain evils in the American economy and polity; in other words, it had a reform program. The outstanding reforms that the New Deal was attempting to effect may be listed as follows. (It will be noted that portions of the recovery devices also had reform aspects.) 1. It succeeded in writing legislation and obtaining Supreme Court approval in the interests of labor's rights to organize and bargain collectively under its own leadership. This undoubtedly was the New Deal's outstanding achievement. 2. It passed legislation looking toward the establishment ultimately of adequate unemployment insurance protection. 3. It laid the basis for an old-age annuity fund, under which, in time, all superannuated workers would receive annuities and not doles. 4. It fought for and obtained the establishment of a minimum-wage and maximum-hour code and the abolition of child labor (on a national scale) as humanitarian measures. 5. It recognized the existence of submarginal farmers and tenants who were economically and socially incapable of functioning and it therefore began to experiment with resettlement projects in which such farmers could become productive once more. 6. It set up the Tennessee Valley Authority for the purpose of rehabilitating, economically and socially, the population of the valley and for the purpose of creating an experiment in the public control of electric light and power. This was to serve as a "yardstick" against which the performances of privately controlled power might be measured. 7. It sought to eliminate unnecessary holding company structures in the power field. 8. It set up an agency for the supervision, in the public interest, of security exchanges. 9. It created an agency to guarantee the savings of small depositors in savings and commercial banks. 10. It sought to rehabilitate the permanently depressed bituminous coal industry by establishing an agency to control prices and production. 11. It tried to come to grips with the problem of soil erosion by paying bonuses to farmers to grow soil-conserving crops. 12. It set up a railroad coordinator in an effort to work out a plan for the coordinating and refinancing of the permanently depressed railroad industry. 13. It was preoccupying itself with the question of the rehabilitation of the American merchant marine. 14. It recognized that the building of decent homes was an outstanding social need and it established an agency which, with government financing and subsidies, was to assist quasi-public authorities to create low-cost housing.

The Politics of the New Deal

It can thus be seen that the New Deal had no intention of overhauling drastically the capitalist system. The mechanism had run down temporarily; it was to be wound up again—after certain repairs had been made and new parts substituted. Having done this, the hope was that there would be suspended in balance and for all time the existing class relations in American society. This was, in brief, an experiment in state capitalism, that is to say, greater government controls over private business and government participation in business directly in those regions where private initiative had definitely failed.

To this extent, therefore, it is possible to characterize the New Deal as being largely a political rather than an economic plan. Its governors did not move over the economic and social scene foot by foot, making adjustments at every point where oppression and injustice had sunk their roots deeply. It operated in those sectors where discontented groups were most effectively organized and whose leadership was most articulate. As a result, the New Deal was able to court successfully the political allegiance of strategically located economic interests; and in this way, therefore, it was able to possess political power.

Thus, in the case of agriculture, the New Deal worked in the interests of the agricultural landlords and commercial farmers almost entirely; and, at that, not all the commercial farmers were assisted. The growers of corn, wheat, and cotton were the most favored; the producers of meat and dairy products and the unorganized growers of vegetables received relatively little support. Landlords having mortgage debts were giving a helping hand; but not tenants whose chief encumbrance was chattel debt. It did next to nothing—its operations were never above the experimental level here—for the great numbers of sharecroppers in the South and the pure subsistence farmers all over the country. It did nothing at all for the more than two million agricultural laborers.

In the case of labor, it worked in the interest of the organized trade unionists; for these, after 1935, had their rights protected by the National Labor Relations Board. But the great mass of the workers of the country were unorganized and had no pressure devices for improving wages and hours and obtaining job security. It was not until 1938 that an hours and wages act was passed to safeguard the industrially underprivileged; and it was still problematical how many persons really could be helped by such legislation.

In the case of business, the New Deal definitely worked in behalf of those interests whose destinies were tied up with foreign trade and investments. It wrote reciprocal trading agreements; it was concerned with the building of a new merchant marine; it sought to safeguard the financial stakes of American investors in those foreign lands where defaults on interest and attempted repudiations of debts were taking place. Notably, its State Department, under Secretary Hull, was adopting an aggressive policy in the Far East for the purpose of protecting the future right of American capital to exploit this backward economic area. Covertly, the same program was being pushed in Latin America.

Put baldly, the New Deal was a political program in behalf of agricultural landlords and big commercial farmers, organized trade unionists, and oversea investors and imperialist promoters.

It must be apparent, after six years of experimenting, that some of the important evils of the American economy were not attacked at their source. Tinkering with prices was an uncertain device for coming to grips with the heavy burden of capital claims. Demands for fair competition was a Canute-like program for checking the onward sweep of monopoly control over prices and production. The problem of excessive saving could not be handled almost entirely through the safeguarding of American rights to invest freely overseas; for this meant imperialist rivalries and the possibilities of war. The taking care of the needy was proper and a humane act. But was it just to demand that the lower middle classes, the workers, and the needy themselves, carry the greater part of the load in the form of heavy concealed taxes on consumption? Such were some of the questions still being asked of the New Deal by more realistic inquirers who wondered what fundamentally had been achieved as the government continued to pile up debt for the purpose of priming the pump of private enterprise.

We must now turn our attention, in the next two chapters, to a specific analysis of the outstanding new government agencies and an examination, in economic terms, of the success of the New Deal planning.

IX. THE NEW DEAL AGENCIES

Agriculture

The program for agriculture was the most elaborate of all those that received the attention of the New Deal planners. The goals were the following: 1. The establishment of parity prices, that is to say, the restoration of the farmer's purchasing power to the position it had had in the immediate prewar years. (The period August, 1909, to July, 1914, was fixed as the base period and it was assumed that at that time the prices farmers paid were in balance with the prices they received.) 2. The establishment of parity income. This concept later on replaced the one of parity price. It was the intention of the Department of Agriculture to obtain for the farming interest the relative income, as compared with total national income, it had been receiving in the prewar years. 3. The adjustment of farm production to meet market requirements. Surpluses were to be held off the market to prevent price derangement. 4. Soil conservation and improved land use. Farmers were to put idle acres into soil-conserving crops. 5. Debt reduction and security against foreclosure at the hands of mortgagees. 6. Rural relief and rehabilitation for submarginal farmers and tenants.

On March 16, 1933, President Roosevelt sent to Congress the administration's first bill for the relief of agriculture. Accompanying the measure, which was based on the unprecedented principle of the grant of subsidies (through rental or benefit payments) to farmers in return for acreage reduction, was a message which stated:

> I tell you frankly that it is a new and untrod path, but I tell you with equal frankness that an unprecedented condition calls for the trial of new means to rescue agriculture. If a fair administrative trial of it is made and it does not produce the hoped-for results, I shall be the first to acknowledge it and advise you.

On May 12, 1933, the Agricultural Adjustment Act was passed and it remained on the statute books until January 6, 1936, when it was invalidated by the Supreme Court. The measure authorized four major lines of action for the purpose of balancing agricultural production. 1. Agricultural prices of certain basic products were to be increased and the surpluses were to be removed from the market. The products originally designated as basic were wheat, cotton, field corn, hogs, rice, tobacco, and milk. To this list later there were added rye, flax, barley, grain sorghums, cattle, peanuts, sugar beets and sugar cane, and potatoes. 2. Farmers' incomes were to be enlarged through direct payments made to them for their participation in the voluntary control, or reduction, programs. 3. The funds necessary to meet these benefit payments were to come from excise taxes imposed on processers. 4. In the cases of farm commodities other than those specifically mentioned, the Department of Agriculture was authorized to draw up marketing arrangements among growers in order to limit production and raise prices. To carry out the provisions of the act there was established within the Department of Agriculture the first of the great *ad hoc* agencies of the New Deal, the Agricultural Adjustment Administration (AAA).

The Brookings Institution, in one of its many analyses of the AAA, explained the mechanics of acreage control in this way:

> Except in the case of rice and dairy products, the programs followed the same general lines. They undertook production control through contracts with individual farmers who agreed to limit their acreage. . . . Each contract established what was known as an "historic base" for the commodity and farm in question. This base was the farm's average acreage . . . of the commodity during a period chosen as having been relatively typical. In signing a contract, each farmer agreed to limit his acreage . . . to a certain percentage of his base. In order to prevent increased production of competing products, the land which was withdrawn could ordinarily be used only for soil-improving crops or for food and feed for home consumption.

It was quickly demonstrated that voluntary acreage reduction could not work, notably in the cases of cotton and tobacco. The weather was too kind—and cotton and tobacco growers had been resourceful in their use of fertilizer. The result was the passage, on April 21, 1934, of the Cotton Control Act and on June 18, 1934, of the Tobacco Control Act, under which growers were to accept production quotas. The Cotton Control Act worked as follows: for the crop year 1934–1935, production of cotton was

Wholesale Price Indexes of Guaranty Trust Company and United States Department of Labor for Years 1919 to 1938. (1926=100.)

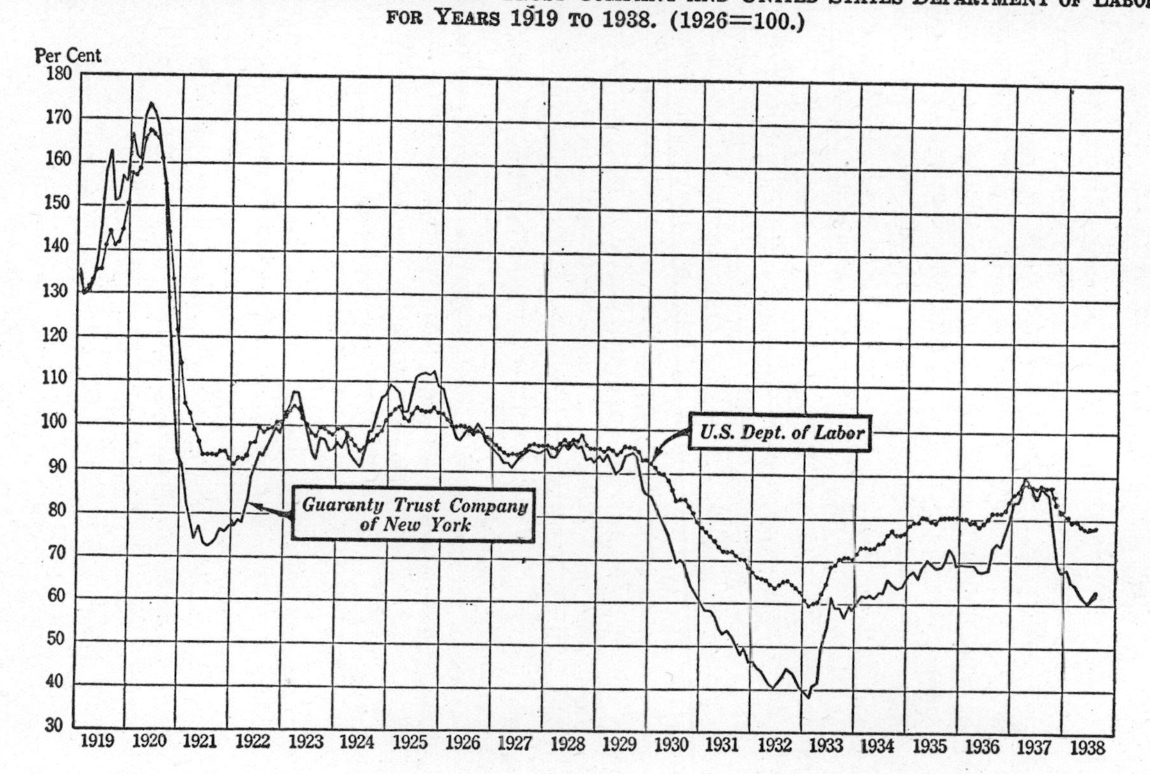

to be limited to 10,000,000 bales; the plan was to be extended by the President for an additional year provided two-thirds of the cotton growers gave their consent; all cotton-growing states, on the basis of their yields over the previous five years, were to be allotted quotas; quotas, in turn, were to be fixed for counties and then for individual farmers, the latter to receive tax exemption certificates, or licenses, for the amounts allotted to them (and, of course, benefit payments); production in excess of the stipulated amounts was to be taxed at the gins at not less than 5 cents per pound.

What did this mean? It meant nothing less than complete governmental regimentation of the cotton (and also tobacco) producers. The economic implications of the device of production control were equally significant. The two laws implied, in effect, the licensing and, therefore, the continuance in production of every grower of a cash cotton and tobacco crop who had previously participated in commercial agriculture—his continuance, that is to say, whether he cultivated marginal lands or not, or whether he used or was in a position to employ technical and mechanical methods in his operations. Clearly, the licensing of farmers might very easily end in the destruction of agriculture's efficiency by government itself.

Through acreage—and, later, production—control, crops were to be reduced. But what of those crops that could not be marketed in an orderly fashion, that is to say, at a sustained price, regardless? The government, in such cases, proceeded to supplement by commodity loans, by marketing agreements, and by government purchases of surpluses. In the first instance, it lent money to holders of cotton on their warehouse receipts (usually around 10 cents a pound) and to holders of corn sealed in bins (usually around 45 cents a bushel). In the second instance, it entered into marketing agreements with milk producers in specific areas (there were some fifty in all such) and with growers of fruits and vegetables, also on a regional basis. In all, some twenty-six crops were covered in this way. These agreements fixed prices, limited the sales of crops to the top grades, called for the suspension of shipments when the market was glutted, and rationed the market among shippers and processors. In the third instance, the government bought up for distribution among the needy surpluses of flour, meats, hides, and the like, for this purpose establishing the Federal Surplus Commodities Corporation.

On January 6, 1936, by a vote of six to three, the Supreme Court found the AAA unconstitutional on the following grounds: 1. The act was a statutory plan for the control of the volume of agricultural production, a power not granted to the federal government by the Constitution. Therefore Congress, in taking such action, had invaded the field of regulation reserved to the states under the Tenth Amendment. 2. The processing taxes and benefit payments were inseparable parts of the same plan. Therefore the processing tax was not a proper exercise of the federal taxing power.

To circumvent the constitutional barriers Congress quickly passed and the President signed (on February 29, 1936) the Soil Conservation and Domestic Allotment Act. Presumably for the purpose of protecting the land resources of the nation against soil erosion and to encourage the utilization of improved methods of cultivation—contour ploughing, terracing, fertilizing, the planting of leguminous crops—growers of staples (wheat, corn, cotton, tobacco) were to receive grants from the government. In this case, the farmers were not to be under contract, but they were to work under the supervision of state and county committees. In order to comply with the Supreme Court's ruling, the act provided that after January 1, 1938, the states themselves were to have full charge of the soil-conserving and soil-building programs and that to them would be voted grants-in-aid for distribution among cooperating farmers.

This, obviously, was only an expedient. It could have no real effects in guiding production; and the Brookings Institution quite properly characterized the program as the subsidy "of uneconomic operations in response to political and sectional pressures." The determination of an overhauled agricultural policy awaited the outcome of President Roosevelt's effort to have the Supreme Court reorganized. The President, as we shall see more fully below, failed in his immediate intention but gained his ultimate objective: the Court became more compliant to the executive will. The upshot was, the passage of the Agricultural Adjustment Act of 1938 (approved February 16) which went even farther than the law of 1933.

The AAA Act of 1938 called for the continuance of the soil-conservation program; and for the support of this Congress was to appropriate out of the general revenue funds. Also producers of wheat, corn, cotton, tobacco, and rice were to receive benefit payments so as to restore the 1909–1914 ratio of farmers' income to the income of other persons (parity income). Commodity loans might also be made. The intention of the commodity-loan feature was to put a floor below which farm prices could not drop. Thus, loans to wheat growers were to go out when the farm price of wheat fell to 52 per cent of the parity price. The loans would have the double purpose of maintaining prices in heavy-yield years and at the same time permitting the government to store adequate reserves against years of dearth. Particularly in connection with wheat, a crop-insurance plan was introduced which protected the country's wheat growers for from 50 per cent to 75 per cent of the average normal harvests. This idea of stabilizing wheat supplies through reserves together with insurance protection was Secretary of Agriculture Wallace's "ever-normal granary" proposal, now written into law.

Also, in order to control the surpluses, the Department of Agriculture was given the right to prorate production for all outstanding crops. A spokesman for the department described the control features in this way:

> Commercial producers of the several major crops will be given acreage allotments so calculated as to produce the supplies necessary to satisfy domestic and foreign demand and to provide carryovers larger than the averages of the past. Producers who keep within these acreages, and who also carry out the soil-conservation practices that may be required, will receive benefit payments and be fully eligible for crop loans. But despite these acreage controls, bumper yields may produce crops larger than are anticipated, or carryovers may prove to be larger than was expected when the acreages were allotted. If the current supplies are in such excess as to provide carryover reserves of some 250,000,000 bushels of wheat or 400,000,000 bushels of corn, then marketing quotas will be imposed. These quotas will restrict sales for the season, with a penalty tax on sales in excess of individual quotas. Marketing quotas will become effective, however, only if two-thirds or more of the farmers to whom they will apply, voting in a referendum, favor them.

It may be pointed out briefly what the implications of the law were. First, agriculture was to be subsidized openly from the public purse. Previous experiences under the AAA indicated that benefit payments, under one guise or another, ran in the neighborhood of from a quarter of a billion to half a billion dollars a year. Second, complete government regulation was applied to the basic crops of the country, so that control was now over *production* and not *acreage*. Third, the government virtually had the right to fix prices for basic crops in good and bad years. Fourth, it was charged with the carrying of great surpluses which (certainly in the case of cotton) meant progressive accumulations and mounting storage charges. Fifth, it protected the growers of food crops at the expense of consumers. The "ever-normal granary" concept was economic nationalism run riot; for, in terms of world production, no real dearth of foodstuffs appeared probable. Sixth, the notion of parity income made of agriculture a special interest. If parity income for commercial farmers, why not parity income for croppers, agricultural laborers, and industrial workers?

We shall have occasion to see, in the next chapter, what effects this program had on agricultural production, prices, and income.

The second part of the farm program had to do with the relief of the credit situation. The Emergency Farm Mortgage Act of May, 1933, authorized the federal land banks to make loans on the basis of "normal" values. At the same time, the Land Bank Commissioner was empowered to make loans upon the security of first or second mortgages in an amount which, together with other indebtedness, would not exceed 75 per cent of the normal agricultural value of farm property. But the bond market was unable to absorb land bank bonds in the amount and at the rate of interest allowed ($2,000,000,000 at 4 per cent); the result was the passage of the Farm Mortgage Refinancing Act of 1934, which created the Federal Farm Mortgage Corporation (under the direction of the Farm Credit Administration). The FFMC was authorized to issue up to $2,000,000,000 worth of bonds, guaranteed as to principal and interest by the government, which it could exchange for the bonds of the land banks and invest directly in mortgage loans. The agency was to a degree successful in obtaining interest reduction and the scaling down of the principal of farm obligations—but at a price. Thus, from April 1, 1930, to January 1, 1935, total mortgage debt on farm lands and buildings was reduced from $9,214,000,000 to $7,645,000,000 (17 per cent). The price was a sharp increase in the government-held debt so that by the end of 1937 perhaps one-half of agricultural long-term paper was in the possession of governmental agencies. In other words, private financing agencies were abandoning the field; and the nationalization of credit was taking place unobtrusively in this sector.

Agrarian political spokesmen were also interested in checking the continued foreclosure of farm properties. The first measure passed, the Federal Farm Bankruptcy Act of June, 1934, was declared unconstitutional by the Supreme Court in May, 1935, because it threatened the rights of the lien holders. Under it, distressed mortgagors had been given the rights to request an appraisal of their farms by a court and to purchase the property by payments over a period of six years, at the same time maintaining occupancy. In its place there was enacted the Farm Mortgage Moratorium Act of August, 1935, under which distressed farmers, with court permission, could enjoy a three-year moratorium against seizure. During this breathing space, the mortgagor was to retain possession of the property upon the payment of a reasonable rental fixed by the court and could possess the farm by paying the appraised value. If the creditors were dissatisfied with the appraised value they could demand a reappraisal or sale at auction; and for ninety days thereafter the debtor had the right to redeem at the sales price.

The third part of the agricultural program had to do with the rehabilitation of submarginal farmers. Originally, the intention was a grandiose one: large numbers of farmers, farm tenants, croppers, and even agricultural laborers, who were destitute or in low-income groups, were to be moved from cutover and other submarginal areas and resettled on subsistence homesteads or in semi-rural villages. Some of the results envisaged by the proponents of the scheme—the initial backers in 1933 and 1934 were Undersecretary of Agriculture Rexford G. Tugwell and Emergency Relief Administrator Harry F. Hopkins—were the following: the surpluses of agricultural goods would be eliminated; more people would live in semi-rural surroundings, at the same time learning to cultivate again a pioneering independence; a long step would be taken toward the decentralization of industry and the reduction of many of those social ills which have flourished with the growth of great cities.

A series of experiments was launched. This included rural resettlement projects, suburban resettlement projects, and loans for rural rehabilitation. What the original planners looked forward to was the establishment of communities administered through local non-profit or limited dividend corporations to which federal funds were to be lent. These in turn were to advance funds to settlers for the lease or purchase of homesteads—the individual property in each case averaging $2500—upon which homes were to be erected. But certain practical questions immediately presented themselves: 1. Was it not impossible to create individual homesteads at so small a capital cost? (This fear quickly was realized. Costs of the first projects ran to at least twice that amount.) 2. Granted the completion of the project, where was the homesteader (who was to be a subsistence farmer) to secure cash with which to purchase those necessaries and semi-luxuries demanded by modern standards of living, which he could not produce on his own plot? 3. Where was the money to come from to pay the interest and the principal of his indebtedness? 4. If this income was to be derived from the sale of surplus agricultural products, would not the subsistence farmer become in effect, partially at least, a commercial farmer and thus a competitor of the man engaged wholly in commercial agriculture, putting both back exactly where they were before? 5. If the necessary income was to be derived from part-time factory employment or even from handicraft industries, would not the subsistence farmer become in fact a "sweatshop" worker and hence a dangerous competitor of the whole-time industrial worker?

Small farmers, tenants, and croppers had other ideas which did not exactly jibe with those of the resettlement experimenters. They pointed out that the basis of settlement was to be the original American small homestead—where the homesteader in time possessed his property in fee simple, operated it as an independent unit, had inadequate capital for the cultivation of anything but cash crops, and quickly became the prey of the money lender and land speculator. One of the spokesmen of this group bluntly said: "We believe that in the cotton South the small homestead visioned in many of the present proposals is an economic anachronism, foredoomed to failure." These people therefore insisted that restrictions be imposed on the easy alienation of the lands of the new settlers, that communities be operated as cooperative enterprises, and that there be close surveillance of planting programs, and the like.

The Division of Subsistence Homesteads of the Department of Interior (established in 1933) and the Resettlement Administration (its successor in 1935) pursued the course originally laid down. They bought up and retired from cultivation substandard lands, setting these aside as grazing ranges, recreation places, forests, and wildlife territory. They made small rehabilitation loans, under careful supervision, to needy farming families for the purchase of seed, tools, and livestock. They resettled stranded families in new rural settlements or on scattered farmsteads, providing them with old-fashioned homesteads ranging from 20 to 160 acres in size. They created projects for homes in rural and suburban communities (three of these were the so-called greenbelt towns) where fully employed industrial workers might also cultivate subsistence kitchen gardens.

The Farm Security Administration (established in 1937), however, was also beginning to strike out in those new and untried directions proposed by the critics of the old program. It began to give heed to the demand for settlement on a cooperative basis, with the homesteaders possessing only a large lot on which was to be located the house and a kitchen garden; the rest of the farm lands—surrounding the community—were to be operated in common, with the use of labor-saving devices and mass-production methods of farming. Also, the transfer of title to the homesteaders was to be withheld for a long period of years. This was a new institutional form for America; but in reality it was a return to that village organization which Western Europe had known before the enclosure of the common lands took place. Indeed, early in 1938, the first such community at Lake Dick, Arkansas, was opened up. The FSA in 1938 was voted by Congress $175,000,000 for its activities. Whether it would be permitted to push the village community settlement idea—in the face of the embittered opposition of old-line farmer organizations, which insisted upon family farms with alienation assured—remained to be seen. In any case, whatever the policy finally to be determined upon, the New Deal's resettlement program was still at an experimental level. The economic and social needs of the underprivileged farmers, who constituted fully two-thirds of America's agriculturists, had barely been analyzed, let alone satisfied.

Industry and Labor

Just as agriculture was to be revived, in large part, by price raising (in this case a return to the price situation prevailing during 1909–1914), so industry and labor were to be saved by the same rule (in the case of industry a return to the price situation of 1926 being the objective, in the case of labor reemployment as a result of shorter hours and minimum wages). To effectuate these ends Congress passed and the President signed on June 16, 1933, the National Industrial Recovery Act. Its important provisions were: 1. The President was to establish an agency to which was to be delegated the powers and functions indicated in the act. 2. Codes of fair competition might be drawn up by trade or industrial associations and submitted to the President for his approval. The President was given the power to approve such codes if the associations were "truly representative" of their industries and if the codes were "not designed to promote monopolies or to eliminate or oppress small enterprises." 3. Once such codes were approved, they were enforceable by law; the courts could issue injunctions against violation on the institution of equity proceedings by the United States district attorneys. 4. The President might prescribe codes for industries if none as submitted was approved by him. 5. The President might make agreements or approve voluntary agreements to further the purpose of the law. He was also empowered to institute a licensing system in any industry if that were necessary to make a code or agreement effective. (This last power was never employed.) 6. Any action under provisions of the law was exempt from the anti-trust acts. 7. Every code of fair competition was to contain the following conditions affecting labor. This was the much discussed section 7(a) of the law and it is quoted in full.

(1) That employees shall have the right to organize and bargain collectively through representatives of their own choosing, and shall be free from the interference, restraint, or coercion of employers of labor, or their agents, in the designation of such representatives or in self-organization or in other concerted activities for the purpose of collective bargaining or other mutual aid or protection; (2) that no employee and no one seek-

ing employment shall be required as a condition of employment to join any company union or to refrain from joining, organizing, or assisting a labor organization of his own choosing; and (3) that employers shall comply with the maximum hours of labor, minimum rates of pay, and other conditions of employment approved or prescribed by the President.

The National Recovery Administration was the agency created to supervise the preparation of the codes of fair competition and enforce their observance. In addition to the Chief Administrator, Gen. Hugh S. Johnson (succeeded later by Donald Richberg), and several assistants, there were provided a compliance board (in charge of enforcement) and advisory boards for industry, labor, and consumers. To protect the rights of labor and to settle by mediation, conciliation, or arbitration all industrial disputes the National Labor Board was created on August 5, 1933. It was headed by Senator Robert F. Wagner and was made up of twelve additional persons, six of whom represented the employers and the other six the workers. The Board was empowered to establish local or regional boards, upon which employers and workers also were to have equal representation, supervise elections in industrial plants where the workers were to choose their own representatives for their negotiations with employers, and refer its findings of violation of section 7(a) of the NIRA to the Attorney General and to the compliance division of the NRA.

The code-making process in most cases was comparatively simple. Representative groups in each industry, usually working through their trade associations, drew up codes which were presented to the NRA for consideration. Public hearings were then held under the direction of deputy administrators, at which the viewpoints and objections of consumers, labor, and other interested parties could be presented; upon the acceptance of these codes by the deputy and division administrators the documents were submitted to the President or the NRA Adminstrator for his approval. After proper approval a code had the force of a statute. With the completion of the code, an agency was set up in each industry called the Code Authority which was, in effect, the agency of self-government in the industry. In most cases the code authorities were merely the old trade associations in new guise, except for the occasional addition of a small number of "public" representatives; labor as such was given a formal place on very few of the Code Authorities. While individual codes were being formulated, a large number of industries operated under what was called the "blanket" code, or the President's Reemployment Agreement. Every employer signing this was entitled to display forthwith the Blue Eagle, the emblem which indicated compliance with the spirit of the NIRA. In time, more than five hundred separate codes were drawn up.

Because of the relatively slight participation of labor in the initial proceedings, only a handful of the codes provided for less than the 40-hour week. Minimum wages ranged in the great majority of cases between $12 and $15, while the labor of children under 16 years was banned. Industry, however, displayed extraordinary ingenuity in devising methods for limiting production and controlling prices, that is to say, inaugurating monopoly practices, and more than one-half of the codes accepted by May, 1934, contained such features. These were usually of seven kinds: (1) the establishment of minimum prices, or the maintenance of resale prices; (2) the fixing of a minimum mark-up (as in the retail code); (3) the prohibition of the sale of commodities below the cost of production; (4) the creation of open-price posting arrangements (which, in effect, meant the establishment of uniform prices); (5) multiple basing-point systems (as in steel); (6) the fixing of prices under governmental control (as in coal and oil); (7) the limitation of production (the usual methods being by the allotment of production quotas to individual units in the industry, by prohibitions of the increase of productive capacity through either the installation of new machinery or the erection of new plants, and by a uniform limitation on machine hours). Another characteristic which led to a tendency of monopoly control was the arbitrary definition of "cost," particularly in determining the fixing of minimum prices. Finally, the codes set out to make sales practices uniform in order to check the taking of unfair advantages.

While industry, during the initial months of the New Deal, glady accepted public intervention and raised few objections to the administration program, it soon became apparent that its acquiescence was to be of brief duration. As the economic processes began again to move, by the midsummer and fall of 1933, complaints began to pour in increasingly of the violation of codes of fair competition by factory and store managers. Indeed, so widespread had the practice become that in a radio address on

October 22, President Roosevelt was compelled to admonish "chiselers" that the penalties authorized by the laws would be imposed.

Serious in itself, this was not nearly as disquieting as the growing protest on the part of industrialists against the basic principles of the New Deal. Increasingly, spokesmen for business (and these were in time joined by leaders of the Republican party and some members of the Democracy, foremost among whom was Alfred E. Smith) began to demand that government retire again to its traditional functions and leave the operations of industrial affairs to private enterprise and the chances of the free market, or at most to industrial self-regulation. This stand was crystallized in a series of discussions taking place during June, 1934, in which participated many of America's greatest industrialists, who had served or were still serving on the industrial advisory board of the NRA. The plan of self-regulation proposed included the establishment of maximum hours of work and minimum wages for labor, the prohibition of child labor, the elimination of unfair trade practices, the relief of technological unemployment, and the conservation of natural resources. Nothing was said of recognizing the workers' right to organize for collective bargaining or of preventing monopoly prices.

If this was disheartening, what was to be said of the growing conviction that the chief function of the NIRA and the code-making process had become exactly that fostering of cartelization, with consequent strangulation of competition and the establishment of monopoly prices, which industrial leaders were proposing to continue forever? The consumers' advisory board of the NRA, after having examined at length the working out of codes, in the beginning of 1934 pointed out that "wholesale prices were rising, retail prices were bound to go up, and the consumer demand must inevitably drop." From every side evidences began to accumulate that prices definitely were getting out of line. The administration was not unaware of these tendencies and exhorted manufacturers and distributors to check too sudden price rises. The admonition was unavailing, and the redistribution of national income, which had been one of the major theoretical objectives of the New Deal, was perhaps as remote as ever before.

The whole controversy came to a head with the release of the initial reports of the National Recovery Review Board on May 21, 1934. This board, largely on the basis of the representations of Senators Borah and Nye that the codes were driving small enterprisers out of business, had been created on February 19, 1934, to hold hearings and collect evidences of repression; the veteran lawyer Clarence S. Darrow had been named its chairman. After having examined the work of Code Authorities in iron and steel, motion pictures, electrical goods, bituminous coal, and a number of lesser industries, the National Recovery Review Board came to the conclusion that the NRA was fostering monopoly and oppressing small industrialists and distributors, that certain codes were openly being administered by monopoly interests, and that prices to consumers were at the mercy of monopoly control.

More sensational than these findings was the supplementary report signed by Mr. Darrow and Mr. W. O. Thompson. It reiterated charges of monopoly, called for transfer of code enforcement and fact-finding from the NRA to the Federal Trade Commission, and insisted that competition no longer could be relied upon to protect the consumer. The report concluded:

> The choice is between monopoly sustained by government, which is clearly the trend in the National Recovery Administration, and a planned economy, which demands socialized ownership and control, since only by collective ownership can the inevitable conflict of separately owned units for the market be eliminated in favor of planned production. There is no hope for the small business man or for complete recovery in America in enforced restriction upon production for the purpose of maintaining higher prices. The hope for the American people, including the small business man, not to be overwhelmed by their own abundance lies in the planned use of America's resources following socialization. To give the sanction of government to sustain profits is not a planned economy, but a regimented organization for exploitation.

Into an atmosphere already overcharged, the Supreme Court decision of May 27, 1935, in the so-called Schechter case, came like a bolt from the blue. By a unanimous vote the Court found the NRA unconstitutional on three grounds: that Congress could not delegate its legislative powers to private individuals (i. e., the Code Authorities) and could not do similarly in the case of the President or other executive officers without first laying down definite principles for their guidance; that the federal government could not legislate about wages, hours, prices, production, or other industrial practices so far as these practices did not directly affect interstate commerce; and that a national emergency did not exist.

The whole NRA, with its codes of fair competition, its limitations on child labor, its efforts to assure the workers minimum wages, maximum hours, and the right of collective bargaining, was thus in ruins. This was a major defeat for the administration and, in the case of industry, all the President could hope for was voluntary cooperation. He sought to salvage something from the wreckage by pressing for the passage of the Wagner-Connery Labor Disputes bill, the Wagner-Lewis Economic Security bill, the Omnibus Banking bill, and a measure to outlaw utility holding companies. The Labor Disputes bill was to make up for the shortcomings in the administration's labor policy: it called for the establishment of an independent labor board with quasi-judicial powers similar to those of the Federal Trade Commission. The Economic Security bill was to take a step in the direction of security for the aged, the unemployed, the physically disabled, and for dependent mothers and children: this was to be accomplished through federal contributions to the states, the building up of a compulsory old age pension fund, and certain encouragements given to the states to create their own unemployment funds. The chief purpose of the Omnibus Banking bill was to give the Federal Reserve Board, as a governmental agency, control over the open-market operations of the member banks; this meant, simply, that Washington and not the private bankers would determine at what time the credit flow of the nation should be expanded or contracted.

In addition, the President launched an undisguised attack upon the Supreme Court: the Court's disregard of the emergency and its insistence upon being bound by the constitutional limitations on federal action imposed when, as he said, the country had been in "the horse and buggy stage" moved him to declare that ours was the only national government in the world which did not have the right to enact and administer laws that had to do with economic and social problems. During 1937, the President pressed for reorganization of the Court to make it more responsive to executive and legislative program making. Of the great controversy that raged about the Supreme Court more will be said in the next chapter.

As regards industry, the President was determined that the interest of government be recognized. Business had opposed beneficent regulation under its own Code Authorities, even in return for the virtual suppression of the anti-trust laws. Very well, then: the anti-trust laws would be enforced once more. For the President and his advisers had come to agree that price inflexibility and production control—the two main devices of monopoly—had to be destroyed if private enterprise was to continue to function. In the message to Congress on April 29, 1938, already referred to, the President inveighed against the growing concentration of economic power in a few giant groups. His analysis read like a text out of a radical handbook. "The statistical history of modern times proves that in times of depression concentration of business speeds up." ". . . the concentration of stock ownership of corporations in the hands of a tiny minority of the population matches the concentration of corporate assets." "Close financial control, through interlocking spheres of influence over channels of investment, and through the use of financial devices like holding companies and strategic minority interests, creates close control of the business policies of enterprises which masquerade as independent units." "Private enterprise is ceasing to be free enterprise and is becoming a cluster of private collectivisms. Masking itself as a system of free enterprise after the American model, it is in fact becoming a concealed cartel system after the European model." "One of the primary causes of our present difficulties lies in the disappearance of price competition in many industrial fields, particularly in basic manufacture where concentrated economic power is most evident—and where rigid prices and fluctuating pay rolls are general. Managed industrial prices mean fewer jobs."

The President therefore called for the effective enforcement of free competition once more. Present agencies (the Department of Justice and the Federal Trade Commission) were to be strengthened in their investigatory powers. Mergers and interlocking relationships were to be scrutinized more closely and methods devised for breaking them up. Financial control over industry was to be checked. Investment trusts, including the insurance companies, were to be circumscribed in their activities. Bank holding companies were to be controlled and in time abolished. Trade associations were to be supervised. And President Roosevelt requested a comprehensive investigation into the workings of monopoly and the creation of means of curbing its growth. This last request the Seventy-fifth Congress, in June, 1938, granted him, voting $500,000 for the purpose.

Meanwhile the President appointed Thurman W. Arnold Assistant Attorney-General and charged him with the rigorous enforcement of the existing anti-trust laws. And the general character of the administration's trust policy was foreshadowed when Mr. Arnold, in an initial statement in August, 1938, announced that his office would raise the following questions in connection with anti-trust prosecutions. 1. "Does the particular combination go beyond the necessities of efficient mass production and become an instrument of arbitrary price control?" 2. "Does any particular arrangement affecting marketing practices tend merely to create orderly marketing conditions in which competitors can exist, or is it an instrument to maintain rigid prices?" This was all very well and seemed like a realistic approach to the problem of monopoly control over prices. But it is exactly at this point that an interesting question presents itself. According to the administration analysis, prices had a tendency to drop sharply as one of the incidents of depression: but these were the prices largely of consumer goods. Such prices—Mr. Arnold called them "starvation prices"—had to be raised to further recovery. On the other hand, the prices in the managed, or monopoly industries, were too high: and these had to be lowered. If, therefore, high prices were to be lowered and low prices to be raised, obviously the market mechanism of free capitalism no longer was to function. It was to be replaced (as had already happened in the case of agriculture) by managed prices emanating from a single directing public agency on top and outside of the market. Did anything prove more clearly the intention and the methods of state capitalism than this policy of differentiating between (and controlling) the prices of different economic sectors?

In the case of industry, therefore, initial experimentation had ended without result; and only in the sixth year of its existence was the New Deal coming to grips—perhaps—with the problem of monopoly first by studying its morphology. This, at any rate, was a beginning. In the case of labor, there was fruition. As has been said earlier, it was in this sector that the New Deal met with its most substantial victories. Section 7(a) of the NIRA, with its promises of the right of collective bargaining, the free choice by workers of their own representatives, and their recognition by industry, was at once regarded by labor as a new charter of liberties; and the wage earners of the country, seizing the opportunity, flocked to join unions affiliated with the American Federation of Labor and quickly resorted to the strike weapon when union recognition and higher wage scales were denied them. From the enactment of the Recovery Act until its annual convention in October, 1933, the A. F. of L. reported the issuance of 700 charters to new federal unions, a great growth in membership in affiliated internationals, and the spread of unionization into industries like steel, automobiles, textiles, tires, oil, and aluminum, where earlier efforts at organization had always proved abortive. Before long the A. F. of L. was claiming a strength of 4,500,000 members, which was in excess of its previous highest development in 1920. In addition, independent unions not affiliated with the A. F. of L. and often having progressive leadership had a membership of at least 250,000 workers; while unions affiliated with the Communist Trade Union Unity League claimed 125,000 members. Particularly significant was the growth of federal unions, organizations directly chartered by the A. F. of L., usually based on single shops and as a rule cutting across the craft lines of the old internationals. Into these new organizations were pouring young, enthusiastic, and militant workers who were unfamiliar and impatient with the conciliatory tactics of the older craft-union leadership and who refused to effect any agreements with their employers short of trade-union recognition. Many of the strikes following the inauguration of the NRA were rank-and-file struggles which were not led by the officers of the old unions but by strike committees made up directly of workers in the shops.

On account of these industrial conflicts and the possibility of a general steel strike, the first in the industry since 1919, which threatened to involve some 400,000 workers, Congress on June 16, 1934, passed the Labor Disputes Joint Resolution which included the following: 1. The President was authorized to establish a board or boards empowered to investigate matters in dispute between workers and employers arising out of the NIRA. 2. Such agencies were to order and conduct elections among the workers in order to determine representation for the purpose of collective bargaining. (It will be noted that nothing was said of majority rule in the case of workers' elections.) 3. The boards, with the approval of the President, were to prescribe such rules and regulations as might be necessary. 4. Boards established under the resolution were to cease to exist on June 16, 1935, the date of termination of the NIRA. 5. Nothing in the resolution was to prevent or diminish the right of workers to strike or engage in other concerted activities. On June 26, the President established the National Longshoremen's Board, to investigate the bitter strike involving thousands of waterfront and marine workers in San Francisco; and on June 28, the National Steel Labor Relations Board was set up. Finally, on July 9, the National Labor Board was abolished and in its place there was created the National Labor Relations Board, of three members, independent of the NRA and working in conjunction with the Labor Department, which was to coordinate the various functions set out in the Labor Disputes Resolution and act as a court of last review for special labor boards.

No more serious challenge to the administration's labor policy was presented than the four-day general strike, in effect a sympathy strike to assist the longshoremen and marine workers, which broke out in San Francisco in July, 1934. While the great mass of workers (some seventy-five thousand had gone out) soon returned to their shops and factories, as a result of a red scare, the strike was of the utmost significance. It revealed an extraordinary solidarity among the rank and file, who were impatient with the half-way measures of the conservative A. F. of L. leadership; and it proved that labor was intending to utilize every conceivable weapon at its disposal to gain the right of collective bargaining promised by section 7(a) of the NIRA.

The striking down of the NIRA by the Supreme Court and, by implication, the invalidation of Section 7(a) forced Congress to enact its third piece of legislation in the interests of labor's right to organize. In July, 1935, there was passed the (Wagner) National Labor Relations Act, which was frankly class legislation, in that it spoke only of industry's duty toward labor: employers were obligated to bargain collectively with their workers and to give up all practices which might prevent employees from properly realizing the objective of free trade unionism. To achieve this end, the act defined specifically a number of unfair practices which henceforth were to be regarded as illegal. The outstanding were: Employers might not in any way interfere, restrain, or coerce workers in their plans to organize. They could not discharge or discriminate against workers for trade-union membership or activities. They could not support company unions. Their refusal to recognize and treat with a union, which had been chosen by a majority of the workers as their representative, was to be held a violation of the law. Closed shop agreements were not to be regarded as illegal.

To enforce the provisions of the act, there was to be set up an independent and quasi-judicial body, the National Labor Relations Board, of three members. This was invested with extraordinary powers. It was to determine what was to be the appropriate unit for the purposes of collective bargaining, that is to say, whether the unit was to be an employer unit, a craft unit, a plant unit, or a subdivision thereof. (In other words, the NLRB might decide that an employer or employers had to treat on the one hand with an industrial or a craft union, and on the other, for a whole region or a whole industry, for a single plant, or only for an individual department.) The Board was authorized to investigate questions concerning the representation of employees, to conduct elections when the workers asked for them, and to certify the trade unions duly chosen by the majority of the workers involved.

The machinery for the prevention of unfair labor practices was to follow closely those devices created by the Federal Trade Commission Act. Whenever workers or their representatives charged that an unfair labor practice had been or was being engaged in, the Board could issue a formal complaint and summon the employer for a hearing before a trial examiner. The employer complained of had the right to file an answer and to appear and give testimony. The Board then reviewed the whole proceeding and if it found the workers' charges substantiated it had the power to issue a cease-and-desist order and petition the appropriate federal circuit court of appeals to enforce it. No penalties were provided in the act for non-compliance with cease-and-desist orders and demands for access to employers' records other than those available to the circuit court of appeals in contempt proceedings.

The Board, as set up by the President, proceeded to carry out these mandates with energy, exploring every contingency that normally was likely to arise in employer-employee relations. This it did for the purpose of obtaining clarifying Supreme Court decisions. It held elections and authorized specific trade unions to speak for the workers. It declared specific labor practices illegal, including the use of violence, the hiring of labor spies, and the organization of vigilante groups. It handed down cease-and-desist orders and requested their enforcement by the circuit courts of appeal. Where it found employers acting illegally, particularly in the discharge of workers, it ordered reinstatement with back pay. It concerned itself with questions that were clearly in interstate commerce and others that were doubtful. Never, in American history, was a body of administrative law more quickly or plainly formulated. And the Board met with a complete success: for, the upshot was, within less than three years, not only did it manage to write a labor code for American industrial relations which was the most advanced in the world but it also obtained the Supreme Court's approval of every exploratory step it had taken.

In a group of five notable rulings, on April 12, 1937, the Supreme Court, by five-to-four decisions (except in one case where the vote was unanimous because interstate commerce was clearly involved), held that the NLRB was within its rights in treating with employer-employee relations, even when the products of the employers were locally manufactured. This was a complete reversal of the position taken by the Court in the E. C. Knight case in 1895. The Court found that the right to organize was a "fundamental right"; that discrimination and coercion to prevent its exercise was "a proper subject for condemnation by competent legislative authority"; and "that union was essential to give laborers opportunity to deal on an equality with their employer." The cases involved virtually every aspect of industry and communication where interstate commerce existed, even if only in a secondary degree. They were: the *Washington, Virginia, and Maryland Coach Co. Case* (an operator of motor buses); the *Associated Press Case* (an organization for dissemination of news via wire services); the *Jones and Laughlin Steel Co. Case* (a manufacturer of steel products); the *Fruehauf Trailer Co. Case* (a manufacturer of automobile trailers); and the *Friedman–Harry Marks Clothing Co. Case* (a manufacturer of men's clothing).

And in 1938, there followed fast at least six other important decisions whose intention was the clarifying of the Board's powers. In one of these, the Court ordered the disestablishment of a company union; in another, interference with picketing was found illegal; in still another, the closed shop agreement was found not a violation of the fundamental constitutional rights of non-union members. Indeed, up to the middle of 1938, in but one instance of the many cases involving the Wagner Act which came before it, did the Court deny review of a decision of a lower court refusing to enforce an order of the Board.

Thus supported, well might J. Warren Madden, chairman of the Board, declare in May, 1938:

> They [many employers] dispensed with their industrial spies, recognized the dignity of their employees and their chosen representatives, and instructed their supervisors and foremen to keep their hands off union affairs. The consequence has been an unprecedented growth of unions old and new, and thousands of new collective bargaining contracts which have given mutual self-respect and stability to labor relations.

And Mr. Madden closed his address with the following ringing declaration:

> We shall continue to try to do a careful and workmanlike job in the interpretation and administration of our law. We shall not modify our policy of vigorous enforcement. We are glad that the Supreme Court was able to say, only the day before yesterday, in one of our cases, "the contention that the respondent was denied a full and adequate hearing must be rejected."

It was significant to note, as well, that the NLRB was pressing its operations into many fields which, hitherto, had scarcely been touched by employer-employee negotiations, or, in fact, by federal regulation. It was taking jurisdiction in cases affecting motion pictures, banks, insurance companies, public utilities, and department stores. At the end of three years of activity (in July, 1938), the Board reported an extraordinary tale of successful functioning. Of the cases coming before it, 55 per cent, covering 1,248,000 persons, were settled amicably and by agreement. Only 5 per cent of the cases went to formal hearing; and in only 2 per cent of the cases did the Board have to fall back upon cease-and-desist orders. It settled 580 strikes involving 150,000 workers, and it held 1280 elections in which 450,000 valid ballots were cast.

Social Security

In another region new trails were blazed: and this was in connection with the passage of federal social security legislation. On August 14, 1935, President Roosevelt approved the Social Security Act, which, in addition to setting up a Social Security Board to administer its provisions, called for federal support of a number of different types of assistance and insurance. The law provided for the following: (1) a system of federal old age benefits, based upon earnings before a fixed retirement age of 65; (2) a system of unemployment compensation, administered under state laws approved by the Social Security Board; (3) grants to states, more or less on a matching basis, for public assistance to the needy aged, the needy blind, and to children under 16 deprived of parental support; (4) grants to states, on a matching basis, for the provision of maternal and child health services, medical and other services for crippled children, and welfare services for the care of homeless, dependent, and neglected children; and (5) payments to states for the establishment and maintenance of state and local health services and for the vocational rehabilitation of the physically disabled.

Prior to the passage of the act, but one state—Wisconsin—had established an unemployment insurance plan. But as a result of the operations of the Social Security Act, by the middle of 1938 every American jurisdiction had passed acceptable legislation, which covered nearly 26,000,000 persons. And by June, 1938, twenty-eight states were paying out unemployment benefits. (In the first six months of 1938, the payments amounted to $180,000,000, with the individual benefits ranging from $5 to $15 a week. The average was $10.50 weekly, and the maximum period was sixteen weeks.) This was effectuated through the laying of a federal tax on all pay rolls, 90 per cent of which was to be credited employers as payments toward state funds, if the states in which they were located adopted approved systems of unemployment insurance. After January 1, 1938, this pay roll tax was to be 3 per cent. In this connection, it should be noted that, unlike the European countries, states were not required to make contributions nor was employee participation made compulsory. However, a few states did begin to pass legislation calling for worker contributions. Also, all contributions made were to be paid into the general fund of the federal Treasury; and against this the states were to draw when they were ready to pay out unemployment benefits. However, even granted the universal adoption of approved legislation, it was estimated that not much more than half the working population would be protected, for farm laborers, domestic servants, casual workers, government employees, and the employees of charitable, religious, and educational organizations were excluded from the benefits of the law.

In the case of the care of the aged, two plans were devised. The first called for the payment of pensions to the aged by the states, with the federal government making matching grants-in-aid to those states which accepted the conditions laid down in the act. These included the following: programs were to be state-wide in their effects; the minimum age limit for pensions was to be 70 years up to 1940 and 65 years thereafter; the period of residence to be required was not to be in excess of five years; and the federal government's maximum contribution to the states for each person aided was to be $15 a month, provided the states made matching grants. The second plan called for the building up of an old-age benefit fund (which, in time, would replace the pensions), out of which aged persons would receive annuities based upon their wage experiences. The fund was to be created out of contributions made by both employers and employees; and these contributions, like the unemployment benefit contributions, were to be paid into the general fund of the federal Treasury. All working persons (except for the same excluded occupations listed above) receiving $3000 or under, or on the first $3000 of their wages or salaries, were to have annuities provided for them after 65 years of age. The employer contribution (in the form of an excise tax) and the employee contribution (a form of income tax, and deducted from pay rolls) were to be equal. Both were to begin at the rate of 1 per cent each in 1937, 1938, and 1939, and increase gradually to 3 per cent after 1948. Old age benefits, from the fund thus built up, were to be paid on a monthly basis, beginning in 1942.

How far-flung the influences of the act were, particularly as regards the care of dependents, may be noted from the fact that toward the end of 1937, 1,500,000 aged persons, 482,000 dependent children in 194,000 families, and 39,000 blind persons were receiving assistance in states whose plans had already received the approval of the Social Security Board.

In May, 1937, the Supreme Court, in three decisions, underwrote the constitutionality of the Social Security Act in all its aspects. One case had to do with the validity of the federal unemployment insurance tax, and this the Court found lawful by a five-to-four decision. Another case had to do with the legality of the old age benefit tax levy; this was approved by a seven-to-two decision. The third passed on the constitutionality of the unemployment insurance law of Alabama; and here the decision was five-to-four.

There was general agreement that the federal government had

made giant strides forward, particularly in the liberalization of provisions for the care of the aged, dependent children, crippled children, and the blind. About the unemployment and old age benefit funds aspects of the act there was less unanimity. Critics pointed out, as regards unemployment insurance, that government itself made no contributions, thus limiting the size of the funds and the benefits to be paid. As regards the old age annuities, it was insisted that those should be built up by government and employer contributions entirely, that the annuities would end by being smaller than the present pensions, and that the act placed an immediate backbreaking burden upon the younger workers in view of the fact that persons reaching the age of 65, after a few years of making contributions, could begin drawing annuities. Most critics were notably concerned over the fact that the reserves for this fund would in time reach a staggering total; indeed, by 1980, when this portion of the act would be generally operative, they would stand at $47,000,000,000, entirely invested in government obligations. As Abraham Epstein properly pointed out: "It is difficult to forecast the consequences of concentrating all governmental debt and securities in one account held and controlled by the government itself."

On June 13, 1938, Congress passed the Wages and Hours Act, also made necessary by the invalidation of the NIRA; this was frankly humanitarian legislation for the purpose of establishing minimum wages and maximum hours and abolishing child labor throughout the country in a fairly large number of trades and industries engaged in or producing goods for interstate commerce.[1] In an opening declaration of policy, the act stated:

> The Congress hereby finds that the existence, in industries engaged in commerce, or in the production of goods for commerce, of labor conditions detrimental to the maintenance of the minimum standard of living necessary for health, efficiency, and well-being of workers (1) causes commerce and the channels and instrumentalities of commerce to be used to spread and perpetuate such labor conditions among the workers of the several states; (2) burdens commerce and the free flow of goods in com-

[1] The act exempted, as regards the maximum hour provisions, employers of labor engaged in the processing of milk and cream, the ginning of cotton, the processing of cottonseed, and the processing of sugar beets or maple sap into sugar or syrup. Also, an exemption of 14 weeks in any calendar year, in the case of maximum hour standards, was granted to first processers engaged in canning or packing perishable fresh fruits or vegetables, or in the handling of poultry or livestock. Seamen, fishermen, and farm workers also were excluded.

merce; (3) constitutes an unfair method of competition in commerce; (4) leads to labor disputes burdening and obstructing commerce and the free flow of goods in commerce; and (5) interferes with the orderly and fair marketing of goods in commerce.

The act, therefore, provided for the establishment of a Wage and Hour Division in the Department of Labor, to be headed by an Administrator who was to appoint boards for all industries; and these boards, representative of the public, the employers, and the employees, were to convene from time to time to draw up minimum wage scales in order to "reach, as rapidly as is economically feasible without substantially curtailing employment, the objective of a universal minimum wage of 40 cents an hour for each industry." For the first year of the act's operation, no minimum wages were to be less than 25 cents an hour; during the next six years, the minimum wage was to be 30 cents an hour; and after the expiration of seven years, it was to be 40 cents an hour. Maximum hours were fixed as follows: a 44-hour week during the first year of the law's operation; a 42-hour week during the second year; and a 40-hour week thereafter. All overtime was to be paid for at the rate of time and one-half. In special cases employees might be permitted to work 12 hours a day or up to 56 hours a week without overtime payments, if such employees were employed in pursuance of a collective-bargaining agreement certified as bona fide by the NLRB and guaranteeing 2000 hours' work a year or 1000 hours of work a half-year or 14 weeks' work in a seasonal industry.

The minimum wage committees of the separate industries might recommend wage differentials; but none of these was to be fixed on solely a regional basis. Factors to be considered in determining such differentials were the following: 1. Competitive conditions as affected by transportation, living, and production costs. 2. The wages established for work of like or comparable character by collective labor agreements. 3. The wages paid for work of like or comparable character by employers who voluntarily maintain minimum-wage standards in the industry. The Administrator might approve or disapprove of the recommendations of these industries committees. Once he approved, after affording interested persons an opportunity to be heard, he could issue an order embodying the wage scales. Employers, on the other hand, had the right of review in circuit courts of appeals.

The provisions as regards the abolition of child labor were as follows: The shipment of goods in commerce produced by "oppressive child labor" was declared illegal. Children under 16 years of age engaged in ordinary employment and those between 16 and 18 years of age in hazardous employment (as defined by the federal Children's Bureau) were to be regarded as the victims of "oppressive child labor."[2] The Children's Bureau, if it found that regular schooling, health, and wellbeing were not being interfered with, might authorize the employment of children between the ages of 14 and 16 years in occupations other than manufacturing and mining.

The penalties section imposed a maximum fine of $10,000 or a six-months' prison term upon violators; called upon employers so found to pay to employees the differences between wages received and the ordered minimums as well as "an additional equal amount as liquidating damages"; and the employer found guilty was to pay the attorney's fee of employees bringing the action against him.

There could be no question that from the social point of view this was welfare legislation of the highest order; what the act's economic effects were likely to be was problematical, however. Conservative critics (disregarding the successful experiences of American states and England with such legislation) insisted that the act was likely to have the reverse effects of the putative ones of stimulating recovery by creating employment and increasing purchasing power. Substandard workers would be dropped. Marginal firms would go out of business. An artificial stimulus would be given to mechanization, in an effort to lower labor costs, and further disemployment would result. Radical critics, on the other hand, maintained that what was necessary was not minimum-wage legislation on an hourly basis but minimum-income legislation on an annual basis. Between the two terminal points of such a wide arc the debate swung; it remained to be seen how tangible achievement was to be. But of the good intentions of the New Deal planners there could be no question.

Currency and Credit

The drive to raise prices and relieve the pressure of the debt burden soon turned the thoughts of the administration to the dual problems of currency expansion and bank credit inflation. The fol-

[2] The child labor provisions did not apply to the labor of persons in agriculture who were beyond the school attendance age, as set by the laws of the states of their residence.

lowing devices were possible and all of them were employed: the devaluation of the dollar; an increase in the amount of outstanding currency; and an increase in the amount of outstanding bank credit. It was also assumed that by such methods a stable price level could be maintained; and indeed, in 1936, the administration began to contract the bank credit base in an effort to force prices down. Our attention, first, must be directed to the monetary activities of the New Dealers. On March 10, 1933, the President issued an executive order to halt the export of gold except when licensed by the Treasury; on April 5, the hoarding of gold coin, gold bullion, and gold certificates was forbidden; and on April 19, the United States formally departed from the gold standard when an executive order stopped the free movement of the metal both within and without the country. To achieve the same result in a somewhat different way the Gold Repeal Joint Resolution, approved June 5, 1933, canceled the gold clause in all federal and private obligations and made contracts and debts payable in legal tender.

The Thomas Amendment to the Agricultural Adjustment Act of May 12, 1933, embodied the first positive efforts to increase the amount of money in circulation. It authorized but did not require the President to use one or all of the following methods in order to inflate the price level: 1. Require the Federal Reserve Banks to conduct open-market operations in United States securities up to the value of $3,000,000,000. 2. Issue up to $3,000,000,000 worth of United States notes. This paper currency could be used by the government only in retiring outstanding federal obligations but, of course, it was to be legal tender for all public and private debts. 3. Reduce the gold content of the dollar as much as 50 per cent; and set up a bimetallic system and provide for the unlimited coinage of both gold and silver at ratios fixed by him. 4. Accept, for a period of six months, silver from foreign governments in payment of their indebtedness to the United States, at a price of not more than 50 cents an ounce. However, not more than $200,000,000 worth of silver was to be taken on the account of the intergovernmental debts. A few weeks before the passage of the act the value of the dollar began to drop and prices to mount, a trend which continued until July, 1933.

Initially, the administration sought to push the value of the dollar down by public pronouncements. A world economic conference had assembled in London on June 12, 1933, and, to the dismay of the conferees, who wanted to discuss currency stabilization, President Roosevelt instructed the American delegation by no means to accept stabilization of the dollar or the renewal of gold shipments. Said the President, about the United States: it was seeking "the kind of dollar which, a generation hence, will have the same purchasing and debt-paying power as the dollar value we hope to attain in the near future." The conference broke up without result; and for a short time the United States, persevering in its own course, was able to note a price rise. But prices began to slip again in the midsummer of 1933, and the President, to still the growing clamor of the inflationists, in October announced a new policy. The government would purchase gold freshly mined in the United States and also foreign gold, at figures to be determined by itself; in this way, a progressively cheaper value on the dollar would be set.

The Treasury at once began buying gold and continued the operation for a number of months; the dollar began to drop in relation to foreign currencies; commodity prices, however, did not rise correspondingly but tended to stand still or actually to decline. Nevertheless, the President continued. On December 21, acting on the authority given him in the Thomas Amendment cited above, President Roosevelt ordered the Treasury during the next four years to buy all the silver mined in the United States—coming to approximately 24,000,000 ounces annually—at 64½ cents an ounce. (This was 21½ cents above the market level on the day in question.) On January 15, 1934, he asked Congress to enact a measure which would directly allow dollar devaluation. The new bill was to give the President power: (1) to fix the limits for devaluation of the dollar at from 50 to 60 cents in terms of its old gold content; (2) to authorize him to "manage" the dollar within these limits, by making such changes in its value as he deemed necessary; (3) to impound in the Treasury the vast stocks of gold held by the Federal Reserve Banks; (4) to assure to the government whatever profit might result from an increase in the value of this metal, by paying the banks with gold certificates on the basis of the previously existing gold content of the dollar; and (5) to use part of this profit to create a fund of $2,000,000,000 with which to "stabilize" the dollar. This so-called Exchange Stabilization Fund was to permit the Treasury to prevent fluctuations in the value of the dollar in terms of foreign currencies, by buying and selling gold, foreign exchange, and United States securities. Congress immediately complied, the bill was carried by both houses and signed January 30, and two days later Mr. Roosevelt fixed the value of the dollar at 59.06 cents in terms of its old parity. As has been said, the leading intention of this Gold Reserve Act was the pushing upward of prices. The nationalization of gold, of course, had a protective feature: it was to prevent the hoarding of gold or its shipment abroad by persons who had lost confidence in governmental policy or were seeking to make profits from fluctuations in foreign exchange. The Gold Reserve Act therefore made it impossible to exchange paper money or bank deposits for gold.

As commodity prices continued sticky, the President turned to still another course: in May, 1934, he announced that he would give his consent to the enactment of permanent silver legislation. He proposed: 1. A new national policy to increase the use of silver in the country's monetary stocks "with the ultimate objective of having and maintaining one-fourth of the monetary value of such stocks in silver." 2. Authorizing and directing the President to purchase silver to attain this objective ultimately, or until the price of silver exceeded $1.29 an ounce. 3. Authority to buy silver at his own discretion, and at whatever prices were necessary. 4. Nationalization of silver, as was done with gold, to be permissive, and to be undertaken when in the President's judgment such a course was wise. Then the present surpluses of silver would be taken over and the government would regulate imports, exports, and dealings in monetary silver. The Silver Purchase Act of 1934, incorporating these provisions, was passed by Congress and approved by Mr. Roosevelt on June 19, 1934. And on August 9, 1934, the President nationalized silver.

The Treasury Department began buying silver at 50 cents (later raised to as high as 78 cents) an ounce, not only in this country but abroad as well. In almost two years, the Treasury put into circulation an addition of about $700,000,000 worth of silver certificates against the silver it held. This was a bagatelle, obviously, since nine-tenths of the country's money was not currency but bank credit. The fact is, the government never made a serious effort to bring the silver bullion stock up to one-fourth of the total monetary stock of the country, as the Silver Purchase Act of 1934 required.[3] But the silver

[3] When the law went into effect the Treasury held $7,856,000,000 of gold, so that it should have acquired $2,619,000,000 of silver, valued at $1.29 per ounce. At the end of June, 1938, the amount of gold in reserves was $12,962,000,000, and after buying 1,687,000,000 ounces of silver, at a cost of about $900,000,000, the Treasury was still short 970,000,000 ounces of the required amount. It is interesting

program did bring relief to the domestic silver miners, even if it did drive Mexico and China off the silver monetary standard. After 1936, when the price of silver remained steady at about 75 cents, the Treasury continued to buy silver intermittently until it possessed an enormous silver hoard for which, from the currency point of view, it had no use whatever.

Apparently, the President began to worry about the possibilities of a runaway currency inflation, for his tinkering with money stopped after 1934. He never devalued the dollar further; his silver purchase program ended by being only a gesture; and he refused to issue any part of the $3,000,000,000 worth of Treasury notes authorized by the Thomas Amendment. When Congress, becoming recalcitrant, in May, 1935, passed the Soldiers' Bonus bill for the purpose of issuing $2,200,000,000 worth of Treasury notes to pay off immediately the veterans' adjusted compensation certificates, the President vetoed the measure. In his message, Mr. Roosevelt said:

> It is easy to see the ultimate result of meeting recurring demands by the issuance of Treasury notes. It invites an ultimate reckoning in uncontrollable prices and in the destruction of the value of savings, that will strike most cruelly those like the veterans who seem to be temporarily benefited. The first person injured by skyrocketing is the man on fixed income. . . . Wealth is not created, nor is it more equitably distributed by this method. A government, like an individual, must ultimately meet legitimate obligations out of the production of wealth by the labor of human beings applied to the resources of nature. Every country that has attempted the form of meeting its obligations which is here provided has suffered disastrous consequences.[4]

The expansion of bank credit became increasingly the reliance of the New Deal's price-control program. It will be recalled that in the Thomas Amendment, the Federal Reserve Banks had been granted the power to buy government securities and this they proceeded to do, so that by midsummer of 1935 open-market purchases

---

to note that foreign purchases totaled 1,353,000,000 ounces, against 333,000,000 bought at home of which 220,000,000 ounces were newly mined.

[4] A somewhat similar bill was repassed over a second veto in January, 1936. This act called for the payment of the veterans' certificates in 9-year 3 per cent non-transferable bonds, which, however, might be redeemed for cash by veterans themselves on demand. In all, up to June 30, 1936, $724,235,500 worth of bonds were redeemed; for the fiscal year ending June 30, 1937, the redemptions totaled $695,531,000; and for the fiscal year ending June 30, 1938, they totaled $82,-624,000.

stood in excess of $2,000,000,000. But another factor had entered to complicate the picture: the inflow of foreign gold. The upshot was the increase in reserves and also excess reserves of the member banks; so much so that by midsummer of 1936, these excess reserves stood at $3,000,000,000.[5] The theory in back of the purchases of government securities by the Federal Reserve Banks had been simple: these open-market activities were to lead to an increase in the cash reserves of the commercial banks; their credit base accordingly would be widened; and in turn the banks would make more private loans, a renewal of business activity would result, raw material stocks would be purchased—and prices would rise. The plan was plain enough; we may anticipate our story a little by pointing out that its result in the large was the creation of a greater liquidity on the part of the banks without any real accompanying expansion of bank credit. The many methods employed by the government to make the banking system of the nation more amenable to public controls so that, through credit expansion (and contraction) prices could be regulated, must now be recounted.

A corollary of the banking reform program, of course, was the stricter regulation of banking practices. As we have seen, two of the reasons for the speculative orgy of the nineteen twenties had been the misuse of bank credit to finance market activities, on the one hand, and the forging of bonds between the commercial banks and their security affiliates, on the other. The result had been, more than six thousand banks had closed their doors following the setting in of crisis after October, 1929. The sensational disclosures of the Senate Committee on Banking and Currency (whose investigations had been begun in April, 1932) had forcefully brought home the need for drastic change in the operations of security exchanges and commercial banks which, through their affiliates, were engaged in the flotation of securities.

The Banking Act of 1933 (approved June 16) came to grips with some of these abuses. The important features of this measure were: 1. Deposits were to be guaranteed through the creation of an agency known as the Federal Deposit Insurance Corporation, whose capital was to be built up by subscriptions from the federal government, every Federal Reserve Bank, and all banks becoming members of the insurance plan. No bank could remain a member of the deposit

[5] See below, for chart showing required reserves and excess reserves, page 287.

corporation after July 1, 1936, unless it became a member of the Federal Reserve System.[6] 2. Within a year, member banks were to be divorced from their security affiliates; also, private bankers were to choose between doing an investment and a deposit business. 3. National banks might have branches anywhere within a state, if the state law permitted state banks to do so. 4. In order to check excessive speculative activity, the Federal Reserve Board was given the power to deny the credit facilities of the system to banks lending too much money for speculation in securities, real estate, or commodities. 5. Executive officers of Federal Reserve Banks were to be prohibited from borrowing from their own banks. 6. Membership in the Federal Reserve System was widened to include industrial and savings banks. 7. Payment of interest on demand deposits by member banks was forbidden.

The second aspect of the program—the extension of public control over the activities of the Federal Reserve Banks and the member banks—did not come until August 23, 1935, when President Roosevelt signed the Banking Act of 1935. Its leading provisions were: 1. The name of the Federal Reserve Board was changed to that of Board of Governors of the Federal Reserve System; the membership was increased from six to seven with ultimately a period of service of fourteen years for all members; and all members were to be appointed by the President (the ex-officio members being eliminated). The President was to designate one of the members to act as chairman for four years. 2. The president of each Federal Reserve Bank was to be the chief executive officer of the Bank; he was to be appointed by the board of directors; and this choice was to be approved by the Board of Governors of the Federal Reserve System. 3. The control over the expansion (and contraction) of bank credits was to be in the hands of an Open Market Committee, consisting of the Board of Governors of the Federal Reserve System and five representatives of the Federal Reserve Banks. Obviously, control of this key committee was in the hands of

[6] All individual deposits from Jan. 1, 1934, to June 30, 1934, were to be guaranteed up to $2500; after July 1, 1934, the Corporation, under a permanent insurance fund, was to guarantee fully all deposits of member banks up to $10,000, and partly insure those above this amount. In June, 1934, the temporary features were ordered retained until July 1, 1935, but the maximum amount insured was fixed at $5000; also, non-member banks were given up to July, 1937, to join the Federal Reserve System if they wished to benefit from the insurance feature. By the Banking Act of 1935, state non-member banks with deposits exceeding $1,000,000 were to be deprived of the right of insurance after July 1, 1942.

the federal government. 4. The purchase of government securities by the Federal Reserve Banks was limited to open-market operations. 5. The Board of Governors was also given the important power of raising the reserve requirements of the member banks up to double the existing maximums. 6. Reserve Banks were permitted to make advances (loans) to member banks upon time or demand notes having maturities of not more than four months. 7. National banks might make real estate loans but they were denied participation in the business of underwriting securities.

As has already been said, based upon the authority of the Thomas Amendment and the Banking Act of 1935, the Federal Reserve Banks had been purchasing government securities in order to expand the credit facilities of the member banks. In other words, they continued to pursue a cheap money policy up to late 1936. This had led to the piling up of the cash reserves of the banks and, because these were not lending money rapidly enough, to their excess reserves. Excess reserves had been further increased by gold imports, Treasury purchases of domestic-mined gold, and the issuance of silver coin and notes. In August, 1936, the Board of Governors of the Federal Reserve System was compelled to take cognizance of this state of affairs: it raised the reserve requirements by 50 per cent; and proceeded to raise them twice again in March and May, 1937, so that the full 100 per cent allowed by the act was reached. This was an example of how the new controls of the system could be used to prevent a too rapid credit expansion which was being threatened largely by the inflow of foreign gold. In December, 1936, the administration took another step in the same direction of contraction of the credit base: it proceeded to sterilize the gold pouring into the country by buying it up through the issue of short-term Treasury bills and refusing to issue gold certificates against the gold for deposit in the Reserve Banks.[7]

Credit expansion was achieved directly as well, that is to say, through government lending. Here the chief agency was the RFC.

[7] It should be pointed out that by September, 1937, the Treasury held more than $1,400,000,000 of such gold in its "inactive" gold account. When recession set in, in the midsummer of 1937, to widen the credit base, the Treasury engaged in an inflationary activity i. e., it desterilized a portion of this gold. This policy was pursued further in the spring of 1938. Then, the Treasury desterilized all the gold it controlled, while the Board of Governors of the Federal Reserve System announced a lowering of member bank reserve requirements. It was estimated that the two operations were going to increase excess reserves by $2,000,000,000, and make possible additional bank loans by many times this amount, as a result.

It has already been pointed out how the RFC had been created by the Hoover administration in its fight on the depression. The rationale of the agency had been based on the assumption that industrial activity would be revived if governmental funds, in the shape of loans, were made available to release frozen assets of the financial institutions of the country; in this fashion, the benefits would flow from the top down into the broad base of industrial enterprise. The act establishing the RFC (and its later amendments by New Deal Congresses) therefore called for the granting of loans, secured by collateral, to banks, trust companies, building and loan associations, railroads, insurance companies, mortgage loan companies, federal land banks, joint stock land banks, intermediate credit banks, and agricultural credit corporations. The RFC was also authorized to subscribe to insurance company preferred stock and to make loans upon or purchase the assets of any banking institution closed between December 31, 1929, and January 1, 1934; it could, too, subscribe to the preferred stock, capital notes, and debentures of banks and trust companies. Further, it was authorized to supply the capital funds of such government-owned financial corporations as the Federal Home Loan Banks, the Home Owners' Loan Corporation, and the Land Bank Commissioner; to lend funds for public and public-guaranteed construction projects; and to make direct capital loans to business men. In connection with this last, the fund for direct loans was to total $580,000,000 and no loan was to exceed $500,000; also, the loans were to be used largely for working capital. (Incidentally, relatively little of this fund was employed.) The RFC's funds came from the capital of $500,000,000 subscribed by the government and the power of the corporation to issue up to $4,075,000,000 of notes, plus such amounts as might be applied to the purchase of preferred stock, capital notes, and the debentures of banks.

The activities of the RFC took on gigantic proportions. From its inception on February 2, 1932 to December 31, 1937, it made loans totaling $6,512,518,000, of which $4,452,121,000 were repaid, and $2,060,397,000 still remained outstanding. The table on page 243 shows the principal such loans (figures are in millions of dollars).

In addition, the RFC purchased securities from the PWA to the total of $552,850,000, of which $420,286,000 were sold or matured, leaving outstanding $132,564,000. Within the same

ACTIVITIES OF THE RFC, 1932–1937
(In millions of dollars)

	Disbursed	*Repaid*	*Outstanding as of Dec. 31, 1937*
Banks and trust companies	$1,989.6	$1,835.9	$153.7
Building and loan associations	117.5	115.4	2.1
Insurance companies	89.7	86.9	2.8
Mortgage loans companies	401.9	273.4	128.5
Federal land banks	386.2	375.6	11.6
Railroads	537.1	181.2	355.9
Industrial or commercial businesses	98.0	23.2	74.8
Financing of agricultural commodities and livestock	725.0	661.9	63.1
For relief and work relief	300.0	17.0	283.0
Purchase of preferred stock, capital notes or debentures of banks and trust companies	1,090.6	504.8	585.8

period the RFC also paid out $2,430,018,000 to other governmental agencies.

Nor was this the whole story. Other agencies were set up (some have already been mentioned) to refinance old debts, to make new loans, and to guarantee debt obligations. Professor Arthur B. Adams has indicated how many these were in the tabulation on page 244.[8]

Another outstanding financial reform was the regulation of the security exchanges. On May 27, 1933, the President signed the Federal Securities Act, as a result of which no new securities were to be offered publicly unless such issues were first registered with a body subsequently created, called the Securities and Exchange Commission. This Commission was to see to it that statements made by a corporation proposing to issue securities were free of misleading sales propaganda. This legislation was followed, in June, 1934, by the enactment of the Securities Exchange Act, which, among other things, provided for: the establishment of a

[8] See his *National Economic Security* (1936), p. 129.

THE THREE CLASSES OF GOVERNMENT FINANCING AGENCIES

For refinancing old debts	*For making new loans*	*For guaranteeing debt obligations*
Farm Credit Administration	Farm Credit Administration	United States Treasury
Federal Farm Mortgage Corporation	Commodity Credit Corporation	Federal Deposit Insurance Corporation
Federal Land Banks	Production Credit Corporation	Federal Savings and Loan Insurance Corporation
Home Owners' Loan Corporation	Intermediate Credit Banks	Home Credit Insurance Corporation
Federal Home Loan Banks	Export-Import Banks	
Land Bank Commissioner	Federal Savings & Loan Associations	
	Banks for Cooperatives	
	Federal Land Banks	
	Federal Home Loan Banks	

Securities and Exchange Commission and the licensing of the stock exchanges by the Commission; vesting of the Federal Reserve Board with power to prescribe rules "with respect to the amount of credit that may be initially extended and subsequently maintained on any security" (i. e., the margining of brokerage accounts); prohibitions against manipulative practices to establish artificial prices for securities; liability at law to customers by dealers or brokers giving false statements about securities; similar rules regulating or preventing members from floor trading for their own account, and in other ways segregating and limiting the functions of members, brokers, and dealers. All listed securities were to be registered with the Commission and information furnished about the organization, financial structure, and nature of the business performed.

POWER AND HOUSING

In the fields of power provision and control the New Deal broke new ground: for here were to be found activities that were frankly state capitalist in character. The first great experiment was the creation of the Tennessee Valley Authority in May, 1933, which had assigned to it not only the customary functions of navigation improvement, flood control, reforestation, and land reclamation but also the proprietary rights of hydroelectric plant construction and the transmission and sale of surplus power. A board of directors of three persons was to be appointed by the President; and these were charged with varied functions. They were to build dams, power plants, and transmission lines; they were to develop fertilizers; and they were also to lay out a general plan for promoting the social and economic welfare of the seven states in the Tennessee Valley region. The power program, obviously, was to be the most important. The TVA was to generate and sell power (priority to be given to public bodies and cooperatives) for the purpose of creating a "yardstick" against which the rates and practices of private utilities could be measured; it was to advance rural electrification by providing transmission lines to farms and small villages not supplied with electricity; it was to fix resale rates and insure rate schedules that were reasonable and fair; and it was to help municipalities acquire their own power plants and other utility properties.

This program the TVA began to push with dispatch. Granted originally $50,000,000 from the funds of the Public Works Administration, it proceeded to work on a comprehensive scheme for the supplying of cheap electrical power to the residents of the states in the region who were within transmission distance of the plant already at Muscle Shoals in Alabama and the ones being erected at the Norris Dam in Tennessee. By 1938, it had completed four dams and had four more under construction; also, its accomplishments as regards flood control and fertilizer production were measurable.

It was inevitable that the TVA should encounter bitter opposition. First, upon what basis were rates, for the purpose of creating the famous "yardstick," to be fixed? The TVA decided to include the following factors in its cost calculations: operation, maintenance, depreciation, amortization, and interest on the investment. But what of taxes and reserves, which were two important elements of costs as far as private operating companies were concerned? The TVA, under pressure, agreed to set aside portions of gross proceeds for these purposes, but critics pointed out that in these areas the government had decided advantages over private enterprise (as it did also in the case of borrowing money). Second, with the right the TVA had of building transmission lines, it was made possible for municipalities in the region to hook in for TVA power and distribute themselves; but private companies already served these areas. Long court litigation followed and it was not until 1938 that the way was cleared—partially—for joint TVA and municipal action. In a decision handed down in 1938, the Supreme Court held that the government's lawful possession of Wilson Dam permitted it to utilize the water power for the generation of electrical energy. This energy, too, might be sold not only at the generating plant but via transmission lines in order "to seek a wider market." The cities of Knoxville, Memphis, and Chattanooga—buttressed by PWA loans (which the courts also had found legal for this purpose)—were now in a position either to build municipal distribution systems or to buy out the plants of the existing private companies. The indications were that the latter alternative was to be followed and, indeed, in the first two cities arrangements for purchase were settled in September, 1938. In other words, federal construction and federal loans were making possible the municipalization of the public utilities in the valley.

All the knotty points involved in the controversy over the TVA were not yet cleared up, for the Supreme Court was still to pass on the law's constitutionality. The chief point at issue was this: Were the dams to be used essentially for power development or for flood control? The private utilities, when they argued in the lower court in 1937, took the following stand: that, if the government's interest was really flood control, low dams at smaller cost would do the job equally well; and that the real purpose behind the construction of high dams had been the development of electric power and the validation of the government's case for public ownership and operation. The lower court found for the TVA, deciding that the dams built were "reasonably adapted" to use for both flood control and power development, and that in the actual operations of TVA the creation of electric power was subordinated to the needs of flood control and navigation. The Supreme Court was still to rule upon the point, which was more than academic. For the whole question of rate-fixing depended upon it, in other words, what proportion of the cost of the dam construction was to be allocated to power production? If a smaller proportion, then the TVA could fix its "yardstick" rates very low and drive the private utilities out of business.

It was this question, too, that led to the outbreak of a bitter feud among the three directors of the TVA. In 1938 the controversy became so acrimonious that President Roosevelt was compelled to step in. Upon the refusal of Chairman Arthur E. Morgan to present evidence supporting the charges he was making against his co-directors, Harcourt A. Morgan and David E. Lilienthal, he was removed. Subsequently, before a Congressional investigating committee set up to look into the TVA, Dr. Morgan accused his former associates of being wasteful and also of fixing the "yardstick" rates before a proper allocation of costs had been made. He also charged that the rates to municipalities and rural cooperatives were arbitrarily determined and at extremely low levels.

Whether the lengths to which the TVA program was being pushed was an earnest of the government's intention in other regions it was as yet difficult to say. The federal government had already constructed or was in process of constructing other great hydroelectric developments at Grand Coulee Dam (Columbia River), Boulder Dam (Colorado River), Bonneville Dam (Columbia River), and Fort Peck Dam (upper Missouri River). The PWA was supplying funds for municipally owned power systems in many parts of the country. The Rural Electrification Administration was building generating plants and rural lines (some 380 projects were already under way in 44 states) to reach isolated rural districts not yet served with electricity. It is true the Supreme Court had issued a warning: the government might not engage in selling power except as an incident of its recognized functions to aid navigation, conserve natural resources, further the national defense, and control floods. Whatever the ultimate design, the New Deal was rapidly advancing toward the realization of the TVA slogan "Electricity for all," and was using great federal funds to achieve this end.

In the domain of power control, the plans were equally comprehensive. Here, the New Deal had encountered the holding company device pushed to its furthest extremes. Said a group of English surveyors (*The Economist*, October 3, 1936) of the corporate structure of this industry:

> The device of the holding company has been used more consistently and carried further towards its logical conclusion in the American electrical industry than in any other. There is some virtue in the device. It may

serve to integrate a number of small companies and to secure for them operating and financial economies. But in the 1920's it was carried far beyond this and made to serve far wider purposes. Different utility magnates used holding companies to build up their rival utility "empires." They were ready to purchase any utility that was in the market, however remote it might be from their existing interests. Pyramiding was carried to fantastic lengths, and in many of these pyramids the operating companies were "milked" for the benefit of the holding companies.

And the background of the administration's power control program was correctly summarized in this fashion:

The depression years brought many of these structures to collapse. There was no catastrophic decline in the income of the industry; its revenues were less than 11 per cent below the best known year even in 1933, which was the worst of the depression. But even this minor setback was sufficient to prick many insubstantial bubbles, and the attendant losses to investors raised a storm of hostility to the industry. Mr. Roosevelt had long been a foe of the utilities, and his beliefs had already been demonstrated during his two terms as governor of New York. His attitude seems to be inspired partly by indignation at the policies—financial and political—which had been pursued by a considerable part of the industry, partly by a strong belief that a general reduction in rates would tap an enormous demand for electricity and set the country on the highway to the "power age."

The Public Utility Act of 1935 laid down the lines of policy. The act's second and less important part enlarged the sphere of activities of the Federal Power Commission, which was given authority to control all utilities transmitting electricity across state lines. Its first part was made up of the Utility Holding Company Act, embodying the famous "death sentence" clause. Under it: 1. All companies were required to register with the SEC. 2. These registered companies in the future could issue only stocks; they could acquire new properties only with the permission of the SEC; their contracts with subsidiaries for the furnishing of services were to be subject to control in order to prevent the taking of exorbitant profits; they might not borrow from their subsidiaries. 3. The SEC was ordered "as soon as practicable after January 1, 1938" to limit the operations of registered holding companies "to a single integrated public-utility system"—that is to say, to a system whose utility assets were physically interconnected, and capable of being operated economically as a single coordinated system confined to a single area. It is important to note, in this connection, that no time limit was set in the statute for the imposition of the "death sentence."

The act was immediately thrown into the courts in a long and involved litigation and it was not until 1938 that the Supreme Court began to clear up some of the complex problems presented by it. The first important victory for the New Deal came when the Court found the registration requirements with the SEC constitutional; the second, when fourteen outstanding holding companies pledged cooperation with the SEC. The SEC, on its part, held out the olive branch. One of its members, writing in 1938, declared:

[The act] means that government will have the right to say something as to the direction of the growth of national utility systems made up of corporations which are said to be devoted to the public service. . . . On the other hand, the Holding Company Act does not mean the nationalization of the utility industry. It does not mean a death sentence for the utility industry or for the utility holding company. It does not mean that we can raise Insull Utility Investments, Inc., from the dead or that we can breathe valuc into securities which it was unfair to issue in the first place. Finally, it does not mean that there is to be a dictatorship over the utility industry.

In the case of power, there were small beginnings and great promise for the future; in the case of housing, there was next to nothing of the first and only the glimmerings of the second beginning to emerge in the fifth year of the New Deal. Building construction in America had always been regarded severely as a private concern. And because construction costs were particularly the victims of monopoly prices—both as regards materials and labor—and unsound financing, the building industry was one of the most speculative in the country. According to Evans Clark, whereas the total value of urban real estate had increased from $64.6 billions in 1921 to $73.7 billions in 1929 (14 per cent), the long-term mortgage debt had increased from $9 billions to $27.6 billions in the same period (208 per cent).

Housing for the upper-middle and middle-middle classes was more than adequate, although priced too high; housing for the poor, on the other hand, was wretched. In most of the cities of the country, great numbers of families lived in dwellings that did not conform to minimum standards of safety, health, and decency.

Their homes were without indoor toilets, bathing facilities, gas or electric cooking, refrigeration, adequate sunlight and ventilation, reasonable fire protection, privacy. Wretched slums abounded in all the great industrial centers—and in the countryside as well. In New York City, for example, about one-fourth of the entire population (1,800,000 persons) lived in filthy and unsafe tenements, many more than thirty years old; and these tenements had 200,000 dark rooms into which the daylight never penetrated. It was agreed by many authorities that the country needed more than 8,000,000 new urban housing units to replace substandard dwellings, and more than 3,000,000 new rural units. The general estimate was—and with this President Roosevelt agreed—that fully one-third of the American population was inadequately housed.

The depression took its toll in two areas. The pressure of the top-heavy debt on mortgagors became intense, so that foreclosures took place, or continued to threaten, in great numbers, leaving financial institutions with great blocks of properties on their hands. New construction, on the other hand, virtually ceased. (During 1920–1930, private residential construction erected annually in urban and non-farm areas 700,000 family units; during 1933 and 1934, the average annual building was 60,000 units—less than the estimated requirements for replacement.) These problems, therefore, confronted the New Deal: 1. The imminent eviction of large numbers of home owners who could not meet mortgage debt charges. 2. The perilous position of many financial institutions which held mortgages or had already possessed houses for which no market existed. 3. The necessity for creating new mortgage money sources. 4. The need for reviving the building industry. 5. Provision of housing for the poor.

The rescue work came first. The Home Owners' Refinancing Act, approved June 13, 1933, and the Home Owners' Loan Act, approved April 27, 1934, set up two agencies to extend relief to home owners either in danger of losing their homes through foreclosure of mortgages or incapable of making necessary improvements because of their inability to obtain financing. The first of these agencies, the Home Owners' Loan Corporation, was to serve the needs of home owners by refinancing mortgage debts; the second, the Federal Savings and Loan Associations, was to provide funds for home construction. The HOLC offered to exchange its bonds for the instrument of the mortgagee; the previous mortgages and all other liens were to be converted into a single first mortgage secured by the home and held by the corporation. Interest was to be at 5 per cent and principal was to be repaid in fifteen years, beginning with June 13, 1936. The corporation's capital stock of $200,000,000 was entirely subscribed for by the Treasury and it was permitted to issue bonds up to $3,000,000,000. When the operations of the HOLC ceased, in June, 1936, it had lent out its three billions in one million new mortgages; in almost every case the transactions had been effected by the exchange of the guaranteed bonds of the HOLC for past due mortgages. How good the assets of the HOLC were, remained to be seen; but it was hard to deny that it had done a piece of social engineering of the first order in its relief of small home-owners. The Federal Savings and Loan Associations were local, mutual thrift, and financing agencies sponsored by the government; funds were obtained from the sale of shares, and shareholders borrowed money using their shares as security.

The second achievement was in the field of housing financing and was designed to relieve financial institutions and to make the lending of money for mortgages safer. In this connection, the President approved the National Housing Act on June 28, 1934, which set up the Federal Housing Administration. In the act, a program of mutual mortgage insurance (covering first mortgages on residential property which were being amortized) was devised; and there were authorized national mortgage associations with the right to purchase and sell first mortgages and borrow money through the issue of securities up to ten times (changed in 1938 to twenty times) their outstanding capital value or the current face value of the mortgages they held. The position of the FHA in this setup was to be unique. It was to standardize methods of construction and financing. It was to guarantee, or insure, mortgages up to 80 per cent of the appraised value of the houses which it approved, with interest rates not in excess of 5½ per cent (of which ½ per cent was the insurance premium payable to the FHA itself). And it was authorized to insure loans made for the modernization of homes, guaranteeing up to 20 per cent of $1,000,000,000 borrowed for this purpose. By amendment in 1938, the FHA was to insure up to 90 per cent of the first $6000 of owner-occupied single-family residences. Also, mortgage interest was not to exceed 5 per cent, and the maximum amortization period for the 90 per cent loans was extended from twenty to twenty-five years. In the four years 1934–1938, the FHA transacted a gross business of $2,500,000,000, of which $1,825,000,000 consisted of small-home mortgages underwritten, $610,000,000 in property improvement loans, and $85,000,000 in loans underwritten for large-scale housing projects. That government assistance helped in reviving the building industry—there were, of course, other factors—may be noted from the fact that during 1935 and 1936 average annual building totaled 200,000 new family units.

The provision of new low-cost housing proceeded at a laggard's pace, however. The only agency covering this field was the Housing Division of the PWA, and in the three years of its active operations (up to the middle of 1936) it was able to provide for not more than 30,000 new family units. Even here, despite the fact that much of the labor costs were being met by the Works Progress Administration, the rental per room per month of these new dwellings had to be in the neighborhood of $7. This had nothing to do, of course, with slum dwelling. The failure of the PWA also clearly demonstrated that housing of this kind had to be regarded as a public utility and subsidized by government.

In 1937, the federal government began to move falteringly in the right direction. Under the National Housing Act of 1937 (amended in 1938) a United States Housing Authority was established and given a fund of $800,000,000 out of which to make loans and grants to local communities in order to remedy "a shortage of decent, safe, and sanitary dwellings for families of low income in rural or urban communities." The USHA was authorized to advance funds to local housing authorities once a "housing need" was established, with the stipulation that a certain amount was to be earmarked for each state. The loans made by the USHA to the local authorities (for 60 years at 3 per cent) were to cover 90 per cent of the costs of construction, with the other 10 per cent raised locally. In addition, the USHA could grant an annual subsidy (if the local authority was prepared to match one dollar for every five dollars thus contributed) upon the provision that building costs were kept at $1000 a room or $4000 a dwelling unit. As an alternative to the local subsidy, tax exemption or tax remission was to be permitted. The act also provided that for every new building built with federal funds, at least one unsafe or unsanitary dwelling must be either repaired or eliminated. And in order to keep the houses for low income groups the act stipulated that rentals could be made only to those tenants whose income was not more than five times the rent (or six, if there were three or more dependents).

In other words, through generous government loans and government subsidies, low rental building was to be encouraged and slum dwellings made habitable. As has been said, this was only a beginning—thus, fifty millions of dollars was the maximum allowed under the act for each state, whereas New York State alone could use several billions—but it was a beginning in the right direction.

Railroads and Shipping

The railroad industry of the country was in a state of collapse: and none of the New Deal's halfway measures succeeded in breathing more than faint life into it. Heavily weighed down by debt, a good deal of its equipment obsolescent, its controls frequently in the hands of holding companies which were milking the operating companies—the industry was incapable of adjusting itself easily to the contracted business of the depression period. In addition, new competitive forms had emerged to cut down the areas of expansion: automobiles and auto buses permanently were accounting for the decline of passenger business; trucks were successfully competing for the light freight; pipe lines were carrying crude petroleum and refined products; transmission lines were seriously affecting the soft coal traffic. Undoubtedly, the most serious factors were the excessive debt burden due to overcapitalization and the existence of unnecessarily duplicating and competing systems (upon which had been superimposed the financially manipulated holding companies). In the nineteen thirties, 62 per cent of the railroad securities were in bonds and these were exacting a toll of a half billion dollars a year annually in fixed charges. It was small wonder that the railroads could not modernize their plants.

The economic solutions were simple: debt had to be squeezed out, the holding companies eliminated, the railroad organizations reformed into a few comprehensive systems. But who was to pay off the chief sufferer—the institutional investor whose portfolios were in considerable measure made up of depreciated railroad securities? Drastic refinancing might necessitate the elimination of as much as ten billions of dollars of railroad values!

The New Deal shied away from the implications of such an act; and it therefore resorted to expedients, which only succeeded in involving the government deeper in an unhealthy situation. The ICC permitted the railroads to raise their rates, and the RFC pumped enormous sums into the systems, so that, at the beginning of 1938, the railroad companies (and their receivers) owed this government agency $356,000,000. Too, when bankruptcies took place, government trustees had to be appointed to protect the public stake in the defaulted lines. An effort was made to formulate a policy in the Emergency Railroad Transportation Act (approved June 16, 1933), but it remained not much more than a paper plan. This law made provision for the establishment of a Federal Coordinator of Transportation, placed railroad holding companies under the supervision of the ICC, and repealed the recapture clause of the Transportation Act of 1920. The Coordinator was to eliminate wastes, improve the financial position of the roads, and bring about a greater degree of cooperation. Certain labor protective clauses were inserted placing restrictions on reductions in the number of employees in the service of a carrier and in their compensation. Joseph B. Eastman, who was appointed Coordinator, in a report to Congress indicated it as his belief that government ownership and operation was likely to be the only solution of the railroad problem; however, he was not prepared to make such a recommendation for the time being because the financial strain of taking over the railroads was likely to be too great.

In the field of shipping, on the other hand, there was a frank movement toward a government-subsidized (if not a government-owned) merchant marine. There was a difference between railroad and shipping, of course: for ships constituted an arm of the naval establishment of the country.[9] This distinction was recognized

[9] Joseph P. Kennedy, chairman of the United States Maritime Commission, in his report "Economic Survey of the American Merchant Marine" (1937), openly confessed this. He said: "It is obvious that national defense is an important, if not the primary, justification for the maintenance of American vessels in foreign trade." And again: "With regard to cargo vessels, the Commission has developed a standardized design for a vessel of 8800 deadweight tons with a speed, fully loaded, of 15 to 15½ knots. This vessel is considered extremely practical from

clearly in the writing of the Merchant Marine Act of 1936 and the activities of the United States Maritime Commission created by that measure. There were other reasons for the recasting of the country's shipping policy: The subsidy program, which was the heart of the acts of 1920 and 1928, had failed. Virtually the whole American foreign fleet—largely because most of it had been built during the World War—had become obsolescent all at once. And public confidence in American shipping had been obviously shaken as a result of a number of marine disasters and a poorly defined labor policy which had led to a good deal of turbulence on the waterfront and at sea. A few comparative figures

FOREIGN TRADE FLEETS OF LEADING SHIPPING COUNTRIES

Nationality	*Total gross tonnage*		*Gross tonnage of vessels 12 knots and over*		*Gross tonnage of vessels 10 years of age and under*	
	Tons *	% †	*Tons* *	% †	*Tons* *	% †
British Empire	13.0	44.7	8.3	47.5	4.7	55.3
Japan	3.0	10.4	1.6	9.2	.8	9.1
United States	2.7	9.2	1.4	7.8	.4	4.9
Germany	2.8	9.6	2.0	11.5	1.0	12.0

* Gross tons, in millions.
† Per cent of combined fleets of the eight principal maritime nations.

show the weak position of the American foreign fleet at the end of 1936. The United States, among the great maritime nations, was fourth in foreign trade tonnage, fifth in respect to the speed of its ships, and eighth as regards modern tonnage in operation. In fact, 88 per cent of the number and 83 per cent of the gross tonnage of the American fleet would be obsolete (over 20 years old) by 1942. In the case of general cargo ships (as distinguished from passenger and cargo vessels), our position was even worse. While we owned 20 per cent of the world's tonnage in this category, our ships had only 7.5 per cent of the cargo tonnage capable of 14 knots or more, and less than 1 per cent of the cargo tonnage had been built within the last ten years.

The Merchant Marine Act of 1936 sought to cope with these

the standpoint of both trade and defense. Cargo vessels converted to tender use are rarely loaded beyond 50 per cent of capacity on a weight system. So loaded, the Commission's proposed cargo vessel would be able to travel with the fleet."

questions. It set up three types of subsidies in place of the old mail contracts: construction differentials to meet the difference between foreign and American construction costs; operating differentials; and countervailing subsidies (to be employed when aid paid to American operators was found to be inadequate to offset the effects of subsidies paid to foreign competitors). The act also sought to prevent the misuse of subsidy funds by prohibiting operating recipients from having financial interests in any allied activities which might divert government grants (stevedoring, ship-repairing, etc.). An effort was made to standardize and improve maritime labor personnel.[10] And all administrative power was vested in a single body, the United States Maritime Commission. This Commission was to lay out the essential routes in which American ships were needed and to report to Congress a "long-range program for replacements and additions to the American merchant marine." (This work, incidentally, was to be done in close collaboration with the Navy Department.) It could also build up, if it found this necessary and if the President agreed, a large government-owned merchant fleet. These ships might be built either at the private letting system or in United States navy yards.

Clarence N. Weems, Jr. has pointed out the extraordinary power of this body:

> Under the subsidy provisions the Commission is, first of all, a fact-finding body with legislative powers. It will not only accumulate data on differentials in construction and operation costs and on maritime labor conditions, but will also act as sole judge of the correctness of its own conclusions and will fix subsidies and working conditions in accordance with these findings. Secondly, the Commission is a board of examiners with final authority to determine the economic need for a subsidy in any given case and the qualifications of the particular applicant concerned. Thirdly, it is the custodian and disbursing agent for subsidy funds, subject only to auditing by the General Accounting Office. Finally, it is also the agency for enforcing the innumerable financial, commercial, and socio-

[10] By amendment, in 1938, the Commission was granted the power not only of prescribing on subsidized vessels minimum wage and manning scales, but as well "minimum" working conditions. Also, there was set up for three years a Maritime Labor Board, authorized to assist in making, maintaining, and interpreting agreements and to mediate in disputes, except those over unfair labor practices and questions of employee representation, which were to continue under the jurisdiction of the National Labor Relations Board.

logical requirements and restrictions to be incorporated in the new subsidy contracts.

What were the prospects of a new merchant marine under such conditions, particularly in view of the fact that all great European nations were also subsidizing their carrying fleets openly? The outlook was not bright. Mr. Kennedy, in his report to Congress on November 10, 1937, declared that "the disparity between the replacement requirements of the American merchant marine and probable construction is so great as to present a discouraging prospect for the industry as a whole." And he pointed out that to replace all ships obsolete by 1942 would require the construction of 7,402,000 tons at a total cost of $2,500,000,000. Private capital was reluctant to enter the ship construction and operation business because of uncertain public policy and the fear that subsidies would be cut once profits were reported. Mr. Kennedy therefore concluded that a government-built and -owned fleet appeared inevitable:

The brutal truth is that the American merchant marine has been living off its fat for the past 15 years; that is, we have been subsisting upon the war-built fleet. That fleet is now nearing the end of its useful life. Many of our operators built their business on vessels which they secured from the government at prices as low as $5 a deadweight ton. Who is going to replace these vessels at $200 a ton? The Commission is forced to conclude that, from all present indications, it will have to be the government.

Foreign Trade

The programs of the New Deal were not all cut from the same cloth. Some were obviously designed to assure a greater measure of economic national self-sufficiency; while others were in the interests of the reestablishment of the international division of labor. Nowhere was this confusion of purpose more clearly evidenced than in our relations with other countries. The World Economic Conference of 1933 broke up because we would not join the other gold nations in the stabilization of currencies; we insisted upon the building up of our own merchant marine, thus depriving foreign debtors from selling us shipping services; we sought to protect our agriculture from the chances of the world market. On the other hand, our State Department devoted itself to the tasks of breaking down tariff barriers the world over and defending American economic interests—

present and potential—in those regions where mercantilist state policies threatened to bar American capital.

As has been said, Secretary of State Hull was the advocate of the latter course, and he persevered so unwaveringly that he was able to wear down or eliminate all forces in the administration hostile to him. He got rid of Undersecretary of State Raymond Moley, whom he held responsible for the economic nationalist position of the United States at the World Economic Conference; in time he was able to reduce to helplessness George N. Peek, who, through the Export-Import Banks, advocated direct bartering arrangements—financed by government funds—with other countries.

Mr. Peek had the presidential ear only for a short time. As a result of his counsels, there were set up in 1934 two banks, the so-called Export-Import Bank of Washington, D.C., and the second Export-Import Bank of Washington, D.C., the first to extend credit facilities to all business men desiring to sell to Russia and the second to do similarly in the case of Cuba; it was subsequently announced that the second bank would also finance trade with all other countries. Mr. Peek, who was made president of the institutions, promised to push vigorously the sale of American farm and industrial surpluses abroad; his statement announcing the opening of the first bank declared in part: [11]

> Due to changing conditions throughout the world, government can and should assist in many directions in the conduct of a sound international trade. I urge industry in its own interest to be temperate in its demands and I invite its fullest cooperation. I want to make it clear that this bank has been created for the purpose of assisting our foreign trade and of providing facilities, not now obtainable in regular banking channels, for financing the seller. . . . Eventually, exports and imports must balance.

Such proposals did violence to all Secretary Hull was seeking to achieve, that is to say, the reestablishment of the international divi-

[11] The Export-Import Bank never got started in its business of financing Russian trade as a result of the decision of its administrators that they would abide by the Johnson Debt Default Act (approved April 13, 1934), which forbade the sale in this country of securities issued by governments which were in default in the payment of their obligations to the United States. This was, of course, only technically true of Russia, for the Russian debt had been contracted not by the Soviets but by the Kerensky government. The move was interpreted as a device for compelling Russia to come to an agreement with the United States over the governmental debts and private claims outstanding. Americans were estimating that the debt and claims totaled $600,000,000.

sion of labor, and so effective was he in his war on Mr. Peek that the latter was soon forced out and the Export-Import Bank permitted to lapse into desuetude.[12] Mr. Hull's prescription for recovery was plain: "full, stable, and durable business recovery can only be effected by the restoration of international trade and finance to an extent mutually profitable." The device was also simple: it was the writing of reciprocal trade agreements with foreign nations, calling for the mutual lowering of tariff barriers, each such agreement to contain a most-favored-nation treatment clause.[13]

In June, 1934, Congress delegated this function—heretofore jealously guarded as a legislative right—to the President.[14] For three years (the measure was renewed for a similar term in 1937), the President might negotiate agreements, without Congressional consent, for the purpose of lowering tariff rates; on his part, he could reduce American rates up to 50 per cent of the existing duties, provided he did not add to or subtract from the prevailing free list. The benefits of all such reductions were to be extended to all coun-

[12] This, in any case, was true until 1938; and then Mr. Hull himself used the Bank to drive the German financial interests out of Haiti. See below, page 318, for this extraordinary use of a public agency as an instrument of imperialist conflict.

[13] Mr. Hull's program for the reestablishment of the international division of labor was furthered not only to achieve recovery for the United States; he looked to it as a device for achieving world peace as well. Thus, on February 6, 1938, he said: "The economic warfare which reached such enormous proportions during the depression years, has been in large measure responsible for the alarming disintegration of all international relationships which the world has recently witnessed. . . . The world desperately needs today international order. . . . The achievement of such order will be impossible, unless nations direct their efforts toward the attainment of economic security and stability, rather than dissipate their energies and substance in destructive economic strife. . . . Our trade agreements program is a standing offer to other nations to join with us in a determined effort to promote economic appeasement and security through making possible the expansion of international trade, along lines of constructive peaceful effort and upon the friendly and universally beneficial basis of equal treatment."

[14] The Trade Agreements Act, of course, did not give the President or the State Department arbitrary powers. The work of preparing new schedules was in the hands of a large group of interdepartmental committees, the most important of which was the Trade Agreements Committee. American interests affected had the right to be heard and to file recommendations and briefs. As Raymond Leslie Buell has pointed out ("The Hull Trade Program and the American System"): "The various committees and departments concerned with the conclusion of a trade agreement study all petitions carefully before making their final recommendations to the Secretary of State. At no time in the history of the United States has tariff formulation been undertaken in such a painstaking and scientific manner, or inspired by such a broad concern for the national welfare." Nevertheless, it should be noted that the President was writing treaties without the ratification of the Senate.

tries not discriminating against the United States, that is to say, they were to receive most-favored-nation treatment.[15]

Between midsummer 1934 and midsummer 1938, Secretary Hull wrote trade agreements with seventeen countries, and opened negotiations for such an agreement with the United Kingdom. The initial understandings were reached with Latin American countries, most of whose exports to us were already on the free list—Brazil, Haiti, Colombia, Honduras, Nicaragua, Guatemala, and Salvador. We promised to retain these free lists; they, in turn, reduced duties on American automobiles, machinery, and cereals. The next agreement was written with Cuba; and under it, Cuba retained her preferential position in our import trade (under the Platt Amendment she had been receiving a 20 per cent reduction on all duties), while we gained advantages for our exports of lard, flour, potatoes, automobiles, machinery, and textiles. The Canadian agreement was the first to arouse opposition on a significant scale—and this came from American farmers. For Canada produces largely raw materials and agricultural goods, many of which the United States itself seeks to sell. The

[15] This does not mean that the United States made concessions without receiving benefits in return. Most-favored-nation treatment meant that each party agreed to give the other party the benefits of any concessions it might subsequently allow other countries. Thus, as a result of a reciprocal treaty with Belgium, when that country in turn lowered its duties on French automobiles, it proceeded to reduce the duties on American automobiles. It should also be noted that Germany is the only country on our "black list," because of its discriminations against American trade; that is to say, the benefits of reductions extended to foreign countries making agreements with us do not apply to Germany, even if it should have a most-favored-nation treaty with the other countries.

It is significant to note that the President's request for power to lower tariff duties received the support of a number of Republican leaders outside of Congress, notably of former Secretary of the Treasury Mills and former Secretary of State Stimson. Thus there were indications that the Republican party might be led to champion the internationalist cause after having steadfastly defended the isolationist position, as regards tariff protection, for more than seventy years. If this reversal was to occur it could be said that the predominant economic interest of the country was no longer industry but finance, no longer industrial capitalism but finance capitalism. Mr. Mills's speech, on January 29, 1934, was frankness itself. In it, he said:

"I prefer to turn my attention to the possibilities, among others, of recovering lost markets and to the stimulation of increased consumption not only through the restoration of purchasing power at home but through the promotion of a greater prosperity and a higher standard of living the world over. Granted that the difficulties are enormous and that much time and patience will be required, this is even more true of the self-containment program. We will have to abandon the present policy of isolation and intense nationalism and to some extent modify recent tariff practices."

United States gave Canada reductions on exports to us of lumber, Cheddar cheese, apples, maple sugar, live poultry, halibut, whiskey; and reduced tariffs on limited quotas of beef and dairy cattle, cream, and seed potatoes.

Further difficulties appeared in the writing of agreements with the industrialized European countries, for specialized American manufacturing interests were now affected. There were mutterings of discontent when conventions were signed with France, Belgium, the Netherlands, Sweden, and Switzerland: for their textiles, glassware, china, and special steel products directly competed with our own. These somewhat muted protests became loud and insistent as a result of the agreement signed with Czechoslovakia on March 7, 1938. The Czechs cut rates on American lard, apples, automobiles, and office appliances; and we granted tariff benefits to 63 items coming from Czechoslovakia. The trouble here arose over the addition of Czech shoes to the reduced lists; the upshot was, Czech shoe imports at reduced duties were placed on a quota basis, with the State Department having the right to raise the tariffs when Czech imports exceeded more than 1.25 per cent of domestic production.

What was the result of this program which Mr. Hull pushed so energetically? As Mr. Buell records it, the State Department succeeded in reducing duties on some 411 imported items of the 3200 tariff commodities. About one-half of the rates were pushed lower than those in the Tariff Act of 1922; but only 68 were lower than those in the Tariff Act of 1913. However, 272 of the items on which reductions were obtained were non-competitive, since American imports of each were worth less than $100,000 in 1936. And how were our own exports affected? They undoubtedly showed increases, although it should be had in mind that our improved export position was due in part to increased sales of American munitions and implements of war and of cereals to countries temporarily having crop failures. Nevertheless, whether the Hull program was responsible or not, it is interesting to record that our exports to agreement countries increased 42 per cent for the two years 1936 and 1937 as compared with the two years 1934 and 1935, whereas our exports to non-agreement countries increased only 26 per cent in the same period.[16]

[16] Imports, however, showed a reverse tendency. For the two years 1936 and 1937, imports from agreement countries were 45 per cent higher than for the two years 1934 and 1935; but imports from non-agreement countries were 51 per cent higher.

There was a significant underlying perplexity here, with which the administration had not yet come to grips. We were a creditor nation; and we were planning to extend our credit balances further by heavy increases in exports and by the provision of our own shipping services. Indeed, the revival of agriculture on an independent footing was possible only through the exploration and conquest of new oversea markets for our surplus crops. This, at any rate, was the hope of Secretary of Agriculture Wallace, who, in an eloquent plea for a "planned middle course," called for the lowering of American tariff walls to such a point that we could import some $500,000,000 more of foreign goods than reached us in 1929; and payments for these would be made in agricultural wares.

But this path was beset with difficulties, for it was not easy to revive oversea markets for our surplus crops. Continental Europe appeared definitely out of the reckoning, since each nation, constantly faced by the threat of war, was bending every effort to produce its own food supply. Great Britain, for long our best customer, was giving preference to her own colonies and dominions. South America was no market, for the countries of that continent produced surplus agricultural products. The Orient remained. We could sell tobacco and wheat to Chinese, Malayans, and Siamese—teaching those peoples to consume wheat instead of rice—but we would end, if successful, by deranging their home economies. Certainly, at the present time, it appeared that American agriculture, by world forces, was being limited to a domestic market.

All of which still left the initial difficulty, flowing from our creditor status, unresolved: if we had to increase our imports, as we did, would these be manufactured goods—or would they in time have to be agricultural goods? We could not, for example, lower duties on foreign woolen textiles, unless we first lowered duties on raw wool. We could not sell to Argentina more unless we bought her corn and meat products. Would we not, sooner or later, have to abandon our agriculture? Some of these fears many farm leaders began to express as early as 1934, when the reciprocal trading agreement plan was first being spoken of. At a meeting of the representatives of organized farmers held in Washington in April, 1934, this thought was voiced as follows:

> We are appreciative of the President's keen interest in the welfare of agriculture, but frankly we are afraid of the State Department, in which Department we know practically all of the work of negotiating reciprocal

trade agreements will be done. Those who are informed about Washington matters know that whenever the State Department gets up against agricultural matters, something slips.

Regarded historically, as a vital economic force—perhaps, too, as a significant political one—American agriculture's sands were running out. And the full implications of Mr. Hull's program of the reestablishment of an international division of labor, in the interests of recovery and world peace, drove this conclusion home. Whether agriculture was to be abandoned as an economic system altogether, or whether through subsidy it would be maintained only because national self-interest in time of war required ready sources of food supply, it was not possible to foretell at the present time.

The reason for the dilemma has been made plain. The growing of staples in America had become unprofitable: world competition, heavy capital charges, a protective tariff system which raised the prices of non-agricultural commodities and at the same time closed our markets to the wares of other nations: these factors were contributing to the debasement of the lot of the farmer. He had served his purpose by permitting American manufacturing to grow to maturity. His surpluses were no longer necessary, as they were from 1865 to 1914, to pay the interest on our loans from abroad and the cost of raw materials needed for American industry. Today, our industrialists, because of their superior techniques, were able to compete in the markets of the world with Great Britain, Germany, and France. To the manufacturer, the investment banker, and the rentier, the abandonment of American agriculture (that is to say, the growing of staples) would not be unwelcome: to sustain agriculture, subsidy would be necessary, and subsidy would mean higher-priced foodstuffs and raw materials, resulting in higher manufacturing costs; to sustain agriculture, again, would make it impossible for debtor nations, whose chief products were agricultural commodities, to repay their loans or to make new borrowings from us. The choice here was the abandonment of the protective system or the abandonment of agriculture.

The other horn of the dilemma was this: to maintain our national isolation, staples of food, cotton, and wool were necessary. And to insure a supply of these commodities, particularly toward the day when our security might be threatened, American agriculture had to be continued. To continue meant to subsidize. Translated into political terms, a policy of nationalism required the support of domestic agriculture; a policy of internationalism permitted its abandonment. And our State Department was pushing us in the latter direction. It remained to be seen whether Mr. Hull was to be successful in his intention of preserving opportunities in the world for an aggressive and expanding American capitalist-imperialist economy.

Public Works and Relief

The Hoover administration had sought to use the device of public works construction as a means of creating employment, and by the Emergency Relief and Construction Act (approved July, 1932) had empowered the RFC to lend to states and local bodies up to $1,500,000,000 for this purpose. But the RFC, at the same time, had had its hands tied by the proviso that all projects thus financed were to be self-liquidating; the upshot was, in a year and one-half, only about $60,000,000 was released. The New Deal proceeded more energetically. The building of public works was to be regarded as an emergency measure of the first importance (it will be noted that it had nothing to do with long-time planning): and by the expenditure of vast sums not only would jobs be provided but a lift would be given to those heavy industries that were in such a bad state of depression (steel, cement, lumber). The second title of the National Industrial Recovery Act, therefore, provided for the creation of the Federal Emergency Administration of Public Works (PWA) and appropriated a fund of $3,300,000,000. The Secretary of the Interior, Harold Ickes, was made Administrator of the PWA.

While a detailed plan for public works was being drawn up, the President was authorized and empowered, through the Administrator or through such other agencies as he might designate or create: (1) to construct, finance, or aid in the construction or financing of any public work projects; (2) to make grants to states, municipalities, or other public bodies upon such terms as he, the President, might prescribe, for the construction, repair, or improvement of any projects; (3) to acquire by purchase or the power of eminent domain any real or personal property in connection with the construction of any such project; (4) to aid in the financing of such railroad maintenance and equipment as might be approved by the Interstate Commerce Commission; (5) to advance the unappropriated balance of the sum authorized by the construction and equipment of an annex to the Library of Congress.

Because of restrictions with which the act and the Administrator ringed around the public works program, it made slow progress and it is doubtful whether the scheme lived up to the expectations of its supporters that it would prime the industrial pump. Thus, only 30 per cent of the cost of labor and materials of the projects could be granted outright; the rest had to go in the form of loans. To cover these, states and local bodies had to give their bonds to the PWA. The difficulty here was the existence of constitutional limitations on borrowings. Again, because the PWA insisted that a good proportion of the funds advanced be spent on materials (instead of simply "made-work" projects), most local authorities had to draw up plans first for PWA approval: an obviously time-consuming task.

Within a single year, that is, by June 16, 1934, the PWA had allotted its entire $3,300,000,000 fund to 13,266 federal projects and 2407 non-federal projects. It is to be noted that the fund was frequently dipped into by Congress for various emergency purposes so that many of the allotments could not be regarded strictly as of a public works character, that is to say, they could not succeed in stimulating private industrial activity on a very large scale. In all, more than one-third of the fund was allotted by Congressional enactment or executive order. Of the remainder, about $1,400,000,000 went to federal construction projects throughout the country and considerably less than $1,000,000,000 went for loans, loans plus grants, or grants alone to various local governments or for construction in the public interest. Later appropriations increased the total of federal money actually earmarked for the PWA to $1,291,000,000.

By the middle of 1935, the New Deal was prepared to abandon public works as a recovery device (it did not create employment rapidly enough and it was too expensive), for the "made-work" projects of the Works Progress Administration; the result was, the Appropriations Act of 1936 carried no funds for the PWA. Up to the end of the fiscal year June 30, 1936, some four billions in all were spent on public works, of which $1,291,000,000 was directly voted to the PWA; $1,567,000,000 was spent on federal projects under the supervision of particular departments; $395,000,000 came from the revolving funds of the PWA (obtained by the sale of bonds of local bodies); and $723,000,000 was spent by the states and municipalities directly. This amount was divided among the following types of projects: 23.8 per cent for public buildings; 15.9 per cent for roads; 9.9 per cent for dams; 8.6 per cent for sewage systems; 7.8 per cent for bridges; 3.4 per cent for housing. The balance was distributed among ships, aids to navigation, railroads, waterworks, power stations, and aviation.

If the public works program initially failed as a recovery measure, it did have significant social effects, for large numbers of smaller municipalities in particular availed themselves of the offer of federal funds to make needed improvements, beautify their cities, and erect schools, hospitals, sewage systems, and public electric light and power plants. As Secretary Ickes characterized these activities, they were "useful and enduring projects which will serve the people."

The New Deal profited from these experiences when it proceeded to lay out a policy for the handling of the "recession" which had set in during the midsummer of 1937. The result was, in the spring of 1938, for the fiscal year 1938–1939, Congress voted the appropriation of $1,462,000,000 for public works construction, of which $1,000,000,000 was to go directly to the PWA. Of this latter amount, at least $550,000,000 was to be set aside for loans to states and local bodies. These localities were to be permitted to borrow up to 55 per cent of the cost of approved projects, with the other 45 per cent coming as a grant; or they could borrow funds covering the total cost of new projects, with the PWA paying the interest. To prime the pump in this instance, all projects thus federally financed were to be started within six months after the law's enactment, and were to be finished within a year and one-half at the latest. The PWA had been examining and approving some 3000 plans during the whole spring of 1938, and with June, began to release funds very rapidly. It was not at all impossible that public works construction as a pump-priming expedient might work this time.

The question of relief of the needy was more insistent and heroic emergency measures were necessary here. The depression of 1930 and after was taking a terrible human toll. At its lowest point, in March, 1933, there were at least 15,000,000 persons out of work. In 1934, the figure still stood at 12,364,000, according to the estimates of the American Federation of Labor. (In fact, by February, 1937, despite enormous expenditures by the federal government and the revival of industrial production, the number of unemployed was still 9,722,000; and in the spring of 1938, in the midst of a new depression, at least 3,000,000 more were added.) Unemployment had its physical and psychological victims, undoubtedly by the millions. Men, women, and children were suffering from malnutrition; were going for years inadequately housed and fed; had long lost confidence in themselves. A whole school generation of youth had grown to maturity without ever having engaged in productive activity.

The Hoover administration came to the relief of the distressed grudgingly. Holding grimly to its assumption that the care of the needy was a local responsibility, it did not obtain authorization for the RFC to use its funds for relief until July, 1932. By this amendment, the RFC might lend to states and local bodies up to $300,000,000 for relief activities; and so slowly did the funds trickle out that for the six months ending December 31, 1932, only $80,000,000 had been borrowed by states and other bodies.

The New Deal brushed aside legal doubts and disregarded the experiences of European nations and private philanthropic enterprise. It experimented with all sorts of devices; and by the middle of 1935 it had beaten out a theory and a program that had many attractive qualities about it. Put simply, it was this: the great mass of persons out of work were not lazy or functionally maladjusted; they were only unfortunate. It was imperative that they be given opportunities to work once more, preferably at their own skills, vocations, and professions, and at wage rates that were the prevailing ones in their localities. In this way they could maintain their own self-respect, continue functioning in their customary modes of work, perform socially useful tasks, and, at the same time, receive a modest subsistence wage until private industrial opportunities once more presented themselves. This embodied extraordinary departures from precedent. For the first time in its history, the federal government acknowledged a public responsibility toward the underprivileged, who were without work through no fault of their own. In the second place, by the continuance of the Works Progress Administration through 1936, when a real business revival was taking place, it tacitly accepted the fact that capitalist production—even at the height of its powers—was no longer capable of providing jobs for all those willing to work.

This, at any rate, was the policy that emerged in the middle of 1935. Before then, the following steps were taken. 1. On March 31, 1933, Congress authorized the creation of the Civilian Conservation Corps (CCC) to give work to young men, largely in the national parks and forests. From its inception through the middle of 1938, more than 2,000,000 youths passed through the CCC camps, the standing force at any one time ranging between 300,000 and 500,000. This, in effect, was a relief measure, for the wages paid to the enrollees went to their families. 2. On May 22, 1933, through Congressional enactment, there was set up the Federal Emergency Relief Administration (FERA) with an initial appropriation of $500,000,000 and a second one of $950,000,000 voted in February, 1934. Unlike the Hoover program, this fund was to be expended on "non-reimbursable grants" to states and local bodies, the states and municipalities, in their turn, being required to match the sums allocated or a percentage of them. Once the grants were made, they became the property of the local authorities which were responsible for distribution and supervision. 3. In October, 1933, the Civil Works Administration (CWA), as a branch of the FERA program, was established. Its purpose was the creation of jobs, of a temporary character, for 4,000,000 unemployed persons, at least half of whom were on the relief rolls, at prevailing wage rates. (For this purpose, $400,000,000 was appropriated from the funds of the PWA.) Because of the speed with which the whole scheme was devised—and carried out, for jobs were actually created—many of the projects undertaken perforce were of a "made-work" character. The entire program was of an emergency nature and the administration had no thought of making it permanent. Consequently, beginning in February, 1934, the CWA was demobilized, the process being completed by March 31. Persons on CWA projects who were unable to obtain private employment were then transferred back to work divisions of local relief administrations. A new federal supervising agency was established, the Work Division of the FERA.

4. There now appeared a new FERA program, which was to continue up to July 1, 1935. Federal grants continued to be made to the states for distribution among the local bodies; but this time, moneys were to be used for works projects as much as possible. The federal controls were more precise: the FERA set up rules for the selection of workers, helped in the planning of projects, and laid down conditions of work. The needs of the workers on relief were looked into, and the FERA established for each one a "budgetary deficiency," which was to be made up by the provision of a job at prevailing wage rates. In short, the federal government became responsible for a minimum family budget for all persons on relief

through the device of "made-work" projects. How it succeeded in staving off starvation at least for many, may be seen from the fact that whereas in May, 1933, the average monthly relief allowance per family in the country was $15, in July, 1935, it was $35. This was significant; but the program had developed an important blind spot. In the words of Nels Anderson: [17]

> . . . the Work Division suffered from the tendency in some communities to unload on FERA many persons who were not strictly victims of the depression. They were the chronic poor, including many types of persons who have always been the legitimate charge of the local welfare agencies. Once the rolls were loaded down with these unemployables, the able-bodied unemployed found it almost impossible to get FERA assignments.

To get around this difficulty, a double-barreled plan was conceived. The unemployables were to be taken care of by social insurance and federal assistance to the states and municipalities. (This was the basis of the Social Security Act, already described.) The employables only were to be given work. This was the basis of the Works Progress Administration's (WPA) activities, which were launched July 1, 1935, to replace those of the FERA. According to Mr. Anderson, the following were the principles of operation of the WPA:

1. The projects shall be useful.
2. Projects shall be of such a nature that a considerable proportion of the money spent will go into wages and labor.
3. Projects will be sought which promise ultimate return to the federal Treasury of a considerable proportion of the cost.
4. Funds allotted for each project shall be actually and promptly spent and not held over until later years.
5. In all cases projects must be of a character to give employment to those on the relief rolls.
6. Projects will be allocated to localities or relief areas in relation to the number of persons on relief rolls in those areas.
7. The program must move, from the relief rolls to work on such projects or in private employment, the maximum number of persons in the shortest possible time.

[17] See his *The Right to Work* (1938), the best description of the government's relief program that has yet appeared. I am indebted to Mr. Anderson for much of my factual material.

The WPA set to work at once, absorbing in time up to 80 per cent of workers taken from relief rolls. Of the WPA, the English surveyors, previously referred to, said:

Against them [the criticisms] must be set admiration for the amazing rapidity with which a vast organization was improvised and for the imaginative humanity with which it has been administered. It is natural for the critics to compare the actuality of relief in a nation which had not admitted the possibility of such a thing five years ago with some theoretical ideal. It is, perhaps, more pertinent to make the comparison with the chaotic misery of Mr. Hoover's last two years.

The diversity of projects inaugurated was simply extraordinary. WPA funds (largely used for wage payments) helped build the great Tri-Borough Bridge in New York City as well as hundreds of thousands of miles of rural roads; and armories, amphitheaters, zoos, swimming pools, sewers, and school buildings in large and small cities and in rural communities. It financed theater companies, music projects, artists, and writers; it helped thousands of research workers and scholars by furnishing them professional assistants; it made possible the opening of adult-education and leisure-time activities classes all over the nation; it restored old public monuments, erected new ones, and drew up a great guide to all the places of interest in the country.

The WPA's wages and hours rules were generous. It paid a minimum "security monthly wage" to various categories of workers, that is to say, common laborers, intermediate workers, skilled workers, and technical and professional workers, based on local wage and relief conditions. Thus, common laborers received from $19 a month in rural southern counties up to $55 in large northern cities, with $50 as the monthly average. Professional workers, on the other hand, received up to $94 a month in northern cities. Originally, all workers were expected to do a monthly minimum of 140 hours of work; subsequently, this ruling was modified to base hours of work on the prevailing hourly wages for each occupation. As a result, the work month varied, according to occupation and hourly rate, from 43 to 140 hours.

How many persons were furnished jobs through the direct intervention of the federal government? According to Mr. Anderson, the month of greatest employment for the Works Program was February, 1936; and then, the distribution of workers from relief was as follows:

In all agencies of the federal government	3,836,087
Workers on WPA	3,035,852
Workers on CCC	459,461
All other federal agencies (including PWA)	340,774 *

* The PWA was giving employment to 41,259 workers from relief rolls and to another 115,000 workers on its own projects.

This was only a works program, and did not take care of all the needy. In fact, in February, 1936, local home relief agencies were aiding 2,130,000 family units, or households. Thus, in this month, no less than 6,000,000 families and individuals were receiving the assistance of the WPA, home relief bodies, and PWA. Averaging 3.1 persons to a household, the approximate population on relief was 18,600,000—pretty close to one-seventh of America's total population! In April, 1938, the figure was even higher. According to WPA estimates, in that month, 6,641,000 households, representing 20,581,000 individuals, were receiving some form of public assistance through direct aid or work relief. Of the total of 6,641,000 households aided, 2,632,000 were on WPA.

Two other parts of the relief program require mention. In June, 1935, the President ordered the creation of the National Youth Administration (NYA), which was subsequently attached to the WPA. This agency was to concern itself with the rehabilitation and assistance of young people between the ages of 16 and 25 years. Two programs were devised, one to furnish student aid for both high school and college attendants, and the other to set up work-relief projects for boys and girls, usually the children of relief recipients, who needed vocational training as a preparation for jobs. The NYA was doing a commendable piece of work, not only in helping youngsters and young men and women complete their educations but in providing useful activity for the idle hands of young people already living in underprivileged homes. At one time or another, the organization had on its rolls as many as 660,000 youngsters and young people. The high school students—helping their teachers in one way or another—were given a chance to earn $6 a month as a maximum; the college students—set to work at a great variety of clerical, statistical, research, laboratory, and library tasks—were given $15 a month as a maximum; while the unemployed boys and girls out of school were engaged on clerical, home-making, and construction jobs at an average monthly pay of $15.75. Up to midsummer 1938, the NYA had spent $125,000,000; and the new relief act of 1938 earmarked for it another $75,000,000.

The Federal Surplus Commodities Corporation (really operating as a subsidiary of the Department of Agriculture) was established in October, 1933, for the purpose of distributing surplus farm products among state relief organizations. In 1933, it functioned on a large scale, and then disappeared into obscurity, only to be revitalized in 1938 when surplus crops, with their threats to price structures, made their appearance in those agricultural sectors not ordinarily covered by farm relief legislation. With $30,000,000 at their command—to which was added $50,000,000 by the relief act of 1938—agents for the FSCC made quick purchases of every manner and variety of marginal agricultural goods, usually from distressed farm cooperatives, and distributed the articles among relief recipients. They bought fresh fruits, vegetables, nuts, cheese, cane syrup, fruit juices, flour, live animals: and their activities ranged all over the United States. From September 23, 1933, to June 17, 1938, the FSCC had made purchases totaling $221,600,000.

This "buy and give" program, as it came to be called, at first was regarded wholly as a form of agricultural relief, with the needy on the receiving end as something of an afterthought. But when, in 1938, the WPA began to apply the principle to the clothing industry—$15,000,000 was set aside to purchase men's and women's clothing (for the needy of course but also to aid overstocked manufacturers and create jobs for unemployed needle trades workers)—then questions began to be asked. If the government was to distribute direct in this fashion, what was to happen to workers in the wholesale and retail business? Was it not likely that an incentive to overproduction would appear everywhere, if government was ready to buy surpluses of consumer goods, particularly when a tie-up with the needy could be indicated? It is true, the operations of the FSCC and the WPA, under the "buy and give" principle, had been to date inconsequential when measured by the activities of business in general, but the willingness to experiment with the idea was an indication of the lengths to which the New Deal state capitalism could be pushed.

How much did the cost of carrying the relief burden come to? It was a gigantic sum. According to federal estimates, the total amount of federal, state, and local funds (all public) spent for direct assistance and work-relief programs from 1933 to the end of 1937 was $13,870,000,000. The ratio of federal to state and local expenditures was 4 to 1 for the whole period; however, by the first half of the fiscal year 1938, states and localities were contributing 37 per cent of the total spent. For the fiscal year 1938–1939, as part of the government spending program in an effort to hasten revival, the President asked for $1,550,000,000 for relief purposes, $1,250,000,000 of which was to be spent on the WPA.[18]

Financing the New Deal

Thus, the New Deal was lending and spending money on a vast scale—lending to distressed banks, railroads, insurance companies, corporations, farmers, home owners, states and municipalities; spending by way of subsidies or grants to farmers and ship builders and operators and low-cost housing authorities, and for work relief projects, old age pensions, the construction of public buildings, flood control, reforestation, road building. It was paying its way through what came to be called "deficit financing." The taxation program of the Roosevelt administrations did not impose oppressive burdens on the wealthy. Up to 1935, the New Deal made no serious effort to finance its spending program through taxation; and though, after 1935, there was a good deal of tinkering with the revenue act, no new tax avenues really were explored. Consumption taxes, open or concealed, continued to be the broad base of the federal —as well as the state and local—tax structure.

In June, 1935, the President called upon Congress to impose a heavier burden upon accumulated wealth in the form of increased inheritance, succession, and gift taxes, higher income taxes in the upper brackets, and graduated corporation taxes in order to penalize the giant corporations. The President's message stressed the social implications of these additions to the tax structure, rather than their possible revenue contributions. Thus, he spoke in the following wise of taxing of large fortunes:

> The desire to provide security for one's self and one's family is natural and wholesome, but it is adequately served by a reasonable inheritance. Great accumulations of wealth cannot be justified on the basis of personal

[18] It is to be noted that the allowance for WPA for 1938–1939 was actually lower than the WPA expenditures for 1937–1938, which were around $1,475,-000,000. In other words, the President's widely heralded spending program called for no increase in relief disbursements.

and family security. In the last analysis such accumulations amount to the perpetuation of great and undesirable concentration of control in a relatively few individuals over the employment and welfare of many, many others.

Such inherited economic power is as inconsistent with the ideals of this generation as inherited political power was inconsistent with the ideals of the generation which established our government. Creative enterprise is not stimulated by vast inheritances. They bless neither those who bequeath nor those who receive.

Congress resisted, but in August it finally passed the Revenue Act of 1935. This measure contained the following provisions. As to estate taxes: there was an increase in rates, beginning with 2 per cent on net estates of more than $40,000 and mounting up to 70 per cent on those parts of the estates above $50,000,000. As to gift taxes: these were raised to approximate three-fourths of the new estate tax schedules. As to individual taxes: there were increases in individual surtaxes beginning with the income brackets above $50,000, and going up progressively to a maximum of 75 per cent on incomes in excess of $5,000,000. As to corporation taxes: these were graduated from a tax of 12.5 per cent on net corporation incomes up to $2000 to 15 per cent on net incomes in excess of $40,000. As to excess profits: a tax of 6 per cent was imposed on corporation profits exceeding 10 per cent and not over 15 per cent and a tax of 12 per cent on corporation profits exceeding 15 per cent of the declared value of corporation stock. As to personal holding companies: an increase in the rates of taxes on the undivided profits of personal holding companies to make them conform to the higher surtaxes.

The President, however, did not regard this as adequate, particularly as it treated corporations. He held that those corporations notably that were failing to distribute their net incomes were furnishing wealthy stockholders with a "method of evading existing surtaxes." As a result of his demand, therefore, Congress in the Revenue Act of 1936 (made applicable also to 1936 earnings) revised the progressive corporation tax, scaling it this time from 8 to 15 per cent; and it added a tax on undistributed corporate profits ranging from 7 to 27 per cent. It is interesting to note that the revenue additions of this tax were inconsequential, because for the years 1936 they brought in only $100,000,000. Also, Congress changed the treatment of capital gains and losses, imposing a heavy tax on the realized gains made in the transfer of capital assets and allowing a deduction of only $2000 from taxable income as a result of capital losses.

Because of the onset of depression in midsummer 1937, these two taxes—the undistributed profits tax and the capital gains tax —were brought under the heavy fire of business economists and conservative newspapers. It was argued that the taxation of capital gains prevented persons of means from launching upon new commitments; and that the taxation of corporate surpluses devitalized corporations so that they could not carry on in periods of depression. These charges frightened Congress; the result was, the Revenue Act of 1938 (which the President refused to sign so that it became law without his signature) overhauled both these tax features. As regards the undistributed profits tax, the 7–27 per cent scale was changed to a flat 2½ per cent to be applied only to corporations earning more than $25,000. And as regards capital gains and losses, the taxpayer was offered favorable rates on gains on long-term transactions, while he was permitted to offset net losses against other income to a larger extent than previously.

What "deficit financing" came to may be seen from the following figures. On June 30, 1933, the gross debt of the country stood at $22,539,000,000, and its net debt was $19,477,000,000. On June 30, 1938, the gross debt was $37,165,000,000. But partly to offset this latter amount, the government had assets of various kinds: it had a proprietary interest in various recoverable enterprises that was put at $4,000,000,000; it had $2,000,000,000 in the Exchange Stabilization Fund, which was a profit from the revaluation of the dollar; it had $2,216,000,000 in the general fund of the Treasury. Allowing for these assets, the net debt was $29,109,000,000. The difference between the positions of the net debt in 1933 and in 1938 represented the major part of permanent government spending to hasten recovery—and the price future generations would have to pay for what reforms the New Deal had succeeded in achieving. This was, at the end of five years of spending and lending, about $10,000,000,000.[19]

[19] In using the concept "net debt" the Treasury made the following comment: "In arriving at a figure showing the net debt of the United States, there has been used as a basis for such a figure, the gross debt and certain outstanding realizable assets. . . . No effort has been made to evaluate the tremendous natural and other resources of the government, such as public lands, highways, harbors, and other

Was this too heavy a price to pay for the New Deal's experiments? The country, apparently, did not think so: for as the deficit rose, the rates the government had to pay for borrowings dropped. The yield on U.S. Government bonds was 3.65 per cent in the second quarter of 1929, and 2.57 per cent in the last quarter of 1937. The fact is, if English experiences were worth anything, the New Deal was correct in assuming it could borrow much more without jeopardizing its credit and bringing on a runaway inflation. According to the English surveyors of *The Economist,* the American debt (in relation to national income) was only one-fourth or one-fifth of the English; and per capita English debt was more than twice that of the American (with no allowance made for the great differences in average annual income).

State Capitalism and the Problem of Bureaucracy

There was no question that the New Deal had come to grips with a series of important and pressing problems. From the social point of view, it deserved much praise; from the economic, as we have seen, virtually every credit to its favor seemed to produce its own debit. It was in the political sector, however, that the New Deal planning was producing some of the most disquieting elements in the whole program. To provide a rough form of social justice, the New Deal had parted company completely with the nineteenth-century idea of the passive state. It is true that the concept of laissez-faire had never been much more than wishful thinking in any case; indeed, except for England, during the years 1850–1914, the state of the western countries had frequently intervened in economic matters. In the United States, it had espoused protectionism, built the transcontinental railroads out of public funds, turned over the natural resources to favored exploiters. But, taken in the large, the state's intervention had been as a rule in the rôle of umpire among enterprisers. This was all very well as long as capitalism possessed dynamic qualities: for, with opportunities for individual enterprise existing relatively on a wide scale, it was possible for the defenders of the system to talk of *equality* of opportunity. Of course, under capitalism, the notion of equality was a fiction pure and simple: but this fiction was able to sustain the middle class, and the frequent

public projects, such as dams, buildings, fortifications, naval vessels, etc., for the purpose of offsetting them against the gross public debt. . . ."

THE UNITED STA

THE FEDERAL

CONS

LEGISLATIVE

EXE

THE CONGRESS

THE

NATIONAL ACADEMY OF SCIENCES

GENERAL ACCOUNTING OFFICE

GOVERNMENT PRINTING OFFICE

LIBRARY OF CONGRESS

THE CABINET

INTERSTATE COMMERCE COMMISSION

ARCHITECT OF THE CAPITOL

DISTRICT OF COLUMBIA

DEPARTMENT OF STATE

DEPARTMENT OF THE TREASURY

WAR DEPARTMENT

DEPARTMENT OF JUSTICE

POST OFFICE DEPARTMENT

BUREAU OF THE BUDGET

FEDERAL TRADE COMMISSION

UNITED STATES TARIFF COMMISSION

FEDERAL POWER COMMISSION

FEDERAL COMMUNICATIONS COMMISSION

SECURITIES AND EXCHANGE COMMISSION

BOARD OF GOVERNORS OF THE FEDERAL RESERVE SYSTEM

FEDERAL DEPOSIT INSURANCE CORPORATION

POSTAL SAVINGS SYSTEM

FEDERAL HOME LOAN BANK BOARD

FEDERAL HOUSING ADMINISTRATION

FEDERAL SAVINGS AND LOAN INSURANCE CORPORATION

HOME OWNERS LOAN CORPORATION

SOCIAL SECURITY BOARD

RAILROAD RETIREMENT BOARD

CIVILIAN CONSERVATION CORPS

FEDERAL SURPLUS COMMODITIES CORPORATION

SMITHSONIAN INSTITUTION

NATIONAL ARCHIVES

UNITED STATES EMPLOYEES COMPENSATION COMMISSION

UNITED STATES CIVIL SERVICE COMMISSION

THE FEDERAL

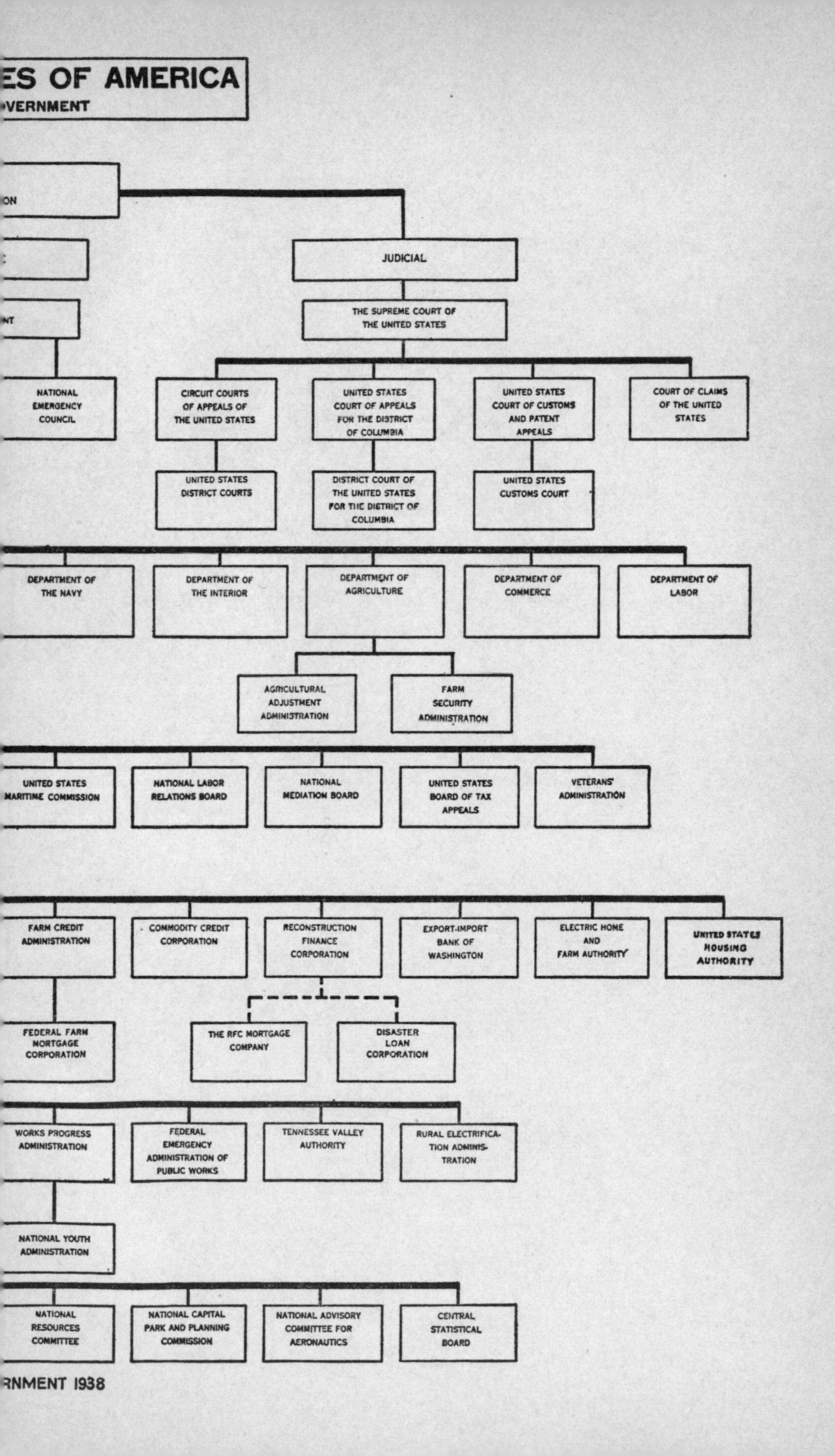
ES OF AMERICA
VERNMENT
ON
NT
JUDICIAL
THE SUPREME COURT OF THE UNITED STATES
NATIONAL EMERGENCY COUNCIL
CIRCUIT COURTS OF APPEALS OF THE UNITED STATES
UNITED STATES COURT OF APPEALS FOR THE DISTRICT OF COLUMBIA
UNITED STATES COURT OF CUSTOMS AND PATENT APPEALS
COURT OF CLAIMS OF THE UNITED STATES
UNITED STATES DISTRICT COURTS
DISTRICT COURT OF THE UNITED STATES FOR THE DISTRICT OF COLUMBIA
UNITED STATES CUSTOMS COURT
DEPARTMENT OF THE NAVY
DEPARTMENT OF THE INTERIOR
DEPARTMENT OF AGRICULTURE
DEPARTMENT OF COMMERCE
DEPARTMENT OF LABOR
AGRICULTURAL ADJUSTMENT ADMINISTRATION
FARM SECURITY ADMINISTRATION
UNITED STATES MARITIME COMMISSION
NATIONAL LABOR RELATIONS BOARD
NATIONAL MEDIATION BOARD
UNITED STATES BOARD OF TAX APPEALS
VETERANS' ADMINISTRATION
FARM CREDIT ADMINISTRATION
COMMODITY CREDIT CORPORATION
RECONSTRUCTION FINANCE CORPORATION
EXPORT-IMPORT BANK OF WASHINGTON
ELECTRIC HOME AND FARM AUTHORITY
UNITED STATES HOUSING AUTHORITY
FEDERAL FARM MORTGAGE CORPORATION
THE RFC MORTGAGE COMPANY
DISASTER LOAN CORPORATION
WORKS PROGRESS ADMINISTRATION
FEDERAL EMERGENCY ADMINISTRATION OF PUBLIC WORKS
TENNESSEE VALLEY AUTHORITY
RURAL ELECTRIFICATION ADMINISTRATION
NATIONAL YOUTH ADMINISTRATION
NATIONAL RESOURCES COMMITTEE
NATIONAL CAPITAL PARK AND PLANNING COMMISSION
NATIONAL ADVISORY COMMITTEE FOR AERONAUTICS
CENTRAL STATISTICAL BOARD
RNMENT 1938

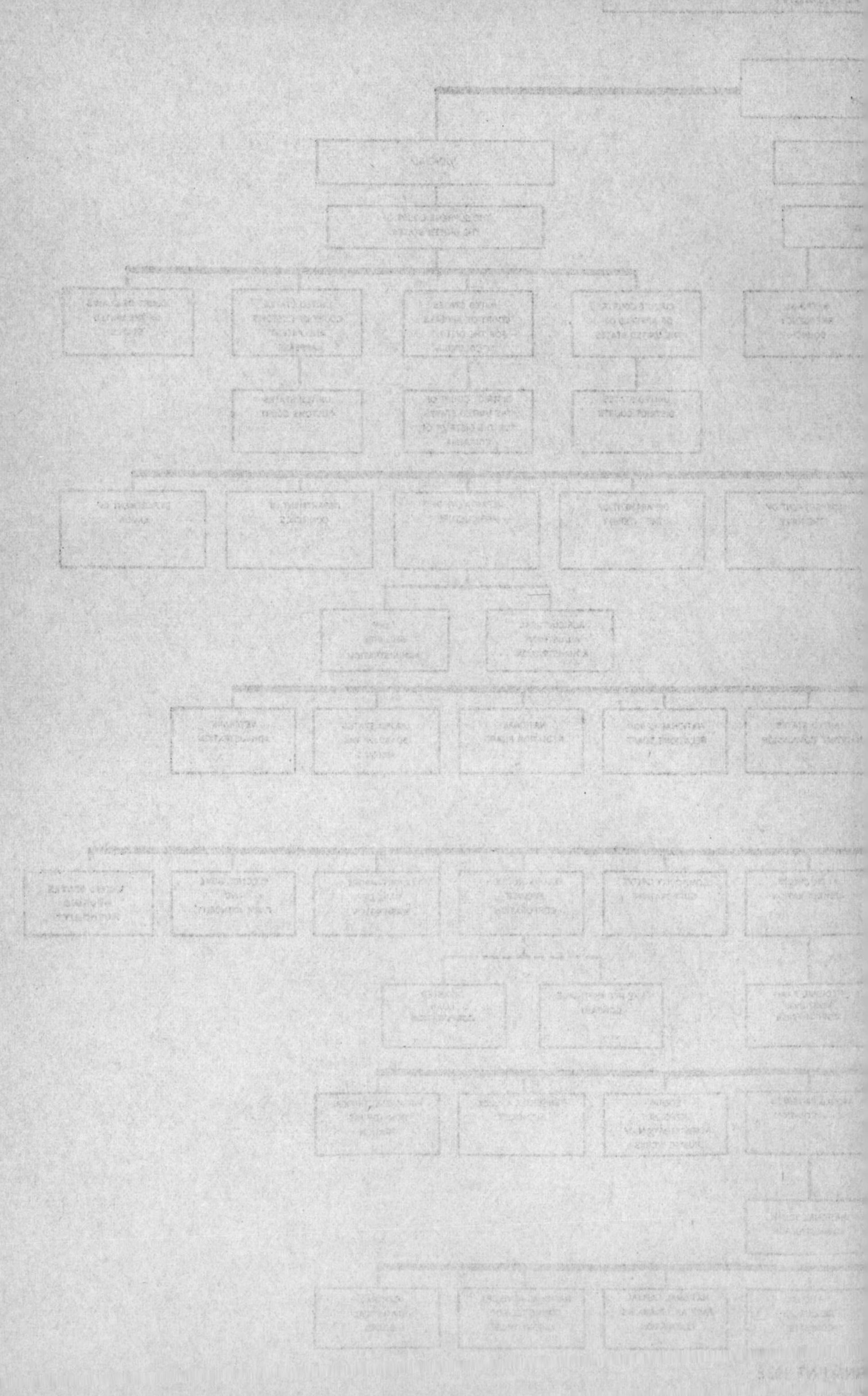

examples of careers from rags to riches, so to speak, gave political authority the justification it required for refusing to come to the assistance of the victims of economic and class oppression.

The depression of 1930 and its continuance indicated clearly enough that capitalist progress had slowed up, if it had not ceased altogether. Now, the state's function changed—virtually over night. Its part as umpire was magnified and extended into other regions—as in the case of the establishment of the National Labor Relations Board and the old-age reserve fund and unemployment insurance fund. Its social service functions were expanded, particularly as regards the handling of the problems of the unemployed, the unemployables, and other forms of dependency. More significant, in terms of the basic nature of the state, it began to initiate projects and enterprises of an economic character. The state, in other words, was beginning to take on the essential color in many domains of private enterprise. It was borrowing money, of course; but it had always done this, although heretofore this had been merely for the maintenance of the civil establishments of government and military defense. This time, however, it was borrowing money for the purposes of buying and selling commodities, processing goods, creating electric power and light, dealing in real estate, engaging in warehousing, the banking business, the operation of ships and railroads, and the like. And it was using the organizational forms of private enterprise: corporations and corporate agencies which possessed assets of their own, reported earned income, had great rolls of employees, some of them running into the thousands—and a few of which, like private business itself, were chartered under the laws of Delaware, Maryland, and other jurisdictions.

This was transformation. The state no longer pretended to be the laissez-faire, or passive, state: it was now the capitalist state. We were beginning to live under the authority of state capitalism. In short, the general theory and functions of capitalism remained: private ownership of the means of production, unhampered individual accumulation, the wage system, inequality of income based upon property possession and not social need, a class society. In some areas, however, the state was beginning to act as enterpriser; and in a few, indeed, as a monopolist enterpriser as in the case of the TVA.

The new corporate activities of this capitalist state were diverse and bewildering. Under the New Deal, some fifty corporations and corporate agencies had been created to engage in business: producing, buying, selling, transporting, distributing, borrowing and lending: and these, by the end of 1937, possessed capital and assets of at least five billions of dollars! To quote Charles Cortez Abbott: [20]

The activities of these bodies range from loans to individuals as small as $10, made by the Emergency Crop and Feed Loans division of the Farm Credit Administration, to single loans amounting to millions of dollars extended by the Reconstruction Finance Corporation. Their operations comprise such diverse undertakings as the insurance of mortgages, as large as $5,000,000 on a single piece of property, by the Federal Housing Administration, the manufacture of rum and the raising of chickens and tomatoes by the Virgin Islands Company, and the operation of the Alaska and Panama Railroads. Their enterprises include the construction and operation of vast hydroelectric undertakings by the Tennessee Valley Authority and the Boulder Dam, Bonneville, and Grand Coulee projects, as well as the financing of consumer purchases of domestic electrical appliances, such as stoves and refrigerators, by the Electric Home and Farm Authority.

This state of affairs, obviously, raised a number of important questions. 1. Was it possible to dismantle the capitalist state and restore it to its original passive rôle? A demand for such a return came from the New Deal critics on the right. They argued that state interference, control, and initiation were hampering and burdening with excessive taxes private enterprise, and the fear of an overweening public authority was preventing the movement of fresh capital into new undertakings. But the return to so-called rugged individualism, it was more and more plain, was out of the question. Rugged individualism left in its train too many casualties: the permanently disemployed, gross inequalities of income, marginal and submarginal producers. With the international division of labor at an end and fewer and fewer opportunities for fresh imperialist adventure existing, the modern capitalist world was confronted by excess productive capacity and excess savings. State intervention was necessary, from the viewpoint of capitalism itself, to prevent social unrest if not profound dislocations.

2. Was state capitalism leading to socialism or communism? This also was problematical. State capitalism was not destroying old class relations: it was simply freezing them. Where the state was ex-

[20] Professor Abbott has prepared a pioneer study of these federal corporations and corporate agencies. See his significant article, "Federal Corporations and Corporate Agencies" in *Harvard Business Review*, Vol. XVI, No. 4 (1938).

propriating property actually or in effect (as in the case of private utility companies competing with the TVA or private insurance companies holding farm mortgage paper), it was compensating: a rentier class therefore was being substituted more and more for an enterpriser class. Nor were the underprivileged being provided for in terms of their social necessities and their full individual potentialities. The wage system was being maintained: it scarcely mattered who was employer, whether it was government or private business. It should also be pointed out that this New Deal state was initiating projects as a rule in those realms where private capitalism had failed. This left a large region of enterprise—by far the greater part—for private ownership and private accumulation.

3. Was the capitalist state a responsive state? It was at this point that one's judgments could be regarded as quite certain. Plainly, the New Deal state was not a responsible authority. It is true, the social agencies—NLRB, WPA, FERA, Social Security Board—were being scrutinized closely: by Congress, the press, independent popular agencies. This was all to the good; for this was one of the ways a democracy functioned and in this way public authority was held responsible. But the same could not be said of the great majority of the corporate agencies, that is to say, these federal corporations which were in business. The pattern was too complex and too obscure for popular control. These agencies came and went, often without hails or farewells. They were created by Congress, sometimes only by implication; by Presidential orders; by intra-departmental memoranda. Often they were run, presumably, by Cabinet officers who, in the nature of things, were compelled to delegate powers to anonymous lesser officials. Frequently, there existed interlocking directorates, so that there was being built up a concentrated financial (and political) power in the hands of a few individuals. The accounts of these agencies were not uniform. Sometimes they reported to the General Accounting Office, sometimes they did not. In some cases, even, annual reports were never drawn up to become public documents. Nevertheless, these agencies were using public funds, borrowing and lending among each other, and beginning and terminating various kinds of businesses.

Where was the danger? Without responsiveness, such a state was likely to develop a bureaucracy with its own institutional safeguards and rhythms of being. For its maintenance (as well, of course, for the carrying out of the programs it was supporting) the productive energies of the nation would have to be dipped into more and more. In short, under state capitalism—as under mercantilism in the seventeenth and eighteenth centuries and under modern-day fascism and, perhaps, too, Soviet-style communism—a constant hemorrhage of capital would be required to maintain an apparatus which, to the bureaucrat, was more important than anything else.[21]

It was a political axiom that authority without responsibility led to tyranny. It was beside the point whether the tyranny was that of an absolute monarchy, an oligarchy, a party, or a bureaucracy. The New Deal was in process of developing such a bureaucracy, whose allegiance was almost entirely to the Executive, only in slight measure to the Legislature and the popular will.[22] In a period of stress and under cover of an emergency, the Executive always can succeed in arrogating to itself extraordinary powers. This had happened during our Civil War and World War; but following them, these powers of the Executive had been terminated. But what of a permanent emergency, if the paradox may be permitted? For the New Deal was pleading the existence of an emergency for whose conclusion it was holding out no immediate hopes. The Executive's powers, therefore, were constantly being expanded, the agencies increased, the lesser and anonymous officials and directors multiplied, and the public pay roll enormously distended.[23]

[21] The absolutist mercantile states of seventeenth-century England and eighteenth-century France both were characterized by such bureaucracies which became in time hopelessly inefficient and venal. They had to be dislodged by revolution—the Puritan Revolution in England and the French Revolution in France.

[22] On this point, Professor Abbott, in the article cited, makes an important observation: ". . . Congress has never enunciated a policy defining the proper scope and purpose of federal corporations and corporate agencies. Nor has Congress firmly established their status in the governmental structure or the methods by which they should be created, financed, and controlled."

[23] Under the New Deal, the number of persons on the public pay roll has increased absolutely and relatively in terms of the total employed. According to the National Industrial Conference Board, in 1929, there were 47,885,000 employed persons, of whom 833,000 worked for the federal government. And in June, 1938, the number of employed persons totaled 42,955,000, of whom 1,194,000 worked for the federal government on its regular pay rolls. In other words, total employment over the period 1929–1938 *decreased* by 10 per cent, while federal government employment *increased* by 43 per cent. If we add to the list of regular federal employees the 2,000,000 to 3,000,000 workers on the WPA, who seemed to constitute a permanent group, then the picture takes on even sharper and more challenging outlines. In 1938, it was being clearly indicated that the WPA could be —and, indeed, already was being—used for political purposes, that is to say, to keep Mr. Roosevelt's supporters in power. In fact, the Workers Alliance, an organization of the unemployed, was already calling for a third term for Mr. Roosevelt!

What was needed, as has been said, was responsibility, so that the democratic processes could be maintained in fluid form. The following desiderata constituted a minimum program for present-day America, notably as regards the federal corporations: (1) reporting to Congress and the General Accounting Office; (2) uniformity of accounting practice; (3) complete control over interlocking directorates. So much government could do. The responsibility of the public was even greater. It was imperative that popular agencies be set up to scrutinize and criticize the activities of the new agencies and call officers who were overreaching themselves to account. The defense of democracy was the task not only of the Executive but of the Legislature and the people as well. For democracy could be imperiled not only from without but also from within.

X. THE NEW DEAL MAKES PROGRESS SLOWLY

The Course of Recovery to Midsummer, 1937

Following an uneven course for the first two years, the line of recovery began to move upward. General wholesale prices as well as agricultural prices improved, the capital goods industries resumed operations, new jobs appeared. There was a sharp drop in business activity from midsummer of 1933 to the end of that year; another upward swing and then an even sharper drop in the second half of 1934; again a climb and a tapering off in the second quarter of 1935. From midsummer of 1935 until the midsummer of 1937, with but brief and unimportant setbacks, American business proceeded forward. By 1936 it appeared as if the economic revival might attain the levels of 1929. It was recovery—but with a difference.

There could be no question that the leading factors in the situation were the New Deal's spending and easy-money programs. Vast sums were being poured out by the government on public works, as subsidies to farmers, in loans to public authorities and private enterprise, in the form of the soldiers' bonus, for relief. These were stimulating heavy goods and consumer goods industries alike. There were other forces exerting significant influences: the administration's devaluation and credit policies were encouraging prices to rise, thus relieving considerably the burden of debt charges; industry was finding it imperative to replace portions of obsolescent plants and machinery, so that the capital goods industries resumed operations naturally; more efficient industries were hastening to introduce labor-saving devices in order to reduce their wage costs; European countries, embarked on rearmament programs, were buying American raw materials and heavy goods.

While the general level of production in the spring of 1937 was reaching the average normal of the nineteen twenties, it was not to be assumed that relatively the American economy was recovering all the ground lost in the depression. Industrial production was almost as high as it had been in 1929; but, on the basis of past performances, it should have been higher. The reasons were plain: for one, the population of the country was larger; again, the rate of productivity in industry was perhaps 25 per cent greater. The upshot was, the spring of 1937 saw 9,700,000 persons still unemployed, according to the American Federation of Labor's estimate. Indeed, the Department of Labor calculated that production and services had to rise 20 per cent above the 1929 mark before there could be any reason for feeling that our economy was resuming where it had left off when the depression began.

The general situation, nevertheless, appeared encouraging. The position of agriculture, in particular, showed improvement. Cash income from the sale of farm products and from government payments in 1937 totaled $8,521,000,000, or about double the $4,328,-000,000 from marketings in 1932, the low year of the depression. It should be noted, too, that as marketing income improved, government payments tapered off. In 1934 and 1935, benefit payments were around $500,000,000 each year; but in 1936, they were $287,-000,000 and in 1937, $367,000,000. The index numbers of farm prices and the purchasing power of the farm dollar continued to mount. The figures on page 284 present the index for prices received and the ratio of prices received to prices paid over the pre-New Deal and New Deal years. (August, 1909–July, 1914 = 100.)

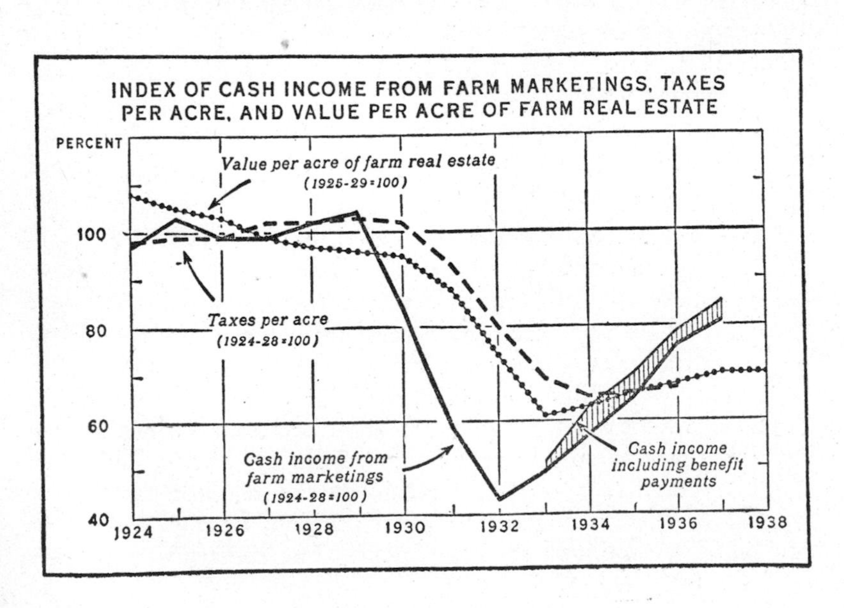

Indexes of Prices Received and Prices Paid by Farmers, with Ratio of Prices Received to Prices Paid, 1910–1937

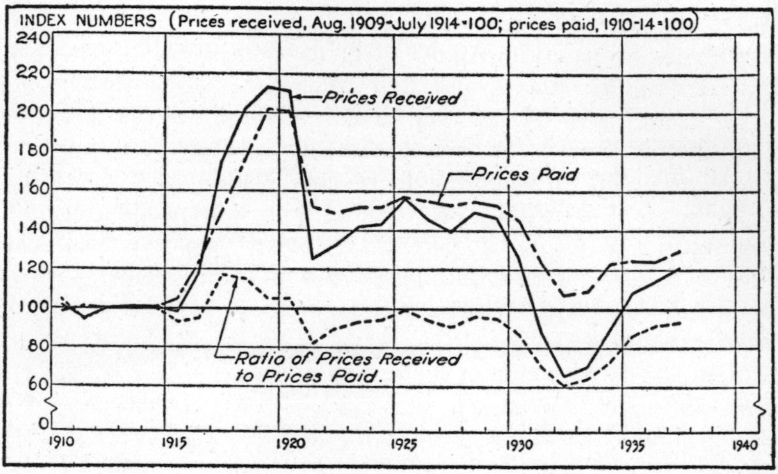

U. S. Department of Agriculture

Year	Prices received	Ratio of prices received to prices paid
1929	146	95
1932	65	61
1933	70	64
1934	90	73
1935	108	86
1936	114	92
1937	121	93

Farm real estate values also increased. From 1933 to 1937, farm real estate values rose 4 per cent each year, and by 1937 were 16 per cent above 1933. For the twelve months ending March 1, 1938, the index of average value per acre of farm real estate stood at 85 per cent of the 1912–1914 period.

If industrial production and agriculture generally were making rapid strides forward, there were other sectors in which the unfavorable aspects still were very marked. The wages index was lagging behind that for industrial production. Freight-car loadings were slow in recovering their former position. Foreign trade, notably imports, continued at a low point. The construction industry was badly mired. Bank debits outside of New York City, representing check payments, or spendings, continued sluggish. The figures in the accompanying table show the spotty nature of recovery, even at the highest point reached under the New Deal direction. The figures also show the consequences of the steep plunge into depression again during 1937–1938.

It has been pointed out that factory employment and pay rolls were moving toward the 1929 levels. But in a number of outstanding non-manufacturing activities, the achievements were not nearly so sizable. The following figures show this state of affairs. They indicate, at any rate as far as two important service industries were concerned, that the factory unemployed were not being absorbed by trade and communications.

STATISTICS OF EMPLOYMENT AND PAY ROLLS

(Monthly average, 1929 = 100)

First quarterly average	*Anthracite mining*		*Bituminous mining*		*Telephone and telegraph*		*Retail trade*	
	Employment	*Pay rolls*	*Employment*	*Pay rolls*	*Employment*	*Pay rolls*	*Employment*	*Pay rolls*
1929	103	104	106	110	95	95	97	96
1933	62	53	80	42	74	72	71	52
1934	74	78	91	64	70	69	80	59
1935	71	58	99	76	70	74	80	60
1936	70	63	99	86	70	76	81	62
1937	63	44	105	98	75	84	86	69
1938	60	47	95	71	76	92	83	69

There were elements in the recovery picture that could scarcely be regarded as reassuring; indeed, their presence encouraged the belief that the possibilities of once more achieving a continuous line of economic progress were remote. The following in particular were to be noted: unemployment continued on a large scale; new capital flotations (the investment of savings in the new securities of corporate enterprise) were slight; despite the easy money policy of the government short-term borrowings from banks did not expand; labor's relative share of the national income dropped off; and while labor productivity increased, labor's relative compensation lagged behind.

Unemployment. The significance of this phenomenon has already been commented upon. Because of the increase in productivity during the depression years, at least 7,000,000 persons were added to the body of permanently disemployed. At the height of the New Deal revival, there were still almost 10,000,000 men, women, and young people out of work.

Capital flotations. Business activity was resuming, profits were being made, and savings were taking place: but, interestingly enough, fresh capital funds were not pouring into the money market for investment in the new securities of corporations. Private enterprise, in short, was not seeking funds with which to make extensions to capital plant and therefore to the nation's wealth. This was a situation which markedly differentiated the New Deal revival from all earlier ones in American experience. It also pointed up an observation previously made, that is to say, that as long as there continued to exist a great gap between productive capacity and effective consumer demand, it was idle to employ savings to add to capital plant. What then, was happening to savings? In considerable measure, these were being placed at the disposal of public agencies—to finance public works, relief, subsidies. That was why the federal government, in particular, could continue to borrow so heavily at low interest rates—and this in the face of a mounting deficit.

The following figures indicate the purposes for which new capital issues were being floated in our money market. The virtually complete disappearance of foreign issues during the depression years is also to be noted. In the tabulation, the "public issues" do not include the direct obligations of the United States government. Issues for refunding purposes are also excluded.

NEW CAPITAL FLOTATIONS

(Figures in millions of dollars)

Year	*Total new capital issues*	*Total domestic capital issues*	*Total domestic corporate issues*	*Total domestic public issues*	*Total foreign issues*
1929	$10,183	$9,420	$8,002	$1,418	$763
1933	710	708	161	547	2
1934	1,386	1,386	178	1,208	...
1935	1,412	1,409	404	1,005	3
1936	1,973	1,949	1,192	757	25
1937	2,083	2,076	1,192	884	7

Banking activities. In this sector, as well, the improvements were not as significant as the New Dealers had expected. As has been

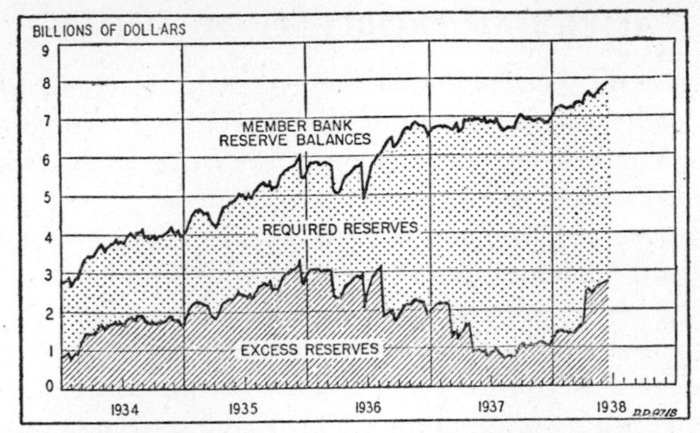

Total Member-Bank Reserve Balances at Federal Reserve Banks

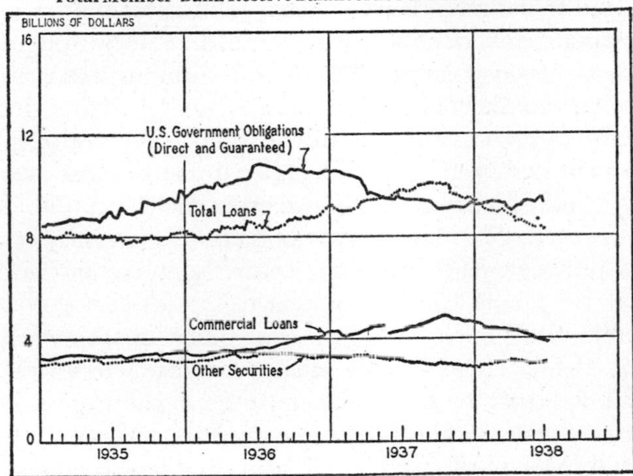

Bank Credit of Reporting Member Banks in 101 Cities, 1935–38

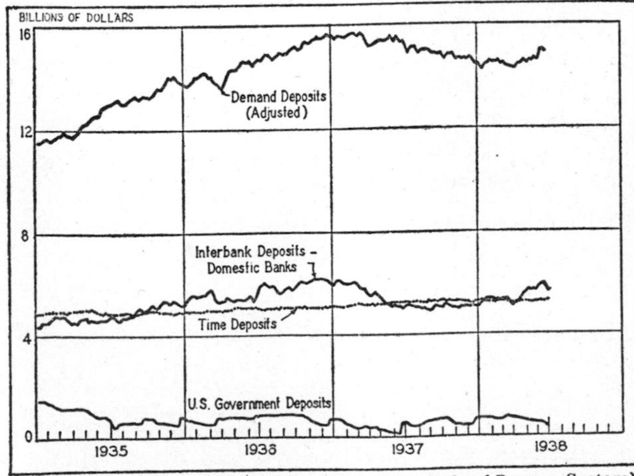

Wednesday Figures (Board of Governors of the Federal Reserve System)

said, the federal government was spending large sums of money, and the receipts for these sums—the government bonds—entered the banks. The Board of Governors of the Federal Reserve System then pursued a cheap-money policy. They bought government bonds, and this action led to an increase in member bank reserves. Too, member bank reserves grew through the inflow of gold from abroad.[1] By these processes, the base of the credit pyramid was expanded; and the hope was that there would take place a comparable increase in commercial loans for the purposes of furnishing business men with working capital. That is to say, increased reserves were to lead to increased bank deposits (through commercial loans) and increased bank deposits were to lead to increased spending. This was the theory of the New Deal's banking policy: but performance fell far short of expectations.

Thus, from July 1, 1933 to July 1, 1937, member bank reserve balances mounted from $2,286,000,000 to $6,900,000,000, an increase of about 200 per cent. On the other hand, deposits (demand and time) increased from $15,931,000,000 to $20,422,000,000, or about 28 per cent. And spending, or check payments (bank debits outside of New York City), increased from $3,562,000,000 for the week ending July 1, 1933, to $4,826,000,000 for the week ending April 24, 1937, or 35 per cent. What was happening was simply this: member bank reserve balances were expanded enormously; deposits grew measurably; but the deposits largely reflected increased holdings on the part of the banks of government securities.

The banks of the country—and this applied to the large and small institutions alike—to put it another way, showed their increased deposits in their investment portfolios rather than in their loan portfolios. They were, in other words, maintaining themselves in an amazingly liquid form; and the first hint of contraction of business sent them further to cover. They liquidated loans and discounts. The position of the fifteen biggest banks in New York City was symptomatic of what was taking place all over the country. The following figures show the distribution of assets of these banks on June 30, 1937, when revival was at its peak, and on June 30,

[1] The process worked in this fashion. The Treasury received the gold, issued gold certificates against it, and deposited the certificates with the Reserve Banks. This deposit credit was then employed for the government's current requirements. As the funds were disbursed they were deposited by the recipients in banks, which in turn deposited them with the Reserve Banks, in this way building up their reserve balances.

1938, when depression was at a low point. The figures are in percentages of total assets.

	June 30, 1937	*June 30, 1938*
Cash	28.5	34.6
United States governments	28.1	29.3
Other investments	7.9	7.9
Loans, discounts, etc.	32.4	25.0
Other assets	3.1	3.2

The key to the New Deal revival therefore appears at this point. It was not due to new capital borrowings; nor was it due to any real expansion in bank credit. It was largely due to public spending; and when public spending was slowed down—as happened from midsummer 1937 to late spring 1938—then depression once more set in.

National income. It was to be expected that national income would fall off sharply as a result of depression experiences; and that it would climb once more as a result of the government spending program. The fact is, "national income produced"—the net value of goods and services turned out in any one year—did increase every year. In 1929, the figure stood at eighty-one billions of dollars, in 1933, at forty-one and three-quarter billions, and in 1937 at almost seventy billions. But—and this was a more important question—how was this income distributed? The following figures show roughly the respective shares of the national income received

NATIONAL INCOME, BY CLAIMANTS

	1929	*1933*	*1937*
Total income paid out	100.0	100.0	100.0
Total compensation of employees	65.6	65.3	67.4
Total salaries and wages	64.4	61.7	61.8
Work relief wages	....	1.5	2.7
Social security contributions of employers	....	....	1.3
Other labor income	1.2	2.1	1.6
Total dividends and interest	14.4	15.7	13.8
Dividends	7.6	4.9	7.2
Interest	6.6	10.4	6.7
Entrepreneurial withdrawals	15.6	15.9	15.1
Net rents and royalties	4.4	3.1	3.7

by capital, labor, owners of realty, and self-employed entrepreneurs (including professional men, farmers, etc.). The figures are in per cents of the total.

These comparative figures are very illuminating. It will be noted that labor in private employment ("total salaries and wages") received a smaller share of national income in 1937 than it did in 1929—and this despite all the New Deal's professions of concern about the improved relative position of the working class. It will also be noted that the returns on invested capital ("dividends"), on the other hand, showed a very real improvement and an approximation to the relative position of 1929; while the returns on lendings ("interest") indeed had a better relative position. Also, self-employed business men and landlords were gaining.

Another comparative analysis may be made which shows that labor was worse off relatively in 1937 than any other economic group in the population. The following figures are the percentages of the income received in 1933 and 1937, based on 1929 income.

	1929	*1933*	*1937*
Total income paid out	100.0	57.7	88.3
Wages (selected industries)	100.0	42.5	82.1
Dividends	100.0	37.0	83.8
Interest	100.0	90.5	89.5
Entrepreneurial withdrawals	100.0	58.7	84.9

In other words, in depression and in New Deal revival as well, the economic group in the population which suffered most severely was the working class.

Income by family groups. Indeed, the distribution of family income, in the midst of New Deal recovery, showed even a steeper pyramiding than had been the case in 1929. A study made by the official National Resources Committee (released in September, 1938) indicated that for the year 1935–1936 the average family income of one-third of the nation was only $471; while 1 per cent of the population, at the top of the scale (whose family incomes were in excess of $10,000), received 13 per cent of the national income. The contrasts between the estimates of the Brookings Institution for 1929 and the National Resources Committee for 1935–1936 were illuminating. In 1929, over 42 per cent of the families in the United States were receiving apiece less than $1500; in 1935–1936, the proportion in the same income group was 65 per cent. Also, in 1929, 71 per cent of America's families were receiving apiece less than $2500; in 1935–1936, the proportion in the same income group was 87 per cent. It is interesting to note, too, that in 1935–1936, the 42 per cent of all the families with incomes under $1000 were receiving less than 16 per cent of the total family income; while the 3 per cent with incomes of $5000 or more were receiving 21 per cent of the total.

Labor productivity and labor cost per unit of output. We have already seen above how greater efficiency of production was one of the characteristic hallmarks of the golden nineteen twenties.[2] This labor productivity continued to increase under the New Deal in every sector. What was equally significant—despite higher wages—was the fact that the labor cost per unit of output did not increase as much as did the output per man-hour. Here was the refutation of those charges so frequently heard that the New Deal, through its encouragement of trade unionism and the work of the NLRB, was pushing labor costs out of line with other costs and in this way was imperiling the return of a real prosperity. The facts showed exactly the reverse: for labor was producing more in 1936 than it was in 1932 and it was *not* getting a comparable increase in wage payments.

The following figures, the work of the Bureau of Labor Statistics, show the uneven position of these two relatives clearly. The index of productivity (output per man-hour) is derived by dividing the index of production by the index of man-hours. The labor-cost index is derived by dividing the index of pay rolls by the index of production. The table shows that over 1932–1936, in all manufacturing industries productivity increased 15 per cent and labor costs increased 6 per cent; in steel productivity increased 31 per cent and labor costs *decreased* 5 per cent; in automobiles productivity increased 38 per cent and labor costs *decreased* 18 per cent; in anthracite mining productivity increased 31 per cent and labor costs *decreased* 23 per cent; in railroading productivity increased 27 per cent and labor costs *decreased* 14 per cent; while, among the outstanding industries, only in the case of bituminous coal did labor costs increase more than productivity.[3]

[2] See above, page 77.

[3] In this case, there existed a special reason. Said the *Monthly Labor Review:* "After 1932 the greatly increased demand for coal, combined with agreements regarding markets and operating conditions, tended to make possible the operation of many comparatively unproductive mines."

Labor Productivity and Labor Cost in Selected Industries, 1926, 1929, 1932, 1936

(1932 = 100)

Industry	*Output per man-hour*		*Labor cost per unit of output*			
	1932	*1936*	*1926*	*1929*	*1932*	*1936*
All manufacturing industries	100	115	131	124	100	106
Blast furnaces, steel works, and rolling mills	100	131	103	95	100	95
Automobiles	100	138	87	75	100	82
Cement	100	121	157	139	100	118
Cotton goods	100	121	166	146	100	130
Woolen and worsted goods	100	140	164	136	100	96
Leather	100	107	131	125	100	125
Flour	100	100	142	128	100	118
Slaughtering and meat packing	100	103	145	146	100	125
Cigars and cigarettes	100	158	196	148	100	77
Petroleum refining	100	127	142	123	100	99
Rubber tires and inner tubes	100	116	210	176	100	120
Anthracite mining	100	131	...	127	100	77
Bituminous-coal mining	100	113	...	162	100	141
Crude-petroleum producing	100	135	...	177	100	96
Class I steam railroads	100	127	104	102	100	86
Telephone industry	...	...	111	116	100	104

The Election of 1936

The stars were favorable in their courses; so that, in a period of rising business activity, President Roosevelt entered the Presidential campaign of 1936 to request popular endorsement of his policies. The Republicans had met first at Cleveland during June 9–12, 1936, and had come out flatly against the New Deal and all its works. Their platform opened with the words, "America is in peril," and in this spirit they submitted the principles and achievements of the New Deal to a bitter arraignment. The President had sought to usurp the powers of Congress and flout the authority of the Supreme Court; he had ridden roughshod over the prerogatives reserved to the states by the Constitution; he had tinkered with the tariff so that the country was being flooded with foreign commodities. The Republicans, therefore, were for a high protective tariff and compacts among the states to make possible such social legislation as the Supreme Court had found unpalatable. It may be said here, in passing, that it was an ironic quirk that the Republican party, which had always claimed descent from the Federalists, should now completely change its position and advocate decentralization of authority. The Republicans also looked upon the NRA experiment and found it evil, calling instead for "the vigorous enforcement of the criminal laws, as well as the civil laws, against monopolies and trusts and their officials." The leading contenders for the nomination had been Alfred M. Landon, Governor of Kansas; Frank Knox, proprietor of the Chicago *Daily News;* William E. Borah, Senator from Idaho; and Arthur H. Vandenberg, Senator from Michigan. When the balloting began to take place, however, no real opposition to the candidacy of Mr. Landon evidenced itself, and he was named on the first ballot. In the same way, Mr. Knox was nominated for the Vice-Presidency.

The Democrats met at Philadelphia, during June 23–26, with President Roosevelt, although absent, obviously dominating the proceedings. The convention was in a defiant mood, largely because of the blows directed against the New Deal by the Supreme Court; and in his keynote address, Senator Barkley threatened that "if, in the future, further amendment [to the Constitution] should become necessary to enable the people to work out their destiny and protect their fundamental rights or to govern some archaic interpretation never intended by its framers, I doubt not that the people will face that duty with the same calm intelligence which has guided them in the past."

The Democratic platform did not go so far; but it did insist upon the right of Congress to legislate nationally for such matters as relief, child labor, minimum wages, hours of labor, soil conservation, flood control, and the like. The rest of the platform was largely taken up with paeans in praise of the New Deal accomplishments. Democratic rule had put the nation "back on the road to restored health and prosperity"; the policies of the government had been "humanized"; the administration intended to continue thwarting "the activities of malefactors of great wealth who defraud and exploit the people." There were also promises made of continued aid to farmers, wage legislation, and a fight on monopoly. President Roosevelt and Vice-President Garner were renominated by acclamation. A significant piece of business completed at this convention was the revocation of the more than one-hundred year rule in existence at Democratic conventions which called for Presidential nominations by a two-thirds vote of the delegates. In this way the Democracy gave notice that its councils were no longer to be dominated by the Solid South.

Other parties entering the contest were the Socialist, which named Norman Thomas; the Communist, whose candidate was Earl Browder; and the newly formed Union party, whose nominee was William Lemke, Republican representative from North Dakota. This last group was made up of an oddly assorted company of dissidents, some of whom had links with old-time Populism; some of whom followed Father Charles E. Coughlin, a Catholic priest whose orientation was fascist; and some of whom followed the star of Dr. Francis E. Townsend, the originator of a plan for high federal pensions for the aged in order to increase purchasing power. Many labor leaders, notably those who agreed with John L. Lewis that the A. F. of L.'s program required serious recasting, organized Labor's Non-Partisan League and campaigned for Mr. Roosevelt. The A. F. of L., on the other hand, announced it would follow its traditional non-partisan policy of endorsement of its friends.

Mr. Landon, due to bad general staff work among his top advisers, got off on the wrong foot. Personally a liberal and sympathetic to many of the New Deal achievements, he began to make a campaign that could appeal only to the extreme bitter-enders. In a sense, his advisers were misled by the support given Mr. Landon by a number of personally disaffected Democrats, among whom were to be found Alfred E. Smith, John W. Davis, James E. Reed, and Joseph B. Ely. It took the Republicans some time before they learned that these were captains without an army. Also, the Republicans alienated labor when Chairman Hamilton of the Republican National Committee called a number of respectable leaders of responsible trade unions Communists, and when Mr. Landon attacked the Social Security Act. Mr. Landon subsequently made efforts to redeem himself; he supported relief expenditures, promised continued aid to agriculture, and even pledged himself to a Constitutional amendment, if necessary, to permit adequate federal control of industry and agriculture. But the whole campaign was conducted ineptly, and it at once became apparent that the Republicans were doomed to defeat.

Mr. Roosevelt made a swing around the circle, beginning on October 9, and defended all his policies vigorously before enthusiastic gatherings. His triumph was unexampled in American Presidential elections. He received a popular vote of 27,751,000 to Mr. Landon's 16,680,000; and even the minor parties were swamped with Mr. Lemke getting only 894,000 votes, Mr. Thomas 194,000 votes, and Mr. Browder 80,000 votes. Mr. Landon carried only two states, Maine and Vermont, so that the electoral vote was 523 to 8. The Democrats also increased their membership in both houses of the Seventy-fifth Congress and left the President's leadership of his party unimpaired. In the immediately following years, Mr. Roosevelt's popularity—despite the reappearance of depression during 1937–1938—did not wane: if there was a devil of the piece in the minds of the American public, it was the standpatter Democratic contingent in Congress and not the President or his body of advisers.

The Supreme Court Fight

On only one major question did the President lose—and then he suffered but a temporary defeat. This was his effort to change the make-up of the Supreme Court, by statute, to enable him to deal freely with social and economic legislation. On February 5, 1937, a Presidential message demanded that the President be empowered to appoint "additional judges in all federal courts without exception where there are incumbent judges of retirement age who do not choose to resign." And a bill accompanying the message—the work of the Attorney-General—provided that in the case of the Supreme Court the voluntary retirement age was to be 70 years and that the President might appoint up to six additional members to supplement non-retiring members. The official reasons presented were that the federal courts were congested, the judiciary was too "static" in its attitude toward laws, and that there existed "inequality, uncertainty and delay" in the determination of Constitutional matters. This, of course, was being less than frank; for what the President sought was a bench that would be more responsive to his and the public will as it had taken shape in Congressional legislation.

There was no question that President Roosevelt had been growing increasingly impatient with the strict constructionism of the Supreme Court, which refused to recognize the existence of a national emergency. In case after case it had ringed around the Presidential power with a whole series of inner breastworks, so that movement into new and unexplored regions was virtually impossible. It had hauled out a body of ancient principles and, by applying them, had been able to throw into the discard some vital parts of the President's program. Indeed, the Court had been ill-advised. In 1935, in a series of Gold-Clause decisions, it had cast an aura of doubt about the President's devaluation measure, and it had found unconstitutional the NIRA, the Frazier-Lemke Farm Mortgage Act, and the Railroad Retirement Act. Similarly, in 1936, the judicial lightning had hit the AAA, the Bituminous Coal Stabilization Act, the Municipal Bankruptcy Act, and even the New York State Minimum Wage Law. This last decision had been a bitter pill to swallow: for, in invalidating the NIRA, the Supreme Court had declared that Congress might not legislate on wages; while, in invalidating the New York Minimum Wage Act, it had also solemnly decreed that neither could the states. Justly, President Roosevelt declared that there now existed a no man's land where both federal and state action was ineffective.[4]

What were these Constitutional principles that the Supreme Court revived in its fight against the Presidential program? Dwight L. Dumond [5] summed them up well as follows: 1. That Congress might not delegate its legislative powers to administrative agencies or individuals. This rule was applied notably in the NRA decision. 2. That Congress might not regulate conditions in industry, using the commerce clause as a pretext. This rule was applied in the invalidation of the Railway Retirement Act. 3. That Congress has no general powers "apart from the specific grants of the Constitution." 4. That Congress might not use the tax power for the purpose indirectly of effecting social and economic reform. This rule was used in the AAA decision. 5. While, when emergencies existed, the states might call upon their reserved powers, the same situation did not apply in the case of the federal government. Constitutional amendment was required to extend the field of federal action.

What to do? The boldest course of action called for legislation to deprive the Court of the right of judicial review. Other proposals ranged from the simple and realistic expedient of packing the bench by additional appointments to the cumbersome device of Constitutional amendment granting both the federal and state governments

[4] Some of the decisions against the administration measures had been by 5 to 4 votes. The fact that a single justice could frustrate the Executive and Congress drew the hottest fire of proponents of the Presidential plan.

[5] *Roosevelt to Roosevelt* (1937).

control over production, wages, hours, and conditions of work in industry. The Republican party, in its 1936 platform, fell back upon an ineffectual compromise: it looked to state compacts in those fields where Congressional action was impermissible. Opponents of this plan were able to indicate the tardiness with which states had passed adequate child labor legislation to point up their argument that only through federal legislation could it be possible to move swiftly and effectively when social or economic crises threatened.

The President chose the easiest means to obtain judicial compliance; his was a packing program, and liberals defended it as such. They stressed the fact that the Supreme Court was not the only guardian of the Constitution of the United States; that the Court had reversed itself a number of times, that is to say, that there was nothing sacrosanct about its decisions; that in a number of cases President and Congress had simply defied the Court when it had gone counter to their wishes; and that the so-called Constitutional method of change suggested—amendment—was cumbersome, undemocratic in nature, and unlikely to produce the results sought. So, Charles A. Beard said of the President's proposal:

> It seems to me in accord with the facts . . . to say that the normal way to overcome adverse decisions against Congress is not to resort to an amendment, to tinker with the Constitution, every time a case arises. The American way in general practice is to use other means—that is, to change the number of judges, to appoint the right kind of judges, and to resubmit issues to the Court for reconsideration.
>
> . . . Congress has the same right as the Supreme Court to be courageous and independent. If Congress believes, with leading students of Constitutional law, if Congress agrees with four of the Supreme Court Justices, that five of the Justices have misread, misinterpreted, and in substance violated the Constitution, then Congress has the civic and moral obligation to bring the Court back within the Constitution. If it so believes, Congress is bound by oath of office to do this very thing. And citizens who believe in the necessity of legislation dealing with agriculture, unemployment, industry, social security, and natural resources, now have a right to expect Congress to do this very thing.

But the President's supporters were not organized; while the opposition was organized and articulate. Great newspapers, bar associations, conservative farmer organizations, college presidents, a number of state legislatures, some of the President's old friends and supporters like Governor Lehman of New York and Senator

Wheeler of Montana, all ranged themselves against the measure. In a hundred and one different ways they rang the changes on the same arguments: what they feared was the destruction of our Constitutional liberties if the Supreme Court was compelled to become the rubber stamp of the Executive. As Senator Wheeler put it: no Supreme Court at all would be better than "a Supreme Court which is subservient to any one man."

The President, stung by tactics which he regarded as unfair, dropped all pretense in two public addresses. Reviewing the unfavorable attitude of the Court in its recent decisions, he declared bluntly that there was "no definite assurance that the three-horse team of the American system of government will pull together"; and that he sought "to appoint justices who will not undertake to override Congress or Legislative policy."

The President could not prevail, however. The chief fight took place in the Senate and, despite the efforts of Senator Robinson of Arkansas, the majority leader, to keep Democrats in line, defections from party discipline were numerous. On June 14, the Senate Judiciary Committee reported the bill out adversely, accompanying its decision by a lengthy report in which the President was openly attacked. The President's supporters were slow to reply and when Senator Robinson was found dead in his apartment on July 14, the administration forces were left leaderless and bewildered. An ineffectual compromise bill was introduced, and because it pleased nobody, the Senate voted to recommit this substitute proposal on July 22. Thus, suddenly, the struggle ended with the President's defeat. All the administration could salvage was a mild measure to improve the procedural machinery in the lower courts.

Chief Justice Hughes played a prominent part in the fight on the President—behind the scenes, of course. He made two public addresses during the period that the conflict was raging, and while he spoke discreetly—he warned, for example, against permitting "dominant groups" to imperil democracy—there could be no question where his sympathies lay. Indeed, he was charged with having devised a stratagem that cut a good deal of the ground from under the President. While the debate was at full flood, on June 1, Justice Van Devanter announced his voluntary retirement from the Supreme Court. Van Devanter had been a consistent foe of the President's measures; his withdrawal meant the appointment of a liberal judge and a swinging of the balance on the Court now in the

President's favor. In other words, the Court thenceforth was likely to uphold the hand of Congress and the President; why, then, pack it? [6]

Indeed, subsequent events proved that victory really rested with the President; for the temper of the Court underwent an extraordinary change. One may only guess at the forces at work: but it is not unlikely that here again the Chief Justice played a leading rôle. The Court had been in serious peril; real statesmanship required that, without the surrender of the Court's authority as an institutional force, it yield before what had really been the popular will. The Court continued to maintain its high estate: but it now spoke with the tongue of the New Deal. For during its 1938 term, it issued a series of decisions which buttressed the New Deal at practically every point. It openly reversed itself on state minimum wage legislation and validated the State of Washington Minimum Wage Law a short year after it had rejected the similar New York State law. It gave the NLRB virtually a free hand. It approved the Social Security Act. It permitted the PWA to lend public funds for the construction of municipal power plants. It called upon public utility holding companies to register with the SEC. It affirmed a municipal bankruptcy act. It defended the government monetary policy in three new gold-clause decisions. And, in a number of public utility cases, it showed a willingness to move toward the liberal doctrine of prudent investment as the basis of rate fixing. Very justly could President Roosevelt declare—as he did in one of his "fireside chats" in July, 1938—that while he had lost a battle he had really won the war.

Labor Organizes

At the same time, a great schismatic struggle was taking place within the ranks of organized labor. A new force arose to challenge the leadership of the American Federation of Labor: this was the

[6] To succeed Van Devanter, the President named Senator Hugo L. Black of Alabama, an enthusiastic supporter of the Presidential policies and the author of a maximum-hour bill which labor endorsed. After the Senate had confirmed the appointment and Black had taken the oath of office, it was divulged that he had been a member of the Ku Klux Klan fifteen years previously. Black did not deny the charge—although he did make a spirited defense of racial, religious, and civil liberties—and the President took no action. Black's later career on the bench justified President Roosevelt's confidence in him. In 1938, another conservative justice quit the bench and Mr. Roosevelt made another liberal appointment, that of Stanley Reed, Solicitor-General in the Department of Justice.

Committee for Industrial Organization. The basis for the conflict was simple: were the unorganized workers to be formed into trade unions on craft lines or on industrial lines? By and large, the A. F. of L. spoke for the use of the older organizational forms of the craft unions, while the CIO spoke for the new type of organization along industrial lines. The A. F. of L. bureaucracy had been presented with two unexampled opportunities to press unionization. The first was during the twenties, when American capitalism was advancing to its greatest heights and job opportunities existed. Then, a militant program of better wages and shorter hours would have led hundreds of thousands, if not millions, of the unorganized into the trade unions. But the A. F. of L. top leadership accepted the slogans of the industrialists and bankers: that every humble individual could rise to fame and fortune in time; that only patience was necessary. The A. F. of L. officials therefore engaged in a policy of collaboration with capital: they frowned on strikes; they themselves sought to become capitalist by entering the labor banking field; they drove the most militant workers out of labor's ranks; they opposed social insurance. Hampered by their own craft structural forms, they found themselves incapable of going into the mass-production industries—steel, automobiles, rubber, radio, oil refining, aluminum—where mechanization and monopoly capitalism were reducing workers to unskilled laborers superannuated by the time they reached 40 years of age. Also, industrialists took the offensive: they formed company unions, engaged labor spies, helped organize vigilante groups: and in this way hampered independent organizational activity.

The second golden opportunity for organized labor presented itself in the first years of the New Deal. The NIRA's section 7(a) in effect legalized trade unions and authorized them to deal with industry through their own selected representatives. Again, there might have been a mass movement into the ranks of the A. F. of L. had its leaders been prepared to forget about craft jurisdictions. But the A. F. of L.—it almost seemed, so slowly did it move—waited for the government to do its organizing. There were exceptions: John L. Lewis rehabilitated the coal miners' union, Sidney Hillman the men's clothing workers' union, David Dubinsky the ladies' garment workers' union; but otherwise the opportunity was missed. In May, 1935, as has been said, the Supreme Court found the NIRA unconstitutional; and organized labor was back where it had been in 1932.

Then revolt broke out openly in the ranks. New leaders, as well as a handful of the old ones, emerged to point out that mechanization and the existence of a growing body of disemployed were imperiling the positions of the few already organized workers. To these forward-looking spokesmen, the only solutions were the organization of all the workers of the country and the creation of industrial instead of craft unions.

When John L. Lewis, of the miners, threw down the gage of combat at the 1935 convention of the A. F. of L., the lines of battle were clearly drawn.[7] He forced a vote on a resolution calling for organizational work on industrial lines in the basic industries regardless of jurisdictional claims and, although he met with defeat on this test of strength, he succeeded in rallying to his support a number of outstanding labor leaders and their unions. With these, he formed the Committee for Industrial Organization for the purpose of working within the A. F. of L. Mr. Lewis assumed the chairmanship of the new committee, an initial fund of $500,000 was collected, a machinery was set up, and organizers were sent out into a vast variety of fields as yet only slightly touched by the trade union ideology. The two outstanding were automobiles and steel; others were flat glass, rubber, radio, municipal and state offices, local traction, white collar jobs, insurance, agricultural labor, and the like. Before 1936 was over the CIO had the backing of ten national and international unions of which the most important were the United Mine Workers of America, the International Ladies' Garment Workers' Union, the Amalgamated Clothing Workers' Union, the United Textile Workers of America, the Oil Field, Gas Well, and Refinery Workers of America, and the International Union of Mine, Mill, and Smelter Workers.

The CIO moved on seven-league boots. The A. F. of L. took two measures to check its growth and counteract its influence. First, the executive committee of the A. F. of L., in the summer of 1936,

[7] To be strictly accurate, the struggle first emerged into the open at the 1934 A. F. of L. convention when, as a result of pressure, a resolution was adopted authorizing the organization of the mass-production industries. However, "the jurisdictional rights of all trade unions organized upon craft lines" were to be protected. Before the 1935 convention met charters were issued to unions in automobiles and rubber, but certain skilled craftsmen and the maintenance employees were excluded.

suspended the ten unions which had joined the CIO; and at the 1936 convention, A. F. of L. delegates gave their formal approval. In 1937, the A. F. of L. convention took the final step of authorizing its executive council to expel any of the suspended unions which would refuse "to return to the ranks of our movement." (Accordingly, nine of the unions were expelled during 1938.) Second, the A. F. of L. launched its own organizational campaign. The year 1936 and the first half of the year 1937 saw both bodies pushing their activities zealously.

The CIO's initial successes were unprecedented. Its first significant field of operations was in automobiles. The United Automobile Workers of America was revitalized (it had been established in 1935 by the A. F. of L.), given funds and direction under CIO leadership, and was supported in a number of preliminary skirmishes with the employers. Then, in December, 1936, the full weight of the UAWA (backed by the CIO) was thrown against one of the mightiest industrial forces of America, the General Motors Corporation. Strikes were called in most of the centers of this company's operations and the new technique of the sit-down (in which the workers refused to leave the plants and defied sheriffs with court orders to oust them) was employed with telling effect. The shutdown lasted for 40 days and in time involved 126,000 workers in 25 cities. It ended with complete success, for in February, 1937, General Motors signed an agreement with the UAWA recognizing it as the bargaining agency for its members in all the company's plants, establishing an hourly wage scale in place of the prevailing piecework scale, and creating grievance committees in the shops. As a result of short strikes, all other automobile companies except the Ford Motor Company quickly fell into line and also signed agreements.

The CIO then pressed into steel, a region in which industry had fought bitterly and with success all efforts at trade union organization. The Steel Workers' Organizing Committee was formed by the CIO and given full powers to act for the workers over the head of the existing paper union. In March, 1937, without resort to industrial conflict, the SWOC and the United States Steel Corporation came to terms, signing an agreement as a result of which the SWOC was recognized as the exclusive bargaining agency for all the workers, without, however, the closed shop. Also, wages were raised 10 per cent, an 8-hour day and 40-hour week with time and one-half for overtime were provided, and a grievance machinery was established. Other steel companies, at any rate, the older ones, followed suit and before the drive was over 260 companies employing 356,000 men had signed up.

So-called Big Steel had capitulated with surprising ease. Little Steel—the Republic Steel Corporation, Youngstown Sheet and Tube Co., and the Inland Steel Co. (these also were joined by the Bethlehem Steel Corporation)—proved a harder nut to crack. Strikes were called on May 26, 1937, and quickly spread over the whole eastern steel region with the leading centers at Chicago, the Mahoning Valley, and Johnstown, Pa. In all, 90,000 workers were involved. Employers' spokesmen not only refused to treat with the SWOC but they forced the fighting: attempted sit-downs were forestalled; vigilante committees were organized locally; plants were armed; and civil rights were suspended in a number of districts. In Ohio and at Johnstown, national guardsmen and state police helped the local police keep plants open. The result was bitter violence. On May 30, as a result of a clash between Chicago police and pickets moving on the Republic Steel works in South Chicago, shots were fired by the police and ten workers were fatally injured.[8] None of the police was seriously hurt. There was also fighting between strikers on the one hand and company guards and municipal police on the other in a number of Ohio communities, as a result of which eight additional lives were lost. The strikes against Little Steel were not organized as effectively as had been the strikes in automobiles; they met with stubborn resistance (backed by the state militia in Ohio); and public opinion, particularly in the small communities where the strikes largely raged, was apathetic to the striking workers or forced into hostility by vigilante bodies. The upshot was, the strike failed by July, 1937.

In other fields, CIO successes were more measurable. The shipping industry, first on the West coast and then on the East coast, was partially organized by a CIO affiliate. A great drive was begun in textiles by the Textile Workers' Organizing Committee. The rubber industry was signed up. Missionary work was begun in areas

[8] The so-called La Follette Civil Liberties Committee (really a subcommittee of the Senate Committee on Education and Labor), after a painstaking investigation, in which it was aided by newsreel films taken during the incident, reported: "From all the evidence we think it plain that the force employed by the police was far in excess of that which the occasion required. Its use must be ascribed either to gross inefficiency in the performance of police duty or a deliberate effort to intimidate the strikers."

where trade unionism never before had seriously raised its head: in the public utilities, meat packing, furniture, aluminum industries. In April, 1937, as has already been pointed out, the Supreme Court validated the National Labor Relations Act and with their legal status thus definitely established, trade unions now could meet employer reprisals with legal weapons. The CIO not only used the good offices of the NLRB whenever possible (so much so that employers and the A. F. of L. began to refer to the NLRB as a CIO agency) but, accepting the split with the A. F. of L. as an irrevocable one, proceeded to set up its own state and municipal federations and councils. The drive thus could continue on a great number of fronts and employ a variety of means. It was no accident therefore that it should be attended by such an extraordinary numerical success.

On November 9, 1935, the CIO began with seven unions and almost 1,000,000 members, of whom the miners accounted for 500,000, the ladies' garment workers 200,000, and the men's clothing workers 150,000. Two years later the CIO was able to boast of 32 affiliated national and international unions with a membership of 3,750,000. Of this number, only 12 per cent, according to Benjamin Stolberg, belonged to paper, or really non-operating, unions. According to its own figures, the CIO could claim 600,000 members in coal, 510,000 in steel, 400,000 in automobiles, 400,000 in textiles, 265,000 in the ladies' garment industries, 200,000 in men's clothing, 125,000 in radio, 100,000 in lumber and furniture, 90,000 in municipal traction, and 75,000 in rubber.

The A. F. of L., on its part, intensified its activities so that, whereas in the summer of 1935 it was reporting 3,154,000 members in all, in the summer of 1937 it was reporting 3,272,000 members exclusive of the membership in suspended CIO unions. In other words, the total gain in trade union strength for the whole country had been almost 4,000,000 members in two years.[9]

[9] An interesting index of the relative drawing power of both organizations was to be found in the outcome of the collective bargaining elections held under the NLRB. From its inception to the end of 1937, the NLRB supervised 966 elections, in 74.8 per cent of which the workers chose established national and international trade unions to represent them. However, of the 500 odd elections in which CIO unions were involved, they were chosen in 81.7 per cent of the cases; while in the 400 odd elections in which A. F. of L. unions were involved, success took place in only 56.1 per cent of the elections. In 208 out of the total of 966 elections, A. F. of L. and CIO unions both sought to speak for the workers. In these elections, the CIO unions won 160 and the A. F. of L. unions 48. To what extent workers participated in these elections may be noted from the following. Before the valida-

Indu
M
M
Prod
Au
Bi
C
E
Lu
Pe
Pi
St
W
Distr
Ca
R

Cash
Empl
E

Pa

Cons
C

Fore
E

In

Fina
C
Se

B
St
Pric
W
C

*

Labor militancy went hand in hand with organizational successes. It is interesting to note, as well, that the outstanding cause for labor stoppage in the New Deal period was trade union recognition instead of wage increases, as had been the case previously. The number of strikes began to mount, and the year 1937 saw the greatest number of industrial disputes in American labor history. However, the number of workers was less than half as great as that involved in strikes in 1919. The following table shows the figures for representative years.

STRIKES, 1919 TO 1937

Year	*Number of strikes*	*Number of workers involved*	*Number of man-days idle*
1919	3,630	4,160,348	*
1929	921	288,572	5,351,540
1932	841	324,210	10,502,033
1933	1,695	1,168,272	16,872,128
1934	1,856	1,466,695	19,591,949
1935	2,014	1,117,213	15,456,337
1936	2,172	788,648	13,901,956
1937	4,740	1,860,621	28,424,857

* Data not available.

THE "RECESSION" OF 1937–1938

While debates such as these were going on, suddenly, without heralding, a new depression hit America in August, 1937. There were no premonitory tremors as had occurred in the summer of 1929; there were also no runaway stock market speculation, no bank failures, no tightening of capital available for bank loans and investments, no high interest level, no sudden collapse of European markets. Nevertheless, business activity went into a sharp and deep decline, the drop continuing precipitously from August, 1937, to January, 1938, and then leveling out on a low plateau into the middle of June, 1938. The fall was more rapid than it had been during 1929; but it never got near the low of 1932.

In every sector, the tale was the same. The decline in agricultural prices and in the value of the farm dollar was almost catastrophic.

tion of the National Labor Relations Act by the Supreme Court in April, 1937, the number of valid votes cast of the total eligible employees was 64.1 per cent; after validation, this proportion mounted to 95.6 per cent.

Whereas in May, 1937, the general index of all farm prices stood at 128, in May, 1938, it was at 92. And whereas the ratio of prices received to prices paid in May, 1937, was 96, in May, 1938, it was 74. Cotton in May, 1937, had been selling at 12.9 cents a pound; and in May, 1938, at 8.4 cents. Corn was worse off, for in May, 1937, it had been selling at $1.21 a bushel; in May, 1938, the price was 52.7 cents. Wheat, in May, 1937, had been selling at $1.18 a bushel; and in May, 1938, at 71.4 cents.

Industrial production was no better. The Federal Reserve index for industrial production (1923–1925 as 100, with adjustments for seasonal variations) in May, 1937, stood at 118; in May, 1938, it was at 76. Iron and steel production in May, 1937, was at 134; in May, 1938, at 47. The automobile production index was at 135 in May, 1937, and at 49 in May, 1938. The lumber and plate glass industries showed similar histories. These were the durable goods industries; but the same was happening in the case of consumer goods industries. The following figures are indexes of production for typical ones in May, 1937, and May, 1938. Textiles, from 123 to 77; cotton consumption from 130 to 81; wool consumption from 132 to 73; leather and products from 133 to 104. As for the state of employment, it may be said simply that reliable estimates put the number out of work at 13,000,000; an increase of 3,000,000 over the summer of 1937.

What were the causes of this new downswing in the business cycle? It was agreed on all sides that this was no major crisis; that what had occurred was a decline in consumer demand. As Alvin H. Hansen phrased it: "The recovery was a 'consumption recovery.' The upswing moved forward under the stimulus of an expanding consumer demand fed by (a) consumers installment credit supporting purchases of automobiles and other durable consumers goods, and (b) governmental expenditures. The recovery, many believe, ceased when these two stimuli played out." Put more specifically, the outstanding factors in bringing on the new depression were the following: 1. The reduction of governmental contributions to the national income, that is to say, the termination of pump priming. Whereas, as Arthur Gayer pointed out, during 1934–1936, the government annually had added between three and four billions of dollars to the national income, in 1937 its contribution was less than one billion. 2. The continued stickiness of prices in many industrial regions under monopoly or partial monopoly control (e. g., steel,

Index of Business Activity, Guaranty Trust Company (Estimated Normal = 100.)

(Ten adjusted Series are included in the combined Index, as follows: Steel Ingot Production, Pig Iron Production, Construction, Automobile Production, Cotton Consumption, Bituminous Coal Production, Factory Employment, Car Loadings, Bank Debits, Foreign Trade.)

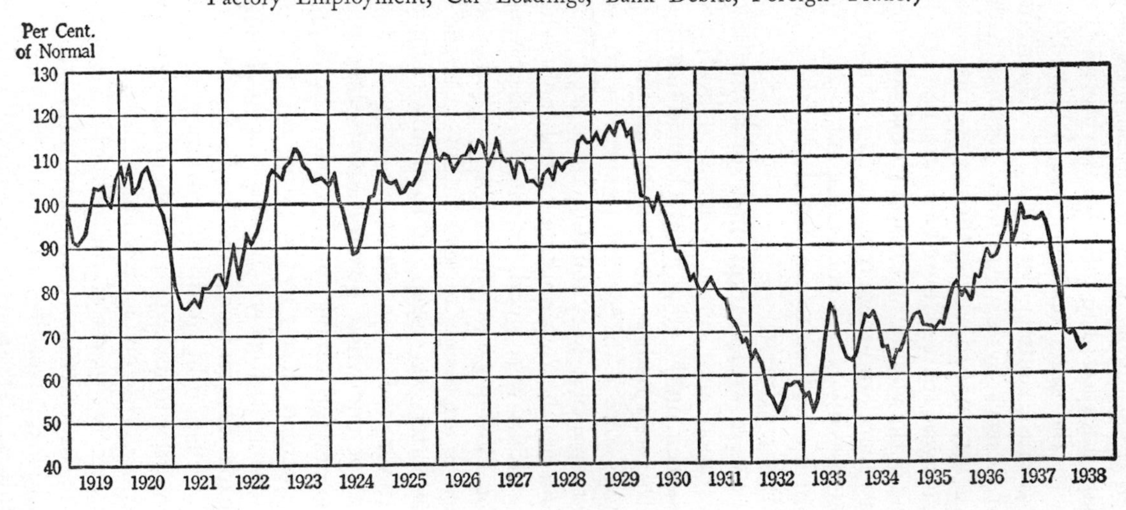

building materials) had held back capital goods expansion. 3. Prices had been rising during 1936–1937 and business men, fearing further sharp advances, had piled up inventories. The same phenomenon—with the same reaction—had followed the passage of the NIRA after the summer of 1933. 4. The Board of Governors of the Federal Reserve System had been pursuing a deflationary policy, after August, 1936, doubling the reserve ratios and sterilizing gold. The result was, there followed a contraction in bank loans and hence a decline in the volume and velocity of deposit turnover. While this was not general and there continued to be large surplus reserves in the system as a whole, some banks, notably in New York and Chicago, felt it expedient to contract closely their commercial loan and investment portfolios.

There were wild charges made of a "strike of capital" by the administration and, curiously enough, by the Communist party. Business men, on the other hand, claimed that the mounting deficits, the unbalanced budget, and the undistributed profits and capital gains taxes were at the basis of a general want of confidence in governmental policies. They could invest in capital plant expansion, add to inventories, borrow working capital, only when the chances for making profits were good. Currently, their spokesmen said, they were not. How much weight such factors had in affecting the general picture it is impossible to say; in any case, the New Dealers and their supporters were prepared to dismiss them as irrelevant.

Whatever the administration's original analysis, in time it adopted the one whose general aspects have been presented here. Its program for coming to grips with the depression—a program which emerged clearly in the spring of 1938—therefore included the following: 1. Renewal of governmental pump priming, through direct expenditures, loans, and grants to states and special authorities. 2. Reflation by gold desterilization and reduction of reserve ratios in order to make possible the mobilization of additional bank resources. 3. The forcing down of monopoly prices.

The first two parts of the plan the President announced in a special message to Congress on April 14, 1938. Specifically, he called for additional governmental expenditures for the fiscal year beginning July 1, 1938, notably for the WPA, the Farm Security Administration, the National Youth Administration, and the CCC. He recommended that the RFC be authorized to lend money directly to business men. He said that the Treasury would be ordered to desterilize the whole of the $1,400,000,000 in gold which the government held, and the Board of Governors of the Federal Reserve System would be requested to reduce reserve requirements by about $750,000,000. And he asked for new legislation (or amendments to existing acts) for the financing of additional housing projects under the USHA, new PWA public works grants and loans, and additional appropriations to the Bureau of Public Roads and for flood control, reclamation works, and the construction of federal buildings.

President Roosevelt's own cost estimate for his entire program was the addition of two billions of dollars to direct Treasury expenditures and another billion to government loans. Functionally, the breakdown could be presented in this way. The appropriations for direct relief—WPA, FSA, NYA, CCC—totaling $1,550,000,000, represented no increase over the expenditures of the fiscal year 1936–1937. For public works—housing, schools, roads, municipal public utilities, flood control, etc.—$1,462,000,000 was to be authorized, some of which could not be moved very quickly. The RFC was to be authorized to lend up to $1,500,000,000 to business. The expansion of bank credits, of course, involved no governmental outlays. The success of the program really depended upon the celerity with which the PWA and the USHA could release large sums for public works construction (thus also making possible an increase in PWA jobs), the RFC lend money, and the banks lend and business borrow sums for working capital and the carrying of inventories.

In any case, a part of Mr. Roosevelt's program was put into effect at once, thus clearing the tracks for recovery. The Secretary of the Treasury released the gold in the gold sterilization fund; and the Board of Governors of the Federal Reserve System lowered member bank reserve requirements by 12½ to 16⅔ per cent to bring about the desired reduction in required reserves. On April 13, 1938, the President signed the bill which broadened the lending powers of the RFC. Under this measure, RFC loans were to be made available to states and their subdivisions for the financing of projects authorized by law and to business enterprise in cases where capital or credit were not otherwise available.

Also, in June, Congress passed the Work Relief and Public Works Appropriation Act of 1938, which carried the funds for direct relief, public works, federal building and housing the President had requested. In addition, a farm parity section (not included in the President's plan but added by the Senate) appropriated $212,000,000 to permit the Secretary of Agriculture to make parity payments to growers of wheat, cotton, corn, rice, and tobacco. On the other hand, the handling of the question of price regulation, notably in those regions where monopoly controls prevailed, was deferred until the completion of the inquiry to be made by the Temporary National Economic Committee established under the O'Mahoney Monopoly Inquiry Act.

The spending and lending program got under way at once. The PWA made grants and loans to public bodies for public works; the USHA approved new housing projects and also made funds available; the Department of Agriculture began lending to farmers on cotton, corn, and wheat; the Farm Security Administration advanced funds for farm purchases and rehabilitation purposes; the RFC began moving credits to business men to permit them to carry inventories; the FHA's new mortgage terms began to stimulate private-house construction.[10] Private enterprise, apparently, caught the fever, for steel announced substantial price reductions without wage cuts and automobiles an augmented production program. As a sign of returning confidence, stock prices began to climb sharply in the last week of June, 1938, and by the middle of July, most indexes were pointing to a renewal of recovery.

Was it to be permanent? One was permitted to doubt. In fact, on the basis of the experiences in agriculture, it was possible to say that the New Deal was producing dislocations every whit as profound as those iniquities it was succeeding in redressing. On balance, it was hard to say that any permanent good had been achieved. The positions of the wheat and cotton growers in 1938, after five years of the ministering care of the New Deal, were symptomatic.

In the case of wheat, the long-term outlook was definitely not bright. Despite all the efforts of the first AAA and the Soil Conservation Act to induce wheat farmers to move into other types of agricultural operations, the preliminary reports for the 1938 harvest promised a crop of 967,000,000 bushels against a domestic consump-

[10] On July 6, 1938, Jesse H. Jones, chairman of the RFC, announced that this agency was making loans to smaller business men at a rapid rate. From February 20, loans aggregating $78,000,000 were approved and applications for loans totaling $93,650,000 were under consideration. Also, up to July, 1938, the Federal National Mortgage Association had bought $43,000,000 worth of mortgages insured under the Federal Housing Act, at the rate of about $285,000 each day.

SELECTED BUSINESS INDICATORS

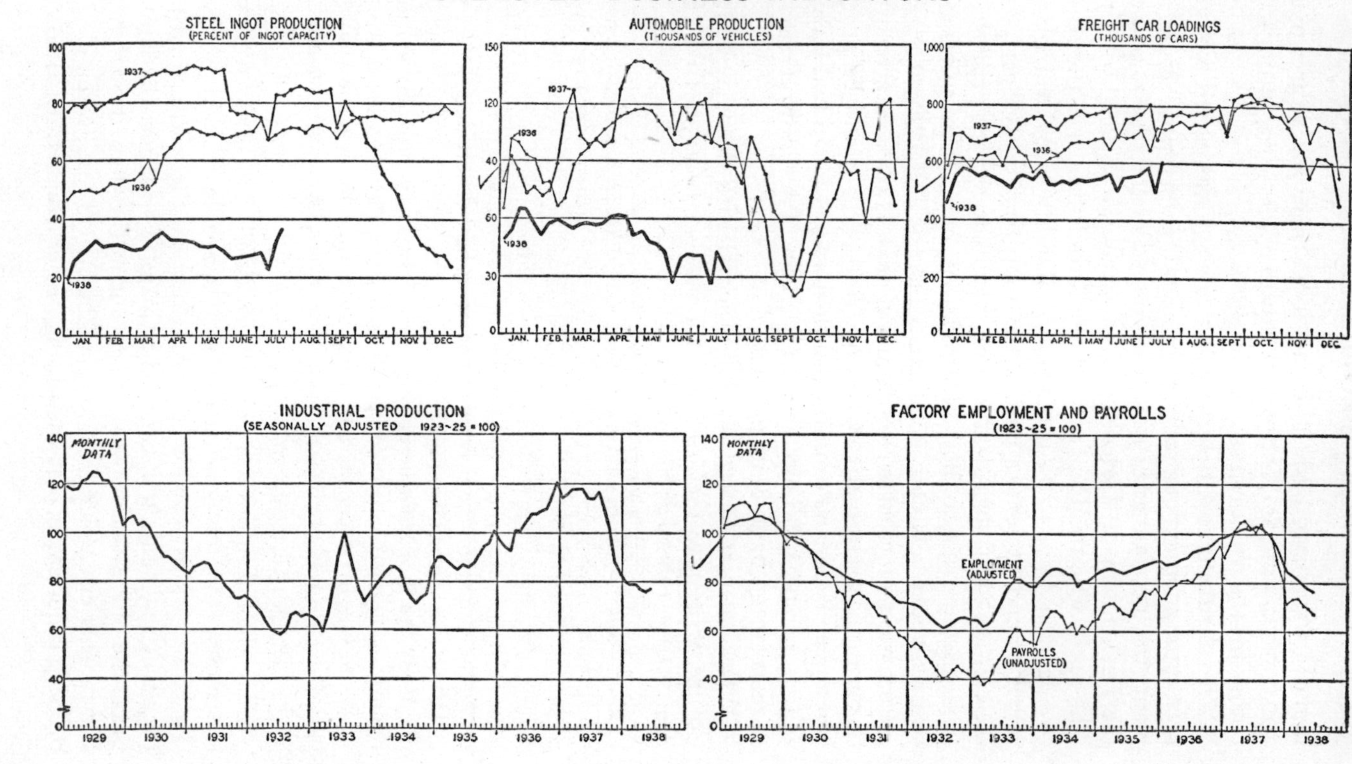

tion of 650,000,000 bushels. In addition, there was a carry-over of 200,000,000 bushels. The world situation for wheat promised no outlets for the American surplus.

The Agricultural Adjustment Act of 1938 was passed too late to permit the adoption of a reduction program; the result was, farmers planted 80,000,000 acres in wheat, instead of the 62,500,000 acres the Department of Agriculture had set as the national allotment. The result was, the Department was forced to finance the season's crop, and in July, 1938, it offered commodity loans averaging between 59 and 60 cents a bushel (or approximately 52 per cent of the existing parity price) at a time when the market price was 70 cents. Because it was not expected that more than 115,000,000 bushels would be absorbed by the loans, the Department of Agriculture was compelled to announce that only 55,000,000 acres would be permitted for the 1939 planting. And these would be prorated first among states and counties and then among individual farmers; and, as a bonus for compliance, cooperating farmers would receive subsidies of 26 to 30 cents per bushel of wheat.

Wheat farmers looked on this proposal with dismay. As J. M. Collins, writing to the *New York Times* on July 30, 1938, from Kansas City, reported:

> Compliance with the AAA's wishes would mean a radical change in the agricultural economy of the Middle West. Farmers have found wheat their most dependable crop. Due to a succession of dry years and grasshopper infestation, large acreages of corn, alfalfa, and other feed crops have been put into wheat and a great quantity of wheat machinery laid in. At the same time the livestock population has steadily declined.
>
> While most agricultural observers agree that the salvation of the Middle West lies in a permanent program of livestock production, time is required to bring this about. First, the farmer must obtain the funds with which to buy livestock, then he must have time to switch his cropping operations to a feed production basis. Meanwhile, he requires income from cash crops.

Thus the difficulties were clearly indicated. The carry-overs were enormous; the foreign market was incapable of taking up the American surplus; the lower prices dropped, the greater had to be the parity payments and commodity loans. To support the domestic price, the only solution was a sharp cut in the domestic allotment. But to what else was the commercial farmer to turn, when his ever-pressing requirement was the raising of immediate cash? The AAA was carrying the wheat farmer with government funds; but the possibilities of the wheat farmer's once more becoming an independent producer seemed remoter than ever.

Cotton's perplexities were even greater. In 1938, cotton acreage was calculated at 27,000,000 acres, the smallest since 1900. And the final yield was estimated at 12,000,000 bales, which about equaled the yearly consumption of the crop. Yet the staple was selling—measured in gold—at the lowest levels in American history! Why was this? There were two reasons: (1) the carry-over at the end of the season was likely to be 13,300,000 bales, the greatest in our experience; and (2) foreign-produced cotton was cutting deeper and deeper into our export markets. In connection with the latter, it was noted that during 1936–1937, the rest of the world used only 5,300,000 bales of American cotton as compared with 17,900,000 bales grown elsewhere; while during 1932–1933 (the last year of unrestricted production in the United States), the rest of the world had used 8,400,000 bales of American cotton as compared with 10,300,000 bales grown elsewhere. In other words, in 1932–1933, 45 per cent of all the cotton consumed outside of the United States came from us; and in 1936–1937, only 23 per cent. The result was, for 1939, the Department of Agriculture was compelled to announce a restriction of planting to 27,000,000 acres, compared with a normal acreage of 40,000,000; also, cooperating growers were to receive benefit payments, or subsidies, of 3.6 to 4 cents per pound of cotton.

The support of cotton under the AAA led to all sorts of direct and indirect costs. It was estimated by J. H. Carmical, writing in the *New York Times* of July 10, 1938, that some of the direct costs were as follows: (1) $750,000,000, the cost of benefit payments to growers over the five years 1933–1938; (2) $75,000,000, the potential loss on the 1,700,000 bales still held as a result of the commodity loan of 12 cents to growers in 1934; (3) a large and still undetermined loss on the 5,300,000 bales of the 1936–1937 crop, also supported by a commodity loan; (4) $26,000,000 annually in storage charges for the 7,000,000 bales still owned by the government. Indirect costs of reduction included the abandonment of corn and wheat lands, which are supplementary to cotton production; the loss of sales of machinery, mules, lumber, and the like, to cotton growers; the losses of employment opportunities in gins and transportation. And Mr. Carmical concluded:

Under the present Agricultural Adjustment Act, any land that is taken out of cotton or other controlled crops may not be used to increase commercial dairy activity and meat production. With these restrictions put on the abandoned cotton acreage, there is not much left for the cotton grower in the South to raise profitably. The enactment of the Wages and Hours Bill also will tend to restrict the shift of industry from a high to a low-cost area and thus prevent those thrown out of employment by the crop-control program from obtaining employment in industry unless they move to other sections, which at present also are suffering from an acute unemployment situation.

The social dislocations caused by the reduction program were equally unsettling. Efficient cotton growers, notably in the Southwest, in an effort to bring costs into closer line with low prices, were introducing tractor cultivation on a large scale, thus cutting down opportunities for the employment of sharecroppers. And a large number of landlords were reducing their plantings not by cuts in their own acreage so much as in the elimination of the holdings of their tenants. The result was a profound transformation in the organizational form of the economy—one that was occurring contemporaneously. The plantation's leading characteristic from colonial times on, when indentured servants had been introduced in Virginia and Maryland, had been its unfree labor supply: a labor supply attached to the soil and representing the most important capital cost of the landlord. The replacement of the indentured servant by the Negro slave in the eighteenth century, and the slave by the black croppers in the nineteenth century and the black and white croppers in the twentieth century, had not changed the essential characteristics of the picture. The croppers had to be provided an improvement, mules, implements, seed, and their "furnishings" (food during the planting and cultivating seasons): and this was necessary in order to maintain a permanent labor supply on the land. And because the cropper was being financed by the landlord during the seasons that he was not productive, his status was a debtor one from which escape was not easy; the cropper, therefore, was also unfree like the indentured servant and the slave before him.

But machine cultivation and crop reduction cut down the size of the necessary number of laborers. And the existence of a permanent body of disemployed made possible the changing of their status. The landlord no longer had to be concerned about anchoring his labor supply to the land; nor did he have to invest such a sizable part of his capital fund in its maintenance. The cropper could be converted into a day laborer: and increasingly this was taking place. The results of this revolution were as follows: 1. The plantation organization of cotton production was in process of breaking up, to be replaced by commercial farms. 2. The former cropper was deprived of shelter and "furnishings" during his non-productive months, and increasingly was dependent upon wages paid only during the cultivating and picking seasons. The rest of the year he had to fall back upon WPA or home relief. 3. The landlord's capital fund now in growing measure could be diverted into other areas of costs: the purchase of fertilizer, cultivating machines, tractors—and the picking machine when it was mechanically perfected. And this process only further contracted the area of employment opportunities for the croppers and quondam croppers.

This then—in the long term—was likely to be the ultimate end of the cotton reduction program: our retreat to a wholly domestic market with a consumption ultimately between 6,000,000 and 7,000,000 bales annually and the cultivation of only 15,000,000 acres (instead of the 46,000,000 acres of 1925!); increasing machine operations on commercial farms instead of plantations; and the elimination of first security and finally even job opportunities for large numbers of small white and Negro cotton farmers. Where were these unfortunates to be moved? The New Deal had no answer to that knotty problem.

The Foreign Policy of the New Deal

In the realm of foreign affairs, it was less easy to note a clear-cut position on which the Executive and Congress were in complete agreement. Taken in the large, the Executive (that is to say, the President and his State Department) favored a wider participation by America in world affairs, while the majority of sentiment in Congress leaned toward isolationism. This, at any rate, was true as regards Europe and the Far East. Most Americans, the memory of our fruitless participation in the World War not completely dimmed, regarded with suspicion the unrolling of events in Europe and the Orient. Distasteful as was the concept of authoritarianism to the great majority and much as our population sympathized with the victims of fascist oppression—the Spanish Loyalists, the Chinese people, the Jews of Germany and Austria—the general feeling existed that Europe's and the Orient's quarrels were not ours. The attempts of those who favored collective security—joint action by the so-called democracies to check fascist aggression—to force the United States into an understanding with Britain and France were regarded with a jaundiced eye. Was the British government, which kept India under heel, showed its open animosity toward the Spanish people, wrote a treaty with Mussolini, and sought to come to terms with Hitler, a democratic power? Or was it not in reality a satisfied empire which was seeking to protect what it had gained by one means or another against the depredations of the dissatisfied nations Germany and Italy? To those who reasoned in such wise an alliance with Britain, or even Secretary Hull's "parallel action," looked very much like our pulling the British chestnuts out of the fire. Or, as Quincy Howe cynically phrased it: "England expects every American to do his duty."

In Latin American relations, the administration's activities were regarded with less misgivings. What Americans learned about them —for there was much that did not enter upon the public record— they were prepared to approve. The President's "good neighbor" pledge, which he had made in his first inaugural address, was being carried out. On December 28, 1933, Mr. Roosevelt had amplified this promise in the following words:

> . . . the definite policy of the United States from now on is one opposed to armed intervention. The maintenance of constitutional government in other nations is not a sacred obligation devolving upon the United States alone. The maintenance of law and the orderly processes of government in this hemisphere is the concern of each individual nation within its own borders first of all. It is only if and when the failure of orderly processes of government affects the other nations of the continent that it becomes their concern; and the point to stress is that in such event it becomes the joint concern of a whole continent in which we are all neighbors.

In line with the above, Washington withdrew the last of the American marines from Haiti by the end of 1934; on May 31, 1934, it abrogated the Platt Amendment as regards our direct interest in the internal affairs of Cuba; it watched, if not with sympathy at least with a fair degree of patience, the experiment in state socialism being carried on in Mexico; and it set out to cultivate the friendship of Latin Americans culturally and economically. So much so, that the Mexican expropriation of foreign-owned oil properties in 1938 led to a diplomatic parting of company by the United States and Great Britain; for Great Britain's sharp demand for the return of the oil properties of her nationals forced Mexico to suspend diplomatic relations, while we indicated our willingness to wait the working out of a proper settlement.[11]

Similarly, our courting of Latin Americans, at the expense of German and Italian interests in Central and South American countries, was apparently meeting with a measure of success, for in 1938 the German coordinated press took to complaining that we were encircling them in the Western Hemisphere. Certainly, in Brazil, this was definitely so, for the Brazilian orientation was turning toward us and away from Germany. The same appeared to be true of Chile and Argentina.[12]

[11] Secretary Hull's only immediate public comment was that as a sovereign state Mexico had the right to expropriate, but that "fair, assured, and effective values" must be paid to foreign nationals. Oil companies estimated that the properties seized were worth $450,000,000, of which the American interest was put at $175,000,000, the rest being largely British. These figures, however, were seriously questioned in many quarters. The Mexican government proposed to pay for the expropriated properties from royalties derived from the sale of oil from government fields as well as those taken over. The oil interests—in an effort to bring pressure to bear on Washington as they had on London—insisted that Mexico's record for compensation was bad. They pointed out that up to June, 1933, the Mexican government had expropriated between 660,000,000 and 950,000,000 pesos' worth of land against which 25,000,000 pesos' worth of bonds were issued. And currently, the bonds were being quoted at 10 per cent of their face value. It began to appear, in 1938, that Washington's attitude was stiffening somewhat. In March, 1938, the Treasury Department announced the temporary suspension of our purchases of Mexican silver, so that, as a result of the withdrawal of this support, the Mexican peso dropped from 3.6 to the dollar to 5 to the dollar. Also, in July, Secretary Hull, in a note to Mexico, in which he commented on the tardiness with which the expropriation of agrarian lands had been compensated, called for "adequate, effective, and prompt compensation." Americans assumed that by implication the Secretary was referring to the oil properties as well. In the case of the agrarian lands Mr. Hull proposed arbitration under the provisions of the Inter-American Treaty of Arbitration of 1929, to which both Mexico and the United States were parties. Mexico replied to the following effect: she refused to recognize the existence of an international legal principle forbidding a sovereign state to expropriate property; she was willing to compensate, but at her own convenience; and she was opposed to the arbitration of what she considered a domestic issue. Mr. Hull rejoined, again proposing arbitration. Also, he called upon Mexico to halt expropriation in the meantime and to put funds aside toward the day when damages would have to be paid. Again Mexico rejected Mr. Hull's position, but she did accept the suggestion that mixed claims commissions be established to pass on the disputes over the value of individual ranches. What was disturbing about the whole exchange was the increasingly stern tone of the State Department.

[12] The trade figures pointed up this state of affairs very clearly. From 1936 to 1937, our exports to Latin American countries increased as a whole from 40 to 90

That the State Department was prepared to use every expedient —even to the point of employing public funds—to resist German penetration into the Western Hemisphere was further demonstrated by an extraordinary measure taken in July, 1938, in connection with the financing of a Haitian loan. The government of Haiti, hard pressed for funds, sought to raise $5,000,000 for a public works program; but American investment bankers regarded the flotation coolly. At this point, two German-controlled banking houses (one with an office in New York) stepped in and offered to take up the issue, partly in blocked marks (to be used for the purchase of machinery in Germany) and partly in real currency. At the same time they demanded guarantees and privileges that would have entrenched German finance firmly in the internal economy of Haiti.

According to Joseph Alsop and Robert Kintner, writing in the *New York Times* of July 29, 1938, the State Department learned of these negotiations. They record the finale of the drama as follows:

The J. G. White Engineering Company, a big firm doing much government business, was induced to take the Haitian public works contract. The Haitian Government gave the engineering company its note for $5,000,000. And the engineering company took the note to the Export-Import Bank, where it was discounted at par, in return for a promise that American materials would be used exclusively in the new Haitian public works.

The arrangement is a remarkable one, for it is tantamount to a loan by the United States Treasury to Haiti. The Export-Import Bank, chartered in the dim dawn of the New Deal to finance American foreign trade, is an agency of the government. Its funds are government funds. And now, by the device of the discount, the bank is using its powers to advance American cash to foreign governments.

That Latin American countries were prepared to accept American leadership was evidenced by the results of the Inter-American Conference for the Maintenance of Peace, held at Buenos Aires late in 1936. Out of the discussions—centering in the single idea that security in the Western Hemisphere was a joint concern and that any threat to peace on the continent necessitated immediate consultation between all governments—there emerged three major treaties. In the words of Secretary Hull, these were designed "to bring into

per cent. The Italian trade increased only 1½ per cent and the German less than 30 per cent.

active cooperation all twenty-one governments whenever the peace of the hemisphere is menaced either from within or without, or whenever a sufficiently grave situation arises elsewhere in the world which may create a threat to the peace of the western world." But the agreements signed at the conference were of equal importance: for their intention was to increase trade, stimulate cultural interchange, and improve methods of communication. Secretary Hull's trade policy won a signal victory when the conference resolved that trade was not to be diverted into artificial channels by bilateral understandings or manipulated by "various systems of control, clearing, and compensation devices" (this was a blow at Germany's activities). And President Roosevelt's "good neighbor" program was approved when the conferees called for plans to increase the educational and cultural interchange between the American countries. This greater cultural affinity took interesting forms: on the one hand, we began to broadcast inspired news about ourselves to Latin Americans; and on the other, we took to sending naval and military advisers and instructors to those countries to the south of us which requested them.[13]

Outside the Western Hemisphere, Congress was less disposed to give the Executive a free hand. Through the agency of the Senate Munitions Committee, headed by Gerald P. Nye of North Dakota, it probed at great length into the workings of the munitions industry, at the same time revealing the connection between finance and big business on the one hand and American entrance into the World War on the other. It passed the Johnson Debt Default Act in 1934, which forbade the sale in this country of securities issued by governments in default in the payment of their obligations to the United States. And with the outbreak of the Italo-Ethiopian conflict in 1935 it passed the first of a series of Neutrality Acts for the purpose of making American involvement in this or any other war difficult.

[13] In order to give the State Department complete control over this cultural work (a skeptic might call it "propaganda"), there was set up in 1938 a new division of Cultural Relations of the State Department. According to Mr. Hull, this division was to concern itself with such matters as the exchange of professors and students; the distribution of books; "supervision of participation by this government in international radio broadcasts," and the like. It will be noted that such work was being done by the Carnegie Endowment for International Peace; but apparently the State Department was beginning to feel that "the dissemination abroad of the representative intellectual and cultural works of the United States" required a political direction.

Majority sentiment in Congress was prepared to surrender without too much of a struggle the traditional concept of the freedom of the seas, that is to say, that neutrals had the right to trade at will with belligerents as long as contraband rules were being strictly observed. Our persistence in claiming such rights during the first years of the World War had plunged us into too much controversy and eventually into war. But who was to guide policy? One group in Congress, fearful of the power of the Executive when passions were running high, was disposed to pass mandatory legislation making it compulsory upon the President to prohibit certain practices once a state of war in which we were not involved had been declared. Another group was less inclined to tie his hands and favored discretionary legislation.

It turned out that the acts written constituted a compromise of these different positions. The first Neutrality Act, the joint resolution of August 31, 1935, was to remain in force until February 29, 1936, and it provided that "upon the outbreak or during the progress of war" an embargo was to be imposed upon the export of implements of war. Also, at his discretion, the President might prohibit Americans from traveling on the ships of belligerent nations except at their own risk. For the purpose of learning to what extent Americans were helping in the arming of foreign nations, the resolution also called for the establishment of a National Munitions Board to register munitions plants and grant export licenses to munitions manufacturers.

The second Neutrality Act, the joint resolution of February 29, 1936, which was to operate until May 1, 1937, further whittled down the area of discretionary action. The President was ordered to apply and extend the embargo on implements of war whenever he found that a state of war existed; also, the embargo was applied to the flotation of securities and loans by belligerent powers in our money markets. The American republics in this case were exempted from the terms of the act.

The third Neutrality Act, the joint resolution of May 1, 1937, was intended to be permanent. Again, the President was to act when a state of war existed; he was ordered to apply and extend the embargo; and he was to prohibit certain practices automatically and at his discretion might ban others. In the first category of automatically prohibited acts were the following: 1. The export of "arms, ammunition and implements of war" to belligerents. 2.

The sale in this country by belligerents of their securities or other financial obligations. 3. Their solicitation of war contributions. 4. The use of American ships to transport implements of war to belligerents. 5. The travel by Americans on belligerent ships. 6. The arming of American merchant ships. And in the second category of acts to be prohibited at the discretion of the President were the following: 1. The transport of *any* commodities on an American ship to a belligerent. (In other words, at his discretion, the President might extend the meaning of the term "implements of war.") 2. Export of any goods to a belligerent until all rights and titles in such goods had been transferred to a foreign government. (This was the so-called "cash and carry" provision, which meant that the foreign government was first to pay for and then be prepared to transport its own purchases before America would release the goods in question. The provision, however, was to remain in force for only two years.) 3. The use of American ports as supply bases for belligerent warships. 4. The use of our ports by foreign submarines and armed merchant ships.

In the eyes of those who were prepared to keep America out of a foreign war at any cost, this was progress of a sort. But critics were ready to point out that there remained many gaps in the neutrality legislation. First, the concept "existence of a state of war" was too loosely drawn. The President, it seemed, was not compelled to act if the international amenities were not being strictly observed. Thus, Japan did not trouble to declare war on China in 1937 when it invaded that country; hence, the neutrality legislation in his mind did not apply. Second, the term "implements of war" required further definition. Were oil, scrap iron, airplane engines, cotton, metals generally, which ultimately were destined for conversion into implements of war, strictly that? Apparently not, unless the President in his discretion decided to extend the terms of the embargo to include them. Third, the prohibition against the flotation here of securities by belligerents was virtually meaningless. It was quickly indicated that in the World War the Allied powers had financed their purchases in America by the shipment of gold, the repatriation of privately owned American securities, and bank credit. It was not until all these resources had been exhausted that recourse was had to the money market. Today in fact, foreign countries—certainly this was true of England and France—were even better situated in this respect than they had been in 1914. Their gold reserves were unimpaired, their nationals owned a large part of the more than $8,000,000,000 worth of foreign deposits in American banks and American securities and properties, and bank credit was only too easily available. In other words, using such means, foreign nations could launch America once more on a tremendous industrial boom and plunge the American economy deeply into wartime pursuits—as had happened during 1915 and 1916—before there was the slightest need for raising funds publicly. By that time our fortunes would have been already deeply involved.

Thus, those who hoped for American neutrality in the full meaning of the term were not content. They wanted explicit legislation; and they also wanted the war-making power resting squarely in the hands of Congress, which, they felt, was more likely to be responsive to the public will. This group—and it seemed to represent the majority of American sentiment—also pressed for the passage of the Ludlow amendment to the Constitution, which called for American participation in a foreign war only after a national referendum had first been taken. On the other hand, there was a group that wanted the President to have a free hand almost completely. He was to have power to impose embargoes at his discretion; in addition, he was to discriminate against the aggressors; [14] and, preferably, he was to act in concert with the democratic nations for the purpose of stopping the continued onward sweep of fascism. Why such faith in the Executive, particularly when the Executive—as the conduct of Presidents McKinley and Wilson had indicated—could withhold significant information from Congress and the people? Realistically, because President Roosevelt was indicating by his words and acts that he himself was moving toward this second position of what came to be called collective security. In brief, the advocates of collective security (which really meant joint action on the part of the United States, England, and France against Germany, Italy, and Japan first to forestall war and then, if necessary, to prosecute it) were backing the President against Congress.

But certainly the President's course was not a clearly charted one. Thus, in January, 1936, the administration had supported

[14] Incidentally, what constituted "aggression"? Historians are still debating, almost twenty-five years after the event, who started the World War. Who, also, started the Spanish-American War?

legislation which would have authorized the President to prohibit the export of all materials to belligerents in excess of "normal quotas"; at that time, too, he was not prepared to discriminate against any belligerent, aggressor or not. Again, to the chagrin and amazement of many American liberals, it was the President himself who asked Congress in January, 1937, to impose an arms embargo on Spain, and this despite the fact that the duly constituted Loyalist government was being fought by insurgents openly supported by Italy and Germany. (It is significant to note in this connection that the arms embargo was not applied to Italy, despite its admitted intervention with men and arms in Spain.) Further, in order to apply the arms embargo to the Italo-Ethiopian conflict, the President had declared a state of war in existence before diplomatic relations between the two countries had even been suspended; and, on the other hand, he had refused to recognize a state of war in China in the face of obvious Japanese aggression. The question could only be raised: Did the President act swiftly in the case of Ethiopia because we had no actual or potential interests in the region, whereas in China our interests were very real? The recognition of a state of war in China would mean that our warships would have to get out of Chinese waters, our nationals would have to remain at their own risk, and American property rights could not be immediately defended. The President, it appeared, was averse to such a line of action: and so we remained in China, while "incidents" which strained relations between us and the Japanese to the danger point multiplied.

The Chinese situation was particularly trying. Japan had opened hostilities at Shanghai in August, 1937, and without declaring war proceeded to extend its operations over a good part of northern and central China. Secretary Hull followed what he called a "middle-of-the-road" policy: that is to say, trade in implements of war with the belligerents did not cease; American marines and warships were maintained in Chinese areas; the property interests of our nationals were watched; but Americans themselves were urged to evacuate danger zones. Notes to Japan poured across the sea in what seemed an unending stream. We insisted that Japan would be held responsible for loss of life and property damage; we announced we would not withdraw our fleet and would accept any necessary risks to defend the rights of Americans still in China; we protested the general aerial bombing of territories where large civilian populations resided. In fact, after one such attack, that on Nanking, President Roosevelt delivered what has come to be called his famous "quarantine" speech at Chicago, on October 5, 1937. After touching in general terms on the unsettled international situation and by implication referring to the Japanese invasion of China and the Italian support of the insurgents in Spain, the President called upon "the peace-loving nations" to make "a concerted effort" to protect the sanctity of international treaties and to maintain "international morality." Then he went on:

> The peace, the freedom, and the security of 90 per cent of the population of the world is being jeopardized by the remaining 10 per cent who are threatening a breakdown of all international order and law. . . . It seems to be unfortunately true that the epidemic of world lawlessness is spreading. When an epidemic of physical disease starts to spread, the community approves and joins in a quarantine of the patients in order to protect the health of the community against the spread of the disease. . . . If civilization is to survive, the principles of the Prince of Peace must be restored. Shattered trust between nations must be revived. Most important of all, the will for peace on the part of peace-loving nations must express itself to the end that nations that may be tempted to violate their agreements and the rights of others will desist from such a course. There must be positive endeavors to preserve peace.

From the outbreak of hostilities in China, our government had consulted with other powers, notably Britain. The policy was called one of "parallel" rather than "joint" action; and in line with this we concurred in the condemnation by the League of Nations Assembly of the Japanese bombing of open towns in China, and also agreed with other nations that Japan by her invasion had violated the terms of the Nine-Power Treaty and the Kellogg-Briand Pact. But the American people were watching such threatening gestures on the part of the Executive with small sympathy. In polls taken by the American Institute of Public Opinion, Americans expressed themselves as opposed to the administration's activities. So, in a poll released on September 4, 1937, 54 per cent of those participating favored the withdrawal of American troops from China; and in a poll released on January 15, 1938, the majority stood at 70 per cent. For this reason, it was generally agreed, the Brussels Conference of November, 1937, called to consider applying pressure on Japan, failed.

The sinking by Japanese airplanes of the American gunboat

Panay, which was evacuating refugees and escorting three American tankers, provoked an official crisis—but left most Americans unmoved. Secretary Hull made strong representations, insisting that American ships were in Chinese waters "by uncontested and incontestable right"; demanded full indemnification; and called upon Japan to assure us that American interests and property would not again be molested. On all these points Japan complied. Washington, however, while agreeing that the incident was closed, took a number of steps that pointed up its general distrustfulness of the Japanese and its intention to remain in China at all costs. American warships participated, as observers, in the ceremonies opening the great British naval base at Singapore. Secretary Hull addressed a letter to Vice-President Garner in which he made the significant statement that the American government was interested in its nationals abroad not simply because of their investments or the foreign trade they carried on. Said he: "There is a broader and much more fundamental interest—which is that orderly processes in international relations be maintained." And both the President and the Secretary of State employed the unusual device, for them, of publicly attacking the Ludlow Resolution, which had been brought out of the House committee as a result of rank-and-file membership pressure. The President's campaign was successful: but not successful enough to prove to the outside world that his foreign policy was accepted without challenge. For the Ludlow Resolution was sent back to committee by a close vote of 209 to 188.

The use of one policy toward Spain and another toward China, the existence at least of a gentleman's agreement with Britain, the sudden demand for a powerful fleet (as we shall see) puzzled many Americans. Senator Hiram Johnson of California stated the position of these when he declared: "I call attention to the fact that the Senate ought to assert itself and learn the foreign policy of the United States before it goes upon this journey which parallels one that we took in 1917." The *New Republic* said: ". . . the United States government has embarked on a policy that is disapproved by a majority of the American people because it involves a genuine danger of war." While the publicist John T. Flynn voiced the unexpressed fears of numbers of persons when he commented in the following fashion on the President's foreign policy and naval construction program:

First, the President is preparing to lead the country into a vast program of armament as a means of spending money to avert another depression—houses for the dogs of war rather than the mutts of peace. *Second,* he is preparing deliberately to sell to this country a war scare as a prelude to the armament program. *Third,* he is attempting to shift the psychological reactions of the nation to the patriotic motif in order to distract attention from the disintegrating domestic situation. *Fourth,* one reason for this is to build up the attitude embodied in the slogan "Stand by the President." . . .

That these were not simply individual vagaries, the representative polls taken by the Institute of Public Opinion plainly revealed. A series of these inquiries was made during the winter of 1937–1938 and the spring of 1938 and they showed the following: Majorities from 65 to 70 per cent were against the participation of the United States in collective action of any kind. The Ludlow Resolution was approved by a majority vote of 70 per cent. War loans to either Japan or China were rejected by a vote of 95 per cent. A majority of 70 per cent favored withdrawal of our citizens, soldiers, and warships from China. Even a private boycott of Japanese goods—despite the popular sympathy expressed for the Chinese cause—was favored by only 37 per cent; while 64 per cent voted against the sending of arms to China to either side.

On the basis of these canvasses of opinion, the Institute concluded that Americans stood for the following:

1. Build a larger army and navy for national defense.
2. Make no entangling political alliances with foreign nations or with the League of Nations.
3. Keep our nationals out of countries at war.
4. Leave the declaration of war up to the people themselves.

The Philippine settlement came to be linked with the Asiatic question, as well. A bill for Philippine independence, the so-called Hawes-Cutting bill, after years of agitation, had finally been passed by Congress on December 29, 1932; had been vetoed by President Hoover on January 13, 1933; and four days later had become law by repassage over the Presidential veto. The measure provided for the establishment of a transitional commonwealth, in effect as an American protectorate, for a period of twelve years and under a Filipino chief executive. The United States retained the right to maintain military posts and naval bases in the islands and decisions by the insular courts were to be subject to review by the United States Supreme Court. During the probationary period the free entry of most Philippine imports into the United States was to cease gradually and regular tariff rates were to be imposed on Philippine sugar, cocoanut oil, and fibers in excess of certain fixed quotas; on all duty-free articles exported to the United States an excise tax was to be put for the purpose of servicing the Philippine public debts; also Philippine immigrants virtually were to be barred from the United States. This measure, however, was voted down by the Philippine legislature on account of its economic and immigration provisions. On March 2, 1934, President Roosevelt reopened the question when he urged Congress to revive the Hawes-Cutting bill. Amendments, however, were to be included to provide for the removal of the American military reservations from the islands and to leave the question of the continuance of our naval bases to future negotiations with a Philippine government. Mr. Roosevelt said nothing of the economic and immigration sections of the old law, thus brushing aside the chief complaints of Filipinos against the independence measure. The Tydings-McDuffie bill, introduced in Congress and signed by the President on March 24, was substantially the Hawes-Cutting law except that the military and naval sections were changed in harmony with the President's recommendations. On May 1, 1934, the Philippine legislature, bowing to the inevitable, gave its approval.

By 1938, Filipinos were contemplating the future with real alarm: for not only did the presence of the Japanese in China threaten their own security, but their imminent withdrawal from the American customs union seemed to promise only economic collapse. Trade figures indicated that the Philippines continued to depend upon the American market for the absorption of their sugar, cocoanut oil, copra, hemp, and minerals as much as ever; and the year 1946, when the Filipinos were to begin paying full import duties on these products, was looming very close. Reverting again to the so-called Japanese threat, it was pointed out that a considerable percentage of the Philippine retail trade was now in Japanese hands, that Japanese were migrating in large numbers to the islands, and that Japan's interest was strengthened by the strategic location of the archipelago. As one writer put it: "On the map, the Philippine archipelago looks somewhat like a large key fitted into a lock composed of Australia, the Dutch East Indies, Singapore, French Indo-

China, and China. Who holds this key may unlock the treasures of southern Asia."

President Roosevelt seemed to be sympathetic to such claims; for in April, 1938, he indicated that he was in favor of extending the Philippine tariff deadline from 1946 to 1960. And the Filipinos themselves were beginning to regard independence now as a mixed blessing. Every indication therefore pointed to Congressional reconsideration of the Philippine settlement before long.

Our sudden determination to build a powerful navy undoubtedly was to be linked with the Executive's growing interest in the maintenance of our uncontested position in the Far East. During 1934–1937 our naval program had been concerned entirely with the building up of the naval establishment to the full strength allowed by the Treaties of Washington and London. It is true, a rift had appeared in the international heavens in December, 1934, when Japan had denounced the treaty of 1930. A new naval conference was called in December, 1935, at London, to reconsider the position of the powers in the face of Japan's demand for parity. But the conference got nowhere: for the United States refused to retreat from the ratio of 5:5:3 set up in 1930. On its part, in the interests of armament reduction, it proposed a flat cut of 20 per cent in navies all around and the continuance of the qualitative limitations of 35,000 tons for battleships and 10,000 tons for cruisers. To those terms Japan refused to accede. In March, 1936, a feeble gesture to check the inevitable naval armament race was made when the United States, Great Britain, and France signed a treaty calling for the maintenance of parity between Great Britain and the United States. Also, the three signatories bound themselves to qualitative limitations in new construction, and the exchange of information about building plans. The treaty contained the inevitable escape, or escalator, clauses; and when, in 1937, Japan announced its intention to use guns larger than the 14-inch ones fixed as the upward limit in the treaty, the three parties to it considered themselves released.

Other than the reporting of this backing and filling on the part of the great naval powers, the administration made no effort to reveal its intentions to the American public. President Roosevelt's message to Congress of January 28, 1938, therefore, came like a bolt from the blue. Calling for new naval construction (without any reference to qualitative limitations), the President took this stand, as he said, "specifically and solely because of the piling up of additional land and sea armaments in other countries, in such manner as to involve a threat to world peace and security." The administration asked for authorization legislation; and its estimates of costs were uncertain, at first the figure being put at $880,000,000 and later at $1,156,000,000. Too, it insisted its intention was to increase the size of our naval effectives by only 20 per cent; critics, on the other hand, declared the figure was closer to 60 per cent.

Congress quickly complied and, despite a mounting protest, passed the administration measure much as the naval experts had drawn it up. The Naval Act of 1938 (approved May 17, 1938) authorized the composition of the Navy in under-age vessels to be raised by the following tonnages: capital ships, maximum increase of 135,000 tons up to an effective tonnage of 660,000; aircraft carriers, an increase of 40,000 tons up to an effective tonnage of 175,000; cruisers, an increase of 68,754 tons up to an effective tonnage of 412,500; and similar increases for lesser craft.

The attack on the Naval bill again and again reverted to the same point: What was the administration's foreign policy? In other words, to what use was such a navy—which would be greater than Britain's and twice the present size of Japan's—to be put? It was pointed out that our present navy was adequate for ordinary police duty in any part of the world; that we already were in a position to repel invasion of our shores by any single power or—in the light of their present political interests elsewhere—any combination of powers; that it was idle to assume that any nation, least of all Japan, would be mad enough to try to cross the thousands of miles of ocean that separated us from the rest of the world for the purpose of landing an expeditionary force here; and that commitment to the resumption of unrestricted capital ship building in the face of the doubts of the invulnerability of battleships from aerial attack was, to say the least, rash. The charge was openly being made that the administration was looking to the building of a two-ocean navy, an unprecedented step in our naval policy: and that the plan was to assure our overwhelming superiority in all foreign and distant waters. The *New Republic*, echoing the sentiments not simply of individuals but of many peace organizations, said flatly: "Few of those who protested would continue to do so if they could be shown that these expenditures were really necessary for defense and were not a possible basis for a diplomacy of force in distant parts of the world."

The administration undoubtedly was taken by surprise, particularly by the charge that it was concealing its foreign policy, for Congressman Vinson, sponsor of the bill in the House, was forced to issue a statement which had every aspect of being official. He said:

> It is declared to be the fundamental naval policy of the United States to maintain an adequate navy in sufficient strength to guard the continental United States by affording naval protection to the coastline in both oceans at one and the same time; to protect the Panama Canal, Alaska, Hawaii, and our insular possessions; to protect our commerce and citizens abroad; to maintain a navy in sufficient strength to guarantee our national security, but not for aggression; to insure our national integrity; and to support our national policies.

America in Two Worlds

Thus, after more than six years of the New Deal, we seemed to be standing in two worlds. In one, our feet seemed for the time being to be planted securely, in the other only perilously. Under the leadership of an energetic state capitalism, we were trying to create for ourselves an island of security in which private enterprise would not be so depredatory or the status of the underprivileged so hopeless. Secretary Hull had set forth the goal of the New Deal, in the dry language of diplomacy, in his note to the Mexican government on July 2, 1938, in these words:

> The government of the United States has itself been very actively pursuing a program of social betterment. For example, it has undertaken to improve the share of the farmer in the national income, to provide better housing, the wider use of electric power at reasonable rates, and security against old age and unemployment, to expand foreign trade through reduction of trade barriers, to prevent exploitation of labor through excessive hours and inadequate pay, to protect debtors from oppression, to curb monopolies; in short, it is carrying out the most far-reaching program for the improvement of the general standard of living that this country has ever seen.

This program, however, was having the leadership of state capitalism, which had supplanted liberal capitalism because of the paralysis of private enterprise. For the initiative and the driving force of enterprisers there had been substituted the energies of the state. But the state could operate only through a bureaucracy—and in this case the bureaucracy was likely to become overpowering because of its size and the necessity for its maintenance. In time, state capitalism really could bring about the attrition of capitalism itself. But the process was likely to proceed at a headlong pace: for the leaders of the New Deal, at the same time they were seeking to create social security at home, were plunging headlong into foreign adventure. Mr. Roosevelt was demanding for the United States a larger rôle in world affairs; he was beginning to speak of the necessity for checking aggression. But was not aggression the other face of the imperialist-capitalist world in which we lived? It was populated by the late aggressors, who were sated because they had enough; and the new aggressors, who were dissatisfied because their share of raw materials, markets, and outlets for accumulations was inadequate. Make them both happy? But the new aggressors could become satisfied only at the expense of the old aggressors, who would yield only at the point of the sword or as a result of defeat in war. And the history of the modern world had clearly taught this lesson: that in foreign wars, all belligerents lost.

Historically, there was a rough parallel for our position. In the third quarter of the seventeenth century, the French nation, under the dispensation of mercantilism, reached unexampled heights. Colbert, the minister of the crown, devoted himself to the social weal by the use of the agencies of the state. The state became the protector of private enterprise and the initiator of new activities: foreign trading companies were encouraged and supported; manufactories for the creation of luxury wear—with subsidies, tax remissions, often completely financed by state funds—were built up; agriculture received the benevolent attention of the state. Rich in natural resources and man power, and its productive energies released because of the state's fostering care, the French nation became the most powerful in the world.

Colbert, however, had a royal master—Louis XIV. And he, personally and dynastically ambitious, used these productive energies to involve France in a bitter series of religious persecutions and foreign wars. France emerged from them with a mountain of debt, a weakened economy—and a state bureaucracy as avid for power as had been that landlordism which it was supplanting.

We are in a somewhat similar situation today. At home, Mr. Roosevelt (like Colbert) labors in the public interest to revive production and increase standards of living through the agency of a state apparatus still in a fluid form and therefore not yet oppressive.

Abroad, Mr. Roosevelt (this time like Louis XIV) is the crusader: he seeks to bring his message of enlightenment into other nations—by peace of course, with the sword if need be. The work of the second Roosevelt is in very real danger of canceling out the work of the first in the short run. And in the long run—even if foreign war is avoided? The topheavy apparatus of state capitalism finds it more and more impossible to support society; rather, its weight is likely to crush it.

BIBLIOGRAPHY

BIBLIOGRAPHY

General

The student of current political and economic developments has at his command a bewildering and ever-growing array of periodicals, which should be consulted for the purpose of keeping abreast of the times. The more important are here enumerated. Published by various agencies of the federal government are the following: *Federal Reserve Bulletin* (by the Board of Governors of the Federal Reserve System); *Survey of Current Business* (by the Bureau of Foreign and Domestic Commerce); *The Agricultural Situation* and *The Land Policy Review* (by the Bureau of Agricultural Economics); *Monthly Labor Review* (by the Bureau of Labor Statistics). The American Federation of Labor publishes the *Monthly Survey of Business.*

The following news letters of outstanding banks contain informative surveys and articles: *Monthly News Letter* (of the National City Bank of New York); *The Guaranty Survey* (of the Guaranty Trust Company of New York); *The Index* (of the New York Trust Company). The Foreign Policy Association, Inc., publishes semi-monthly its authoritative *Foreign Policy Reports.* See also its two series, more popular in treatment, "Headline Books" and "World Affairs Pamphlets."

Also to be consulted are the following: *The New York Times; The American Observer; The Nation; The New Republic; Time; Newsweek; Business Week; The Annalist; The Commercial and Financial Chronicle.* The following monthly and quarterly magazines from time to time contain informative articles: *Harper's; The Atlantic Monthly; Current History; Foreign Affairs; The Yale Review; Virginia Quarterly Review; Bankers' Magazine; The Annals* (of the American Academy of Political and Social Science); *Fortune.* Outstanding learned journals include: *The American Economic Review; The American Political Science Review; The Political Science Quarterly; The Journal of Political Economy; The Quarterly Journal of Economics; Social Research; Journal of Land and Public Utility Economics; Harvard Business Review; American Sociological Review.*

The Brookings Institution, at Washington, D. C., and the Twentieth Century Fund and the National Industrial Conference Board, at New York City, frequently publish reports of surveys and investigations. For brief descriptions of federal agencies, as they come and go, the loose-leaf manual *The United States Government Manual* (prepared by the National Emergency Council) should be consulted. Indispensable to a proper understanding of basic economic matters is, of course, the *Encyclopaedia of the Social Sciences,* 15 v. (1930–1935).

I. POLITICS IN THE NINETEEN TWENTIES

POLITICIANS AND POLITICAL MOVEMENTS. James C. Malin, *United States After the World War* (1930); Preston W. Slosson, *Great Crusade and After,*

1914–1928 (1930); R. V. Peel and T. C. Donnelly, *The 1928 Campaign* (1931); W. A. White, *Masks in a Pageant* (1928); Anonymous, *Washington Merry-Go-Round* (1931); Anonymous, *Mirrors of 1932* (1931); Arthur Capper, *Agricultural Bloc* (1922); Nathan Fine, *Labor and Farmer Parties in the United States, 1828–1928* (1928); Calvin Coolidge, *Autobiography* (1929); W. S. Meyers and W. H. Newton, *The Hoover Administration* (1936).

II. LEADING LEGISLATIVE PROBLEMS OF THE NINETEEN TWENTIES

THE TARIFF ACTS. F. W. Taussig, *Tariff History of the United States* (revised edition, 1931); J. M. Jones, *Tariff Retaliation* (1934).

CREATING A MERCHANT MARINE. James C. Malin, *United States After the World War* (1930); Brookings Institution, *United States Shipping Board* (1931); National Industrial Conference Board, *American Merchant Marine Problem* (1929); J. P. Kennedy, "Economic Survey of the American Merchant Marine" (1937); C. N. Weems, Jr., "Rebuilding the United States Merchant Marine" (*Foreign Policy Reports* of Foreign Policy Association, v. xiii, no. 20, 1938).

THE RAILROAD PROBLEM. Rogers MacVeagh, *Transportation Act, 1920: Its Sources, History, and Text* (1923); D. Phillip Locklin, *Economics of Transportation* (1936); H. G. Moulton and Associates, *The American Transportation Problem* (1933).

THE PUBLIC DEBT AND TAX REDUCTION. H. L. Lutz, *Public Finance* (1936); Twentieth Century Fund, *Facing the Tax Problem* (1937).

THE REGULATION OF POWER. C. O. Hardy, *Recent Growth of the Electric Light and Power Industry* (1929); H. S. Raushenbush and H. W. Laidler, *Power Control* (1928).

III. AMERICA IN TWO HEMISPHERES

GENERAL TREATMENTS. S. F. Bemis, *Diplomatic History of the United States* (1936); R. L. Buell, *International Relations* (revised edition, 1931); Quincy Wright, editor, *Interpretations of American Foreign Policy* (1930); C. A. Howland, editor, *Survey of American Foreign Relations*, 4 v. (1928–1931). See also the publications of the World Peace Foundation and the Carnegie Endowment for International Peace.

THE UNITED STATES AND LATIN AMERICA. J. Fred Rippy, *Latin America in World Politics* (third edition, 1938); Carleton Beals, *Mexican Maze* (1931); Waldo Frank, *America Hispaña* (1931); Foreign Policy Association, "Mexico's Social Revolution" (*F. P. R.*, v. xiii, no. 10, 1937), "Church and State in Mexico" (*F. P. R.*, v. xi, no. 9, 1935); M. M. Knight, *Americans in Santo Domingo* (1928); H. L. Stimson, *American Policy in Nicaragua* (1927); A. Alvarez, *Monroe Doctrine* (1924); U. S. State Department (prepared by J. Reuben Clark), "Memorandum on the Monroe Doctrine" (1930); Foreign Policy Association, "Trade Rivalries in Latin America" (*F. P. R.*, v. xiii, no. 13, 1937), "American Occupation of Haiti" (*F. P. R.*, v. v, nos. 19–20, 1929).

RENEWAL OF THE PEACE MOVEMENT. J. S. Bassett, *League of Nations*

(1928); M. O. Hudson, *Permanent Court of International Justice and the Question of American Participation* (1925); D. H. Miller, *Peace Pact of Paris* (1928); J. T. Shotwell, *War as an Instrument of National Policy* (1929); Foreign Policy Association, "The Weakness of Peace Machinery" (*F. P. R.*, v. viii, no. 14, 1932), "Are Sanctions Necessary to International Organization?" (Pamphlet No. 82–83, 1932), "The League of Nations" (Pamphlet No. 61, 1931), "Revision of the Versailles Treaty" (*F. P. R.*, v. v, no. 8, 1929), "The Permanent Court of International Justice" (*F. P. R.*, v. v, no. 21, 1929).

NAVAL LIMITATION. R. L. Buell, *Washington Conference* (1922); Yamato Ichihashi, *Washington Conference and After* (1928); Foreign Policy Association, "The National Defense Policy of the United States" (*F. P. R.*, v. viii, no. 13, 1932).

INTERALLIED DEBTS AND REPARATION PAYMENTS. C. Bergman, *History of Reparations* (1927); National Industrial Conference Board, *Inter-Ally Debts and the United States* (1925); H. G. Moulton and Leo Pasvolsky, *World War Debt Settlements* (1926) and *War Debts and World Prosperity* (1932).

RUSSIAN RELATIONS. Foreign Policy Association, "The Outlook for Soviet-American Trade" (*F. P. R.*, v. x, no. 11, 1934), "The Outlook for Soviet-American Relations" (*F. P. R.*, v. ix, no. 1, 1933).

IV. CAPITAL AND LABOR

GENERAL TREATMENTS. F. L. Allen, *Only Yesterday* (1931); President's Conference on Unemployment, *Recent Economic Changes*, 2 v. (1929); President's Research Committee on Social Trends, *Recent Social Trends in the United States*, 2 v. (1933); H. T. Warshow, *Representative Industries in the United States* (1928); T. N. Carver, *Present Economic Revolution in the United States* (1925).

MASS PRODUCTION. Taylor Society, *Scientific Management in American Industry* (1929); James T. Adams, *Our Business Civilization* (1929); Charles A. Beard, editor, *Whither Mankind?* (1928); Stuart Chase, *Tragedy of Waste* (1925), *Men and Machines* (1929), *Prosperity: Fact or Myth* (1930); R. S. and H. M. Lynd, *Middletown* (1929); Lewis Corey, *Decline of American Capitalism* (1934); R. G. Tugwell, *Industry's Coming of Age* (1927).

THE POSITION OF LABOR. S. Perlman and P. Taft, *History of Labor in the United States, 1896–1932*, v. 4 (1935); C. R. Daugherty, *Labor Problems in American Industry* (revised edition, 1938); Edward Berman, *Labor and the Sherman Act* (1930); Felix Frankfurter and N. Greene, *Labor Injunction* (1930); P. F. Brissenden, *History of the I. W. W.* (1920); J. S. Gambs, *Decline of the I. W. W.* (1932); L. L. Lorwin, *The American Federation of Labor* (1933); E. E. Witte, *The Government in Labor Disputes* (1932); David J. Saposs, *Left-Wing Unionism* (1926); James Oneal, *American Communism* (1927); Paul H. Douglas and Aaron Director, *Problem of Unemployment* (1931).

THE SUPREME COURT AND PROPERTY. Charles Warren, *Supreme Court in United States History*, v. 3 (1922); J. R. Commons, *Legal Foundations of Capitalism* (1924); Louis Boudin, *Government by Judiciary* (1932); E. S.

Corwin, *The Twilight of the Supreme Court* (1934); Felix Frankfurter, editor, *Mr. Justice Brandeis* (1932); J. P. Pollard, *Mr. Justice Cardozo* (1935).

Mergers and Anti-Trust Legislation. H. R. Seager and Charles A. Gulick, Jr., *Trust and Corporation Problems* (1929); H. W. Laidler, *Concentration in American Industry* (1931); A. A. Berle, Jr. and G. C. Means, *The Modern Corporation and Private Property* (1932); J. C. Bonbright and G. C. Means, *The Holding Company* (1932); W. J. A. Donald, *Trade Associations* (1933); Frank A. Fetter, *Masquerade of Monopoly* (1931); W. Z. Ripley, *Main Street and Wall Street* (1927); National Industrial Conference Board, *Mergers and the Law* (1929); Arthur R. Burns, *The Decline of Competition* (1936); D. M. Keezer and Stacy Macy, *Public Control of Business* (1930); John T. Flynn, *Security Speculation* (1934); Harold G. Moulton, *The Financial Organization of Society* (revised edition, 1938); Lewis Corey, *House of Morgan* (1930); Anna Rochester, *Rulers of America* (1936); Ferdinand Lundberg, *America's 60 Families* (1937); Twentieth Century Fund, *Big Business: Its Growth and Its Place* (1937) and *How Profitable Is Big Business?* (1937).

V. FOUR OUTSTANDING PROBLEMS OF THE TWENTIES AND THIRTIES

Prohibition. E. H. Cherrington, *Evolution of Prohibition in the United States* (1920); Peter Odegard, *Pressure Politics: The Story of the Anti-Saloon League* (1928); Charles Merz, *The Dry Decade* (1931); Herman Feldman, *Prohibition, Its Economic and Industrial Aspects* (1927); National Commission on Law Observance and Enforcement, *Report on the Enforcement of the Prohibition Laws of the United States* (71st Congress, 3d Session, House Document No. 722, 1931); L. V. Harrison and Elizabeth Laine, *After Repeal* (1936).

Immigration Restriction. H. P. Fairchild, *Immigration, A World Movement and Its American Significance* (revised edition, 1925); R. L. Garis, *Immigration Restriction* (1927); W. J. Lauck, *Immigration Problem* (1913); John R. Commons, *Races and Immigrants in America* (1907); Manual Gamio, *Mexican Immigration to the United States* (1930).

The Decline of Agriculture. J. D. Black, *Agricultural Reform in the United States* (1930); Wilson P. Gee, *Place of Agriculture in American Life* (1930); Edwin G. Nourse, *American Agriculture and the European Market* (1924); Clara Eliot, *Farmer's Campaign for Credit* (1927); E. R. A. Seligman, *Economics of Farm Relief* (1929); Bernhard Ostrolenk, *The Surplus Farmer* (1932); J. M. Goldstein, *The Agricultural Crisis* (1935); Louis M. Hacker, "The Farmer Is Doomed" (John Day Pamphlets, 1933).

Economic Imperialism. Julius Klein, *Frontiers of Trade* (1929); Paul M. Mazur, *America Looks Abroad* (1930); Hiram Motherwell, *The Imperial Dollar* (1929); Benjamin H. Williams, *Economic Foreign Policy of the United States* (1929); Charles A. Beard, *The Idea of National Interest* (1934) and *The Open Door at Home* (1934); Scott Nearing and Joseph Freeman, *Dollar Diplomacy* (1925); Scott Nearing, *Twilight of Empire* (1930); Ludwell Denny, *We Fight for Oil* (1928) and *America Conquers*

Britain (1930); Nicholas Roosevelt, *America and England?* (1930); R. W. Dunn, *American Foreign Investments* (1926); Max Winkler, *United States Capital in Latin America* (1928); C. Lewis and K. T. Schlotterbeck, *America's Stake in International Investments* (1938); Commission of Inquiry into National Policy, *International Economic Relations* (1934); U. S. Bureau of Foreign and Domestic Commerce, "Handbook of American Underwriting of Foreign Securities, 1914–1929" (Trade Promotion Series No. 104, 1930), "A New Estimate of American Investments Abroad" (Trade Information Bulletin No. 767, 1931), "American Direct Investments in Foreign Countries (Trade Information Bulletin No. 731, 1930), "American Direct Investments in Foreign Countries—1936" (Economic Series No. 1, 1938); Brooks Emeny, *The Strategy of Raw Materials* (1934).

VI. LIFE, LETTERS, AND ART IN THE MACHINE AGE

General and Special Treatments. Charles A. and Mary R. Beard, *Rise of American Civilization*, v. 2, chap. xxx (1927); F. T. Allen, *Only Yesterday, An Informal History of the 1920's* (1931); P. W. Slosson, *Great Crusade and After, 1914–1928* (1930); Harold E. Stearns, editor, *Civilization in the United States: An Inquiry by Thirty Americans* (1922); Harold Rugg, *Culture and Education in America* (1931); R. S. and H. M. Lynd, *Middletown* (1929) and *Middletown in Transition* (1937); Randolph Bourne, *Untimely Papers* (1919) and *History of a Literary Radical and Other Essays* (1920); Van Wyck Brooks, *America's Coming of Age* (1915) and *Letters and Leadership* (1918); Waldo Frank, *Our America* (1919) and *Rediscovery of America* (1929); Walter Lippmann, *Preface to Morals* (1929); J. W. Krutch, *Modern Temper* (1930); Arthur Feiler, *America Seen Through German Eyes* (1928); André Siegfried, *America Comes of Age* (1927); Dixon Ryan Fox, editor, *Quarter Century of Learning* (1931); I. L. Kandel, editor, *Twenty-five Years of American Education* (1924); E. W. Knight, *Education in the United States* (1929); D. A. Robertson, editor, *American Universities and Colleges* (1928); H. L. Barber, *Story of the Automobile* (1927); W. M. Seabury, *The Public and the Motion Picture Industry* (1926).

VII. CAPITALISM IN CRISIS

The Course of the Depression. Lionel Robbins, *The Great Depression* (1930); W. B. Donham, *Business Adrift* (1931); F. W. Hirst, *Wall Street and Lombard Street* (1931); M. A. Hallgren, *Seeds of Revolt* (1933); Evans Clark and others, *The Internal Debts of the United States* (1933).

The Causes of the Depression. Lewis Corey, *Decline of American Capitalism* (1934) and *The Crisis of the Middle Class* (1935); A. A. Berle, Jr. and G. C. Means, *The Modern Corporation and Private Property* (1932); Walton Hamilton and Associates, *Price and Price Policies* (1938); Twentieth Century Fund, *Big Business: Its Growth and Its Place* (1937) and *How Profitable Is Big Business?* (1937); G. C. Means, *Industrial Prices and Their Relative Inflexibility* (Senate Document No. 13, 74th Congress, 1st Session, 1935); Anna Rochester, *Rulers of America* (1936); Maurice Leven and others, *America's Capacity to Consume* (1934); Edwin G. Nourse and Associates,

America's Capacity to Produce (1934); Harold Loeb, editor, *Report of the National Survey of Potential Product Capacity* (1935); H. G. Moulton, *The Formation of Capital* (1935); Works Progress Administration, National Research Project on Reemployment Opportunities and Recent Changes in Industrial Techniques, "Unemployment and Increasing Productivity" (1937); National Resources Committee, *Technological Trends and National Policy* (1937).

WHAT TO DO? C. A. Beard, *The Future Comes* (1933); Stuart Chase, *A New Deal* (1932) and *Economy of Abundance* (1934); George Soule, *A Planned Society* (1932) and *The Coming American Revolution* (1934); Mordecai Ezekiel, *$2500 a Year, From Scarcity to Abundance* (1936); H. A. Wallace, *New Frontiers* (1934); R. G. Tugwell, *Industrial Discipline and the Governmental Arts* (1933); Howard Scott, *An Introduction to Technocracy* (1933); John Strachey, *The Coming Struggle for Power* (1934); Norman Thomas, *The Choice Before Us* (1934); Franklin D. Roosevelt, *Looking Forward* (1933); Donald R. Richberg, *The Rainbow* (1936).

VIII. FROM AN OLD TO A NEW DEAL

THE FIRST STEPS OF RECOVERY. E. K. Lindley, *The Roosevelt Revolution, First Phase* (1933); C. A. Beard, *The Future Comes* (1933); Anonymous, *The New Dealers* (1934); F. D. Roosevelt, *On Our Way* (1934); A. A. Berle, Jr. and others, *America's Recovery Program* (1934); W. F. Ogburn, editor, *Social Change and the New Deal* (1934); A. N. Holcombe, *The New Party Politics* (1934); R. G. Tugwell, *The Battle for Democracy* (1935).

THE THEORY AND TACTICS OF THE NEW DEAL. PRO: Franklin D. Roosevelt, *The Public Papers and Addresses*, 5 v. (1938); Jerome Frank, *Save America First* (1938); Mordecai Ezekiel, *$2500 a Year, From Scarcity to Abundance* (1936). CONTRA: Columbia University Commission, *Economic Reconstruction* (1934); William MacDonald, *The Menace of Recovery* (1934); Walter Lippmann, *The Method of Freedom* (1934); L. P. Ayres, *Economics of Recovery* (1934). ACADEMIC: Arthur B. Adams, *Our Economic Revolution* (1933) and *National Economic Security* (1936); Alvin H. Hansen, *Full Recovery or Stagnation* (1938); Brookings Institution, *The Recovery Problem in the United States* (1937).

IX. THE NEW DEAL AGENCIES

AGRICULTURE. Wilson Gee, *American Farm Policy* (1934); H. A. Wallace, "America Must Choose" (1934); Mordecai Ezekiel and L. H. Bean, "Economic Bases of the Agricultural Adjustment Act" (1933); Special Committee on Farm Tenancy, "Farm Tenancy" (House Report No. 149, 75th Congress, 1st Session, 1937); Jonathan Daniels, *A Southerner Discovers the South* (1938); H. C. Nixon, *Forty Acres and Steel Mules* (1938); E. G. Nourse and others, *Three Years of the Agricultural Adjustment Administration* (1937); E. G. Nourse, *Marketing Agreements under the AAA* (1935); Works Progress Administration, Division of Social Research, *Landlord and Tenant on the Cotton Plantation* (1936).

INDUSTRY. L. S. Lyon and others, *The National Recovery Administration* (1935); Arthur R. Burns, *The Decline of Competition* (1936); Twentieth Century Fund, *Big Business: Its Growth and Its Place* (1937) and *How Profitable Is Big Business?* (1937); H. S. Johnson, *The Blue Eagle From Egg to Earth* (1935).

LABOR. C. R. Daugherty, *Labor Problems in American Industry* (revised edition, 1938); Twentieth Century Fund, *Labor and Government* (1935); Marjorie Clark and S. Fanny Simon, *The Labor Movement in America* (1938); National Labor Relations Board, Division of Economic Research, "Governmental Protection of Labor's Right to Organize" (1936); Leo Huberman, *The Labor Spy Racket* (1937); U. S. Senate, Subcommittee of the Committee on Education and Labor ("Civil Liberties Committee"), *Hearings and Reports* on "Violation of Free Speech and Assembly and Interference with Rights of Labor" (1936–1938).

SOCIAL SECURITY. Abraham Epstein, *Insecurity, A Challenge to America* (revised edition, 1938); Eveline M. Burns, *Toward Social Security* (1936); Paul H. Douglas, *Social Security in the United States* (1936); D. D. Lescohier and Elizabeth Brandeis, *History of Labor in the United States, 1896–1932*, v. 3 (1935).

CURRENCY AND CREDIT. W. H. Steiner, *Money and Banking* (1933); W. Randolph Burgess, *The Reserve Banks and the Money Market* (1936); H. G. Moulton, *The Financial Organization of Society* (revised edition, 1938); John T. Flynn, *Security Speculation* (1934); Foreign Policy Association, "The United States Silver Policy" (*F. P. R.*, v. xii, no. 15, 1936), "Currency Stabilization and World Recovery" (*F. P. R.*, v. xi, no. 13, 1935), and "Hot Money: An International Problem" (*F. P. R.*, v. xiii, no. 7, 1937).

HOUSING. L. W. Post, *The Challenge of Housing* (1938); M. W. Straus and T. Wegg, *Housing Comes of Age* (1938).

RAILROADS AND SHIPPING. Joseph B. Eastman, "Report of the Federal Coordinator of Transportation" (Senate Document No. 152, 73rd Congress, 2nd Session, 1934) and "Report of the Federal Coordinator of Transportation" (House Document No. 89, 74th Congress, 1st Session, 1935); J. P. Kennedy, "Economic Survey of the American Merchant Marine" (1937); Foreign Policy Association, "Rebuilding the U. S. Merchant Marine" (*F. P. R.*, v. xiii, no. 20, 1938).

FOREIGN TRADE. R. L. Buell, "The Hull Trade Program and the American System" (*World Affairs Pamphlets*, No. 2, 1938); H. S. Patton, "The Midwest and the Trade-Agreements Program" (Department of State, Commercial Policy Series, No. 27, 1936).

PUBLIC WORKS. Arthur D. Gayer, "Public Works and Unemployment Relief in the United States" (1936); J. M. Clark, "Economics of Planning Public Works" (1935); Public Works Administration, "The First 3 Years" (1936).

RELIEF. Nels Anderson, *The Right to Work* (1938); Betty and E. K. Lindley, *A New Deal for Youth* (1938); Louise V. Armstrong, *We Too Are the People* (1938).

FINANCING THE NEW DEAL. H. L. Lutz, *Public Finance* (1936); Twentieth Century Fund, *Facing the Tax Problem* (1937).

X. THE NEW DEAL MAKES PROGRESS SLOWLY

THE COURSE OF RECOVERY. Arthur B. Adams, *National Economic Security* (1936); *The London Economist*, "The New Deal: An Analysis and Appraisal" (October 3, 1936).

THE SUPREME COURT FIGHT. U. S. Senate, Committee on the Judiciary, "Hearings . . . on S. 1392, A bill to reorganize the judicial branch of the government," 6 pts. (1937); Morris Ernst, *The Ultimate Power* (1937); Irving Brant, *Storm Over the Constitution* (1937).

LABOR ORGANIZES. Edward Levinson, *Labor on the March* (1938); Mary Heaton Vorse, *Labor's New Millions* (1938); Benjamin Stolberg, *Story of the CIO* (1938).

THE "RECESSION" OF 1937–1938. *The New Republic*, Special Section, "The Depression" (February 2, 1938); Alvin H. Hansen, *Full Recovery or Stagnation* (1938).

THE FOREIGN POLICY OF THE NEW DEAL. F. L. Schuman and George Soule, "America Looks Abroad" (*World Affairs Pamphlets*, No. 3, 1938); Hubert Herring, *And So to War* (1938); *The New Republic*, Special Section, "National Defense: A Progressive Policy" (March 30, 1938); Foreign Policy Association, "The Mexican Oil Dispute" (*F. P. R.*, v. xiv, no. 11, 1938), "America's Rôle in the Far Eastern Conflict" (*F. P. R.*, v. xiii, no. 23, 1938), "The Neutrality Act of 1937" (*F. P. R.*, v. xiii, no. 14, 1937), and "U. S. Neutrality in the Spanish Conflict" (*F. P. R.*, v. xiii, no. 17, 1937); J. T. Shotwell, *On the Rim of the Abyss* (1936).

INDEX

INDEX

Abbott, Charles Cortez, 278, 280.
Agricultural Adjustment Administration (AAA), 207-213, 312.
Agricultural Marketing Act of 1929, 124-127.
Agriculture, its prosperity during the 1900's and 1910's, 113-115; in the World War period, 114-115; depression in, 115-121; tenancy in, 116-118; and foreign trade and competition, 118-120; and domestic market, 120-121; and legislation during the 1920's, 121-127; and farm credit, 122; and equalization fee and export debenture schemes, 123-124; and Mr. Hoover, 124-127, 192; and imperialism, 131-132; dependence upon foreign trade, 141; and the depression, 190-191; and the politics of the New Deal, 204-205; under the AAA, 207-213; regimentation under New Deal, 210, 213; and the "ever-normal" granary, 212; and credit and debt relief under the New Deal, 213-214; and rehabilitation of marginal and sub-marginal farmers, 214-217; and Canadian reciprocal trade agreement, 260-261; and Mr. Hull's efforts to reestablish the international division of labor, 262-264; its probable permanent decline, 263; and the Federal Surplus Commodities Corporation, 272; and recovery, 283-284; and the "recession" of 1937-1938, 305-306; and renewed recovery, 310; its final position under the New Deal, 310-315.
Aldrich, Winthrop W., 187.
Alsop, Joseph and Robert Kintner, 318.
American Institute of Public Opinion, 324, 326.
Anderson, Nels, 269, 270-271.
Anderson, Sherwood, 163, 164.
Arbitration treaties of 1928 and after, 50.
Architecture in America, 168-169.
Arnold, Thurman W., 224.
Arvin, Newton, 165.
Automobile in America, 158, 159.
Aviation in America, 161-162.

Balance of international payments, and agriculture, 118-119; while we were a debtor nation, 133; as a creditor nation, 134-139, 262-264.
Bank for International Settlements, 59.
Bank reserves. *See* Federal Reserve System.
Banking, "holiday" during 1933, 197; Emergency Banking Act, 197-198; bank failures, 239; and deposit insurance, 239-240; and the Banking Act of 1935, 240-241; and the RFC, 242-243; and New Deal recovery, 286-289. *See also* Federal Reserve System.
Banking Act of 1933, 239-240.
Banking Act of 1935, 240-241.
Beard, Charles A., 154, 167, 297.
Bemis, S. F., 60.
Black, Hugo L., 299.
Blue Eagle, 219.
Bonus, soldiers'. *See* Veterans.
Boston police strike, 10.
Bourne, Randolph, 166.
Boycott, and labor, 83-84.
"Brain Trust," in 1932 campaign, 195.
Branch factories, 129, 136.
Briand-Kellogg Pact, 49-50, 55, 324.
Brookings Institution, 182, 184, 185, 208, 211.
Brooks, Van Wyck, 166.
Brussels Conference of 1937, 324.
Buell, Raymond Leslie, 259, 261.
Bureaucracy. *See* State capitalism.
"Buy and give" program, 272.

Cabell, James Branch, 165.
Canada, and reciprocal trade agreement, 260-261.

Capacity to produce and capacity to consume, 179, 182-184, 191, 199.
Capital flotations, 185-187, 286.
Capital gains tax, 274-275.
Capper-Volstead Cooperative Act, 122.
Caribbean, and United States, 43-48, 316.
Carmical, J. H., 313-314.
Cather, Willa, 162, 164-165.
Child caring services, under Social Security Act, 230.
Child labor, and the Supreme Court, 91; under NIRA, 219; under the Wages and Hours Act, 233-234.
China, and the United States, as result of Washington Conference, 54-55; and immigration, 111; and our silver policy, 238; and our attitude toward Japanese invasion of, 323-326.
Civil Works Administration (CWA), 268.
Civilian Conservation Corps (CCC), 198, 267-268.
Class structure in America, 179-180, 199, 204.
Clayton Act, and labor, 84-86; and Supreme Court, 91; and Big Business, 97.
Codes and Code Authorities. *See* National Industrial Recovery Act.
Collective security, 131, 316, 323.
Collins, J. M., 312.
Committee for Industrial Organization (CIO), 299-304.
Commodity loans, 210, 212, 312.
Communism, the Third International and the United States, 65; in America, 88-90; the wooing of the democracies, 90; support of Roosevelt, 90; under the NRA, 225; and the "recession" of 1937-1938, 308.
Concentration, industrial. *See* Monopoly.
Conciliation treaties of 1928 and after, 50.
Conference for Progressive Political Action, in 1924 campaign, 13-15.
Coolidge, Calvin, election and Presidency, 9-15; veto of veterans' bill, 35; veto of power bill, 40; and Nicaragua, 43-44; and World Court, 52; and Russia, 63-64; veto of equalization fee bill, 123.
Corey, Lewis, 179, 191.
Corporations, public, 277-281.
Cotton Control Act of 1934, 208, 209.
Cox, James M., 4.
Credit, revival of, 201; plans for expansion under the New Deal, 238-243; agencies for, 243-244; spotty character of, 285.
Creditor status of the United States, 119, 133-139, 262-264.
Criminal syndicalist laws, 88, 91, 92.
Criticism, literary, in America, 166.
Cuba, and reciprocal trade agreement, 260; and Platt Amendment, 316.
Currency expansion, under New Deal, 234-238; off gold standard, 235; and the Thomas Amendment, 235, 236; and silver, 235, 236, 237-238; and the Gold Reserve Act, 236-237; and the Soldiers' Bonus bill, 238.

Darrow, Clarence S., 221.
Davis, John W., 12, 14.
Dawes Plan, 58.
"Death sentence," for utility holding companies, 248-249.
Debs, Eugene V., 83, 88.
Debt, in agriculture, 115, 116, 121, 213-214; during the depression, 192-193, 200; tactics of New Deal concerning, 202; relief of housing debt, 250-251; and the railroads, 253. *See also* Public debt.
Debtor status, of the United States, 118-119, 133.
"Deficit financing," of the New Deal, 273-276.
De Leon, Daniel, 88.
Democracy, under state capitalism, 279-281.
Democratic party, in 1920 campaign, 4-5; in 1924, 11-14; in 1928 campaign, 16-17; and the Prohibition question, 105; in 1932 campaign, 194-196; in 1936 campaign, 293-295.
Depression of 1930 and after, onset, 20; and the Mellon tax reduction program, 33-34; and agriculture, 115-116; and effects on philanthropy, 152; course of, 177-179; causes of, 179-191; proposals concerning, 191-192; Mr. Hoover's program, 192-193; Mr. Hoover's analysis of, 194; Mr. Roosevelt's analysis of, 196; and

prices, 200-201; and credit, 201; success of New Deal in handling, 205-206; bank failures during, 239; and housing, 250; and railroads, 253; general nature of, 277; and recovery, 282-285; and weak spots in recovery, 286-292; and "recession" of 1937-1938, 305-308; program for recovery in 1938, 308-310. *See also* Hoover, Herbert; New Deal; Roosevelt, Franklin D.
Dewey, John, 166-167.
Direct investments, 134-138.
Dollar devaluation. *See* Currency expansion.
Dominican Republic, termination of occupation, 43.
Dreiser, Theodore, 162, 163-164.
Dumond, Dwight L., 296.

Economic nationalism, as result of tariff of 1930, 26; and New Deal agricultural program, 213; and foreign trade program, 257-258; in Europe, 262; the rôle of agriculture under, 263-264. *See also* Imperialism.
Economist, London, survey of New Deal, 247-248, 270, 276.
Economy Act of 1933, 198.
Education in America, 152-154.
Eighteenth Amendment, 99-105.
Election, of 1920, 5; of 1924, 14; of 1928, 17; of 1932, 196; of 1936, 295.
Emergency Banking Act of 1933, 197-198.
Emergency Farm Mortgage Act of 1933, 213.
Emergency Railroad Transportation Act of 1933, 254.
Emergency Relief and Construction Act of 1932, 264.
Emigration, from United States, 112-113.
Epstein, Abraham, 150, 232.
Equalization fee plan, 123.
"Ever-normal" granary, 212, 213.
Exchange Stabilization Fund, 236, 276.
Export debenture plan, 23-24, 123-124.
Export-Import Banks, 258-259, 318.

Far East, and Washington Conference, 53, 54-56; and Stimson doctrine, 55; and Mr. Hull's policy, 323-328.
Farm Credit Administration (FCA), 213.
Farm Mortgage Moratorium Act of 1935, 214.
Farm Mortgage Refinancing Act of 1934, 213.
Farm Security Administration (FSA), 216-217.
Farmer-Labor party, in 1920 campaign, 4, 5; in 1924 campaign, 13-14.
Federal Alcohol Administration (FAA), 106.
Federal Coordinator of Transportation, 254.
Federal Deposit Insurance Corporation, 239, 240.
Federal Emergency Relief Administration (FERA), 268-269.
Federal Farm Bankruptcy Act of 1934, 214.
Federal Farm Board of 1929-1933, 124-127.
Federal Farm Mortgage Corporation (FFMC), 213.
Federal Housing Administration (FHA), 251-252.
Federal Intermediate Credit Act, 122-123.
Federal Power Commission, 19, 37-39, 248.
Federal Reserve System, cheap money policy during the 1920's, 187; under Thomas Amendment, 235, 238; reserves of member banks, 239, 241; open-market operations, 238-239, 240-241; under the Banking Act of 1933, 239-240; under the Banking Act of 1935, 240-241; cheap money policy under New Deal, 241; and margin accounts, 244; and New Deal recovery, 286-289; and the "recession" of 1937-1938, 308; and the President's program for renewed recovery, 309.
Federal Savings and Loan Associations, 250-251.
Federal Surplus Commodities Corporation (FSCC), 272.
Federal Trade Commission, 96-97.
Finance capital, leadership in business, 180-181. *See also* Imperialism.
Flynn, John T., 95, 325-326.

Foreign trade, with Russia, 64-65; and agriculture, 118-120; and raw materials required by America, 127-128; character of, 139-145; and the depression, 190; and the tactics of the New Deal, 202; and the politics of the New Deal, 205; under reciprocal trading agreements, 257-261; the probable future history of, 262-264.
Foundations in America, 151.
Frost, Robert, 165.

Gayer, Arthur, 306.
Germany, and reparation payments, 59-60, 62; and American imperialism, 134; and reciprocal trade agreements, 260; and the Export-Import Banks in Haiti, 259, 318; and Mr. Hull's policy of encirclement, 317-318.
Gold, foreign, 239, 288; sterilization of, 241; desterilization of, 308, 309. *See also* Currency expansion.
Gold-Clause decisions, 296, 299.
Gold Repeal Joint Resolution, 235.
Gold Reserve Act, 236-237.
"Good neighbor" policy, 316-319.
Great Britain, and the United States, and naval limitation, 54, 56; imperialist rivalry, 127; and Mr. Hull's "parallel action" with, 316, 324, 325; and naval treaties, 328.

Haiti, termination of occupation, 43, 316; and Export-Import Banks in, 259, 318.
Hansen, Alvin H., 306.
Harding, Warren Gamaliel, election and Presidency, 3-9; and naval armaments limitation, 53.
Hawes-Cutting Act of 1932, 326-327.
Haywood, William D., 88.
Holding companies, and the Federal Trade Commission, 97-98; and savings during the 1920's, 186; and power, 247-249; and railroads, 253, 254.
Home Owners' Loan Corporation (HOLC), 250-251.
Home Owners' Refinancing Act of 1933, 250.
Hoover, Herbert, election and Presidency, 15-20; and the tariff, 23-25; and veterans' legislation, 36; and power, 39-40; and Haiti, 43; and Nicaragua, 44; and the World Court, 52; and reparation moratorium, 60; and Russia, 63; Law Enforcement Commission, 101-105; and quota laws, 111; and agriculture, 121, 124-126, 142; and the Open Door principle, 131, 132; and the RFC, 192; and the depression, 192-193, 194; in the 1932 campaign, 194-196; and public works, 264; and relief, 267, 268; and veto of Philippine bill, 326.
Housing, mortgage debt, 249; inadequacy of, 249-250; relief of mortgagors, 250-251; relief of mortgagees, 251-252; establishment of Federal Housing Administration, 251-252; slum clearance and low-cost housing, 252-253; under the recovery activities of 1938, 309-310.
Howe, Quincy, 316.
Hughes, Charles E., as Secretary of State, 41; on World Court bench, 51; and World Court protocol reservations, 51-52; fight on for Supreme Court bench, 19, 93-94; and Roosevelt's fight on the Court, 298-299.
Hull, Cordell, and the Far East, 56, 205; and Latin America, 205; and foreign trade, 257-261; and the international division of labor, 262-264; and rôle in Roosevelt's foreign policy, 316-325; and his analysis of the New Deal, 330.

Immigration Commission of 1907, 108.
Immigration restriction, 107-113.
Imperialism, American, in Caribbean, 44-45; and Latin Americans, 47-48; struggle of imperialist powers of Europe, 48-49; and German reparations, 60; and American labor, 80; of the United States, 127-139; our unpopularity abroad, as a result, 128-130; the political debate concerning, 130-132; the United States as a debtor nation, 133; as a creditor nation, 133-139; our foreign trade under, 139-145; and the depression, 190, 191; and the politics of the New Deal, 205; and

the Republican party, 260; agriculture under, 263-264; and the present-day struggle for power, 316-322.
Income, national, from 1909 to 1929, 72-73; of labor, 79-80; during the depression, 183-184; under New Deal recovery, 289-291.
Industrial Commission of 1898, 107.
Industrial Workers of the World (I.W.W.), 87-89.
Industry, in the United States, its growth, 71-75; industrial research, 76; and labor productivity, 77-79; and concentration in, 94-96; and the Supreme Court, 91-94; and the politics of the New Deal, 205; and the NIRA, 217-224; reactions to the NIRA, 219-220; recovery under the New Deal, 282; and relations with labor during 1920's, 300; under the "recession" of 1937-1938, 306, 307; under the 1938 recovery, 310.
Injunction, as a weapon against labor, 82-86, 91.
Interallied debts, 57-62, 132.
Inter-American Conference for the Maintenance of Peace, 318-319.
International division of labor, 257-259, 262-264, 319.
Interstate Commerce Commission, 29-31, 92, 254.
Investments, overseas, 133-139; foreign investments in United States, 137-138; investments during 1920's, 185-187; and the possibilities of maintaining American neutrality, 321-322.
Isolationism, 131-132, 315-316, 319-323, 324-325, 326.
Isthmian policy, of United States, 45-46.
Italo-Ethiopian War, 319, 323, 324.

Japan, and United States, and naval limitation, 54, 56-57; and Stimson doctrine, 55; and immigration to United States, 111; and our attitude toward her invasion of China, 323-328; denunciation of naval treaties, 328.
Johnson, Hiram, 325.
Johnson Debt Default Act, 62, 258, 319.
Justice, Department of, scandals in, 7-8; and red hunts, 89; and Big Business, 96.

Kellogg, Frank B., as Secretary of State, 41; and Briand-Kellogg Pact, 49; on World Court bench, 51; and American imperialist policy, 132.
Kennedy, Joseph P., 254-255, 257.
Ku Klux Klan, and Democratic party, 11.

Labor, increased standards of living, 79-80; and trade unionism, 80; and the Negroes, 82; and the injunction, 82-86; and strikes during the 1920's, 86-87; radicalism and, 87-90; and immigration, 109, 113; and the depression, 178, 183-184; tactics of New Deal concerning, 201-202, 203; and the politics of the New Deal, 205; and Section 7(a), 217-218; under the NIRA, 219, 224-225; under the labor boards, 225-229; and social security, 229-234; and wages and hours legislation, 232-234; under the New Deal recovery, 285-286, 289-292; in 1936 campaign, 294; and the struggle between the A. F. of L., and the CIO, 299-304; and strikes, 305.
Labor, American Federation of (A. F. of L.), during the 1920's, 80-82, 87; Communist tactics in, 89-90; under the NIRA, 225; and the struggle with the CIO, 299-304.
Labor, Department of, and immigration, 112-113.
Labor boards, 218, 225-229.
Labor disputes, in South, 74; during the 1920's, 86-87; led by I.W.W., 88; under the NIRA, 225; San Francisco general strike, 226; and automobiles, 302; and steel, 302-303; statistics of, 305.
Labor Disputes Joint Resolution, 225-226.
Labor productivity, 77-79, 191, 283, 291-292.
La Follette, R. M., 12-14, 92.
La Follette Civil Liberties Committee, 303.
Land values, 115, 118, 284.
Landon, Alfred M., 293, 294-295.
Latin America, and arbitration treaties, 50-51; and the "good neighbor" policy, 316-319; and our official propaganda in, 319.

League of Nations, in 1920 campaign, 3-5; in 1924, 11-12; unofficial American dealings with, 48; distrust of, 49-51; and American imperialism, 132.
Lemke, William, 294.
Lewis, John L., 301-304.
Lewis, Sinclair, 162, 163, 164.
Lindsay, Vachel, 165.
Liquor control, 106-107.
Literacy test, 108-109.
Loans, foreign, to Germany, 60, 134; to Russia, 63; and prosperity during the 1920's, 190. *See also* Export-Import Banks.
London Conference, for naval limitation, 53, 56-57.
Ludlow Amendment, 322, 325, 326.
Lynd, R. S. and Helen M., 147.

McNary-Haugen bill (equalization fee), 123.

Madden, J. Warren, 229.
Manchukuo, Japanese invasion of, 55.
Manufactures, growth of, 73-75; labor productivity in, 77, 78; concentration in, 94-96. *See also* Industry.
Marin, John, 162, 168.
Marketing, changes in, 74-75.
Mass production, 75-76.
Masters, Edgar Lee, 165.
Maximum hours, 232-233.
Means, Gardiner C., 188.
Mechanization, social effects of, 71-72; and mass production, 75-76; and technological unemployment, 78-79; and labor, 81; and American society, 146-148; in agriculture, 114, 121, 314-315.
Mellon, Andrew, as Secretary of the Treasury, 32-34; and reparation payments, 62; and Russia, 63.
Mencken, Henry L., 166.
Mercantilism, 280, 331.
Merchant Fleet Corporation, 26-28.
Merchant marine in 1920's, 26-28; under the New Deal, 254-257.
Merchant Marine Act of 1936, 255-256.
Mergers. *See* Monopoly.
Mexico, its constitution, 41-42; its Petroleum Law and Alien Land Law, 41-42; and Dwight W. Morrow, 42; immigrants from, 110, 113; and our silver policy, 238; and Mr. Hull and the land controversy, 316-317.
Minimum wage laws, and the Supreme Court, 91, 296, 299; under the NIRA, 219; and the Wages and Hours Act, 232-233.
Monopoly, during the 1920's, 94-98; during the 1930's, 180, 181; and effects on prices, 187-188; under the NIRA, 219, 220-221; and Mr. Roosevelt's program for, 223-224, 310; Mr. Arnold's views on, 224.
Monroe Doctrine, and Isthmian policy, 46; and "Roosevelt" corollary, 46-47; and Briand-Kellogg Pact, 49.
Morgan, House of, 181.
Most-favored-nation treatment, 260.
Motion pictures in America, 159-160.
Moulton, Harold B., 185, 186-187.
Mumford, Lewis, 169.
Munitions Committee, 319.
Muscle Shoals, under Mr. Hoover, 39-40; under TVA, 245-246.
Music in America, 170-172.

National Housing Act of 1934, 251.
National Housing Act of 1937, 252.
National Industrial Conference Board, 280.
National Industrial Recovery Act (NIRA), purpose, 201; passed, 217; administration of, 218-219; codes under, 218-219; industry's reaction to, 219-220; and fostering of monopoly practices, 219, 220-221; invalidation of, 221-222.
National Labor Board, 218.
National Labor Relations Board (NLRB), 226-229, 256, 299, 304-305.
National Recovery Administration (NRA). *See* National Industrial Recovery Act.
National Recovery Review Board, 221.
National Survey of Potential Product Capacity, 182.
National Youth Administration (NYA), 271-272.
Naval armaments, limitation of, 53-57.

Naval construction program of 1938, 325-326, 328-330.
Negroes, migrations north, 82; and labor, 82.
Neutrality, legislation, 62; as affected by foreign investments in the United States, 138; Neutrality Acts, 319-323.
New Deal, and art projects, 172; its inauguration, 196; emergency measures of, 197-198; establishment of CCC, 198; theory of, 198-200; tactics of, 200-204; program for reform, 203-204; politics of, 204-206; as state capitalism, 204; success of, 205-206; and agriculture, 207-217; and regimentation of agriculture, 210; and resettlement of farmers, 214-216; and industry, 217-224; and labor, 224-229; and social security, 229-232; and wages and hours legislation, 232-234; and currency expansion, 234-238; and credit expansion and banking reform, 238-241; and the RFC, 241-243; and securities and exchange, 243-244; and power, 244-249; and housing, 249-253; and railroads, 253-254; and shipping, 254-257; and foreign trade, 257-264; and public works, 264-266; and relief, 266-273; financing of, 273-276; tax program of, 273-275; "deficit financing" of, 275-276; and the problem of bureaucracy, 276-281; and democracy, 279-281; in aiding recovery, 282-285; spotty nature of recovery, 285-292; and the "recession" of 1937-1938, 305-310; program for renewed recovery, 308-310; the questionable permanence of New Deal planning, 310-315; its foreign policy, 315-328; its naval program, 328-330; and its short-term and long-term prospects, 330-332.
New Republic, 325, 329.
Newspapers in America, 154-156.
Nicaragua, termination of American occupation, 43-44.
Nine-Power Treaty, 54-55, 324.
Norris-LaGuardia Federal Anti-injunction Law, 86.
Novel in America, 163-165.
O'Fallon case, 29, 92, 93.
Oil scandals, 8-9.
Old age, under Social Security Act, 230-231, 232.
O'Mahoney Monopoly Inquiry Act, 223-224, 310.
O'Neill, Eugene, 162, 170.
Open Door, and Nine-Power Treaty, 54-55; in the 1920's, 131.
Open-market operations. *See* Federal Reserve System.

Packers and Stockyards Act, 121-122.
Painting in America, 167-168.
Parity prices, 207, 212, 312.
Peek, George N., 258.
Periodical press, in America, 148, 156.
Philanthropy in America, 150-152.
Philippine Islands, 326-328.
Philosophy in America, 167.
Planning, proposals for during the depression, 193.
Plantation, probable disappearance of, 314-315.
Platt Amendment, 316.
Poetry in America, 165-166.
Population of the United States, 69-71.
Portfolio investments, 134-138.
Power, efforts to regulate during 1921-1932, 36-40; under the New Deal, 244-249; TVA, 244-247; control of public utilities, 247-249.
Price control, in 1920's, 96; during the depression, 187-188, 192, 193; under the NIRA, 219-220; and Mr. Roosevelt's analysis of, 223; and Mr. Arnold's analysis of, 224; as a cause for "recession" of 1937-1938, 306, 307; question of treating deferred, 310.
Prices, agricultural, 114, 115, 116, 208, 213, 305-306; restoration of by New Deal, 200-201; price raising as result of the NIRA, 217, 219-220; program for under New Deal (through currency expansion), 234-238; program for under New Deal (through credit expansion), 238-241; nature of price recovery, 282-284; and "recession" of 1937-1938, 306, 307.
Processing taxes, 208, 211.
Productivity. *See* Labor productivity.
Prohibition, 99-106, 108.

Public debt, under Mellon, 32-34; under New Deal, 275-276.
Public Utility Act of 1935, 248-249.
Public Works Administration (PWA), and the RFC, 242; and the TVA, 245-247; Housing Division of, 252; establishment and activities of, 264-266, 271.

"Quarantine" speech of Mr. Roosevelt, 324.
Quota laws, 109-113.

Radio in America, 160-161.
Railroads, act of 1920, 28-30; new competitors, 31-32, 253; difficulties of, 253-254; under the New Deal, 254.
Railroad Retirement Act, 296.
Rate regulation, 92-94; under TVA (the "yardstick"), 245-247; under the chastened Supreme Court, 299.
"Recession" of 1937-1938, 305-310.
Reciprocal trade agreements, 259-261, 319.
Reconstruction Finance Corporation (RFC), established, 192, 194; under the Emergency Banking Act of 1933, 197-198; under the New Deal, 241-243; and the railroads, 254; and public works, 242, 264; and Hoover relief, 267; and the program for renewed recovery, 308, 309.
Relief, Mr. Hoover's attitude toward, 194; tactics of New Deal concerning, 202-203; failure of PWA as a relief agency, 265; New Deal program for, 266-273; and the CCC, 267-268; and the FERA, 268-269; and the WPA, 269-271; and the NYA, 271-272; and the FSCC, 272; and the "buy and give" program, 272; cost of relief, 272-273.
Religion in America, 148-150.
Reparation payments. *See* Interallied debts.
Republican party, in 1920 campaign, 4-5; in 1924, 11-14; in 1928 campaign, 15-17; and the Prohibition question, 105; in 1932 campaign, 193-196; in 1936 campaign, 292-295, 297; and imperialism, 260.
Resettlement Administration (RA), 215-216.
Revenue Act of 1935, 274.
Revenue Act of 1936, 274-275.
Revenue Act of 1938, 275.
Robinson, Edwin Arlington, 165.
Rochester, Anna, 181.
Roosevelt, Franklin D., and Russia, 64-65; supported by the Communists, 90; and Big Business, 98; and the Prohibition question, 105; and American imperialism, 138; fought by press, 155; on concentration of wealth and income, 180, 181-182; attitude toward debt and the depression, 192-193; in the 1932 campaign, 194-196; his previous record, 195; his theory of recovery, 196; attitude toward the RFC, 197; belief in a balanced society, 200; and prices, 200-201; and agriculture, 207; and his fight on the Supreme Court, 211, 222, 295-299; and the NIRA violations, 220; and reactions to Supreme Court's invalidation of the NIRA, 222; and his program for monopoly control, 223-224; and the London World Economic Conference, 236; and the Soldiers' Bonus bill of 1936, 238; on housing, 250; on taxation, 273-274, 275; power under New Deal, 280-281; and the election of 1936, 292-295; and his program for renewed recovery after "recession" of 1937-1938, 308-310; and his program for American participation in world affairs, 315-330; and his ambitions as a world leader, 330-332. *See also* New Deal.
Rosenfeld, Paul, 171.
Rural Electrification Administration, 247.
Russia, and the United States, 62-65; and Export-Import Banks, 258.

Sandburg, Carl, 165.
San Francisco general strike of 1934, 226.
Saposs, David J., 81.
Savings, capital, and imperialism, 127, 128, 134; during the 1920's, 184-187; and the depression, 192-193.
Section 7(a), 217-218, 300-301.

Securities and Exchange Commission (SEC), 243-244, 248-249.
Security affiliates, 240.
Sharecroppers, 117, 205, 314-315.
Sherman Anti-Trust Law, and labor, 83-84; and agriculture, 122.
Shipping. *See* Merchant Marine.
Silver. *See* Currency expansion; Mexico.
Smith, Alfred E., 12, 15-17, 294.
Social Security Board (SSB), 229-232.
Soil conservation, and tenancy, 117; and the agricultural act of 1936, 211; and the agricultural act of 1938, 212.
Soil Conservation and Domestic Allotment Act of 1936, 211.
South, industrialization of, 74; tenancy in, 117.
Spanish Civil War, 323, 325.
Stabilization corporations, under Agricultural Marketing Act of 1929, 125-126.
State capitalism, New Deal as, 204; and farm mortgage operations, 214; and control of prices, 224; and the problem of bureaucracy, 276-281; and its short-term and long-term prospects, 330-332.
Stimson, Henry L., in Nicaragua, 44; and American Isthmian policy, 45-46; and Monroe Doctrine, 47; and Japanese in Manchukuo, 55; and reparations, 59.
Stock ownership and income, 181-182.
Stock speculation, 177-178, 186-187, 240, 243-244.
Strikes. *See* Labor disputes.
Subsidies. *See* Agriculture; Housing; Merchant Marine.
Subsistence homesteads, 214-217.
Supreme Court, and labor, 83-86; and property rights in the 1920's, 91-94; and trade association, 96; and the AAA, 207-208, 211; and farm mortgage relief, 214, 296; and the NIRA, 221-222; and the NLRB, 228; and social security, 231; and the TVA, 246-247; and the Utility Holding Company Act, 249; and the Republicans in the 1936 election, 292-293, 297; and the Democratic party, 293; Roosevelt's fight on, 211, 222, 295-299; its chastened spirit, 299.
Tariff Act of 1922, 21-22; of 1930, 19-20, 23-26, 124; and our unpopularity abroad, 128-129; future policy concerning, 131; and reciprocal trade agreements, 259-262.
Tariff Commission, 22, 23, 24-25.
Taxation, under Mellon, 32-34; and reparation payments, 62; under the New Deal, 273-275.
Temporary National Economic Committee, 223-224, 310.
Tenancy, in agriculture, 116-118, 205, 314-315.
Tennessee Valley Authority (TVA), 203, 244-247.
Theater in America, 169-170.
Thomas Amendment, 235, 236, 238, 241.
Thompson, W. O., 221.
Tobacco Control Act of 1934, 208, 209.
Trade Agreements Act, 259.
Trade associations, 96. *See also* National Industrial Recovery Act.
Trade unions. *See* Labor; Labor, American Federation of; Committee for Industrial Organization; National Labor Relations Board.
Transportation Act of 1920, 28-32.
Twenty-first Amendment, 105-106.
Tydings-McDuffie Act of 1934, 327.

Undistributed profits tax, 274-275.
Unemployment, technological, 78-79; in the depression, 178, 191, 197; under the Social Security Act, 230-231, 232; under the New Deal, 266-267, 283, 285-286.
United States Housing Authority (USHA), 252-253.
United States Maritime Commission, 254-257.
United States Shipping Board, 26-28.
Urbanization, of the United States, 70-71.
Utility Holding Company Act, 248-249.

Veterans, under Economy Act of 1933, 198; under the Soldiers' Bonus bill of 1936, 238.
Veterans' Bureau, scandals in, 7; liberalization of law affecting, 34-36.

Wages, 77-79, 290-292.
Wages and Hours Act of 1938, 232.
Washington Conference, for naval limitation, 53-56.
Wealth, national, 72.
Work Relief and Public Works Appropriation Act of 1938, 309-310.
Workers. *See* Labor.
Works Progress Administration (WPA), during the 1936 revival, 267; establishment and activities of, 269-271; and "buy and give" program, 272; appropriation for 1938-1939, 273.
World Court, in 1920 campaign, 3-5; in 1924, 11-12; and fight for protocol's ratification, 51-53; and American imperialism, 132.
World Economic Conference of London, 235-236, 257-258.
World War Foreign Dept. Commission, 57.
Wright, Frank Lloyd, 162, 169.

Yellow-dog contract, and labor, 84, 86.
Young Plan, 58-60.